# The Stadium and the City

# The Stadium and the City

## Edited by
## John Bale and Olof Moen

KEELE UNIVERSITY PRESS

First published in 1995
by Keele University Press
Keele, Staffordshire

Composed by Keele University Press
and printed by Hartnolls, Bodmin, England

The Stadium and the City

ISBN  1 85331 110 3

# Contents

# List of Contributors

**Hans Aldskogius**
Department of Social and Economic Geography, Uppsala University, Sweden.

**Tommy D. Andersson**
School of Economics, University of Gothenburg, Sweden.

**Robert A. Baade**
Department of Economics, Lake Forest College, Illinois, USA.

**John Bale**
School of Human Development, Keele University, Staffordshire, UK.

**Susan Brownell**
Department of Anthropology, University of Missouri, St Louis, USA.

**Henning Eichberg**
Institute for Research on Sport, Body and Culture, Gerlev Idrætshøjskole, Slagelse, Denmark.

**Roman Horak**
Institute for Cultural Studies, Vienna, Austria.

**Per Jørgensen**
Danish Institute for Sport and Physical Education, Copenhagen, Denmark.

**Bruce Kidd**
School of Physical and Health Education, University of Toronto, Canada.

**Joseph Maguire**
Department of Physical Education and Sports Science and Recreation Management, Loughborough University, UK.

**Olof Moen**
Department of Social and Economic Geography, University of Gothenburg, Sweden.

**Niels Kayser Nielsen**
Department of Cultural Studies, Odense University, Denmark.

**Kimberley S. Schimmel**
Department of Physical Education, Health and Sport Studies, Miami University, Ohio, USA.

**Jim Toft**
Centre for Sports Research, University of Copenhagen, Denmark.

**John Williams**
Sir Norman Chester Centre for Football Research, Department of Sociology, Leicester University, UK.

# Acknowledgements

The initial versions of the chapters in the pages which follow were presented at an international and interdisciplinary seminar on the 'Stadium and the City', held in Gothenburg in October 1993. The seminar, and hence this collection, could not have been assembled without the support of the Swedish Association of Local Authorities and the School of Economics and Commercial Law of Gothenburg University. The ability and willingness of the authors to transform their first thoughts into the chapters now found between these covers is greatly appreciated. We would finally like to thank Lucia Crothall and her colleagues at Keele University Press for nursing the book from the proposal stage to final publication.

John Bale, Keele
Olof Moen, Gothenburg

# 1
# Introduction
## *John Bale*

The stadium is a phenomenon of modern urban life. It is in the stadium rather than in city squares, the concert hall or the cathedral that we find the largest urban congregations, at pre-ordained times and at regular intervals, to witness sporting rituals and records. Stadiums come in all shapes and sizes, ranging from massive examples of urban monumentalism to humble and homely sites deserving the more modest appellation of 'grounds'.[1] An icon of modernity, the spherical or rectangular stadium is essentially a product of the late nineteenth century (though see Chapter 16), yet it is a physical structure which is arguably 'more like its ancient precursor than anything else in the modern world looks like its architectural ancestors'.[2] It is the prime container of the modern urban crowd but few interpretations of its significance have been proffered.

The stadium is an ambiguous place. Various metaphors have been used to describe it. With its rows of seats and its geometrically segmented form, the container architecture, the pervasiveness of video-surveillance (arguably a modern form of Foucault's panopticon), and the presence of large numbers of police, it is hardly surprising that some stadiums have been likened to penitentiaries. For the American visitor, used to tailgate parties and a carnival atmosphere before the start of a game, the European stadium often appears to have 'a security system more suitable for a prison'.[3] Indeed, in times of political unrest, when secure places of incarceration for large numbers of internees are needed, some stadiums have been prisons. This image, however, is based on a highly selective sampling and more benign metaphors can be found to describe it.

An enclosed expanse of greenery in the urban area frequently gives sport a pastoral image – *rus in urbe* – a concept most often applied to baseball and cricket. This view of a residual element of nature in the concrete and pollution of the modern city is tutored by myth, but is, nevertheless, a powerful and pervasive image. Giamatti likens the stadium to a garden of *paradise* (derived from the Persian word for enclosure or park). He notes that 'we have always envisioned it as a garden … an enclosed, green place', the stadium becoming an adult version of the *kindergarten*.[4] And it is worth recalling how many stadiums and arenas continue to be called gardens and parks, despite the absence of flowers, shrubs and trees within them.[5]

The prison and the garden – respectively symbolizing human confinement and freedom, the closed and the open – perfectly exemplify the ambiguity and perhaps the attraction of the stadium. But many other metaphors could and are applied to the 'conjunction of arena and field, of city and garden'.[6] For example, the stadium could be called a theatre, providing as it does the forum for dramatic performances. As spectators become increasingly confined to seats, they resemble the more passive nature of the modern theatre audience (see Chapter 15). Gazing from individual seats in rows, as regimented as the geometries of the sports they are watching, the audience appears as part of the society of the spectacle.[7]

The stadium could also be called a cathedral, displaying to the public a modern form of religion, a new opiate of the masses. But it could equally be described, by those with a neo-Marxist disposition, as a machine, generating as it does a consumable product and, at the same time, providing income for some of the residents of the city and region around it and for the workers who 'play' inside it. The political economy of stadium development is one of the subjects of current concern among a number of political theorists and urban analysts (see Chapters 7–10).

The main surge of modern stadium growth occurred at the end of the nineteenth century. Open spaces where crowd events had previously taken place were replaced by ordered and enclosed spaces. They grew incrementally and were not without controversy. Various interest groups, then as now, contested the decision to erect permanent structures in what had previously been open spaces or land proximate to residential areas. Whereas municipal gardens may have enhanced the value of residential property, a sports stadium often tended to reduce the price of housing in its vicinity. Local residents often opposed such developments, frequently seeing them 'as a threat to their safety and tranquillity', but rarely could they stop the project.[8] Throughout the twentieth century, stadiums have grown in number and in size. The largest, the Maracana Stadium in Brazil, accommodates over two hundred thousand people. Those who own or occupy stadiums, traditionally sports teams but, increasingly, municipalities, have often favoured relocation – at both city and national levels of scale – adding a spatial dynamic to the historical pattern of stadium development.

Stadiums are invariably associated with sports. In most cases sports are expressions of masculinity and it is not surprising, therefore, that stadiums have been termed 'men's cultural centres'.[9] In much of Europe, the masculine culture of the football (soccer) ground (traditionally never a 'stadium' with all its connotations of image upgrading) is a residual bastion of blue-collar masculinity and its associated cultural baggage. While this is slowly changing – even in Britain – it remains a place of ritual, with its clients often succeeding, through various forms of resistance, in preventing its conversion into a sanitized space. The rituals of sport would seem to require a special arena. But how special can the *modern* stadium be? Can 'character', a sense of place, or *genius loci* be built into the concrete saucer or the bunker architecture of many modern sports facilities? The answer must be yes. And it has been shown to be the case in some of the newer developments in stadium design (see Chapter 11).

As we approach the end of the twentieth century, stadiums are in the news. They are, and always have been, viewed as sources of good and evil, a dualism already suggested by some of the metaphorical allusions noted above. They are often viewed in much the same way as another icon of the modern urban arena, the shopping mall – places for mixing business with pleasure, leisure laced with spending. As cities try to outbid each other for hosting the Olympics or, as in the USA, for attracting a professional sports franchise, stadiums are increasingly viewed as 'the contemporary US version of that ancient cargo cult practice in Papua, New Guinea, of building an air strip in the hope of luring a jet liner to earth'.[10] Stadiums feature on the business pages as much as in the sports columns as new arenas are perceived by city boosters as symbols of success, of urban machismo and vibrancy, as magnets to attract new industry and development, and to provide a much-wanted – or, at least, much-perceived – multifunctional leisure facility. If it often said that a city is not a city without its stadium.

At the same time, as the experience of football in 1980s Britain has so graphically illustrated, the worn-out stadiums of yesteryear, like the worn-out infrastructure of the nation, are recipes for disaster. The events of the 1980s at Bradford, Brussels (Heysel) and Sheffield (Hillsborough) shifted public attention to stadiums away from the sports pages to the political and social agendas.[11] Decaying fabric, unruly crowds, and an intense form of aggressive localism, combined to give the stadium a bad name and the appellation of another metaphor – the stadium as slum. These arenas also generate what are widely perceived as negative impacts on the neighbourhood in which they are situated. Instead of being a source of pride, they become a sign of stigma. There may indeed be positive benefits of having a stadium in the city, but for a sizeable number of the city's residents, their proximity to it (rather than its accessibility) brings them more sport (or other stadium-based events) than they would freely choose. They are unwilling recipients of the stadium's negative externalities, only one of which is the reduced value of their property. In Britain, and else-where, the major nuisances have been found to be parked cars, traffic congestion and crowding. Hooliganism is an unwanted intrusion but is less significant than the tabloid press would have us believe.[12]

Studies of sports stadiums are relatively few compared with other major physical structures of modern urban life. Some good books on the architecture of sports buildings, including stadiums, do exist[13] and the large amount of sociological writing provides much of use and interest. But interpretive studies from scholars in other subjects are few in number. The chapters in this book seek to fill that gap.

## Overview

The contents of the pages which follow reflect the multi-faceted world of the modern stadium. Authored by an international and inter-disciplinary team of scholars from the social sciences and humanities, this book reviews the historical, economic, political, geographical and social dimensions of the modern stadium, illustrated in a wide variety of national and cultural contexts.

In Chapter 2, Niels Kayser Nielsen exemplifies the modern stadium's ambiguity, illustrating a tension between the rationalization of space and its home-like character. While, on the one hand, the stadium tends towards 'placelessness' it also tends towards a much-loved place, a source for 'topophilia'.[14] Using a wide range of illustrative material from an equally wide variety of national contexts, Kayser Nielsen explores the integration of these apparent contradictions. Taking the sports stadium as a text, Joseph Maguire also provides an overview in Chapter 3, in his exploration of the 'meaning' of stadium space. His approach is explicitly sociological and he focuses particularly on the work of Georg Simmel as a source of ideas around which studies of the stadium can be concep-tualized. Maguire argues that Simmel's concepts of sociation, social geometry and social space are central to an understanding of the sta-dium in the modern metropolis. In a sense, these two chapters set the scene for the remainder of the book.

The construction and development of major edifices such as sports stadiums do not take place in a political vacuum. The political history and geography of stadium development is illustrated in Chapter 4, in which Jim Toft builds on Harvey's assertion (quoted in Nielsen's chapter) that space (including that of urban structures such as the stadium) is never neutral in social affairs; this is a recurring theme in this book. Toft examines the transformation of an area of common land in the northern part of Copenhagen, the *Fælled*, from a public open space to an enclosed football stadium known as *Idrætspark* and its subsequent replacement in 1990 by an icon of high modernity, *Parken* (This new development is the subject of more detailed treatment in Chapter 9).

The history of *Idrætspark* is seen as the outcome of political contestation between various nineteenth- and early twentieth-century interest groups. It is also shown that the playing of modern sports became increasingly confined in space (and time), the 'open play' on public, common land becoming enclosed within the segmented world of the private stadium.

As the stadium evolves, two possible scenarios often emerge which may give rise to a conflict of interests. The first is the spatial reorganization of the stadium *in situ* and the second is the possibility of relocation. This latter scenario is examined in an historical-social context by Roman Horak who, in Chapter 5, explores the changing geographical pattern of football stadium locations in Vienna. A twentieth-century trend, that of suburbanization, is apparent. More significantly, however, is the effect of stadium relocation on supporters' allegiance to the club that occupies it. Horak finds that a strong 'sense of place' exists in respect to particular stadiums. Indeed, clubs which have relocated and subsequently returned to their 'home turf' have been found to more than treble their attendance with such a move. In addition, Horak notes the *embourgeoisement* of Austrian football – the 'rational' proposal of mergers of clubs which would each play in the same stadium, the emergence of the 'placeless' team, and the suggestion of more discriminating spectators. The fact that links between the stadium crowd and the immediate locality are today restricted to the lower division clubs is a pattern unlikely to be particular to Austria.

It would be erroneous to think that, in the early twentieth century, the colonization of urban space by sport was restricted to the nations of the 'western world'. Like so many aspects of European culture, the cult of sport followed the imperial flag, and cities of Africa and Asia experienced the emergence of new cultural landscapes of which various forms of recreational and sports facilities were part. In Chapter 6, Susan Brownell traces the emergence of 'sports space' in the city of Beijing, focusing particularly on its role as one of a number of 'disciplinary technologies' of the Chinese State. Tracing the early forms of recreational land use in the city, Brownell highlights the role of existing urban morphology in contributing to the location of twentieth-century sports space. Temple grounds were a particularly important location in pre-Communist times. The stadiums of Beijing during the Communist period are described as veritable icons of State power, their most important function, aided by their architectural style, being to serve as a backdrop for national ceremonies. It is clear that they possess great political symbolism, both in their architecture and in their function. The hierarchical character of Chinese stadium space is carefully analysed and is shown to contrast with the more economically structured spaces of the European and American stadium. In China, the power of the State is actually *presented to* the people, something that is not so self-evident elsewhere.

Chapters 7 to 11 each deals in its own way with the stadium as a phenomenon caught up in urban development and the politics of 'growth' and 'modernization'. In Chapter 7, Kimberley Schimmel provides a necessary background to the urban studies literature on local development policy and on sociological issues of structure and agency. A detailed overview is also provided of the current situation regarding 'stadiumization' in the United States, where something akin to 'stadium mania' can be said to exist. The general focus of Schimmel's chapter is the *political* dimensions of stadium development – who are the actors in these urban dramas and how is the contestation which is invariably involved in both stadium (re)location and construction actually articulated? Different political perspectives on such developments, ranging from rightist local politicians to structural Marxists, are outlined. But the general picture is supplemented by a detailed study of the situation in Indianapolis, a city with a dying downtown and traditionally possessing a zero image, yet seeking a new, vibrant image to attract jobs and investment, through the development of the Hoosier Dome and the attraction of the former Baltimore Colts football team.

Continuing the theme of urban and regional political contestation Per Jørgensen, in Chapter 8, returns us to Copenhagen and explores the role of the various interest groups, including the city council, in the construction of the new Danish National Stadium, *Parken*. He takes us on from Toft's chapter and demonstrates, with a detailed case study, the way in which a stadium was not only seen to 'belong' to the capital city, but the ways in which that location was secured in the face of alternative geographical scenarios. He also illustrates the difficulty of opposition by community groups to local stadium development and the way in which, in this particular case, capital triumphed over community.

The Copenhagen case study illustrates the modernization of the stadium, something currently being undertaken in Britain. In North America it could be argued that a post-modern stage of stadium design has already arrived. In Chapter 9, Bruce Kidd explores the phenomenon of the SkyDome in Toronto. As in the previous chapters, Kidd focuses centrally on the urban political dimensions in the construction of the 'world's greatest entertainment centre'. The SkyDome is an ambiguous structure *par excellence*. Its retractable roof makes it both indoor and outdoor; it is more than a sports stadium, housing as it does a hotel, several restaurants and other leisure facilities. It typifies a multi-functional use of space, in contrast to the more conventional single sport user. Funded by local government for use by private organizations, Kidd explores the 'vigorous politics' upon which the SkyDome was erected.

Do fans become sated with new stadium facilities and yearn to return to the more homely provisions of yesteryear? This is the scenario found in Chapter 10. Olof Moen's study is of two stadiums: New (*Nya*) Ullevi and Old (*Gamla*) Ullevi, in the Swedish city of Gothenburg. Moen identifies the local political and economic background to the 'two Ullevis', but also sets his study within the broader Swedish cultural context. He identifies Gothenburg as traditionally championing 'workers' culture' in contrast to the high cultural emphasis of the capital Stockholm. In this context, he describes the remarkable revival of Old Ullevi with the decision of three local football clubs to return there to play their games, having previously occupied the high-tech facility at nearby New Ullevi. In addition Moen provides a model of the spatial dynamics of both the modern and late modern (postmodern?) stadium.

It is arguable that it has been in Britain that stadiums and their social and economic impacts have been most newsworthy at both national and international levels in recent years. Indeed, a lengthy list of problems associated with spectator disorder and safety has been catalogued in the British popular (and increasingly the academic) press since the 1920s. These have been well documented by members of the 'Leicester School' and others.[15] Since the publication of the British government's Taylor Report into the 1989 Hillsborough disaster, changes in stadium design and construction have been implemented. Such changes, both locational and *in situ*,[16] form the subject of Chapter 11. Here, John Williams argues that since the Hillsborough disaster the milieu of British football really has changed. He provides evidence by describing the new stadium developments at Millwall, Huddersfield and Leicester, but the tensions between tradition and change are not ignored in Williams's chapter. He recognizes the viewpoints of those who support and those who oppose a modernization of the physical environment of the game that England gave to the world. Yet the inevitability of the shifting contours of British society suggest a new world for the 'people's game', although not necessarily carrying the negative connotations of a 'brave new world'.

The next three chapters take a more explicitly economic position with regard to stadium development and impact. It is well to remember that stadiums of modest size, in comparison with those of Beijing, Indianapolis, Gothenburg, Toronto, and Copenhagen, are also part of the local economy. In Chapter 12, Hans Aldskogius focuses on the fact that in the small Swedish town of Leksand, the ice-hockey stadium is a branch of the local economy. Leksand is a case of a major ice-hockey club being located in a small place.[17] The ice-hockey stadium is a modest but nevertheless central feature of the urban scene, not only geographically but also socially and economically. In a detailed micro-geographic study of 'ice-rink space' Aldskogius identifies the regional and national economic linkages which Leksand has with the world outside the arena and reminds us of the links that the stadium has with those who never use it.

From the small town of Leksand, Chapter 13 shifts the focus of economic attention to the stadium boom in large American cities. In this chapter, Robert Baade is concerned with establishing the relationship between new stadium construction and urban economic growth. This is an important subject because it is widely assumed that stadium growth means economic development for the cities and regions within which new arenas are located, through increased spending on local goods and services. A careful quantitative analysis reveals, however, that this is a myth. Baade concludes, therefore, that the public should be wary when local authorities promise new-found wealth through the development of stadium complexes. Although set in the North American context, Baade's study has much relevance to stadium developments in other parts of the world.

A rather different approach to the economic impact of stadium events is explored in Chapter 14 in which Tommy Andersson considers the success of stadium events in terms of the spectators being the primary beneficiaries. In other words, the emphasis is switched from the benefits of stadium events for those outside the stadium, to those inside. Andersson also draws attention to the fact that stadiums, ostensibly built for sports events, are increasingly diversifying their activities and including rock concerts and other such activities in their precincts. He considers three stadium events, a soccer match, a motorcycle race and a rock concert and suggests methods for evaluating the economic effects of such events by using a model based on the notion of customers' 'willingness to pay' and opportunity costs.

Stadiums clearly provide economic benefits and disbenefits. They are also centres for social interactions. The two final chapters accordingly attend more to social-spatial interpretations. In Chapter 15, John Bale is concerned with the notion that the changing internal layout of the stadium, and the alleged confinement of spectators, has had the effect of making it more analogous to a modern theatre than hitherto. The theatre metaphor, however, should not be seen as being appropriate only to the *modern* stadium or to the more modernized (rationalized) sports played within them. Indeed, different forms of theatrical performance are mirrored in different kinds of sporting performance. The segmentation of intra-stadium space does not inevitably create a hardening or an impermeablity of intra-stadium boundaries; indeed, the very opposite is the case in certain sports. As a result, the ambiguous nature of the stadium is reflected in the liminal zones which characterize much stadium space.

The concluding chapter draws together a number of themes touched on in several parts of this book but, at the same time, adopts various novel perspectives. Henning Eichberg, in a wide-ranging and interpretive analysis, applies to the stadium his idea of a social trialectic.[18] In addition to some fascinating historical insights concerning 'stadium-like' projects, where he argues against a single historical line of stadium 'development', Eichberg distinguishes between three possible configurations of the gaze or view in stadium contexts. Accepting that the stadium can exemplify a panoptical view, he also notes that the panopticon is inverted in the case of the stadium crowd: it is not the élite who are watching the crowd, as in the school or prison, but *vice versa* (although, of course, the crowd is also being watched). The ambiguity of the stadium is again recognized. Eichberg identifies not only the pyramidal view resulting from the hierarchical ordering of stadium space, but also the labyrinthine view from within and below the outer shell of the stadium, providing a sense of foreboding rather than exhilaration. A third view is described as 'zapping' – stadium sport as a simulation, TV screens supplementing the stadium and a world of 'virtual sport'. These alternative (but ideal-type) scenarios raise interesting questions for the future shape of spectating space.

The chapters in *The Stadium and the City* reveal the complex backgrounds to the evolution and siting of stadiums, the nature of their economic impacts, and the 'meaning' of stadiums in the (post-)modern world. There can be no doubt that the stadium, like the shopping mall and the theme park, will continue to attract the interest of scholars from a wide variety of academic disciplines. The aim of the present collection is to map out some existing academic terrain upon which other scholars might build.

## Notes

1. For examples of detailed and descriptive accounts of stadiums associated with particular sports see Simon Inglis, *The Football Grounds of Great Britain* (London, 1987) and *The Football Grounds of Europe* (London, 1990), and P. J. Lowry, *Green Cathedrals* (Reading, Mass., 1992).
2. A. Bartlett Giamatti, *Take Time for Paradise; Americans and their Games* (New York, 1989), p.33.
3. William Arens, 'Playing with Aggression', in Jeremy Cherfas and Roger Lewin (eds), *Not Work Alone* (London, 1980), pp.71–83.
4. Giamatti, *Take Time for Paradise*, pp.42–3.
5. John Bale, 'Sportplätze als Gärten und Parks', *Zeitschrift für Semiotik* (1995, in press).
6. Giamatti, *Take Time for Paradise*, p.67.
7. Guy Debord, *Society of the Spectacle* (Detroit, 1987).
8. Steven Reiss, *City Games* (Champaign, Ill., 1989), p.217.
9. Quoted in D. Whitsun, 'Leisure, the State and Collective Consumption', in J. Horne, D. Jary and A. Tomlinson (eds), *Sport, Leisure and Social Relations* (London, 1987), pp.229–53.
10. David Harvey, 'From Managerialism to Entrepreneurialism: the Transformation of Urban Governance in Late Capitalism', *Geografiska Annaler*, Vol. 71B, 1 (1989), pp.3–17.

11. Several studies undertaken at the Sir Norman Chester Centre for Football Research at Leicester University focus on the stadium in the context of 'football hooliganism', See, for example, Eric Dunning, Patrick Murphy and John Williams, *The Roots of Football Hooliganism* (London, 1988); Patrick Murphy, John Williams and Eric Dunning, *Football on Trial* (London, 1990); John Williams, Eric Dunning and Patrick Murphy, *Hooligans Abroad* (London, 1990).

12. The research into the negative impacts of stadiums is reviewed in John Bale, *Sport, Space and the City* (London, 1993).

13. See, for example, Hans Lynsgaard, *Idrætens Rum* (Copenhagen, 1990) and Martin Wimmer, *Olympic Buildings* (Liepzig, 1976). The spatial segmentation of the British football stadium is described in Bale, *Sport, Space and the City*, Ch 2. Note also Simon Inglis's two excellent books (see note 1). A more explicitly visual treatment is provided in Søren Nagbøl and John Bale, 'A View of Football; Sport and a Sense of Place', *Occasional Paper*, 83 (Jyväskylä, 1994). The different symbolisms of the Stockholm Globe are explored in an unusual way by Allan Pred, *Recognizing European Modernities* (London, 1995).

14. The notion of 'topophilia' in a football context is examined in John Bale, 'Playing at Home: British Football and a Sense of Place', in John Williams and Stephen Wagg (eds), *British Football and Social Change* (Leicester, 1991), pp.130–44. The notion of 'placelessness' is explored in Edward Relph, *Place and Placelessness* (London, 1976). Its application to the stadium landscape is dealt with in John Bale, *Landscapes of Modern Sport* (Leicester, 1994).

15. See note 11 above.

16. For further details see Bale, *Sport, Space and the City*, Ch. 6.

17. For a broader analysis (in Swedish) of the economic geography of Leksand see Hans Aldskogius, *Leksand, Leksand, Leksand!* (Hedemora, 1993).

18. Eichberg's notion of a trialectic has been applied to numerous sport-related themes in recent years. See, for example, Henning Eichberg, 'Body Culture as Paradigm: the Danish Sociology of Sport', *International Review for the Sociology of Sport*, Vol. 19, 1 (1989), pp.43–63.

# 2

# The Stadium in the City: A Modern Story

*Niels Kayser Nielsen*

## Introduction

A sports stadium is one of the few places in a city where an urban crowd can gather regularly on a legal basis. For this reason alone, it is a unique phenomenon in urban life. Furthermore, it assists in influencing city life by providing a framework for the outward representation of the city. That is to say, the city influences the stadium, just as the stadium influences the city; the stadium landscape is both staged by the city and a staging of the city. It is an extension of the city's streets and street life, while, at the same time, it differs in that, as in the duality found in the theatre, it provides on the one hand a distinct, formalized and aesthetic staging, and, on the other, an arena for the 'agon', which in the city streets is silently expressed. Whereas normally this duality is a silent constituent of the city and the street, it finds, in the stadium, expression in the form of a demonstrative production for the public – for the crowd's interpretive conception of city life.

The stadium landscape is more than a mere locality. In terms of space, it is limited only by the diversity of events which themselves vary according to their place in time and history. If one wants to understand the full meaning of the stadium, counting the number of visitors will not suffice. The same can be said of it as of any other space, that it is never 'neutral in social affairs' as the stadium and the life taking place there both collect and throw off history.[1] However, history is always coded; it may be created again and again, but, it is always defined by certain norms of expression that have been handed down. In other words, it is a characteristic of the life of the stadium that it is influenced by style, not any particular style, but a stylized exertion, which is direction-determined and determining, yet also so broad that it leaves room for improvization and new creations.

The object of this chapter is to discuss this in further detail, first, by focusing on the disciplinary role of the stadium; second, by looking at the stadium as a theatrical free space, an arena; and finally, by shifting the focus of the discussion to the integration of these two key features into the very life that is taking place within the stadium culture.

## The Rationalized City Landscape of the Stadium

More than anything, the development of the sports ground is an expression of a rationalization of the landscape, in which the multi-functional landscape is replaced by a patchwork of mono-functional locations specialized to handle certain tasks. These spatial enclaves also contain a more or less hidden element of power, inasmuch as they are always supervised.[2] This supervision can be related to property, as in the right of private property over space, or it can be of an administrative kind, as in the decisions of the public (represented by State, county or lower-level administrative boards) with regard to the appearance and tasks of the space.

In order to describe this combination of space and power, one might adopt Robert David Sack's term, 'territoriality', whereby one understands a limited area bound together by dispositions of power, as opposed to the open, unenclosed landscape.[3] In contrast to the conventional understanding of a territory as a static, defended space, Sack sees it as a process, an intended or unintended striving to affect or to control people and social relations by determining the borders of, and exercising control over, a certain geographic area. 'Territoriality', in other words, is something 'that happens'. It connotes a social process, which takes place among people as a socially-constructed form of spatial relations which determine who controls whom and with what purpose. Thus, 'territoriality' does not so much express the power over a space as the control over bodily and mental movements taking place in that space. In other words, who moves in the space, who comes and goes, with what purpose, and how? Here, naturally, the question as to how one moves in a given space is also determined by the construction of the space *vis-à-vis* its architectural layout and the influence of this on people in a bodily, kinaesthetic sense.

Sack does not mention sports and stadiums. Rather, it is from the work of John Bale that we are able to appreciate the usefulness of the term 'territoriality' in relation to sports facilities. This is nowhere more evident than in the stadium, in that one of its characteristics is that people have limited access to space, and when it is accessible, it is to designated seats only. During the week, the stadium lies deserted, with its gates closed. Once a week these gates are opened and people may take their seats, but only as spectators. The term 'territoriality' seems particularly appropriate in connoting this kind of space; a space which is periodically filled up and emptied.

As we shall see below, the stadium also has an expressive free-space, but as a starting point one must focus on its pre-organized relation to both players and crowd. Certain behavioural patterns become a necessity, not in the sense of a violent disciplining of the bodies, but by means of a certain spatial distribution, such as is analysed by Foucault in his work *Discipline and Punish*.[4]

Foucault's concept of distribution and Sack's term 'territoriality' deal with different aspects of the same matter, namely the ostensibly force-free, yet permanent vesting of power in the space, with its subsequent consequences in terms of discipline. This discipline is primarily of a movement-economic and body-distributive nature, which, however, does have certain decisive consequences. As Foucault points out, it is the overall aim of any modernist influence on space to ensure an economic distribution of bodies. That is, it is not certain forms of bodily gestures and behaviour that one should direct attention to: the bodies are not to be trained and castigated. In other words, it is imperative that, once the bodies have been allocated, a free-space does exist, but one which is confined to the cell. In principle, one may behave as one wants – as long as one is allocated and knows one's place.

This bodily distribution, as can be observed in prisons, schools and factories, is, even though disciplinary in its basic structures, not without civilizing qualities. It is at the roots of the modern mass-production of goods and knowledge, and it is, at the same time, part of the production of the crowd as a modern phenomenon. Ultimately, it is also the prerequisite for the understanding of the democratic mass-citizen, in that it is also the prerequisite for modern popular sport, with its foundation of equal conditions within a standardized physical-spatial framework, where violence has been eliminated and competitions of a mimetic nature are conducted.[5]

The standardization specific to sports, in terms of equal competitive conditions resulting from distribution based on age, gender, weight, etc., is obvious here. However, in this context it is more relevant to focus on equal conditions in terms of landscapes that are a prerequisite for sports competitions and hence, ultimately, also inter-urban representations. In other words, we must consider the stadium from the perspective of standardization.


## The Placelessness of the Stadium

In order to describe the homogeneous space, which is a prerequisite for any competition, the concept of 'placelessness'[6] is useful. This concept is based on the fact that many of today's city landscapes are characterized by an increasing tendency towards 'placelessness' or 'sameness', which refs both to the actual place and to its characteristics.[7] This applies equally to the wholesale warehouses of the cities' main access roads, to suburban housing blocks and tower blocks, to public buildings with office landscapes, to fast-food outlets and to international airports. All project a standardized design, which leads to every such place, regardless of city, looking the same. The similarities are so predominant that one may rightfully claim that young people from the larger cities of different countries have more in common with each other than they have with their fellow country men from rural areas. Supermarkets and petrol stations are virtually identical all over the world.

The stadium too, is just such a placeless site, encouraging the same behaviour among both athletes and crowd. As far as the stadium is concerned, this is not only due to the fact that it is part of a series of modern, depersonalized buildings, aimed at regularly servicing a large crowd of people who do not know each other, but also because of the homogenization, which necessarily marks a space for sports. Fundamental to any competitive sport, is the space in which it occurs, both in terms of spatial organization and the physical surroundings which relate to the actual arena in which the sport takes place. These should be as identical as possible and thus disregard any local or global idiosyncrasy. The objective is a disregard for local and regional differences. Stadiums in Manchester, Djakarta or Rio de Janeiro must be identical in terms of ground layout, otherwise it would not make sense to use the word stadium. Hardly any other place in the modern city faces such stringent requirements – only in sports stadiums can one observe identical geometric dimensions everywhere. This adds a certain degree of anonymity to the sports stadium, and at the same time makes stipulations on social interactions which extend beyond the arena itself. The homogeneity of design and construction ensures a common code which is predictable and invariable from one place to another.

With the growing use of synthetic materials, local spatial idiosyncrasies are reduced even further, to an absolute minimum. That is to say, the tendency towards standardization and surveillance, demonstrated for instance with regard to the seats of the spectators, is accompanied on the actual sports ground by an increasing tendency towards homogeneity. The stadium is gradually becoming an isotropic landscape, aimed at identical conditions for production and achievement. Both the athletes and the spectators are spatially restrained. However, this trend does imply that the different parts of the stadium-space must correlate to a certain extent with each other, from place to place and from city to city. This condition can be further accentuated in the direction of one or two overall abstract features of the urban landscape.

The zenith of abstraction in this description will, at the same time, be used as an axis of reflection, by turning around and subsequently descending to another and more 'tangible' side of the stadium-reality in the city.

## The City as Pure Shape and as a Domicile for the Other

In the stadium, the urban tendency towards the isotropic landscape is condensed, a tendency which is intertwined with the city's development towards pure shape: the place of the meeting, the place for getting together, a homogeneous space. This is where indifference is produced, where the different is brought together and becomes identical in a 'piecemeal' shape, which has no contents, but to which everything submits. It has the nature of a tangible abstraction. Thanks to this process of abstraction, the city becomes a social object, which – as a re-organizer – tries to fragment its own preconditions before joining them together again.

In the stadium we see this clearly in the inclination towards homogenization of spectator accommodation, in the uniform, numbered plastic seats, the compartmentalization of the high stands, and in the tendency towards elimination of nature by the use of synthetic materials for the running tracks and – in some places – for the football ground itself. In both cases, we observe a pattern of centralization, which adapts, conforms and homogenizes, and which makes calculation, quantifying and programming possible. The shape is geometrical – either square or circular – and thereby permits symmetry and repetition.

The configuration of the city is displayed nowhere more obviously than in the territoriality of the parking lot. In this abstract space, which is emptied and refilled anonymously by impersonal things with a human inside, absolute centralization and placelessness rule in a well-ordered, practical sequence, which, if anything, homogenizes the different. As a pure shape – a functional expanse finding its meaning in its own emptiness, the parking lot lies there, repeating the empty possibility for humans to find their place in the city, in a continuous 'provisorium' designated by others. This is the epitome of the urban landscape: synthetic materials, 'serialization', surveillance, and a territorial coming and going; controlled movement and repetition in a completely neutralized landscape free of any meaning other than its own empty presence. In Baudriallard's terms, it is a hyper-real and obscene place, repeating itself in its own practical reference to the same, and which is the same, beyond real and unreal, beauty and hideousness.[8]

However, this repetition also opens up the possibility for reading and decoding, so that the city becomes a familiar space in which to move, in all its 'alikeness'. Paradoxically, it is exactly this managing, administration and control, biased towards staging and homogeneity, which also renders possible orientation in time and space. The urban production of simultaneousness, and the homotopic production of space, play the part of handwriting, that is, as a rational ordering of elements which stand in relation to each other. For this reason, we are able – without much trouble – to find our way around Madrid, Berlin and Palermo. Similarly, we can – without too much trouble – go to a stadium in Copenhagen, Reykjavík and Buenos Aires. Because of its isotropic landscape, the space of the city, in general, and the space of the stadium, in particular, become familiar spaces in which to move.

As emphasized by Henri Lefebvre, however, the city is also the domicile of the Other. It contains not only homotopy, but also heterotopy: in the urban space there is always something certain happening. Patterns of relation are constantly changing; differences and opposites clash and turn into conflict.[9] Rationality breaks down and the other side of the urban emerges: the city is also mysterious and occult.[10] The ostensibly well-ordered transparency and regularity is broken by disorder, spontaneity and difference. Regulation and organization are contrasted by ambiguity and passion. This implies a weakening of the centre and the possibility of poly-centrality or omni-centrality: a breakaway from the centre, a breakaway from manipulation and control.[11] However, it also opens up the possibility of losing the code and ending up in despair, conflict and chaos, as we know from the hooliganism of the stadium world and the traffic chaos of the stadium parking lot.

Overall, the urban landscape is thus characterized by a duality of order and disorder, organization and disorganization, restraint and letting go, adaptation and breaking up, unity and multiplicity, repetition and 'Einmaligheit',[12] depersonalization and subjectivity, placelessness and 'Heimat'.[13] This duality is echoed in the stadium. So far we have pursued the track of order, while emphasizing power, surveillance, control and force. The second part of this chapter concentrates on the antithesis of homotopia, the dimension of 'Heimat'. Having thus parked the car in this epitome of placelessness, the parking lot, we can – in a throng of people – enter the stadium having handed off 'seriality'.


**The Stadium and Topophilia**

To describe the antithesis of placelessness, which includes both the attitude towards the place and its characteristics, one may use Gaston Bachelard's concept of topophilia,[14] as it has been developed further by the Chinese-American geographer Yi-Fu Tuan and, in the context of sport, by John Bale.[15]

Topophilia refers to the ties that unite humans and their material surroundings, especially the ties that combine emotion and place. The starting point for such an idea, is that landscapes and places are not only coincidental visual backgrounds for social behaviour and emotions, but rather, even the most homotopic of them forms an integrated and obliging part. The concept of topophilia refers to both the physical-spatial surroundings and to the more or less mysterious – and possibly quasi-religious – aspects of the experience. The place with which topophilia is basically concerned is characterized as authentic, carrying from time to time the stamp of the secular shrine; that is to say, a place, which does not derive its meaning from habit or incidental hunches.[16]

In his discussion of the stadium and a sense of space, Bale concentrates analytically on five versions of topophilia, which, individually and together, shed light on the distinctive sense of locality, which marks the attachment to the city stadium. To demonstrate his contention that the stadium is a 'sacred place', he quotes a soccer fan from Chester, who for many years frequented the city's stadium at Sealand Road:

> Sealand Road has been part of my life for thirty years, it is more than a football stadium – it is a way of life, not only for me, but for thousands of people – dead or alive – whose lives have formed around the Stadium. It is more than bricks and mortar; it is almost something spiritual.[17]

Though one should be careful in making too far-reaching comparisons between sports and religion, it is obvious that similarities do exist in a whole range of areas where ball games in general, and soccer in particular, have become – in the words of the Argentinean social anthropologist Eduardo Archetti – 'rituals comparable to religious ceremonies'[18] and where the stadium assumes the nature of a church.[19] Sports and religion have in common both the striving for perfection, built on discipline, and the aim of integrating body and soul.[20] Both have created rituals and symbols related to humans, procedures and places, and both have developed ceremonies and a liturgy, which, within the framework of locations with particularly 'sacred' qualities, develop cult-like behaviour, where players and coaches may perform with the same charisma as priest and preachers, and where the stadium itself carries – in the words of Yi-Fu Tuan – 'poly-immense meaning'[21] (see Figure 2.1). In this context, it is decisive that Anfield Stadium in Liverpool has, on certain occasions been used as a graveyard, fans having their ashes scattered over the the stadium, and that a former stadium cat has been buried underneath one of the goal lines.[22]

The stadium may also be perceived in terms of domicile or home, inasmuch as the confidentiality of the place, with its singular, unique and tangible, spatial configuration invites home-like emotions.[23] In this context, it is interesting to notice the level of opposition from supporters,

**Figure 2.1** At a stadium event such as the opening of the Olympic Games (as here at Lake Placid in 1980), the spontaneity of the spectators is deemed to disturb the ceremony

which surfaces immediately when plans for changing the location of the home ground are revealed. In Hamburg, it is unthinkable that the supporters of St Pauli FC would consider watching the club's matches if they were to take place at Volkspark Stadium in the city's north-west, Mercedes neighbourhood, rather than at the smaller, but more intimate stadium, Am Millerntor, in the dockland area, where the club belongs. As for England, where quite a few clubs, forced by economic circumstances, have been interested in moving to new locations, these plans have consistently run into fierce opposition.[24] The bonds with the symbolic home have been too strong.

In Gothenburg, the Swedish Premier League football club GAIS, in the early 1990s had plans for constructing a new stadium complex. One of the places being considered was the large recreational area of Slottskogsvallen in the western part of the city centre. However, the proposal was dropped because of the already existing grounds in the area, which were used by smaller local clubs and rented to spontaneously formed groups.[25] GAIS enjoy good relations with these smaller clubs, which are a constant source of talented young players for the club.[26] Therefore they chose to refrain from robbing them of their home ground. The local cultural costs would have been too large.

But the question of stadium-home has played an important role in the sporting world of Gothenburg in another way. The large Nya (new) Ullevi Stadium, housing forty thousand people, was established in an area where the Heden Stadium complex, rich in tradition, with several gravel grounds, has raised some of Sweden's best-known players. Also nearby, and equally rich in tradition, Gamla (old) Ullevi Stadium can be found. With plummeting numbers of spectators for the soccer matches, where a crowd of five thousand looks small in the large Nya Ullevi, and hence finds it difficult to feel comfortable, the three large clubs – IFK Gothenburg, GAIS, and Örgryte – have, since 1992, played their matches at Gamla Ullevi, with its cosy, wooden, high stands and spectators close to the ground (see Chapter 10). Here, to a larger extent, the players and the crowd could experience a sense of connection, and could feel at home. This story bears evidence of a reaction to a consumption-oriented approach to the stadium experience. There is much more at stake than merely watching a match. The confidentiality of the surroundings is notoriously decisive. A place with character performs a potent, socially-integrative part and produces a sense of belonging and participation in a community, especially when the place in question is welcoming.[27]

Closely related to the stadium as a home is the element of topophilia attached to local patriotism and place-pride. The events taking place at the stadium are the outward representation of the local and the regional. The city and the neighbourhood show themselves to the surrounding world by being brought together in one place – at the stadium. Here is the quintessence of the city bringing it together. Yet other buildings also possess such representational value as objects of local patriotism, albeit never staged in the same articulated mass-manner as in the stadium. Stadium life constitutes a form of cultural maintenance of the city's representation, which, as opposed to other versions of cultural enactment, is emphatically tied to a particular place. Whereas a city's annual celebration may take place in many different urban locations, the cultural self-enactment of the city at the stadium is necessarily connected to the place as a place in its own right – regardless of how placeless the configuration of the stadium may be. This is the home ground, and precedence over guest spectators is enjoyed due to the local anchoring, and one's own contribution to the sustaining of this precedence. At the stadium, the city celebrates itself inasmuch as its *genius loci* is concentrated there. The stadium is the experienced and 'inspired' place, where it is possible to identify with the close local ties within a given order and composition, as well as with a broader sense of belonging, whether cosmic, ideological or cultural. The sense of place and 'Heimat' exceeds, in this case, the sense of mere location and allocation.

The stadium is also the place where the city and its inhabitants inherit themselves.[28] Here, the city's sense of history is expressed, not only through museum-like antiquity and the aura of the stadium buildings, but also through the lived history prolonged by the sustained traditions and myths which are an integral part of stadium culture.

In relation to the nursing of heritage as an aspect of an identity-creating conscience of history, it is possible to distinguish between two processes: historic heritage as it takes place among people, and historic heritage as it is constructed, enacted and supervised for people. The latter is normally materialized in certain buildings, landscapes and places with a monumental air about them. Parliament buildings are often such monuments. Edifices that mark national historic events and landscapes, where important battles were fought, can also perform this role. Such places materialize the historic heritage in such a way that makes it seem natural, given and indisputable, so that these buildings and landscapes become part of the conscience of history of the area referred to – something one is let into, voluntarily or involuntarily. Such places sustain history, and in that way assist also in creating it. They are places of objective memory – constructed, institutionalized fixed-points, which act as 'time islands' that are above the time of everyday life. They act as archives of common historic material, which in its everyday-transcendence is oriented towards the given time.

The need for these kinds of historic memory-landscapes, with their objective memory, is inversely proportional to the lack of history of the actual environment. That is to say that during the epochs, where history and life-history do not go together, but where the speed of history erodes life-history and makes it 'memoryless',[29] there is a predilection towards an objective and institutionalized historicism, which is not only characterized by storing history in museums, but which also – existence-philosophically – seeks to turn life into history on a range of different levels and in different areas of life, ranging from interest in antiques and local history societies to the flea-market culture. In this context, the nurturing of certain historic locations that are reconstructively and selectively ascribed historic significance, without being in their own right historic, also plays a part.

Considering the myths and the consciousness of tradition related to the stadium and considering the everyday transcendence and its function as a 'time-island', it seems obvious to group the stadium with this kind of historic landscape and objective place of remembrance. Beyond the temporal aspect, one should also, however, take into consideration the spatial side of these matters. The stadium also performs the part of a 'space-island' (note the opposition against moving it which is mentioned above). Situated a few miles out of the town centre, the stadium, with its dual nature of both permanence and permanent change, functions as a kind of a refuge of historic stability, which has been historically, and for purposes of identification, conquered by the city's citizens – and not only by sports spectators. But in contrast to the actual *lieux de mémoire*, the stadium is also (and in this respect quite uniquely) a forum for a different kind of consciousness of history: the communicative everyday remembrance, which is not everyday transcendent.[30]

The stadium is available for orientation with an archive of material of remembrance, which, as opposed to the history of historic-cultural monuments, can, at any time, be exchanged 'anecdotally' with others; and where the involved parties may, at any time, change roles and positions, in order that they themselves pass on experienced material of remembrance, or lend a willing ear to stories and encounters of incidents, experienced by others. In each case, the prerequisite is a certain common ground so that the communication of recollections is based on and helps to establish social communication and group relationships. The stories of the stadium thus become, in the words of Clifford Geertz, (hi)story, told 'for one another'.[31] At the same time, they are creators and interpreters of identity; a meta-social comment on being a citizen of a city, which people exchange among themselves or read about in the city's newspaper on Monday mornings – after the weekend's occurrences at the stadium.

Both as a place of objective remembrance and as a communicative everyday memory, the stadium performs its part as an inward object of identification in relation to the local users. But it also carries significance outwardly in relation to inhabitants of other cities: it plays a part from a tourism point of view. It may even be a tourist attraction in its own right, a museum that requires a ticket, typified by the Olympic Stadium in Munich, Wembley in London, or Old Trafford in Manchester. Equally important from a visitor's perspective, however, are the signs, displayed on all access roads to the city to help out-of-town visitors. Here, the city presents itself to others and refers demonstratively to its forum, its stage, its arena – as it does to other important places in the city, such as the town hall, church, museum and theatre. In a similar way, the stadium announces to everyone: Welcome to a civilized city, which has an arena of representation, where we, from time to time, present ourselves to the surrounding world for purposes of identification. Here, more than in any other place, it is evident that the stadium does not merely represent sports; it is a matter of relevance for all citizens as a whole – in relation to the surrounding world and its reading of the city.

Regardless of the evident tendency towards the placelessness that characterizes the stadium, there is always more at stake. It is the turning point for the duality marking the city as a whole: anonymity and abstraction versus sense of locality and sense of 'Heimat'. Due to this duality, the stadium functions as the representative logo of the city. It is the place of the conflicting tendencies in the life of the city, in the area of tension between alienation and vivacity.

## Crowd Life at the Stadium

This duality is expressed not least in the crowd life which can be observed at the stadium. On the one side, there is the piecemeal and crowd-dissolving character which accompanies placelessness as it has been described above. On the other hand, crowd life which is connected to the topophilic aspect of city life, and which is expressed not least in the stadium, can also be observed. There may be good reason to use, as a starting point, the purely phenomenological fact that it is actual bodies which come to the stadium – bodies which are eyes and mouth, sense of smell, hands and feet, long before they recognize any emotion which might form the idea that this physical being represents 'me'.[32] This pre-subjective condition can also be found in the behaviour of the crowd, as stressed by Elias Canetti in particular.[33] It may be that the crowd is disciplined and distributed, but in its purely phenomenological presence the body recaptures itself physically – by moving around. The crowd, which sets in motion towards a certain place, such as a stadium, takes on the character of a massive bodily offensive against the city. It makes itself felt by its own physical presence, partly due to the fact that each member of the crowd occupies nine square feet of the city's space and partly because the crowd as such seizes the city's streets, squares and public means of transportation, thus bodily possessing them.

Thomas Leithäuser, influenced by Merleau-Ponty, stresses that such possession of space in a physical-bodily sense is tantamount to establishing a new sense of space, hence enabling another condition of conscience as well as that determined by distribution. From having been an indifferent, empty space decomposed to mere distance, the social space becomes a virtual space of collective exertion.[34] On the way to the

stadium this rearranging of space is compressed and ultimately condensed within the stadium itself.[35] During the walk in the street, the
bodies themselves transform the body space, which becomes a common
social space. This is no longer a diffuse and placeless space of competition, with uniformed bodies heading for some coincidental spot, but
the space of united action or solidarity.[36]

However, the temporary creation of a space of this kind is not so
much an expression of a desired, 'political' action as a testimony to the
bodies' silent, yet absolute presence in the city by means of being exactly
that, a body forming a part of the landscape. The experience of taking
up space and filling up the street becomes, to the participants, a 'living
experience', which goes beyond and lies underneath language and
rationality – and which develops, when many are present, into a crowd-
experience.[37] By means of their gathering and crowding together,
the stadium spectators demonstrate their force, strength and potential
threat (see Figure 2.2).

Elias Canetti has stated that the crowd, which shows itself and presents itself as a gathering of people, cannot be broken. The ring it
constitutes is closed and homogeneous. It seems to be a ring of flesh and
blood. This effect is produced not least by the bodily homogeneity
prevalent within the crowd: 'It is absolute and indisputable, and the
crowd never questions it. It is so fundamentally important that it is
possible to define the state of the crowd as a state of absolute homogeneity. A head is a head, an arm an arm, and differences among them
are irrelevant.'[38] The crowd is there first and foremost in a bodily
sense. That is to say, not as a representative for anything else, but as
a presentation of itself. This, when repeated, attains the nature of a
symbolically, ritually and patterned drama, which helps to create the
'social order' of the city, not just as an abstract uniformed order, but also
as a bodily order, which cannot be reduced to planning and strategy.[39]
The body is not, in this case, its own representative symbol referring, to
begin with, to itself and its own bodily crowd-order, and only afterwards
to eventual political and cultural conditions and strategies. With the
body-crowd, the individual supersedes his uniformed closeness and
alienation. The crowd transcends by its conduct.

Crowd-life does not equal chaos, but order. But it is a different kind
of social order from the common strategic one, inasmuch as the Other
emerges from the bodies' restructuring of the city's landscape and a new
social experience of space of a practical-bodily kind is created, which –
albeit temporarily – puts an end to the placelessness of city space. The
social and geographical space is seized and not distributively filled up.
However, seen from the point of view of the crowd, this does not take
place as a result of a conscious, manifest 'ideology', but as a presentation
of the Other way of being a man of the city, a citizen, namely a way

**Figure 2.2** The ambiguity of the modern stadium: joy behind the fences

which lies beneath or ahead of planning and distribution and which regularly creates its own urban 'scope',[40] by demonstrating through routine and repetitive action that one belongs to a certain place, in a certain time; that is to say, one is specific in a temporal and spatial 'historicity'; one creates history rather than just being created by history; and history is created with the body substantial.[41] The crowd may be an historic product, yet, in its crowding together – such as at the stadium – it dismisses this product-likeness and recreates it(self), not as mere distributed nitwits, but as an historic being making its presence known and making a great fuss about it.

## The Stadium between Pre-modernity and Post-modernity

Letting its presence be known, is probably the stadium crowd's most important characteristic, not least from its own point of view. At the same time, the way in which this happens is an expression of urban tradition which exceeds the city's tendency towards placelessness. First and foremost, it takes place by means of noise; be it produced by shouting, singing, horns, drums or other musical instruments like trumpets and trombones, as is the tradition at Dutch stadiums in particular. However, it may also stem simply from the noise level which is inevitably brought about when many people come together in one place. In most cases, on a quiet day, the shouts, the applause and the noise can be heard from one or two miles away – and the cones of light at evening matches can be seen from a considerable distance. When there is a match at the stadium, it never passes off quietly. The stadium and its crowd assert themselves to an extent not seen at other massive citizen's manifestations in the city, whether at theatre visits, train-station crowding or restaurant life. The noise is the stadium's primary means of expression.

The nature of this noise is pre-modern. Despite the fact that common popular traditions never played as large a part in the world of sports as might be expected, there is reason to allude to older elements in modern sports, not least in relation to the behaviour in the stands.[42] Here, the pre-modern, noisy culture is significant. In accordance with the Charivari culture of Middle and Southern Europe, and inspired by the *commedia del'arte* culture, the satirical songs accompanied by clapping, stamping and drums play a decisive part at the stadium. The away team is harrassed as badly as possible, while simultaneously, the assets of the home team are emphasized. At the same time, the undercurrent of the songs create their own space of sound, not unlike the sound-world found at other arena-like occurrences such as rock concerts and church services, where one also identifies with a self-referential sound.

In addition there are certain carnivalesque expressions in the stadium, including animal analogies often related to fables. At Möngersdorfer Stadium in Cologne, the billy-goat, Hennes, has always had its place in front of the spectator seats.[43] Similarly, players' nicknames around Europe have often contained reference to animals: the Russian goalkeeper Lev Yashin, renowned for his quick reflexes, was often referred to as 'The Cat'; in Gothenburg, one of IFK's fastest and most colourful wingers was referred to as 'The Colt'; similarly, GAIS team members are referred to as the 'Mackerels' due to their green and black shirts – a reincarnation of the port and fishing town on the Swedish west coast; in Germany, there is Peter 'de Aap' Müller and 'Ente' Lippens; from Aarhus Stadium in Denmark there is 'Tarok' Hyldgaard, a slow defensive player, who was lovingly and ironically nicknamed after Denmark's fastest racehorse. In all cases, preferences show affinity to general patterns of movement and orientations of action with players in their total physiognomy, and not to specific technical skills in a parcelled-out bodily pattern. In other words, what is referred to is a more homogeneous, cosmic man/animal world, than the one of segmented 'physicality' which otherwise characterizes the physical exercises of modernity, i.e. sports.

A third archaic and pre-modern cultural element is the noise and the bodily tradition of the circus culture. In Prague, before the Communists took over in 1948, it was a tradition that, close to the Sparta stadium, a platform in front of a circus tent was put up, and with much commotion and ballyhoo, circus director Soukup would challenge 'strong men' among the street crowd to try their strength in a fight with his boxers and wrestlers in the tent before they went on to the match at the stadium.[44] Certain other forms of grotesqueness and half-time clowning similarly form part of the action at stadiums throughout Europe. The culture critic would say, of course, that this is just to lure people into coming. However, it is decisive that it is such folkish elements as shooting competitions, beauty contests, balancing acts, etc. which are used.

Folkish food elements such as beer and hot dogs are never in short supply at stadiums on the European mainland. Regardless of whether one can appreciate the ritual aspect of this consumption of food, it would be unthinkable for spectators to have a vegetarian dish at the stadium, or to drink a sophisticated wine or an elegant cocktail. Instead, they have the traditional, continental 'stadium platter': beer and hot dogs.

Here, we see a central element in the relation between stadium and city: the clash between plebeian, mass-cultural ways of articulation with ritual features and modern forms of culture, unique in their nature. The alarming noise level from the crowd – uncensured and unrestricted shouting at the referee and the away team – which can be observed at the stadium, stands in harsh opposition to the analytic and rational modern reflection normally used to measure and judge city culture. Such low-life expressions as 'black bastard' (about the referee) belongs nowhere in city culture but is commonplace at the stadium. The unrestricted practice of making a fool of the away team's players generally far exceeds civic-democratic principles of fair play and gentlemanly culture. Stadium-delights go way beyond subdued affections and restricted emotions. But it also far exceeds the premeditated outcry, the political mass manifestation and the critical broad view carrying the seed of popular rebellion. Likewise, it goes beyond mere safety-valve behaviour, allowing for a regular catharsis. What can be heard is people celebrating and making noise with no other thought than expressing themselves without any reservations.[45] City culture's a-rationalism finds in this a vehicle of expression. It is precisely that; it is not anti-rationalistic; it defies that kind of categorization.

In the noise of stadium, the pre-modern and pre-rational culture of common people is tied together with post-modernity's suspension of the demand for meaning and depth in expression. The stadium culture is not a counterculture; it is not defined in opposition to the authoritative culture of the city, but exists beyond this, measured by other standards – otherwise, it would probably long since have been radically transformed to a more urban and civilized way of expression. Articulation takes place within other discourses of orientation such as sense of locality and local patriotism, and not within discourses of abstract civic principles such as meaning and reason. Or rather, in this case, meaning and reason are not defined concepts, but are defined *in casu*.[46] This constitutes their real historic dimension. The spectators are not bearers of culture, but creators of culture, beyond ideas of good and evil, beauty and wonder, justice and injustice. The stadium culture is not poetic but historic. It is ethically and aesthetically without norms; it follows historicism's own norms, which are actual and characterized by 'Einmaligheit'.

## Stadium Culture between Style, Fashion and *Habitus*

The duality of conformity without history and situative existence, on the one side, and history-creating, unique behaviour, on the other, have so far been treated separately for analytic reasons. However, stadium culture is distinctive in that these aspects are intertwined in many areas, forming a synthesis containing many contradictions.

That stadium culture is ethically and aesthetically without norms is not tantamount to it being pre- and post-modernly 'wild' and contingent; as pointed out several times above, it contains its own social order. The final part of this chapter discusses this contradictory order, which, for lack of anything better, is termed stadium-style – in the hope of capturing the duality of collectivism and individual uniqueness which is present. To that end, insights from the previous year's fashion and life-style analyses seem relevant, insofar as they deal with exactly the social tension between a historic order and disorder in history. Therefore, while keeping Pierre Bourdieu's concept of *habitus* in mind,[47] this chapter argues in favour of the view that stadium culture relates to a play between central elements of life-style and fashion.

More than anything, the contrast between individualized enactment and conformity, between the chosen, distinctive expression and the abstraction as contents, is a characteristic of the idea of life-style. In the desire to express a certain life-style, individual propensities are excluded in a constructed cultural expression, thereby hoping to express the individual and the specific. However paradoxical it may seem, it is exactly this combination of cultivation of the sign for its own sake and the sign as representation which is at the core of every desire to display life-style. Life-style is an attempt at endowing conformity with cultural variation in a structural-spatial sense – as opposed to fashion which also bears on the relation between the general and the specific, but in a 'timely' sense. Fashion is always in pursuit of novelty, based on the familiar, whereas life-style desires to distinguish permanence as variability, even though it is also continuously threatened by cultural inflation. After all, when too many cultivate the same life-style, it loses its distinctive, identity-creating qualities, so that it must again install some means of making itself permanent.[48]

For reasons of clarification, it is pertinent also to relate fashion as life-style to Bourdieu's concept of *habitus*. Where fashion seeks the unique and the specific, and life-style cultivates permanence, *habitus* equals the inertia that is related to longer-lasting traditions, which one may claim not to live by, but which one cannot act without, and which therefore tacitly mark one throughout life. The *habitus* thus denotes the oldest layers of cultural behaviour; life-style denotes the second oldest, striven for, desired expression sought, garnished with aura; whereas fashion always lives off its novelty, and only relates to the past in an indirect sense inasmuch as fashion will always consider the past dead, over and done with. The life-blood of fashion is its confrontation with permanence, which life-style seeks and *habitus* cannot be without. In other words, where *habitus* is history and life-style seeks to create history, fashion is determined – in a way so typical of modernity – by its continuous confrontation with history.

However, life-style's creation of history is not without norms. Becher shows that the much discussed concept of life-style attempts more than anything to stylize.[49] In this is included the combination of form and contents, code and raw material, which, as we shall see, characterize stadium life. The anarchistic, private self-enactment is impossible in this case, inasmuch as it would not be noticed in the mass-intercourse. At the same time, a too-conforming behaviour would not create life in the spectators' seats. On the other hand, one must keep in mind that, despite its inclination towards style and its limited number of possible dispositions, life-style renders feasible an almost unlimited number of possibilities of action within the given stylized framework.[50] The chances of novel creations in fashion are legion, if only they are conducted in accordance with the norms of style, as could be observed in the ostensibly force-free and anarchistic demonstrations in the cities of Europe during the 1970s and 1980s. Here, seemingly individual exertion only took place in accordance with certain given stylistic norms of how to behave when 'demonstrating'. The same goes for the stadium in areas such as food and drink, clothes, and battle cries/applause. Here too, life-style and fashion wrestle with each other.

## Permanence and Novelty

Among other things, the consumption of beer, hot dogs, chips, and sweets *en masse*, at European stadiums at least, is characteristic of stadium-style. This takes place not only to satisfy basic, individual needs such as hunger and thirst. It goes beyond the realms of necessity and enters the sphere where the consumption of foodstuffs has more of a socially-functional meaning than a biological-substantial one. The consumption of food and drink has more to do with ritual than with food as such. It is part of the actual conduct and experience of 'being at the stadium'. With beer and hot dogs one confirms one's temporary identity as a 'stadium person'. It may be the individual stomach that is filled up, but this happens as a symbolic demonstration, which 'belongs' to the stadium, just as the white wine belongs in the theatre lobby during the break. In other words, the beer, the sweets and the hot dogs all play a part as elements which help to identify and maintain a certain style characteristic of the stadium alone. They do not characterize the individual as such; rather, the individual establishes his identity and individual idiosyncrasy by means of this code of inclusion, by being at the stadium, with the oddities that mark the specific stadium-code.[51]

This stylized behaviour is remarkably similar to the unity of individual enactment and conformity, of confirmation and breaking up, of adaptation and challenging, found in the world of fashion. Just as fashion seeks to enroll the individual into the group by means of small, unique idiosyncrasies in the realization of the general, the stadium spectator seeks, by going to the hot-dog stand or to the toilets, to realize the general by breaking uniquely into a sequence which the group goes through. The group is presented with the individual playing the part of the example.

The same game in relation to conformity and distinction can be found with respect to equipment and clothing. A few years ago Borussia Dortmund's supporters introduced the banana as an accessory at the stadium. This was partly because the yellow and black colours matched the club colours and partly because it presented a novel and innovative demonstration. The supporters acted, not as private individuals, but as spectators on the stage, in a play between conformity and idiosyncrasy. The banana, a timeless and transnational symbol, was used, in this case, as a historically distinctive sign of Borussia Dortmund supporters, as part of a stylized code of an identity-instituting kind. What was signalled here, by means of fashion, was a certain style, which, at the same time, in its playing with exoticism and samba culture, kept an ironic distance from the traditional perceptions of Borussia Dortmund and its club *habitus*: that as a working-class club in the Ruhr district, they would live mainly on pork and cabbage, and 'Strammer Max'. Furthermore, the banana kept its symbolic significance as a traditional phallic symbol for masculinity and toughness.

That spectators put on the colours of the favoured team when they come to the stadium is also part of the play between style and fashion. The style is determined, but the possibilities of variations of this style are many, as always with clothing. Each detail in the decoration and the enactment is decisive in its duality of a shared framework of reference and individual distinction of permanence and relativity, of tradition and short-lived ideas.

Nowhere is this play between permanence and novelty more obvious than in the field of battle songs and battle cries. The style-level is given, and must submit to bodily and culturally passed-down dispositions, but the variations on this theme, in terms of fashions, are innumerable. An individual spectator may shout his own spontaneous line or start his own song, but without compatibility with the tradition and the level of style, it will be unsuccessful. Each year, the stadium sees its innovations, but the relations to preceding years always shine through, thereby securing the development of tradition, which is so characteristic of behaviour at the stadium with its sophisticated playing with repetition and innovation.

At stadiums in Argentina, the battle cries and battle songs are repeatedly variations on the machismo theme. What is expressed here, in pure, concentrated form, is a special Argentinean style, characterized by long, epic sequences accompanied by distinct, rhythmic music. The core of this stylized praising of manhood is not so much a masculine versus a feminine world; rather, it is the question of strong men versus weak men, that is to say, a hymn to force, strength, courage, independence and strong will. In terms of expression, this foundation of meaning centres around two themes: father as opposed to sons, and 'real' men as opposed to homosexuals. When wanting to ridicule the opponents, spectators will insult and humiliate them with hints of sexuality while at the same time confirming their own masculine identity:

> Have you seen, have you seen
> A bunch of plodders.
> Now, when they go home
> We will split their asses,
> As it was the easiest thing in the world.[52]

The style, in this case, is clearly closely related to the *habitus* which is handed down culturally. In other cases, the style lies closer to fashion and the spontaneous comment. When Argentina beat England in the 1986 World Cup, the victory was celebrated by singing:

Thatcher, Thatcher, Thatcher
Where is she?
Maradona is looking for her
So that he can screw her.[53]

During the first half of the 1992 season, the supporters at the Aarhus Stadium in Denmark demanded, on a banner, that AGF's Norwegian player Jan Halvor Halvorsen be appointed Mayor of Aarhus. The banner was filmed by Danish television and was shown on some sports programmes. It soon set 'standards'. When, in the summer of 1992, Denmark won the European Soccer Championship at Nya Ullevi Stadium in Gothenburg and the victory was celebrated in the streets, supporters in Copenhagen were carrying a standard which read, 'Schmeichel for Pope'. The reference to the banner at the Aarhus Stadium is obvious enough, but this standard carried a more subtle message, inasmuch as Peter Schmeichel has Polish grandparents, both of whom were killed during the Second World War, which explains his often-voiced opposition to the Germans, whom Denmark defeated in the final. Thus the standard was also an expression of traditional Danish scepticism about Germans. This 'fashionable' statement embodied at the same time a more or less hidden element of tradition. Several other variations on the same theme can be expected in future years, until the idea disappears like any other phenomenon of fashion.

No matter how different the stadium cultures of Argentina and Denmark may be, the shared and significant element in each is that stadium-style, just like life-style, constitutes a system of coherent forms of expression that signal a certain pattern of orientation, whereby it becomes the genial soil for a sense of belonging to a certain group and a certain culture, located at a certain place. In other words, the stylized expression and its variations are expressions of a sense of locality and longing for a domicile, a home.

## Imitation and Original

Thus, the stadium demonstrates again and again and in a series of different areas, its function as a play with innovation and tradition, imitation and original. Here, in one of the city's meaning-creating points of condensation, the conflicting tracks between history and ahistory, anonymity and idiosyncrasy, distinction and conformity, sense of locality and indifference, come together. At the stadium, the city builds an arena, which is, at the same time, characterized by sanitized emptiness and temporary, socio-cultural exuberance. Its own drama is about the many paradoxes related to being a citizen in a modern city, with continuities and breaks, where being well rooted is not a given foundation of society; rather, it must be continuously reconstructed and founded in certain spatially-limited enclaves, such as the stadium. At the stadium, one is both at the home ground, but also out in deep waters, where one must probe forward innovatively, exposed to the double condition of safeness and searching, condition and possibility, in a continuous interpretation of life as a 'city-zen' – in the area of tension between being exposed and being comfortable, and between placelessness and a 'homely' sense of locality.

## Notes and References

1. David Harvey, *The Condition of Postmodernity* (Oxford, 1989), p.239.
2. John Bale, 'Rustic and Rational Landscapes of Cricket', *Sport Place. An International Magazine of Sports Geography*, Vol. 2 (1988), pp.5ff.
3. Robert David Sack, *Human Territoriality* (Cambridge, 1986); see also John Bale, *Landscapes of Modern Sport* (Leicester, 1994).
4. Michel Foucault, *Discipline and Punish. The Birth of the Prison* (New York, 1979), pp.135ff.
5. Johan Aspund, *Rivaler och syndabockar* (Gothenburg, 1989), *passim*; Gunter Gebauer, 'Festordnung und Geschmacksdistinktionen', in Gerd Hortleder and Gunter Gebauer (eds), *Sport-Eros-Tod* (Frankfurt am Main, 1986), p.113. In both cases René Girard's philosophy about mimetic rivalry is used as a basic theory.
6. John Bale, 'Homotopia? The Sameness of Sports Places'. Paper presented at the seminar 'Räumliche Dimensionen von Bewegungskultur und soziale Identität', Fønsborg, Denmark, August 1991.
7. Edward Relph, *Place and Placelessness* (London, 1976), p.90.
8. Jean Baudrillard, *Der symbolische Tausch und der Tod* (Munich, 1991), *passim*. Note in particular the section on the order of simulacrums, p.77, and the impropriety of fashion, pp.131ff.
9. Henri Lefebvre, *La révolution urbaine* (Paris, 1970), p.173.
10. Ibid, p.162.
11. Ibid, p.161.
12. This German term is very difficult to translate into English and will be used throughout the text. The closest that one could come to a similar English expression would be something like 'once-only-ness'.
13. This German term is not translatable into English and will be used throughout the text. It refers to feelings about home in its widest sense. It could be compared to the feelings evoked in an Englishman when seeing the White Cliffs of Dover on returning home from a long stay abroad.
14. Gaston Bachelard, *The Poetics of Space* (Boston, 1987), where topophilia is used to term 'the happy space' and 'the praised space'.
15. John Bale, 'Playing at Home: British Football and a Sense of Place', in

John Williams and Stephen Wagg (eds), *British Football and Social Change: Getting into Europe* (Leicester, 1991), pp.130ff.

16. Yi-Fu Tuan, *Topophilia* (Englewood Cliffs, 1974), p.99.

17. John Bale, *Sport, Space and the City* (London, 1993), p.65.

18. Eduardo Archetti, 'Argentinian Football: a Ritual of Violence', *The International Journal of the History of Sports*, Vol. 9, 2 (1992), pp.209ff.

19. Janet Lever, *Soccer Madness* (Chicago, 1983), pp.8ff., spec. p.15.

20. The ideas of games as belonging to a 'sacred' sphere of festival and ritual is clearly displayed by the Spanish philosopher José Ortega y Gasset in his ratio-vitalistic philosophy.

21. Tuan, *Topophilia*, p.99.

22. Bale, *Sport, Space and the City*, p.67.

23. From a phenomenological point of view it is interesting to note, as Bachelard has done, the round shapes endowing a place with tranquillity and fullness (Bachelard, *The Poetics of Space*, pp.233ff.). At the stadium the round shapes can be found in both the circle formed by the crowd and in the firmament.

24. Bale, *Sport, Space and the City*, p.69.

25. 'GAIS/ Leif Stenström Markprojektering AB', *GAIS-gården*, *Förslag 4, Dalen, Slottskogsvallen*, unpublished paper. This material has been kindly put at my disposal by the football club GAIS.

26. Per Nilsson, *Fotbollen och moralen. En studie av fyra allsvenska fotbollsföreningar* (Stockholm, 1993), p.205.

27. K.E. Løgstrup, *Solidaritet og kærlighed og andre essays* (Copenhagen, 1987), p.88.

28. Bale, *Sport, Space and the City*, pp.74ff.

29. Heinz-Dieter Kittsteiner, 'Über das Verhältnis von Lebenszeit und Geschichtszeit', in Dietmar Kamper and Christoph Wulf (eds), *Die sterbende Zeit. Zwanzig Diagnosen* (Darmstadt and Neuwied, 1987), p.73.

30. Jan Assmann, 'Kollektives Gedächtnis und kulturelle Identität', in Jan Assmann and Tonio Hölscher (eds), *Kultur und Gedächtnis* (Frankfurt am Main, 1988), pp.9ff.

31. Clifford Geertz, 'Deep Play: Notes on Balinese Cockfight', *Daedalus*, Vol. 101 (1972), p.26.

32. Bernhard Dieckmann, 'Der psychoanalytische und der endlose Körper', in Dietmar Kamper and Christoph Wulf (eds), *Der andere Körper* (Berlin, 1984), p.120.

33. Elias Canetti, *Macht und Masse* (Frankfurt am Main, 1989), *passim*.

34. Thomas Leithäuser, *Untersuchung zur Konstitution des Alltagsbewusstseins* (Hannover, 1972), pp.186ff.

35. In Aarhus, in Denmark, the crowd can be observed covering an area of two miles. The effect is that much more obvious, inasmuch as one can see the crowd growing with every street corner – constituting a star-shaped race from all sides. The same observation can be made in Prague on the long east–west running street Horákové in the northern part of town, as well as a more diffuse gathering from the north and south.

36. Leithäuser, *Untersuchung zur Konstitution des Alltagsbewusstseins*, p.199.
37. Mark Harrison, *Crowd and History. Mass Phenomena in English Towns 1770–1835* (Cambridge, 1988).
38. Canetti, *Macht und Masse*, p.26.
39. Mark Harrison, 'Symbolism, Ritualism and the Location of Crowds in Early Nineteenth-Century Towns', in Denis Cosgrove and Stephen Daniels (eds), *The Iconography of Landscape* (Cambridge, 1989), pp.194ff.
40. Leithäuser, *Untersuchung zur Konstitution des Alltagsbewusstseins*, p.203.
41. Paul A. Pickering, 'Class Without Words: Symbolic Communication in the Chartist Movement', *Past and Present*, Vol. 112 (1986), p.150 *et passim*.
42. Richard Holt, *Sport and the British – a Modern History* (Oxford, 1990). Holt's book is written in opposition to the vacuum thesis in English cultural history writing: that industrial capitalism after *c.*1820 destroyed pre-modern plebeian folk culture in Britain, which only rose again in a working-class framework after 1850, with no links to traditional folk culture. Cf. Niels Kayser Nielsen, *Fra Robin Hood til fodbold* (Odense, 1992), where an equal defence of the continuity in British working-class culture in the first half of the nineteenth century is being adduced.
43. When one goat dies of old age, the next Hennes billy-goat is presented at the stadium in Cologne.
44. Lubor Vorel, *Prager Lokale mit Gerichten und Geschichten* (Prague, 1991), pp.170ff.
45. Rolf Lindner, 'Die Sportsbegeisterung', in Utz Jeggle *et al.* (eds), *Volkskultur in der Moderne. Probleme und Perspektiven empirischer Kulturforschung* (Reinbek bei Hamburg, 1986), pp.249ff.
46. Rather, the sports activities at the stadium are planned so as to pay tribute to civic principles of freedom and equality, with which the game is ideally endowed. Cf. Niels Kayser Nielsen, 'Sport, kultur og utopi', in Niels Kayser Nielsen and John Thobo-Carlsen (eds), *Sport og fascination*, Bidrag no. 13–14 (Odense, 1981), pp.39ff.
47. Pierre Bourdieu, *Outline of a Theory of Practice* (Cambridge, 1977), p.72 *et passim* and *The Logic of Practice* (Cambridge 1990), pp.52ff.
48. Bernhard Giessen, *Die Entdinglichung des Sozialen. Eine evolutionstheoretische Perspektive af die Postmoderne* (Frankfurt am Main, 1991), p.235.
49. Ulrike A.J. Becher, *Geschichte des modernen Lebenstils* (Munich, 1990), pp.12ff.
50. Hans-Georg Soeffner, *Auslegund des Alltags – Der Alltags der Auslegung* (Frankfurt am Main, 1989), spec. pp.158ff.
51. Bernhard Giessen, *Die Entdinglichung des Sozialen. Eine evolutionstheoretische Perspektive af die Postmoderne* (Frankfurt am Main, 1991), pp.234ff.
52. Eduardo Archetti, 'Latinamerikas storbyer emmer af fodbold', *Kontakt*, Vol. 5 (1985/86), p.17.
53. Archetti, 'Argentinean football', p.225.

# 3

# Sport, the Stadium and Metropolitan Life

*Joseph Maguire*

Sports stadiums are sociological entities which are formed spatially. Such an assertion might seem, at first sight, somewhat bold and at odds with the obvious spatial and physical qualities that stadiums exhibit. That is not the tack I wish to follow here; I wish to explore stadiums as a lived, sociological experience. Sports stadiums are not unique in being socio-logical entities. Other leisure venues, such as concert halls or theatres, can be understood in the same way. Of course, such venues are part of the broader metropolis. If we take heed of Georg Simmel, we can note that the city itself is 'not a spatial entity with sociological consequences, but a sociological entity that is formed spatially'.[1] Here, then, I will draw on aspects of Simmel's work to provide a framework in which the sociological exploration of sport, the stadium and metropolitan life, can be undertaken. My substantive comments about stadium life will, by necessity, be preliminary in nature.

Given that the study of sports stadiums is in its relatively early stages of development, I also want to strike a cautionary note and emphasize that the phenomenon has and can be subject to a variety of different readings. The city, and thereby the stadium, can be understood as a metaphor for modernity itself. City life is one of the key features of modernity. Reading accounts of what makes cities – and sports stadiums – tick, how and why they have changed and what it was and is like to live through these changes, can reveal how modern ways of seeing and making sense of these phenomena come into being. We need, then, to be sensitive as to how certain forms of analysis, certain forms of discourse about the city, the sports stadium and urban planning come into being; how they develop and maintain a degree of dominance, become contested and replaced by competing approaches. The ongoing debate concerning the role, function and meaning of soccer stadiums in the UK is a case in point.[2] Before turning to a discussion of the implications of Simmel's work for the study of the stadium, let me, in a rather speculative manner, explain what I have in mind.

## The Sports Stadium as Text

In perhaps a somewhat polemical vein, let me suggest that there is no such 'thing' as a city or a sports stadium. These terms designate the 'space' produced by a set of interwoven figurational tendencies. These include: the interweaving of temporal and comparative structured processes; social relations of production and reproduction; the practices of the State and forms of media communication. Conceptions of the city are, above all, representations that never fully capture the labyrinth in all its complexity. Given this, social scientific explanations of the social processes associated with sports stadiums arguably need to examine two main themes. Firstly, the material determinants of this social space require exploration. Secondly, the discourses, symbols, metaphors and fantasies through which observers ascribe meaning to the modern experience of sports-stadium interaction need analysis. Let me explain a little further what this might involve.

Though I will not concentrate on them here, the following interwoven elements appear relevant in a social scientific study of the sports stadium. I am thinking of, for example: the organization of production, work and commerce within the economy of sport and in the broader nexus of economic relations; issues of control, supervision and regulation of the expression of conduct – violent or otherwise; the form taken by communities and gender relations; networks of communication, both physical and semiotic; the form of political institutions and the rights of citizens to 'free' assembly. In addition to these elements, another area of enquiry appears crucial. I am thinking of the symbolic and cultural forms of the sacred, the profane, the quest for exciting significance and the controlled decontrolling of the emotions embodied in the relative importance and disposition of churches, civic monuments and sports/leisure stadiums. At this stage of enquiry, however, we simply do not have the substantive evidence to hand to provide firm evidence to address these issues.

If we also examine how the city has been conceptualized over time, and especially since the mid-nineteenth century, several questions arise that are equally applicable to the study of global sports/leisure arenas. For example, what concepts, images and metaphors have reformers and planners used to make sense of the city? In addition, how have these been translated into plans and policies for rationalizing and managing the intended and unintended aspects of the interaction that occurs? Further, in what terms have people experienced, imagined and envisioned the city forms that have resulted? A variety of ways of imagining sports/leisure stadiums are also evident. Some accounts emphasize control issues and rational planning. Official British reports into football hooliganism and crowd safety have clearly stressed these issues. Other approaches stress notions of community solidarity in the construction and use of such stadiums. These images appear to be giving way to ideas revolving around notions of flow and movement. Elite sports stadiums have become universal pleasure domes, criss-crossed by the global flow of people, technology, capital, images and ideologies. Observe the world-wide movement of musicians, artists and sports stars performing in the redesigned spatial amphitheatres of late modernity. Such monuments to late modernity include Stockholm's Globe and the Palais Omnisports in Paris. Considered in this light, are not sports stadiums also metaphors for issues surrounding the debate regarding high or post-modernity and the reconstruction of globalized local identities?

It is important, however, to distinguish between how the stadium is imagined and how it is experienced. Michel de Certeau's work on the city can provide us with some signposts.[3] Though it is possible to think in terms of 'concept city', or for that matter, concept stadium, it is equally possible to view the city/stadium nexus as less of a machine and more of a matrix. That is, as a living labyrinth that has a blend of rational and carnivalesque qualities. In the latter respect, the focus would be on the experiential and unpredictable dimensions of stadium life. On this basis the stadium can be viewed in such terms as a temple of commodity capitalism and/or as a popular theatre of mythical dreams revealing fundamental truths about 'society'. The preservation of some sports stadiums in the USA and Sweden, for example, may also be bound up in broader social currents concerning a nostalgic longing for a past golden age and a sense of dislocation with the present. People want a sense of 'heimat'. Some local stadiums – and the representatives of the local people who attend and spectate – perform this function.

What these observations are leading to is a call for the investigation of how the stadium figuration reflects and affects people's psychic well-being and social mores. Stadium life arguably involves an orchestrated staging of embodied emotions – both for those who are 'there' and for those who receive its images represented through the media/sport production complex. Writers such as Bourdieu, Elias and the feminist scholar Doreen Massey all provide insights that would assist the investigation of the stadium figuration. For example, Elias's study of the changing experience of the social space of court life has much to say concerning the 'civilizing' of sporting spaces and the controlled decontrolling of the emotions. Likewise, the masculine world of many sports stadiums can be fruitfully explored from a feminist perspective. Should we be surprised that, just as with the sports process in general, sports stadiums are 'male preserves'? Neither of these asides does justice, however, to the fruitfulness of the approaches mentioned. They are meant as a reminder that there is a variety of ways of viewing the stadium. Here I want to concentrate on the work of Simmel.

There are two broad respects in which Simmel's conceptual framework is useful to the study of the sports/leisure stadium and the city. Drawing on Simmel's formal sociology, it is possible to use his work on social geometry, sociation and the use of space to help make sense of stadium life and experiences. The problems of sociation – of conflict and of co-operation – and of the disciplining, rationalization and the commodification of the social space of the stadium can all be seen in sharper relief by drawing on such Simmelian concepts and ideas.

Simmel's study of metropolitan life also provides a useful framework for the sociology of sport and leisure in general, and his analysis of the relationship between objective and subjective culture can be productively applied to the study of stadium life. Can the stadium be seen as an 'escape route' from what Simmel terms the 'tragedy of culture' or does objective culture pervade the stadium experience? Further, Simmel's analysis of the qualities associated with metropolitan life allows the researcher to question the authenticity and value of stadium culture. Is the entertainment served up in these modern temples shallow and superficial or enriching and purposeful? Let us turn to a discussion of these issues in greater detail.

### The Stadium, Sociation, Social Geometry and Social Space

Clearly it is not appropriate to provide a comprehensive review of Simmel's work; this has been done elsewhere.[4] Nevertheless, to understand more adequately the relevance of his work to the study of sport/leisure stadiums, it is necessary to give some brief attention to elements of his *formal* sociology. For Simmel, human interaction involves the expression of meanings in a dense, multi-layered reciprocal exchange between knowledgeable social actors. He paints an image of a 'web' to convey how the countless number of actions of people creates reciprocal effects and what we thus call 'society'. The 'threads' of this web 'are spun, dropped, taken up again, displaced by others, [and] interwoven with others'.[5] Everything interacts in some way with everything else. For Simmel, then, society is not a 'thing', a reified totality lying outside human consciousness. 'Society', according to Simmel, 'is only the synthesis or the general term for the totality of these specific interactions ... Society is identical with the sum of these relations.'[6] Simmel was also aware that short-term interactions interweave to form connections of a more enduring kind. As he noted, the 'interactions we have in mind when we talk about "society" are crystallised as definable, consistent structures such as the state and the family'.[7] The institutions and social structures of 'society' then constitute the forms taken by the social content of the interaction he describes.

Here, however, the problems of the individual and society, and agency and structure, arise. Simmel uses the terms society and sociation interchangeably and, indeed, sees 'society everywhere, where a number of human beings enter into interaction and form a temporary or permanent unity'.[8] This double usage is evident throughout his work. Though there is no general theorization of society contained within his formal sociology, in *Philosophy of Money*, he studies the rationalization of social life. In this he probes the broader genesis of this 'labyrinth', which human interaction creates. For Simmel, only when sociologists have substantively investigated the complex, and multi-layered forms and dynamics of sociation, can they grasp how the 'new entity', 'society', comes about. Given that Simmel argued that, 'society is everywhere', sociologists could legitimately study the so-called 'serious' or the 'mundane' forms of sociation. For our purposes, the study of stadium sociation is no exception. The stadium figuration exhibits broader social currents. Let me explore this a little further.

In a series of essays, Simmel pointed to the various elements that characterize social relations, or what he termed social geometry. These include numbers of people, degree of distance, position, the degree of self-involvement and symmetry. These elements interweave in different combinations in different types of interaction (sport and leisure practices being no exception). The configuration of stadium design, access to designated areas and the extent and form of interaction between different groups of people can all be investigated using these analytical tools and sensitizing concepts. What we need, however, are substantively-grounded studies of the social geometry of stadium life.

For Simmel, in the cut and thrust of such 'triadic' interaction, an entangled web of larger and larger groups forms. One consequence of this is that the individual becomes increasingly separate from this emerging structure – even though the individual is part of its composition. The individual grows more alone, isolated and segmented from others within the groups in which he/she interacts. Could it be that the triadic interaction of the stadium reverses, however fleetingly, this process? Here, however, we see one of the contradictions that Simmel suggests characterizes everyday life. That is, while this emerging structure (society) allows for the development of individuality and greater freedom, it also impedes, constrains and ultimately threatens, such choices. Game contests clearly show the processes involved. Consider two-person games such as chess or tennis and compare these with more fluid, multi-person games such as basketball, soccer and rugby. Games in general, and sports games in particular, are patterned by the very same elements that characterize social relations. Sports – and the interaction that occurs within sports stadiums – are a particular form of sociation and are also part of the wider matrix of interaction, society.

Sports contests provide almost paradigmatic examples of interaction. This interaction has different degrees of symmetry of reciprocity and degrees of distance and closeness (vertical and horizontal). Examples include not only different types of games, (invasion, striking and fielding) with different numbers of participants and objectives therein, but also varying degrees of symmetry of reciprocity and closeness that distinguish sports cultures more broadly. These different degrees of symmetry and closeness would involve the varying quality of and strategies deployed by the interacting teams. What applies for the players also pertains to others involved in stadium sociation. It would also include referee and player, coach and athlete, élite performer and fans, and agent and media personnel entanglements. Here too, different degrees of symmetry of reciprocity and degrees of distance and closeness are evident.

Though individuals in sports contests – as spectators or participants – enter reciprocal interaction with each other, it should not be taken to suggest that this reciprocity is synonymous with notions of order and harmony. Conflict is central to understanding the web of group affiliations. It is the dynamic by which people are attracted to or repelled by, each other. This occurs within a series of uneasy, shifting combinations, interactions and groups. Spectators, as allies and foes, are mutually entangled, and this entanglement is in a constant process of flux that undergoes different rates of change – sometimes slower, sometimes more rapid. Conflict and rivalry can take various forms in the sports stadium. More broadly, conflict entails a 'synthesis of elements that work both against and for one another' and functions to resolve the tension between contrasts.[9]

This is also one of the unifying features of sport. In sport-stadium venues, as noted, different degrees of reciprocity and closeness exist within and between teams and fans. Without mutual acceptance of the rules governing the contest – on and off the field of play – no resolution of the anticipated conflict between the teams can be attempted. As rivals, opponents are bound to each other. In this connection, Simmel discussed at some length the role of antagonistic games. He observed:

> In its *sociological motivation*, the antagonistic game contains absolutely nothing except fight itself … But there is something else more remarkable: the realization of precisely this complete dualism pre-supposes sociological forms in the stricter sense of the word, namely unification. One *unites* in order to fight, and one fights under the mutually recognized control of norms and rules … these unifications … are the technique without which such a conflict that excludes all heterogeneous or objective justifications could not materialise. What is more, the norms of the antagonistic game often are rigorous and

impersonal and are observed on both sides with the severity of a code of honour – to an extent hardly shown by groups which are formed for co-operative purposes.[10]

In stadium-based sport forms, as well as in 'outdoor' sports, elements of exchange, conflict and sociability characterize encounters between rival opponents. Even with bitter rivals, a reciprocal set of rights and responsibilities govern the contest.

Closely connected to this study of conflict is the role of competition. Again, this analysis is heavily laden with implications for the sociological study of leisure, and sports stadium patterns of sociation. For Simmel, competition is a particular form of conflict in which opposing elements are synthesized. Discussing various types of competition, Simmel observes:

> In many other kinds of conflict, victory over the adversary not only automatically secures, but itself is, the prize of victory. In competition, instead, there are two other combinations. Where victory over the competitor is the chronological first necessity, it itself means nothing. The goal of the whole action is attained only with the availability of a value which does not depend on that competitive fight at all … The second type of competition perhaps differs even more greatly from other kinds of conflict. Here the struggle consists only in the fact that each competitor by himself aims at the goal, without using his strength on the adversary.[11]

A variety of examples is given by Simmel to illustrate these types of competition. Referring to the second type, where the competitor aims at the goal without using force to prevent his/her opponent(s) from producing their optimal performance, Simmel notes that 'this strange kind of fight is exemplified by the runner who only by his fastness … aims to reach his goal … the subject of the final goal and the object of the final result interweave in the most fascinating manner'.[12] If the actual contest highlights webs or networks of interaction/sociation, so too do the supporters of the clubs involved. Significantly, for present purposes, Simmel discusses the role that 'social clubs' play in counterbalancing the presence – or absence – of serious competition in the lives of specific groups. Simmel notes:

> Thus, the members of a group in which keen competition prevails will gladly seek out such other groups as are lacking in competition as much as possible. As a result businessmen have a decided preference for social clubs. The estate-consciousness of the aristocrat, on the other hand, rather excludes competition within his own circle; hence, it makes supplementations of that sort [i.e., social clubs] largely

51

superfluous. This suggests forms of socialization to the aristocrat which contain stronger competitive elements – for example, those clubs which are held together by a common interest in sports.[13]

Considered in this light, sports and leisure stadiums can be the forum for forms of sociation that provide a counterbalance to the presence or absence of competition in different people's lives. Though Simmel himself wrote very little about sport – and nothing at all about sports stadiums – he did write about the 'excitement and euphoria', the 'momentary rapture' provided by the physical act of climbing. Though he regarded the joy gained from 'playing with danger' as 'the highest that life can offer', no explanation for the source of this human need is provided. One motivation for undertaking such journeys, and seeking out new adventures, was, however, to escape from the 'contradictions of modern existence'. That is, from the contradictions between 'objective culture' and 'subjective culture' that were so evident in the metropolis. Could it be that the 'adventures' provided by the spectacles occurring within modern sports and leisure pleasure domes perform a similar function?

With this in mind, it is also relevant to consider Simmel's work on social space. Not surprisingly, in painting an image of the metropolis, Simmel points to the web or network of intersecting spheres. These entangled social circles include the division of labour, distribution, communications, money economy, commodity exchange and intellectual/cultural circles. It is within this set of intersecting circles that we can situate sports and leisure stadiums. Clues to the relative status, function and meaning of the patterns of sociation that occur within such arenas can be derived from an analysis of their place within the interweaving set of social circles of the modern city.

In his study of the metropolis, emphasis is placed 'upon the sphere of circulation and exchange, not merely of money and commodities but also social groups and individuals, a dynamic interaction of social circles'.[14] The circulation and exchange of goods, commodities, images and practices, create a need in metropolitan people to create a distance between their inner selves and the kaleidoscope of impressions they are confronted with. According to Simmel, this social distance can be created by various forms of differentiation, social, physical and psychological. Clearly, leisure practices reflect these forms of spatial distantiation. The exclusion of specific groups from clubs and leisure forms, the segregation of sports practices on lines of gender, and the quest for novelty, adventure and excitement promised by tourism, mountaineering and seafaring, are all examples of the establishment of types of social distance. The separation of players from spectators and one set of supporters from another, can also be understood in terms of Simmel's notion of social distance. In the stadium, however, it is also possible to meet what Simmel termed 'the stranger': that person who brings to the interaction that which cannot stem from the existing fan group itself. The key to understanding leisure then appears to lie in the metropolis and the problems engendered there by modernity. Let me briefly expand on some of these points.

Several of the issues of social distance identified are connected to Simmel's work on social space. Such work has considerable significance for both the socio-geographic study of leisure and sport forms and for an analysis of crowd behaviour at sports stadiums, pop concerts and the like. For Simmel, sociation involves the use and experience of space; it involves sharing space. In this way social relations can be said to assume a spatial form. This space/place functions as a context for action. Several basic qualities of sociation involving a spatial dimension are identified by Simmel. These include: the exclusivity or uniqueness of space; the partitioning of space; the degree of fixity that space offers to social forms; spatial proximity and distance; and, finally, movement through space. Yet his work on the sociology of space involved neither spatial determinism (as is the tendency with some geographical studies of leisure and sport), nor social constructionalism. In this way he could conclude that the city is 'not a spatial entity with sociological consequences, but a sociological entity that is formed spatially'.[15] Likewise, to paraphrase Simmel, the sports stadium, concert hall or theatre are not spatial entities with sociological consequences, but are, as noted, sociological entities that are formed spatially.[16]

If the basic qualities of sociation involving a spatial dimension are borne in mind, then sports and leisure 'places' can be understood in a different light. Consider the different exclusivity or uniqueness associated with places such as the venues of the US Masters Golf tournament at Augusta and the New Year's Day concert from Vienna. Think about the partitioning of space in the form of national parks, nature reserves and sites of special scientific interest. Reflect on the gradual development of spatial boundaries in sport and the growing separation of performer from spectator. Ponder the intimacy and degree of intermingling involved in the 'local pub' and contrast this with the segregation of rival groups of football supporters. Observe the global movement of musicians, artists and sports stars 'performing' in Sydney's opera house, the new section of the Louvre in Paris and Toronto's Skydome. Recognize how the media/sports production complex – as a part of the 'objective culture' to which Simmel drew attention – shrinks space. No longer do we have to be physically present; at the Olympic Stadium, for example, people can 'be together' without sharing space. Taken together, these insights provide a powerful lens by which to re-focus attention on the socio-spatial dimensions of leisure and sports practices.

## The Stadium, the Metropolis and Mental Life

Simmel is understood by some observers as having viewed modernity as being associated with 'the dissolution of our contact with the external world through concrete practice' – if this is the case, then the study of the experience of modernity becomes vital.[17] The ethnographic study of patterns of stadium sociation can be illuminating in this respect. If we examine the themes concerning the separation of objective and subjective culture, it becomes clear, in Simmel's *The Philosophy of Money*, that people do produce the culture of modernity, but because of their ability to reify social reality, this cultural world comes to have a life of its own. The cultural world of objective culture comes to dominate social actors who, in everyday interaction, continually help to recreate it. With modernity, objective culture grows and expands. Different components of this cultural realm not only become more extensive but also increasingly intertwined. The growth and expansion of the money economy in the modern metropolis transform cultural forms into external objects. For Simmel, then, 'every day and for all sides, the wealth of objective culture increases, but the individual mind can enrich the forms and contents of its own development only by distancing itself still further from that culture'.[18]

Though subjective culture – of the kind exhibited in some leisure forms – is used as a refuge by the individual, the overall impact is the domination of objective over subjective culture. With the division of labour, the growing complexity associated with entangled social circles of urban interaction and the emergence of a decentred culture, culture itself becomes more rationalized and less fulfilling. Individuals too, are affected. They become more indifferent, calculating and alienated. The estrangement of individuals from others, and a growing inner restlessness, are related themes that Simmel explored. As he observes, 'the lack of something definite at the centre of the soul impels us to search for momentary satisfaction in ever-new stimulations, sensations and external activities'.[19]

Simmel thus paints a downbeat, pessimistic view of life in the modern metropolis. Subjective culture becomes rationalized, personally less enriching and dominated by objective culture. Objective culture is seen as the 'great leveller' of standards and talent. It creates – in the money economy – mass consumption. 'Cheap trash' is produced for this mass of consumers. Individual culture atrophies. Yet, out of this passivity comes the emergence of what Simmel terms 'excitement' and 'stimulation', and a desire for novel, constantly updated, attractions. Here is what he says:

> There emerges the craving today for excitement, for extreme impressions, for the greatest speed in its change ... the modern preference

for 'stimulation' as such in impressions, relationships and information – without thinking it important for us to find out why these stimulate us – also reveals the characteristic entanglement which means: one is satisfied with this preliminary stage of the genuine production of values.[20]

In the emerging 'boundless pursuit of pleasure', titillating, non-fulfilling activities are avidly consumed. Could we not view sports-stadium culture in a similar vein? The individual becomes atomized, isolated, more dependent, less knowledgeable and is enslaved by an overwhelming objective culture. This then, for Simmel, is the 'tragedy of culture'. Yet, another aspect of *The Philosophy of Money* emphasizes the contradictory nature of the processes involved. Just as it is subjective culture that creates and recreates the objective culture that then comes to dominate it, the development of human potential comes to depend, in part, on this very expansion of objective culture. The irony is, therefore, that there are some 'liberating effects' to this process. Several can be identified. These include the extent to which this process allows individuals to engage with many more people; the obligations of the people involved become specific and not so all-embracing; a greater range of gratifications is available and people enjoy more 'freedom' to develop their individuality. People also have a greater potential to protect their 'inner selves'. Could not some leisure-stadium activities act as an enclave in which these liberating effects be maximized?

For Simmel, the satisfaction derived from the consumption of metropolitan culture was not that fulfilling or authentic. The consumption of cultural goods and spectacles reflected less the meeting of real needs and desires, and more the creation of mass markets of the money economy. In this way, leisure became associated with the possession of things and the escape from the mundane existence of everyday life. The possession of cultural artefacts reflected more the dominance of objective culture over subjective culture then the skilled choice of the individual. Though the metropolis was the 'genuine showpiece of this culture', where new sights, sounds, smells, tastes and feelings could be found, to what extent these exciting cultural practices reflected real needs remained in doubt. The same is true of modern sports stadiums – the showpieces of high modernity. Like the metropolis in general, they are sites for the production, consumption, circulation and exchange of goods and services. They provide a bewildering choice. But it is a choice determined by the market. Do these glitzy places of entertainment – that are seen as 'non-serious' and apolitical – provide a diet of shallow amusement and a superficial intoxication of feelings? Or are they forms of 'popular theatre'?

In some leisure-stadium activities, metropolitan dwellers can find an escape from the demands of external life. In leisure forms such as art, music and travel, 'real' opportunities for 'genuine individuality' could be created and experienced. For Simmel, adventure, travel and tourism were also the frontiers of human imagination, feeling and fulfilment. Yet even these were under threat in his period. The standardization and commodification of the modern sports stadium, vividly illustrated in the redevelopment of Twickenham, the traditional 'home' of English rugby, may have deeply compromised its potential to perform a similar role.

## Conclusion

In this chapter I have sought to highlight, in a preliminary and speculative manner, how the sports/leisure-stadium nexus can be understood. Throughout I have emphasized that this nexus is a sociological entity with time and spatial dimensions. This nexus is also subject to a variety of readings. The stadium as text reveals much about how more powerful groups see society more generally. It is also possible to view this nexus from several theoretical traditions. Here, the work of Simmel has been focused on. Given his concerns with sociation, social geometry, social space and metropolitan life more generally, I have suggested that there is much within this set of analytical tools and sensitizing concepts to enable us to investigate substantively the stadium figuration.

## Notes

1. Georg Simmel, cited in David Frisby, *Simmel and Since: Essays on Georg Simmel's Social Theory* (London, 1992), pp.112–13.
2. Richard Giulianotti, 'Social Identity and Public Order: Political and Academic Discourses on Football Violence', in Richard Giulianotti, N. Bonney and M. Hepworth, *Football, Violence and Social Identity* (London, 1994), pp.10–36.
3. M. de Certeau, *The Practice of Everyday Life* (Berkeley, 1984).
4. See Frisby, *Simmel and Since*; David Frisby, *Sociological Impressionism: a Reassessment of George Simmel's Social Theory* (2nd edn. London, 1992); see also Grant Jarvie and Joseph Maguire, *Sport and Leisure in Social Thought* (London, 1994).
5. G. Simmel, 'The Problem of Sociology' in K. H. Wolff (ed.), *Essays in Sociology, Philosophy and Aesthetics* (New York, 1959), p 328. See also the special edition on Simmel in *Theory, Culture and Society*, Vol. 8 (1991).
6. T. Bottomore and David Frisby (eds and trans.), G. Simmel, *The Philosophy of Money*, (London, 1978), p.175.
7. G. Simmel, 'Sociability' in K. H. Wolff, *The Sociology of Georg Simmel* (New York, 1950), p.9.
8. G. Simmel, 'Zur Methodik der Sozialwissenschaft', *Jahrbuch für*

      *Gesetzgebung, Verwaltung und Volkswirtschaft*, Vol. 20 (1896), pp.575–85, cited in Frisby, *Simmel and Since*, p.12.

9.   K. H. Wolff and R. Bendix (trans), G. Simmel, *Conflict and the Web of Group-Affiliations* (New York, 1955), p.14.

10.  Ibid., p.35.

11.  Ibid., pp.57–8.

12.  Ibid., pp.58–9.

13.  Ibid., p.156.

14.  Frisby, *Sociological Impressionism*, p.101.

15.  Simmel, cited in Frisby, *Simmel and Since*, pp.112–13. For further discussion of Simmel and space see F. J. Lechner, 'Simmel on Social Space', *Theory, Culture and Society*, Vol. 8 (1991), pp.195–203.

16.  Such insights could be profitably be used in conceptualizing sports and leisure stadium disasters such as at Hillsborough, the stadium of Sheffield Wednesday.

17.  Frisby, *Simmel and Since*, p.66.

18.  Simmel, *The Philosophy of Money*, pp.446–8.

19.  Ibid., p.484.

20.  Ibid., p.275.

# 4

# The Copenhagen Idrætsparken: From Democratic Institution to Private Enterprise

*Jim Toft*

## Introduction

This chapter charts the evolution of the first large stadium in Denmark, built in Copenhagen in 1911. The stadium was called 'Idrætsparken'[1] and was one of the first pluralistic and democratic institutions in the young democracy of Denmark. It was demolished in 1990 and taken over by a private enterprise called Baltica – one of the largest insurance companies in Denmark – which constructed the modern stadium of Parken (see Chapter 8). It is, furthermore, a story of a political fight going on for more than four hundred years between the State, the Copenhagen municipal corporation and council, and different political and socio-cultural groups in Copenhagen. The basic construction and the ideologies behind 'Københavns Idrætspark' (KI)[2] as a democratic institution reflected a decisive step toward a mass culture based on what one could call 'modernization' and a political step toward a democratization of access to the Copenhagen environment. From one perspective, therefore, the genesis of KI and Fælledparken as a sports space indicates a 'positive' history, but, from another perspective, the ultimate outcome of the development from Idrætsparken to Parken bears witness to a commercialization of sports space and hence an alienation of sports activity and space.[3]

The transformation from Idrætsparken to Parken mirrors at many levels the historical development and modernization of Denmark in the twentieth century. Firstly, KI was founded as a self-governing pluralistic institution and pluralism became a significant part of the democratic development in Denmark. KI was, and still is, the organization providing widespread facilities for mass participation in the field-sport activities financed by the local political authorities in Copenhagen. Secondly, the history of KI reflects a shift from the egalitarian social democratic ideology, which became the basic political and socio-economic idea in the local authorities in Copenhagen at the turn of the twentieth century and later on by the State (with Copenhagen as the experimental pioneer), through lineages of Danish apprenticeship of early urban modernity under a Social Democratic regime, toward a culture determined by market economy in the 1980s. The shift within the social democratic culture policy was an adaption to these lineages. And last but not least, the political decision process and the handing over from the pluralistic institution to a private enterprise bears witness to a manipulation, which the Social Democrats (and the socialist wing) have to take on their own shoulders, which again indicates the above-mentioned shift.

In a cultural-geographical sense, the history of Idrætsparken began on the Fælled in an open landscape outside the ramparts of Copenhagen. The landscape was transformed from 'un-touched' nature to a culturalized football pitch with a lonely house or stand in 1911, to the first large stadium in Denmark. Gradually, with the increasing popularity of football as entertainment the landscape became a closed space, hidden behind terraces and stands.[4] 'Idrætsparken' became the home ground for the national team from the very beginning until it was demolished in the autumn of 1990. It was always a sacred place, with the same reputation and status in Denmark that Wembley has in England. Furthermore the most famous football clubs (mostly upper-class clubs in Copenhagen) have played their matches in Idrætsparken, using it as their home ground.

Idrætsparken constituted only one part of a larger sports complex within the KI institution, and was situated in the largest park in Copenhagen. The KI was, and still is, the domicile for many sports like athletics, tennis, boxing, wrestling, gymnastics, hockey, fencing, shooting, cricket and, today, asiatic sports too. But while, on the one hand, the number of different sports activities found in the grounds of KI increased, at the same time, from the 1960s until 1986, the number of spectators fell. The consequence of falling figures meant that, with the concomitant substantial fall in income, the stadium was not renovated after 1955. The growing success of the Danish national football team from the mid-1980s accentuated the need for a restored or even a brand new stadium in Denmark. This was especially advocated by Dansk Boldspil-Union (DBU) which was responsible for the national team.[5] This situation was the beginning of the end of Idrætsparken. The old KI could not afford to build a new stadium in 1990 on its modest financial means and with very low spectator figures. It had to give up, and a private insurance company – Baltica – bought the old stadium from the local authorities for a very low price and built a new complex in 1990–2. In other words, the history of Idrætsparken reflects a historical transformation from a democratic institution to a private enterprise based strictly on commercialism. This process also reflects a more general development within Danish society itself and for Denmark as a member of the European Community.

To understand the configurational scene and background of the transformation, a look at Danish history in general, and the development of sport in particular, is essential.

## The Early History of Sport in Denmark

The first step towards a decision to build a stadium in Copenhagen was taken in 1904. At this time, organized sport was still in its initial phase and it is very important to understand that the genesis of the sport movement in Denmark came much later than that of England. Sport came from England to the European mainland in the wake of industrialization, which imposed – voluntarily or not – new economic and political structures and terms. The new conditions and changes included different ways of using and contemplating the body:for the first time in history the body became a medium for expansion – an object for results, which is the basic logic of sport – a bodily incarnation of the logic of industrialization and capitalistic economy.[6] This process has of course its own momentum. Sport in Denmark was introduced in the middle of the nineteenth century by a small progressive *avant garde* group, generally inculding members of the upper class who had strong linkages to the mentality of urban life. Sporting interest was first confined to horse-racing and sailing, but more in the way of a functionalized interest to achieve better results in the new logic of industrialism, technical revolution and a reckoning against the ancient regime, than as part of a new physical activity.[7]

One of the reasons for the new orientation toward English culture can be found in at least two conditions: firstly, the increasing political tension between Denmark and Germany, and secondly, the globalization caused by the English economy and industialization.[8] In the 1864 war between Denmark and Germany, Denmark lost a large part of southern Jutland. The Danish defeat in 1864 initiated a wake of nationalism, which, together with the growing impact of English industrialization and globalization, resulted in a radical new political decision – that the already-planned railway from Copenhagen to Germany (north–south) was changed to east–west, towards the North Sea and England. This change in the direction of the railway mirrors a radical change of Danish consciousness and cultural orientation. The bias for English culture penetrated Danish society in many ways, replacing old German-inspired culture. Even military strategies became English. What is more, English vocabulary became more and more common in everyday conversation in Denmark in the late 1800s. The ideal for behaviour and habits should be 'gentleman-like' and 'lady-like', just as in England. Sport became the most visible change in the realm of bodily habits and one of the most widespread leisure activities. In short, Denmark stood at a threshold; the old agrarian economic and political domination was subsequently replaced by new urban phenomena and powers.

The interest in sport increased from the middle of the nineteenth century. But it was strictly an urban activity until the mid-twentieth century and it remained in general an upper-class orientation for the last three decades, from 1870 to 1900. On the threshold of the twentieth century, only very few working-class people were exercising through organized sport.[9] The passion for strength in working-class culture became related to sport through activities such as weightlifting, boxing and wrestling. The working class did not play football on a large scale until 1900 – a trend which was very different from other European countries like England, Germany, Austria, and Sweden.[10]

*Sport and outdoor life in an absolutist town*

As mentioned above, the pioneers in the sport movement were recruited from the upper class in Copenhagen. Early sailors and rowers found sites along the coast on the outskirts of Copenhagen, as did horse-riders and cyclists. Houses in the middle of the city were bought for fencing and gymnastics but all ball sports and the outdoor life in general appeared constrained. Due to the philosophy and ideology of the time, the old bourgeois regimes in the local authorities considered sport as a strictly private activity, which meant that in general it was confined to the wealthier members of the population. If one needed a place for football, cricket or tennis, one had to buy or rent a ground. But among the pioneers were a number of army officers, who willingly allowed the first football club (also recruited from the upper classes) to use the drill ground for their games. It was located by the military barracks at Rosenborg Castle in the centre of the town, and the first football, cricket and tennis matches were played here. But its surface of gravel and stones meant that the ball bounced unpredictably and players were easily hurt if they fell, which of course was very unsatisfactory.

Because the drill ground was the only place to play football, old absolutist Copenhagen was in no way a suitable town or place for sport in the nineteenth century. Town planning before the twentieth century was a disaster and outdoor life and sports activities were influenced by these conditions. So as soon as a sports culture began to develop in Copenhagen, clubs and sports associations tried to induce the municipal council and corporation to build, or simply to give, them space for their activities – but without success.

**Figure 4.1**  Horses grazing on the Fælled at the turn of the century

*The Copenhagen Fælled*[11]

Outside the ramparts were the old Middle Age commons known as the Fælled. It was these that the cricket and football clubs began to use during the late 1880s. The first large stadium in Copenhagen was built on this common and was finished in 1911, but from about 1884 until 1911, the huge Fælled was the space and place for the growing sporting life in Copenhagen.

The Fælled surrounded the whole town. Originally the area was a large expanse of pasture owned by the Copenhagen citizens and the villages nearby (see Figure 4.1). In 1536, the King gave all the common greens to the city, with the decisive restriction that the military had a continuous right to drill on the whole area.[12] The common was an important part of the defence system of Copenhagen, which meant that the government of war tried to hinder any use of the area.[13] This situation had serious consequences for those who lived inside the ramparts, because the increasing population was packed together without a water and sewer system – a totally unbearable and unhealthy situation. The government of war had to give up – under great resistance – the restrictions and easements for some of the area in 1867.[14] The ramparts were delegated to the Copenhagen council and were the only breathing spaces for the citizens. Parks were made on these ramparts (the well-known Tivoli is placed on an old rampart), whose only purpose was for promenades.[15] But the common green outside the ramparts (the Fælled) was still under military control and still used for drill. The area extended more than 150 acres and farmers and citizens still retained their right to graze their cattle there. The local authorities worked hard for more than 25 years to wrest the remainder of the area from military control; the Fælled became a symbol of what Copenhagen needed – a place for outdoor life for the mass population, the so-called 'lungs of Copenhagen'.[16] From the late 1870s it became a constant popular and political claim that the military had to loosen the easement bonds of the Fælled. Teachers were pleading for playgrounds and more outdoor space for children; doctors were calling for more healthy conditions in general. Both professions were pioneers in the new sports movement and called attention to the unhygienic inner town and the unhealthy consequences of the new housing outside the ramparts. The Fælled was therefore looked upon as a possibility for release. Philanthropic societies were also pleading for it to be used as a new sports area. It became a recurrent theme in journals for architects, doctors, teachers, engineers and sports enthusiasts.[17] The growing political influence of Liberal and Social Democratic parties in the 1880s was bolstered by emphasizing the Fælled issue in their campaigns.[18] But the State and the government of war neglected it and didn't regard it as a popular problem. They did not consider sport as a requisite for health and modernization. In the late 1800s, the military still had an important political role and considerable power inherited from pre-democratic days (before 1849).

### The Fælled as sports ground

Nevertheless, the local military authority in Copenhagen allowed cricket and football clubs to play on the ground in the Fælled for an annual fee of Dkr.1 per club (a worker earned approximately Dkr.2 per day, so it was quite cheap). The richest of the clubs rented an apartment close to the Fælled which was used as a changing room and a place to store equipment. The poorer clubs (working class) had no such facilities, changing at home or more usually in the open air. They kept football and cricket equipment in the local pub, and the host then expected better sales after training.[19] As mentioned above, horses and cattle were still grazing on the Fælled, so if one was unlucky (as was often the case) horse- or cow-pats were encountered. These conditions were, of course, the background for the applications to the Copenhagen municipal corporation for the Fælled as an official place for sport. The chairman, Frederik Markmann, of the upper-class club KB, wrote an open letter in the sports journal *Dansk Sportstidende* in 1888 in which he proposed to the Copenhagen council that a part of the Fælled should be handed over to the cricket and football clubs.[20] The time of the publication of the letter was chosen with care; he knew that the State and the Copenhagen council were negotiating to abolish the military easement to the Fælled.[21] But the negotiations did not succeed and the government of war continued to keep their rights, but only for another five years, until 1 May 1893, at which time the military would have to move out to a new rampart system on the outskirts of Copenhagen – everyone looked forward to 1893. In fact, the easements were not abolished in 1893, but the Copenhagen council did finally get a juridical provision ensuring the takeover of the Fælled by the city, although a specific date was not declared.

## From Fælled to Fælled Park and Idrætspark: A Contested Ground

*The emerging social democracy*

After more than four hundred years of political battle between the State and the government of war on one side, and the local authorities and the citizens of Copenhagen on the other, the Fælled was taken over by the Copenhagen municipal council in 1893 with two modifications: firstly, the council had to accept a significant surrender of territories to the State and the government of war on the outskirts of the town; and secondly, the time of delegation was not fixed, which meant that the State still had the area at its disposal. To persuade the government, the Copenhagen council had to give up 40 acres of the Fælled out of a total of 160 acres, and a further 90 acres in different locations on the outskirts of the city, in order to get possession of the remaining 120 acres.[22] One could not call it a victory – but after more than four hundred, years the city and the citizens of Copenhagen had ensured their future right to the Fælled; a huge area was now at its disposal, close to the heart of the city.

The decision to lay out a park and to build sports facilities was taken by the new Social Democratic government in 1904. But in the first instance, the area was not used for sport. In the years from 1893, the bourgeois-dominated council and corporation wanted it to be sold as an extension of the house-building programme of Copenhagen, one of the main reasons being that the sale could provide an enormous income for the city. Another, and more suspicious, reason was that a number of council representatives were landowners and an extension of the city housing programme on the Fælled would, of course, have increased the value of the area enormously. The Conservative politicians justified their plans by appealing to the ideologies of liberalism – the new economic and political movement at this time in Denmark – and hence they rejected the appeals of sports organizations and interest groups with arguments that provision and acquisition of exercise and outdoor life should be a private matter. In the 1890s, the young Social Democratic Party (founded in 1872) tried to break the power of the 'conservative' bourgeoisie at the city hall. But it was difficult: on the one hand, undemocratic obstacles made it impossible for the party to take over; and, on the other hand, the Social Democratic ideology and strategy known as 'Proletarian Reformism' had for two decades isolated politically the working-class party. The shift in the political profile and self-understanding in the 1880s made it more plausible for other political groups to co-operate with the Social Democratic Party and it attracted a broader and more widespread mass support.[23]

The first democratic election in Copenhagen was held in 1840 (the first in Denmark based on an authorised democratic constitution), but the working class and other lower social groups were still excluded from participation. To gain the right to vote in 1840, one had to be (a) male; (b) 30 years old; (c) a propertied holder of real estate; and (d) a tax payer. As a result, no more than 1,929 males of a total population of 120,000 in Copenhagen held the suffrage in 1840. The possession of real estate excluded practically the whole working class, but franchise reform came in 1865 and prescribed that (a) males of 25 years, and (b) those who paid tax of Dkr. 400 (tax was not paid for the first Dkr. 600, so you had to earn Dkr. 1,000 p.a.) had suffrage. From the 1860s to the 1880s no more than about 5–10% had the right to vote.[24] But the number of workers' votes increased in the 1880s, caused by inflation and growing salaries (the amount of Dkr. 1,000 was fixed), so workers began to reach the threshold of economic qualification. Simultaneously, the 'progressive' Liberals and the Social Democrats agreed on a common political programme for the elections with the purpose of breaking 'conservative' power. The first members were elected in 1893 and in 1898. The coalition won a majority, but there was still one obstacle left before they got the real power.

The municipal constitution was a bicameral system divided into a council and a corporation. The corporation was made up of members elected by the council for six years and the mayor was elected for life by the council. So despite a majority in the council from 1898 the coalition couldn't make the decision to stop the housing programme on the Fælled area.[25] In short, the system's inertia hindered rapid changes. Paradoxically, to get the real power, the Social Democrats had to wait until the death of a mayor. They had to wait five more years – the leader of the finance section, the most powerful position in the corporation, died in 1903, and since they now had a majority in the council they were able to elect the first Social Democratic mayor of Copenhagen, Jens Jensen.

Jens Jensen was not only the first Social Democratic mayor in Copen-hagen, but also in Denmark and he was met by his political counterparts and enemies with scepticism and arrogance.[26] He was a skilled craftsman and was educated politically in the Social Democratic trade union. He became Chairman of the Painters' Union and a key person in the early workers' movement. He had been elected to the Copenhagen council as the first Social Democrat in 1893 and hence he had ten years political experience in the municipal council before he became mayor of the finance corporation. Denmark has only one large metropolis, Copen-hagen, and it has been the bourgeois stronghold for centuries. The bourgeoisie viewed Jensen as the black sheep of the golden metropolitan crown of the nation. But their prejudices against him, and working-class culture in general, were put into the shade during his twenty-one-year period in the mayoral seat.

Nevertheless, one of the first initiatives in his position as mayor was to appoint a common committee in 1904, with members both from the council and the corporation, to consider the future of the Fælled, with special reference to the establishment of a park on the area.[27] 'We (Copenhagen city, the citizens and the people) shall have our own London Hyde Park' said Jensen at the council meeting.[28] A common committee was to work on this principal commission, the council deciding that the plans should be worked out in a formal architectural competition with a deadline of October 1905.

Some years later Jensen was asked in an interview in a sports maga-zine what the background for the park decision was and why exactly this project became the first major piece of legislation of his mayoral term. He answered that he had lived at Vesterbro (one of the town-planning disasters of Copenhagen and a working-class area) with no fresh air, no sun, no space for play and sport, so he knew how important it was to give space for physical activities and fresh air. Another important reason was that, as Chairman of the Painters' Union in 1887, he had tried to introduce cricket to the workers who had played on the open Fælled, but this had proved impossible because of the wind and the animal droppings. From that moment, he thought of the Fælled as a park with trees as a shield from the wind and with grass lawns for sport.[29]

*The Fælledpark and Idrætsparken*

The laying out of the park began when the first tree was planted by Mayor Jens Jensen in April 1909 and was finished in March 1911. The basic idea of the project was to divide the Fælledpark into two separate parts: the Fælledpark and, within it, Københavns Idrætspark (KI). The total area of the Fælledpark was approximately 37 acres and, inside it, the KI was created, extending over 9.34 acres. The Fælledpark was established as an open public park with a variety of different possibilities and facilities for the citizens. It was to provide promenades, playgrounds for children and kindergartens, areas for rendezvous and picnics, concerts, skiing in the winter, a variety of sports and informal meetings; even a speakers' corner was made (modelled on Hyde Park). What made this park unique regarding sport was that the authorities laid out twelve permanent football fields for both organized and unorganized football clubs, which could use it freely, in principle, all day long. This principle is retained today.

In 1907, sports organizations were invited by the Copenhagen council to participate in the planning and elaboration of the KI. These invited organizations included the Danish central sport organization (DIF) and the central football organization (DBU), representing different sports, namely football, hockey, athletics, boxing, wrestling and swimming.[30]

KI consisted of sports grounds, facilities and buildings and was the first large modern sports stadium and arena in Copenhagen (and Denmark). For the first time in history, the working class and other lower social groups had access to outdoor sports facilities within the realm of a public authority. The broader context can now be elaborated.

### The craftsman and John Maynard Keynes

In 1908, the whole project was recommended for ratification by the mayor, Jensen, and was accepted. The total budget was about Dkr. 1.6 million.[31] Even at that time it was an enormous amount. The total budget at the Copenhagen Town Hall in the same year was Dkr. 26.6 million.[32]

An interesting perspective comes to light in the project; namely a new economic strategy in the political takeover by the first Social Democratic municipal administration in Denmark. One of the decisive Social Democratic arguments for the park project was the economic crisis and the growing unemployment within the construction industries in the early 1900s. The argument was that the project would have a catalytic impact on economic development, despite an apparent deficit on the balance sheet. The strategy was that work on the park project would create employment and contribute to economic growth.[33] To budget consciously with deficit was a totally new way of thinking and a clear sign of the changing ideologies of the time – the Social Democratic economic policy and welfare system was dimly emerging. In 1909, the deficit was Dkr. 2.3 million and Dkr. 4.7 million in 1910, approximately 10–20% of the total budget.[34] Later on, this kind of budget politics became one of the fundamental keys in the work of John Maynard Keynes. The Social Democratic Parties in Europe adopted the ideas of Keynes from the 1930s in order to cope with unemployment and state budgets in general. This was three decades after Mayor Jensen had begun to use the so-called social-liberal economic strategies in the finance section in the Copenhagen municipal corporation from 1903–1924.[35]

### Københavns Idrætspark – a self-governing institution

When the whole ground complex was finished, a meeting between the Copenhagen municipal council and corporation and the Danish Sport Federation (DIF) on 11 March 1911, formally delegated the KI to be a self-governing institution.[36] All facilities were delegated without any charge. The leadership of the institution was formed by the Copenhagen local sections of the DIF, by representatives from the Copenhagen municipal corporation and council and by shareholders in the 'sport fund' for financing the buildings.[37] The Copenhagen sports sections had the majority in the council of KI, but representatives from the town hall had the right of veto.[38] The final result was, for Denmark, a huge modern football stadium, together with modern buildings and facilities for a variety of different sports. The whole complex was delegated from the authorities to KI for a period of ninety-nine years.[39]

### Idrætsparken, the Fælled Club House and the working class

The early 1911 version of the stadium was very primitive and consisted only of the Fælled Club House and its field (see Figure 4.2). The field was under the jurisdiction of the self-governing institution, but the Fælled Club House remained under the jurisdiction of the authorities. The stand was built at the back of the house but only had seating for four hundred spectators. The total capacity of the ground was less than ten thousand. It was therefore a small and rather basic stadium, but nevertheless the first larger public arena in Copenhagen (see Figure 4.3).

The Fælled Club House was built for the many new clubs, which were formed from 1900 onwards and which played football on the old open Fælled. The purpose of the building was to give them their own facilities and a home for a 'cultural' club life. The clubs had to apply to the municipal corporation for rooms and obtained permanent facilities for an annual fee of Dkr. 100, which in 1911 was very cheap.[40] Outside the Idrætspark and the Fælled Club House, the municipal corporation

**Figure 4.2** A football match during 1914, with the grand Fælled Club-house, built in 1911, dominating the scene

**Figure 4.3** Idrætsparken, the Fælled and the northern suburbs of Copenhagen in the 1930s

70

had laid out twelve football pitches for the Fælled clubs. For the first time in the history of Copenhagen, the non-ground-owning clubs got facilities to bath and dress and they even had access to permanent football grounds with goals, corner flags etc. But the so-called Fælled Club House was the one exception in the delegation to KI. This was the only building financed by the municipal authorities, but it was not included in the delegation to KI and was still under the explicit jurisdiction of the authorities. When the whole project was ratified in 1908, and built from 1909, nothing indicated that the Fælled Club House had a special position, so why this exception?

If the local authorities had not kept the Club House out of the realm of KI, an 'insurrection' would have broken out. The background lay in the upper-class hegemony within the Danish football federation, DBU.[41] The federation was totally dominated by upper-class clubs and was represented by them in the self-governing institution, so all the smaller working-class clubs playing football in the Fælledpark came under their control. This was of course very frustrating for the Social Democratic vision of the project, namely that the stadium and the Fælled Club House should symbolize a new era of mass-integrated culture – symbolizing an egalitarian nation. But such was the political background in the decision to take the Fælled Club House out of the delegation document.

The relationship between the upper-class clubs and all other clubs in Copenhagen had developed into a relation of hatred from the middle of 1900 to 1911. The reason why DBU was founded in 1889 was that there was no place to play football under acceptable conditions, but the DBU aspiration to own football facilities failed totally, which this story indicates in itself. The upper-class clubs, which ruled DBU, began individually to apply to the bourgeois-dominated municipal corporation for permanent places to play football. Three clubs were successful. An application by a non-upper-class club was denied (in 1901) but confirmed in 1904, when it applied to the Social Democratic corporation. Four clubs had, by 1911, achieved this status and were located in different places in Copenhagen. These four ground-owning clubs alone controlled DBU. By virtue of this power they forced all the other member clubs to play all official soccer matches on the ground-owning clubs' pitches, which gave them an enormous economic advantage and income.[42] The monopoly was broken with the opening of the new stadium, Idrætsparken, in 1911. As a result, if the ground-owning clubs wanted to stay in power and secure their incomes (which became more and more difficult as more football clubs emerged at the beginning of the twentieth century and became members of DBU) they had to exclude all the new clubs from influence by changing the rules in the federation. The upper-class clubs changed the rules in 1908 and 1911 and kept power. But more importantly, they could define the role of the new stadium and hence the federation could control the Idrætsparken. The federation decided that the stadium could only be used as a home ground by the national team and by First Division clubs, i.e. the ground-owning club themselves. In effect, the propertied decided to exclude the unpropertied clubs. With actions like this, the ground-owning group was in power until after the Second World War. After this abuse of power, the two groups became alienated from each other and many clubs chose to stay outside the federation. The Fælled Club House was meant to be not only for members of DBU, but also for football clubs outside the federation. Many clubs, both inside and outside, did not want to see the 'enemy' as the head of the Fælled Club House. In short, this was the decisive background for the decision by the authorities not to delegate the Club House to the self-governing institution. The final result was that the Fælled clubs got homes for their leisure life and a 'home ground' in the park, but the dream of becoming independent of upper-class hegemony, with the new stadium administered by a 'democratic' institution, was never fulfilled. The 'right' to arrange football matches was still under the auspices of DBU – in other words, the stadium was in the hands of KI and the Fælled Club House was in the hands of Copenhagen city.[43]

*Football as space and time mediation of different 'socio-sport' appearances*

I have already described the various sport biases within the different social groups. In the early days of Danish sport, sailing, horse-racing, hunting and rowing were very popular among the aristocracy and bourgeoisie. Among workers, the most popular sports were boxing, wrestling and weight-lifting. At this time, football was not diversified and common. Spatially, all aristocratic sports took place in the open space without any defined limits, e.g. woodland, the sea and landscapes in general. It could be said that they occurred in nature and the outdoors. At the same time, no well-defined and fixed time existed for such activities. Working class sports, however, usually took place indoors. Spatially, the boxing ring, the wrestling mat and the weight-lifting stage are relatively small and well-defined. The time orientation is very short, reduced to the decisive moment of the knock-out, the fall and the lift. Physically, the boxers and the wrestlers squeeze, hug and fix their sweating bodies close to each other, while sailors, horse-riders, and rowers 'never' touch or are forced by the activity itself to have bodily contact.[44]

Football can be seen as a mediation of these 'socio-sport' forms. The football space is enclosed by lines but defined by open nature (in fact the space is vertically open and horizontally closed). Football takes place inside the lines in out-of-door landscapes. The time is defined: ninety minutes, which is rather long compared to boxing but short compared to hunting. The defending team tries to close the space of the attacking team, tackling with body contact, while the attacking team tries to avoid physical contact. This analysis could continue but, in short, football consists of elements and time and space orientation from both upper- and working-class sport activities. This could perhaps explain the football penetration and diversification as the first mass-sport activity. The Fælledpark, Idrætsparken, and The Fælled Club House were the first sports facilities contributing to the underlying development of football as a mass cultural form in Denmark.

## The Good, the Bad and the Ugly Years of Idrætsparken

*From 1911 to 1989*

The working- and middle-class clubs in the centre of Copenhagen never played a decisive role among the top-level football clubs. The élite clubs were, for several decades, strictly recruited from upper-class football clubs, with very few exceptions, and they won the national championship nearly every year from the beginning of a nationwide soccer tournament in 1913 until the late 1960s. As a result, the smaller clubs never considered playing in Copenhagen's only large stadium, and, anyway, they were consistently excluded by the upper-class clubs which controlled the DBU and hence representation on the self-governing board of the KI.

Idrætsparken became the sacred stadium for all the popular teams in Copenhagen and for the national team. When it was built in 1911 there had never been more than six thousand spectators assembled for a single match. But from 1911 until the mid-1950s, football, and sport in general, became a widespread mass movement and in particular the number of spectators increased enormously, reaching a peak in the 1940s and 1950s, which apparently mirrors the pattern all over Europe.[46] In this period, football was totally dominated by four or five teams from Copenhagen, which all played their home matches in Idrætsparken. Simultaneously, the Danish national team was very popular. It was a great time for the stadium and Idrætsparken generated considerable revenue.

Retrospectively, KI became the largest sports organization in Copenhagen. Today it runs more than eighty different sports grounds and sports facilities are spread all over town. The budget for KI is more than Dkr. 100,000 million per year, paid by the local authorities. The sports complexes are open to everybody and are a significant part of the welfare system. In short, one could say that KI administers the sporting life in Copenhagen on instructions negotiated between them and the authorities. Out of eighty sports grounds and buildings, twenty-three have football facilities and several of these have stands at their stadium. All grounds are financed by the authorities. But Idrætsparken is an exception. From the very beginning, a contract between KI and the council prescribed that the former had to finance, administer and renovate the stadium (Idrætsparken), but in return it had the full right and disposition over the entrance income and proceeds. From 1911 to 1955, the popularity of soccer developed rapidly and so did the extension and modernization of Idrætsparken. Before the demolition in 1990 the last huge investment was the Grand Stand built on the place where the old Fælled Club House lay. For several years this was the highest stand in Europe and the greatest investment in the history of Idrætsparken. The tremendous spectator rates in Idrætsparken at this time made the investments evident and profitable.

The Fælled Club house was a 'proud' building, an integrated house in the park, designed by an English architect, built in artisan materials and style. When the new Grand Stand was built, however, all the Fælled clubs living in the old Club House were sent down to the basement of the new Grand Stand, into dark, sterile, concrete rooms without windows. Today they are still there (the stand is preserved in the new Parken). The decision was taken by the upper-class football federation in the executive committee in the Idrætsparken, but more paradoxically approved by the Social Democratic mayor. The cultural spirit of 1911 was fading.

The number of matches played in Idrætsparken from 1915 to 1989 declined steadily. From a figure of 47 in 1915, the number rose to 106 in 1946. Since then, decline set in, reaching a figure of only 38 in 1989.[47] From the beginning of the 1960s, the suburban Copenhagen clubs began to oust the city clubs and the new up-and-coming teams chose to stay at their own smaller grounds on the outskirts of Copenhagen. The crisis became worse with dramatically falling spectator figures in the First Division. The average figure for the 1978 season for the First Division was 2,752. This was the year when professional football was introduced in Denmark, and it should have been one of celebration, but it became instead the worst season in terms of attendance. Under these conditions, it would have been absurd to play in Idrætsparken and it would have caused a deficit for the clubs.

In 1911, the stadium's capacity was about 10,000. It grew steadily to over 52,000 by 1955, but was reduced to under 46,000 in the 1980s because of security measures and the conversion from stands to seats. From the mid-1960s, spectator interest fell enormously and the 1970s were catastrophic years for KI. More than a million people went to Idrætsparken in 1950 and no more than 186,000 in 1975. In 1950, 91 matches were played but there were only 36 in 1975. Revenue followed the same pattern and the consequence was disastrous. Very little was renovated from 1955 to the mid-1980s as a result of this decline and Idrætsparken was criticized for its lack of services, notably toilets, foodstuffs, emergency exits, and TV-facilities. At the same time middle-class norms and ideas penetrated cultural life and the management in the football clubs. Meanwhile, stadiums were transformed into standardized designs and materials, often planned with the TV-media as the most significant and decisive factor. Stadiums all over the world became more and more like each other and gradually assumed a sense of 'sameness' and 'placelessness'.[48] But when journalists, spectators and TV viewers looked around in the space of Idrætsparken they were 'replaced' into the standards and design of the 1930s and 1950s and in the 1970s and 1980s the stadium was subjected to much criticism. With a bad economy and very few spectators, it was unrealistic to invest more than Dkr. 250 million. Stipulated budgets made by KI showed that this was the 'saturation' point, based on incomes from the national squad, one First Division club, rental incomes from offices and two concerts per annum. In short, the financial background was totally out of proportion to be realistic in a budget with loans of more than Dkr. 250 million.

### The ugly years and the final fall of Idrætsparken

Many things happened in Denmark in relation to football in the 1980s. In 1968, the top forty-eight clubs founded an organization called Divisionsforeningen, designed to take care of the interests of élite football. Subsequently, Divisionsforeningen played an increasingly significant role in the Danish football federation (DBU), a role reinforced after the rather late introduction of professional football in 1978. In addition, in the previous years DBU underwent a democratic development due to the egalitarian years of the 1960s when the 'masses' gained influence in DBU affairs and hence on the boards of the KI, but without any current value. Today, they all play at a very low level without significant numbers of spectators. But in the early 1980s, the Danish national team was successful in international matches, and Elkjær, Laudrup, Simonsen, Jesper Olsen, Morten Olsen, etc., became well-known football household names in Europe. In the 1970s, no more than 10,000 (on average) watched the national team, but after the victory at Wembley in September 1983 and the subsequent qualification for the European Championship in France, the World Championship in 1986 in Mexico, the European Championship in West Germany in 1988, and successful matches with the European Cup victory in 1992 in Sweden, Idrætsparken could not cope with the new situation. At the same time, another aspect of the globalization and internationalization trend influenced the show sport – the payment by the TV for the right to broadcast from the stadiums, and at the same time, their demand for better facilities, e.g. light, platforms, speaking and interview facilities, scheduled time for kick-off, etc.

Divisionsforeningen representing the First Division clubs, and DBU representing the national team, strongly insisted on the rights and profits from the TV and advertising incomes that KI had previously received. The conflict between KI and the football organizations escalated into hatred. Relations between the personnel became so strained that they could not even be in the same room together. The professional football clubs are today ruled by commercial businessmen with strong links with the higher echelons of politics and business. Danish private enterprise and the football leaders decided to do anything to circumvent KI and its future plans of renovation. The 'permissive days' of folk-culture, 'egalitarian' and democratic ideas were replaced by a 'modern', more realistic calculating commercialism. The last nail in the coffin was the FIFA demand for all-seat stadiums for matches after 1992. The demand coincided with the conflict in 1987 between KI and the football organizations. These were the events and political background which preceded the decision to demolish Idrætsparken and build Parken – the new stadium for the national team (see Chapter 8).

## The End of Idrætsparken

A new all-seat stadium with a capacity of between forty and fifty thousand people would cost something like Dkr. 500 million or even Dkr. 750 million, a figure well beyond the resources of KI. At the same time, the city of Copenhagen was threatened by bankruptcy, so any economic subsidies and support from the local authorities to KI was absolutely out of the question. The economic analysis elaborated by KI showed that costs extending to more than Dkr. 250 million would not be profitable in Copenhagen. The story of Parken is told by Per Jørgensen in Chapter 8.

The fate of Idrætsparken was in many ways predestinated. The ideologies of the management in the football organizations are based on the notion of football as economy rather than on town planning, cultural values, democratic constitution or historical roots. The FIFA demand for all-seat stadiums expressed a global view of uniformity, independent of national specificities and characteristics (see Figure 4.4). Sport is, perhaps, the most distinguished representative and buffer of world cultural tendencies. Journalists and the FIFA football management constitute a decisive group, defining the world-wide sporting culture typified by football in a very narrow and un-historical perspective. After all, in the eyes of sports journalists or football politicians,

**Figure 4.4**   Parken in late 1992. The open space of the Fælled is still present. The historic community of Brumleby (see Chapter 8) is among the trees to the left of the stadium. (Source: Polfoto, Copenhagen)

Idrætsparken was an old-fashioned, public, democratic institution com-pared to Silverdome, San Siro, Möngersdorfer, Nou Camp and Parc de Prince.

## Notes

1.  Park means the same in Danish and English. Idræt is an ancient Nordic concept, which means sport, play, walk and physical activities in general. Idræt is a broader concept than sport, but it is close to the concept of 'making sport'.
2.  København is Danish for Copenhagen. KI is the administrative and formal political department of the stadium Idrætsparken. Idrætsparken forms only one of many sports grounds under the jurisdiction of KI.
3.  'Fælled' means common green.
4.  See John Bale, 'The Spatial Development of the Modern Stadium', *International Review for the Sociology of Sport*, Vol. 28, 2–3 (1993), pp.121–34, and Chapter 2 in this volume. See also Niels Kayser Nielsen, *Stil og ballade* (Odense, 1994).
5.  Dansk Boldspil-Union (in short DBU) means Danish Football Asso-ciation/Federation. In 1993 the association had 260,000 members, which makes it by far the biggest association in Danmarks Idræts-

Forbund (Denmark's Sport Federation), which has 1.5 million members. The total population of Denmark is 5.1 million.

6. The modern Olympic movement is the clearest and most significant example of the new time and mentality concerning sport. One would expect ancient Olympism to be the historical link backwards to prove the overall un-contemporary witness of human craving to compete and make sport. Norbert Elias has described and elaborated the core essence and the difference between Greek Olympism and modern sport. The ancient Greek Olympic Games were extremely violent and can only be understood in another modern configuration and within the context of civilization. Ancient Greek Olympism has to be understood in a totally different political and cultural structure, which ultimately gave thanks to the gods for the strength they had bestowed on human kind. Norbert Elias, 'The genesis of sport as a sociological problem', in Eric Dunning (ed.), *The Sociology of Sport* (London, 1970), pp.88–115.

7. Ove Korsgaard, *Kampen om kroppen* (Gyldendal, 1982), pp.128ff. and Jørn Hansen, 'Sportens vej til Danmark – hestevæddeløb', in Else Trangbæk, *Den engelske sports gennembrud i Norden* (DHL, 1989).

8. Joseph Maguire, 'Sport, National Identities and Globalization' in John Bale (ed.), *Community Landscape and Identity: Horizons in a Geography of Sports*, Keele University, Department of Geography, Occasional Paper 20 (1994), pp.71–93.

9. Jim Toft, *Fodboldbanen kridtes op* (Copenhagen, 1990); and Jim Toft, 'Fodbold mellem myter og kilder', in Jørn Hansen and Henning Eichberg (eds), *Idrætshistorisk årbog* (Odense, 1993).

10. See Chapters 5 and 10 in this volume and Tony Mason, *Association Football and English Society* (Brighton, 1980).

11. See note 3.

12. Nørlund *et al.* (eds), *København 1888–1945* (København, 1948), p.lxxxix.

13. The area outside the ramparts of the city should be an open space so as to make the enemy visible.

14. *Samling af bestemmelser vedrørende Københavns Kommune 1864–1874* (København, 1878); *Samling af bestemmelser vedrørende Københavns Kommune 1875–1887* (København, 1904); *Samling af bestemmelser vedrørende Københavns Kommune 1888–1896* (København, 1898).

15. The decision about the use of the ramparts was taken with Vienna as a model, which had done the same ten years earlier in 1857. Axel Holm and Kjeld Johansen, *København 1840–1940* (København, 1941).

16. *Borgerrepræsentationens Forhandlinger* (BRF), Københavns Kommune, BRF 65. aarg, 1904–1905, 3 Oct. 1904.

17. *Tidsskrift for Sport, Dansk sportstidende, Architekten, Husvennen,* etc.

18. Hans Helge Madsen, *Østerbros herligheder* (København, 1986), pp.42–4.

19. Beer and football have always been connected as two inseparable phenomena.

20. *Dansk Sportstidende* (1888), pp.384–5.

21. *Borgerrepræsentationens Forhandlinger* (BRF), Københavns Kommune, BRF 47. aarg, 28 Feb. 1887; BRF 48. aarg, 12 Mar. 1888; and BRF 49. aarg, 5 Nov. 1888.

22. Ibid., Københavns Kommune, BRF 53. aarg, tillæg 12 Dec. 1892; BRF 54. aarg, 10 Apr. 1893; and BRF 54. aarg, 8 May 1893.

23. Niles Ole Finnemann, *I broderskabets aand* (Gyldendal, 1985); and Gunhild Agger and Anker Gemzøe, *Arbejderkultur 1870–1924* (Medusa, 1982).

24. Poul Møller, *Københavns bystyre gennem 300 aar* (København, 1967), pp.324–9.

25. *Københavns kommunale forhold* (København, 1897), pp.18–21.

26. 'Hedebol', in Nørlund *et al.*, *København 1888–1945*, p. xciii.

27. 'Common' because it consisted of members both from the council and from the corporation. *Borgerrepræsentationens Forhandlinger* (BRF), Københavns Kommune, BRF 65. aarg, 3 Oct. 1904.

28. Ibid.

29. *Idrætten, 1911* (København, 1911), pp.22–3.

30. Andreas Harsfelt, *Københavns Idrætspark 1911–1936* (København, 1936), p.14. DIF (Dansk Idræts-Forbund) is the Danish Sports Federation. See note 5.

31. *Borgerrepræsentationens Forhandlinger* (BRF), Københavns Kommune, BRF 69. aarg, 4 May 1908.

32. Holm and Johansen, *København 1840–1940*, p.314.

33. *Borgerrepræsentationens Forhandlinger* (BRF), Københavns Kommune, BRF 65. aarg, 3 Oct. 1904.

34. Holm and Johansen, *København 1840–1940*, pp.311–14.

35. Mariann Brandt *et al.*, *Socialdemokratisk agitation og propaganda i mellemkrigsperioden* (Aarhus, 1979), *passim*, Chapter 1.

36. Harsfelt, *Københavns Idrætspark 1911–1936*, pp.15–16. DSA was founded in 1896 and later became the nation-wide head association for all sport associations.

37. *Borgerreprsentationens Forhandlinger* (BRF), Københavns Kommune, BRF 72. aarg, 21 June 1910.

38. The veto has never been used.

39. Harsfelt, *Københavns Idrætspark 1911–1936*, p.14.

40. *Borgerreprsentationens Forhandlinger* (BRF), Københavns Kommune, BRF 71. aarg, 27 June 1910; and BRF 72. aarg, 8 May 1911.

41. Toft, 'Fodbold mellem myter og kilder', pp.105ff.

42. Ibid., pp.110ff.

43. Ibid., pp.106ff.

44. Martin Zerlang, *Underholdningens historie. Fra antikkens gladiatorer til nutidens tv-serier* (Gyldendal, 1989).

45. Toft, *Fodboldbanen kridtes op*, and Niels Kayser Nielsen, 'Sport kultur og utopi', *Bidrag* Vol. 13/14 (1981).

46. See Chapter 5 in this volume and Eric Dunning *et al.*, *The Roots of Football Hooliganism* (London, 1988).

47. All figures are based on annual reports of Københavns Idrætspark, 1911–93.

48. John Bale, 'Running towards modernity: a one-way street', *International Journal of the History of Sport*, Vol. 10, 2 (1993), pp.215–32.

# 5

# Moving to Suburbia: Stadium Relocation and Modernization in Vienna

*Roman Horak*

## The Topography of Viennese Football

*The beginnings*

The process by which the new urban masses claimed the emerging metropolitan areas as their own, in the late nineteenth and early twentieth centuries, took many forms. Among these was the political conquest of the street by the organized labour movement which, especially in Vienna, was able to press its demand for universal suffrage by staging mass demonstrations. The latter had specific goals in the case of the electoral reform movement, the achievement of formal legal equality for all citizens. Though they sometimes degenerated into chaos, they were often centrally planned and organized.[1] The appropriation of urban areas by the common people also took less dramatic forms, notably the new mass entertainments, which progressively changed the face of the metropolitan cities.[2] Among these popular spectacles, the game of football took on a particular significance, becoming a spectator sport and regularly mobilizing large crowds of supporters at the weekends.[3]

Let us first examine the manner in which Vienna's football geography took shape during this period. In the early days, soccer was played on meadows on the outskirts of the city, and only later do we find proper football pitches (in 1900, there were only three). Thereafter, the number of grounds grew rapidly, in line with the rising number of teams being founded, especially in the densely-populated working-class districts. Another consequence of the burgeoning interest in football was a trend towards laying out single-purpose soccer grounds. The early 1920s saw the construction of a number of major sports facilities and stadiums, especially in the southern and western working-class districts, and those in the north, beyond the Danube. This led to one of the fundamental characteristics of the geography of Viennese football: unlike those of some British cities, the Viennese stadiums are located on the outskirts.

81

Between the wars, Vienna's suburbs differed significantly from those of most other major European cities. They were essentially 'grey areas', where urban and agrarian cultures merged into one another, and, as such, reflected the progressive encroachment of urban structures into the countryside. Yet the *Vorstadt* (suburb) was also associated with distinct lifestyles and mentalities, unique spheres of cultural, political and aesthetic experience. In many respects, these reflected the transitional character so typical of the urban periphery as a whole, in that a rural consciousness and lifestyle co-existed with rapid industrialization and urbanization. During the last three decades of the nineteenth century, the industrialization of the periphery was almost completely unregulated. Nevertheless, a typical pattern of urban expansion emerged, characterized by an intermingling of residential and industrial developments. These were interspersed with extensive open spaces, devoted neither to agricultural nor to industrial use. Being 'no man's lands', these spaces were largely free from social control. Such locations became settings for primary socialization, especially in the case of a group to which the stigma of revolt naturally attached, namely suburban youth. They were appropriated for social use, and became a focus for cultural learning and leisure activities. It is thus no surprise that football took on such importance in the suburbs, and that the latter supplied the majority of the spectators and players. But the *Vorstadt* was not just a reservoir for the now booming new spectator sport of football; particular suburban parts of Vienna became closely linked with their own football clubs. What has been shown in reference to English football,[4] namely the idea of 'local pride' connected to a particular local football team, was clearly also very important in Vienna in the 1920s and 1930s. But whereas the geographical structure has not changed much, these very cultural meanings attached to it have – more or less – vanished in the Second Republic.

*The post-war period*

An analysis of the situation in Vienna with regard to sports facilities over the past forty years shows the following trends. In all, there are 75 football grounds in the Vienna area today, but many of these have more than one pitch (e.g. Wiener Stadion has 10; Post, Hanappi and Horr stadiums each have four). In addition, there are about 10 football grounds that are not used by any of the clubs organized in the Vienna Football Association (WFV). The majority of these facilities belong to the major sports clubs (offering a variety of sporting disciplines), or are privately owned. There are also 17 football pitches at various youth club and school playing fields which are available for general use. The total

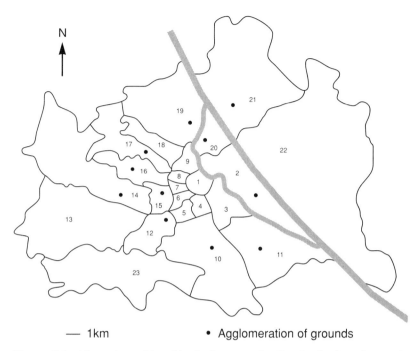

N

— 1km          • Agglomeration of grounds

**Figure 5.1**   Vienna's traditional football geography: the distribution of grounds in the 1920s

number of playing fields that can be used for football runs to about 160[5] (see Figure 5.1).

It is no longer possible to arrive at the precise number of football grounds in the early days of the Second Republic. The only comparison that can be made is of the number of sports grounds offering facilities for football, and this shows a rather modest increase from 58 to 75 football grounds. Growth is almost exclusively concentrated in outer districts, namely those beyond the Danube (21st and 22nd), as well as Liesing (23rd). The reduction in the number of clubs during this period cannot serve as an explanation, as it was more than made good by the increase in the numbers of youth leagues and hobby teams, and by the gradual development of women's football.

It would also be misleading to think of this growth as an uninterrupted process. In fact, it is only possible to point to significant construction of sports grounds up to the start of the 1960s, and it can be taken that there has been a continuous decline in the number of grounds during the past two decades. The immediate post-war period was one of an extreme dearth of playing facilities, owing to war damage. In 1947, an investigation by Vienna City Council of the position with regard to sports grounds revealed major shortages, which the introduction of football pools (1949/50 season) was intended to remedy, the profits being partly earmarked for the creation of new facilities.

These measures contributed to a rapid rise in the number of sports grounds, partly through the reconstruction of existing facilities and partly through the creation of new ones, mainly on the outskirts of the city. Data from the 1960s show a peak of 83 football grounds in the Vienna area.[6] However, this total was not maintained, as grounds were repeatedly sacrificed to building projects, especially Council housing schemes, and sufficient resources were not provided for replacements. At times, the available funds were not even sufficient to rehabilitate or modernize existing facilities.

Today, subsidies from Vienna remain inadequate to redress the 'woeful state' of the city's sports provision (about AS 20 million were budgeted for 1992[7]), though it has been criticized for decades. The amounts available are just sufficient to rehabilitate existing facilities, but not to build new ones. A study of Viennese football grounds, undertaken in 1990, indicated an urgent need for expenditure of about AS 150 million on renovation work alone. In many cases, without private initiative football would cease to be played under acceptable conditions.

Increasingly, football can only be played in an organized context, as young people's access to spaces that used to be open to all (alleyways, commons and fields) is becoming ever more restricted. The building up of numerous green spaces in the outer districts has left only a few parks, part of the Prater and the Donauinsel (Danube Island) for kick-arounds.

The fact that youth competitions have continued on the same scale as in the past is primarily due to immigration by Yugoslav and Turkish families, whose children account for a large proportion of the youth teams of many Viennese clubs. Problems have arisen from the inability of all but a few clubs to understand their 'multicultural' function[8] and from the fact that, for various reasons, the integration of young immigrants has by no means been trouble-free. Moreover, clubs with a high percentage of foreigners are penalized by blanket application of a clause in the Vienna Football Association rules governing the number of 'imported players' who can be picked for a first team. Since the success of a club is still thought to stand or fall by that of its league team, the incentives for including foreign children in the youth scheme are correspondingly limited.

The transformation of football into an increasingly organized sport was one of the main trends of the 1970s and '80s, and has changed it almost beyond recognition. Previously, one of the advantages of the game, and one of its main attractions, was the fact that it could be played almost anywhere, with only a minimum of equipment. Today, football is becoming one of those sporting disciplines that cannot be practiced unless a specific infrastructure is in place.

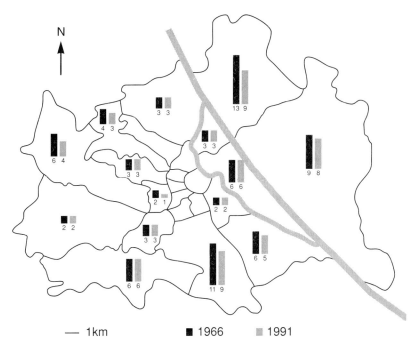

**Figure 5.2**  Number of football grounds per district in 1966 and 1991

As regards the places where this organized football is (and is allowed to be) played, a significant change is also apparent (see Figure 5.2). True, the affinity to the Viennese suburbs is undiminished. Even though many of the geographical associations have become blurred, at least as far as the locations of the football grounds are concerned, the almost exclusive link with the periphery has persisted to this day. In the Second Republic there was not a single football ground in the 4th–9th districts or the 18th district – all traditional middle-class areas.

Leaving aside the areas of Lower Austria bordering on Vienna, we still find a remarkable concentration at the periphery. The stadiums are clustered in Donaustadt (22nd District), Favoriten (10th District), Floridsdorf (21st District), Leopoldstadt (2nd District), Liesing (23rd District), Penzing (15th District) and Simmering (11th District). The overall shifts in the distribution of grounds since 1945 have been minimal; increases occurred only in the 21st, 22nd and 23rd districts (see Figure 5.1). Here, however, direct comparison over time is impossible, as, in 1954, parts of Lower Austria were incorporated into the city, while the 21st district encompassed the entire area on the left bank of the Danube till that year.

It is scarcely surprising that many stadiums are no longer where they were fifty years ago, and that new grounds have often been built nearer to the edge of the city. As many football grounds were (and still are) owned by the City Council or the Federal Government, there were obvious attractions in using the more central properties as sites for schools, housing or other buildings, and creating new grounds on previously unused land. Examples of former football fields are: the Red Star ground (now the Vogelweidpark in the 15th District); the Wacker ground (now the Schoenbrunn sports centre in the 12th District); the Donaufeld ground (now a gymnasium); the FAC ground (occupied by a Council estate); and the Columbia ground (likewise in the 21st District).

Today, more than ever, the decentralization of Viennese football has a major impact on the game itself. While the large clubs (especially Austria and Rapid) can draw support from all districts, the Second Division clubs are far less capable of doing so. Clubs in the Provincial or lower leagues primarily depend on spectators from their immediate neighbourhoods, and are made painfully aware of these local loyalties if they are compelled to move. For instance, when a Provincial League club, Simmering, had to play home games at another ground for three years because its own was being renovated, attendance was roughly halved, though the substitute facilities were barely a kilometre away. Upon the club's return to its traditional home, crowds more than trebled.

## Stadium Relocation and Modernization

I should now like to examine a significant case of stadium relocation in Vienna, in the light of the developments outlined above. This case study concerns Admira and, in its final stages, Wacker Wien, both Viennese clubs with long traditions. It falls within the period that can be characterized as the 'modernization phase' in Viennese and Austrian football, which began in the early 1960s and continued well into the 1970s. In the course of modernization, the ties between clubs and given quarters of the city were progressively loosened. However, it must be noted that this did not apply to all clubs in equal measure, and that the recurrent references by the 1950s media to the 'local allegiances' of given clubs often reflected a mythological recreation of pre-war culture. In this connection, a comment found in a weekly paper is of interest. Here, it is argued that: 'in the Austrian First Division, the choice of grounds has for many years normally been of only secondary importance. Even where they have a choice, many clubs play on grounds other than their own, or hold their matches at the Prater Stadium.'[9]

By way of explanation, it should be noted that, in the early post-war period, many Viennese clubs were forced to play their games at 'away' grounds, owing to the slow progress of repairs to bomb damage. Also, it should not be forgotten that the introduction of so called 'double bills' at the Wiener Stadion, with two league fixtures staged in immediate succession, began undermining the importance of the 'home ground' at an early stage.[10] This is not to say that there were no longer district clubs, closely bound to 'their' stadium, in the Second Republic. It is precisely the classic suburban clubs Rapid Wien (the 'Huetteldorfer'), Admira (the 'Jedleseer'), or Wacker Wien (the 'Meidlinger') which merged with Admira at the start of the 1970s, that were always associated with their 'home ground' by supporters and opponents alike. Depending on a supporter's allegiance, playing there meant either entering a lion's den or watching a team that was 'unbeatable at home'.

Bearing these qualifications in mind, let us turn to the story itself. This concerns the history of the Admira, which was founded in 1905 as a suburban club with a catchment area beyond the Danube. The club took possession of its first ground in October 1911, and in 1933 moved to the new stadium, situated among factories and gardens, not far from the first, with which it was to be linked until the mid-1960s. Between the wars, Admira was spoken of as a typical Viennese 'suburban club', on a par with Rapid. This image stemmed from a cautious, solid style of business management (in 1924 the city became the first on the Continent to legalize professional football), and of course, its close relationship with the home district. In 1927, Hugo Meisl, the creator and manager of the 'Wonderteam', described the club as follows: 'As regards the structure and nature of Admira, the team is a unique kind of line-up. In the past few years, Admira have beaten Czechoslovak and Hungarian clubs and won important trophies with players drawn solely from a single district of Vienna.'[11]

Admira won the championship for the first time in 1927, and remained highly successful throughout the 1930s and during the Second World War. After the War, things took a turn for the worse, and the decline in the club's sporting fortunes culminated in its ending the 1959/60 season at the foot of the table and being relegated to the Second Division. This was the beginning of the end for Admira as a local Floridsdorf (more precisely, Jedlesee) team.[12] To the failures on the pitch were added financial troubles. These appear to have originated in an ill-starred tour of Malaysia. In those days, before the rise of sponsorship and marketing-oriented football, extended tours in distant countries during the winter break and summer close-season were among the main sources of finance, especially for the larger clubs. However, the Malaysian tour in question seems to have ended in financial disaster, and greatly exacerbated the club's problems. According to the conservative Viennese daily, *Die Presse*, Admira's indebtedness reached AS 250,000 in the autumn of 1959, then a considerable sum.[13]

The following course of events is not historically verifiable, as I was unable to examine original documents. My account is essentially based on information from senior club officials involved at the time, and on newspaper reports. According to these sources, Viktor Muellner, who was the Deputy Governor of Lower Austria and also the chief executive of the Lower Austrian energy utilities, NEWAG and NIOGAS, wanted to attract a First Division football club to the new southern suburbs of Vienna. His prime concern was clearly that of enhancing the (sporting) image of his Province.[14] However, the political implications should not be omitted: a significant motive was that of using an explicitly 'bourgeois', Lower Austrian club to break the footballing hegemony of socialist Vienna. Muellner is said to have made an approach to the Admira board, using a former Admira player as an intermediary. The board evidently saw no other means of saving the club, and therefore agreed to a merger with the NEWAG and NIOGAS sports club. From now on, the club was called 'Amira – NOe – Energie'. Only a few weeks before, a Vienna-based daily paper, the *Kurier*, had headlined a story about the impending merger: 'Lower Austria to annex Floridsdorf'.[15]

For the time being, however, the club remained in Floridsdorf. The sports pages got into the habit of dubbing it 'Admira-Energie', and there was thus no direct reference to Lower Austria. The financial shot in the arm certainly brought results. By the 1960/61 season, the club was back in the First Division, and 1965/66 saw it win the championship for the first time in over a quarter of a century. However, this was also the signal for the move from Floridsdorf. In the autumn of 1966, the club began playing its home games at the stadium of a Lower Austrian provincial league club, Moedling, not far from its future home, which was already under construction. The 'modernizers' and the represen-tatives of NEWAG and NIOGAS had finally gained the upper hand over the 'traditionalists' on the board, who wanted to stay in Jedlesee/Floridsdorf. The arguments of the former, to the effect that the club must be professionally run and needed a proper, modern stadium, were in line with the spirit of the times. On the occasion of the move to Moedling, the *Presse* published the following commentary, headlined 'Uncensored!':

> The romantic age of football is gone forever. Before, the teams used to spring up from the ground of a city or district, and their roots were the source of their strength. They were the products of a natural enthusiasm for the game. Today, a football team that aims to reach international standard can only in part evolve naturally. So much must be grafted on to the original stem that scarcely remains visible. A modern club team is a manipulated fraternity, the attractions of which lie in its skills. It follows that one can also take a good team and transplant it to another location.[16]

It is probably of more than coincidental importance that the same year witnessed the collapse of the grand coalition between the socialists and

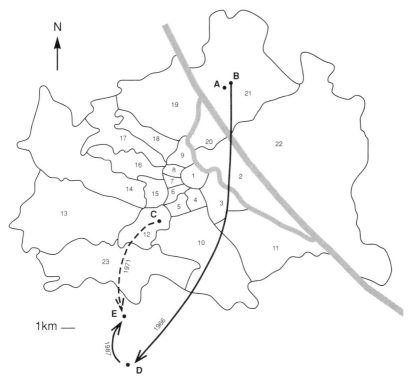

**A**   Admira's home ground 1911–1933
**B**   Admira's home ground 1933–1966
**C**   Admira's home ground 1966–1971
**D**   Ground of the provincial league club 'Mödling' where Admira played
their home matches from autumn 1966– spring 1967
**E**   'The Suedstadtstadium', Admira's home ground since 1967; ground of
Admira-Wacker since the merger of 1971

**Figure 5.3**   Stadium relocation in Vienna: the story of Admira and Wacker.
The map shows the relocation of the two clubs' grounds

conservatives that had set its stamp on the political and social history of
Austria since 1945, and its replacement by a one-party conservative government. The latter's programme, based on a rightward leaning, technocratic interpretation of modernization, aimed among other things at
the dismantling of institutions associated with traditional working-class
culture, which were regarded as incompatible with a 'modern Austria'.[17]

But let us return to Admira. Now a Lower Austrian club, from the
outset Admira-Energie attempted both to attract its existing Floridsdorf
support to the Suedstadt where the new stadium was handed over in

March 1967 and to find new supporters in this southern dormitory suburb (see Figure 5.3). For the former group, there were regular special trains and free buses from Floridsdorf to the southern fringe of Vienna. Special offers such as free tickets for children aged from four to 14 (and school students up to 18), as well as pre-match and half-time tombolas, were probably mainly aimed at the local middle-class population. The latter efforts, which had already begun in Moedling led a newspaper commentator of the day, in autumn 1966, to conclude that football was increasingly turning into 'show business'.[18] On the basis of the official league attendance figures, it is by no means easy to say how the target groups reacted to this marketing strategy, as there was an overall decline in the attendances of the Viennese clubs in the second half of the 1960s. If anything, there was a slightly disproportionate fall in the crowds, but this was not necessarily due to the move. It should be noted that the figures in previous years had also been well below the Austrian average. This suggests that the relatively smooth relocation was connected with a weakening of the club's local roots that had already taken place. As for the recruitment of spectators from the new suburban catchment area, this has never been crowned with great success. The leisure habits of the local population run more towards weekend outings, gardening or tennis club memberships. This is an area where the impact of football, as a spectator sport, is confined to television.

Arriving at the start of the 1970s, we find that the conservative, technocratic modernization drive had run its course. The 'bourgeois' one-party government was supplanted by a social democratic administration, and the country stood at the threshold of the 'Kreisky era',[19] with its social-liberal reform programme. Austria entered a phase of 'soft modernization' that drew its impetus from the wind of change of the late 1960s. Kreisky, in his youth an exponent of Austro-Marxism, opened up the Socialist Party and attempted to free it from the ossified remnants of its socialist traditions. One of the reasons for the success of his 'policies for all Austrians' was the gradual decay of traditional patterns of leisure use, which were no longer directly associated with party allegiances. True, there were still large social democratic and 'bourgeois' sports associations, but increasingly their facilities were simply taken advantage of, and the ideological connotations forgotten. Thus, gymnastic or other sports clubs were often chosen purely on the basis of geographical convenience or the quality of the facilities (good infrastructure and modern equipment), without regard to the political affiliations of the associations to which these clubs belonged.

The economic boom of the 1960s, and the emergence of an affluent society, led to particularly dramatic changes in the leisure culture of the capital. Football as a spectator sport, once the quintessence of male, working-class suburban entertainment was increasingly losing its role.

Club loyalties were weakening and crowds were thinning. Great clubs of the past were declining into insignificance or disappearing altogether.

The next chapter of our story should be seen against this backdrop. In the summer of 1971, Wacker Innsbruck became the second non-Viennese club in Austrian footballing history to win the league championship. In the capital's press, the 'dissipation of Viennese strength' was bemoaned and there were calls for clubs to 'unite their forces'. In an article headlined 'Time to pull together!',[20] a well-known sports reporter gave vent to his anger in the pages of the country's second-largest daily. He lambasted the collapse of the planned merger between Admira and Austria Wien (the club associated with the old liberal Jewish bourgeoisie in the inter-war period), blaming 'traditionalists'.

Mergers were the talk of the town. In June, rumours circulated of the impending 'wedlock' of two historic clubs, Wiener Sportklub and Rapid, but on 1 July came the news that the Wiener Sportklub members' meeting had rejected the planned merger – the 'traditionalists' were still a force to be reckoned with. Just two days later, there was renewed merger talk, this time concerning Admira and the local Meidling club, Wacker Wien. The Wacker board approved the link-up with Admira on 7 July. In an apparent attempt to pacify dyed-in-the-wool Wacker supporters, an interesting structure was arrived at. Two new clubs were founded: Admira-Wacker, which would compete in the First Division, playing its home games in the Suedstadt; and Wacker-Admira, which would continue to use the old Wacker ground in Meidling, as a district-based team in the Second Division. In fact, however, as early as autumn 1971 many Wacker-Admira fixtures were already being played in the Suedstadt stadium, as double bills with those of big brother Admira-Wacker.

A look at Admira-Wacker's attendance figures shows that the local Meidling supporters, of whom there was still a considerable number during the last year of Wacker's existence, did not follow their team to the Suedstadt (see Figure 5.4). This was also noted by a newspaper commentator in the summer of 1973.[21] Why was this so? Wacker Wien was evidently still more deeply rooted in its district. In 1921, the club had settled at a ground that slotted neatly into the surrounding council estate, and it remained there until the merger. It was part of the way of life of its district, and the players generally displayed a strong loyalty to the club, seldom moving elsewhere. Such transfers as did occur were generally attended by difficult negotiations. The club had won the 1946/47 league championship, and had been numbered among the big four of Austrian football in the 1950s (together with Austria, Rapid and Vienna). Even in the 1960s, when it regularly migrated between the First and Second Divisions, it had loyal support, which often exceeded that of more successful teams.

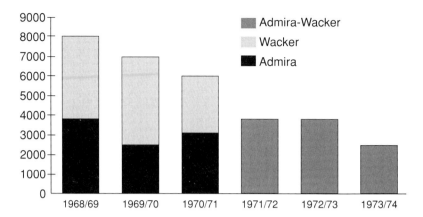

**Figure 5.4** Average number of spectators at home matches: Admira, Wacker and Admira-Wacker

The meagre source material available to me gives no indication as to the reasons for the merger, but they were presumably financial. What can be said with some certainty is that the demise of Wacker Wien marked the end of the role of the big district clubs in Viennese football. Rapid Wien, once a classic example of a district club, may still have local roots, but has in reality become a Vienna-wide (or even all-Austrian) club. Retaining close links with a given district, expressed in a tendency to cling to the 'home stadium', only plays a significant part in the lower reaches of the Viennese game – that world described by Matthias Marschik, as football's 'second culture'.[22]

## Notes

1.  Cf. W. Maderthaner, 'Das Entstehen einer demokratischen Massen-partei: Sozialdemokratische Organisation von 1889 bis 1918', in W. Maderthaner and W. C. Mueller (eds), *Die Organisation der Sozial-istischen Partei Oesterreichs* (Wien, 1994), pp.12–77; W. Maderthaner and S. Mattl, '"… den Strassenexcessen ein Ende machen" Septem-berunruhen und Arbeitermassenprozess 1911', in K. R. Stadler (ed.), *Sozialistenprozesse. Politische Justiz in Oesterreich 1870–1936* (Wien, 1986), pp.117–50.
2.  I. Chambers, *Popular Culture. The Metropolitan Experience* (London, 1988); A. Huyssen, *After The Great Divide: Modernism, Mass Culture and Postmodernism* (London, 1988).
3.  Cf. regarding the Austrian (Viennese) development W. Schmieger, *Der Fussball in Oesterreich* (Wien, 1925); L. Schidrowitz, *Geschichte des Fussballsports in Oestereich* (Frankfurt am Main, 1951); R. Horak, 'Viennese Football Culture. Some Remarks on its History and Socio-logy', in *Innovation in Social Sciences Research*, Vol. 5 (1992), pp.89–95;

R. Horak, '"Austrification" as Modernisation: Changes in Viennese Football Culture', in R. Giulianotti, J. Williams (eds), *Game without Frontiers. Football, Identity and Modernity* (London, 1994), pp.41–64.

4. C. Critcher, 'Football since the War', in C. Critcher, J. Clarke and R. Johnson (eds), *Working Class Culture. Studies in History and Theory* (London, 1979), pp.161–84; I. Taylor, 'Spectator Violence around Football: the Rise and Fall of the "Working Class Weekend"', in *Research Papers in Physical Education*, Vol. 4 (1976), pp.4–9; R. Holt, 'Football and the Urban Way of Life in Nineteenth-Century Britain', in J. A. Mangan, *Pleasure, Profit, Proselytism: British Culture and Sport at Home and Abroad 1700–1914* (London, 1992), pp.67–85; C. Korr, *West Ham United* (Urbana, 1986); J. Bale, *Sport, Space and the City* (London, 1993).

5. *Handbuch der Stadt Wien*, 105, Jahrgang, 1990/91 (Wien, 1991), p.288.

6. Langisch, *Geschichte des oesterreichischen Fussballsports* (Wien, 1966), p.54.

7. *Wiener Sport am Montag*, no. 51 (1991), p.11.

8. U. Mauch, 'Multikulturelle Fussballvereine. Ein Bericht ueber den tuerkischen und jugoslawischen Fussballnachwuchs in Wien', *Salto*, 25 November 1991, p.15.

9. *Welt am Montag*, 1 March 1951.

10. These double fixtures were extremely popular. Thus, on 1 May 1950, the Rapid/Austria and Wiener Sportklub/Admira games attracted a total of 54,569 spectators.

11. Quoted in *75 Jahre Admira & Wacker* (Wien, 1980), p.16. The indirect reference in this quotation to a specific Central European football culture is also of interest.

12. Floridsdorf is the name of the 21st District; the particular area where the club had its traditional ground is called Jedlesee.

13. *Die Presse*, 24 October 1959.

14. It is also rumoured that Muellner wanted to set up a Lower Austrian provincial capital there; and this would have had its own football club, representing the Province.

15. *Kurier*, 24 October 1959.

16. *Die Presse*, 5 September 1966.

17. Cf. A. Pelinka, 'Die oesterreichische Volkspartei', in H. J. Veen (ed.), *Christlich-demokratische und konservative Parteien in Westeuropa* (Paderborn 1983), pp.195–265; W. C. Mueller, 'Conservatism and the Transformation of the Austrian Peoples' Party', in B. Girwin (ed.), *The Transformation of Contemporary Conservatism* (London, 1988), pp.98–119.

18. *Kurier*, 3 September 1966.

19. H. Fischer, *Die Kreisky-Jahre 1967–1983* (Wien, 1994); F. Weber and T. Venus (eds), *Austrokeynesianismus in Theorie und Praxis* (Wien, 1993).

20. *Kurier*, 20 June 1971.

21. *Die Presse*, 25/26 August 1973.

22. M. Marschik, 'The "Other World" of Football. Several Considerations on "non-league" Football seen as an Urban Phenomenon'. Paper for the conference 'Le pratiche sportive in ambiente metropolitano', Rome, 29/30 November 1993.

# 6

# The Stadium, the City, and the State: Beijing

*Susan Brownell*

As I thought about the topic of 'the stadium and the city' with respect to Beijing, I realized that one cannot do so without also thinking about the State. When one traces the history of stadium development in Beijing since the founding of the People's Republic of China in 1949, one traces the history of state power. Following the approach laid out by Foucault,[1] and applied to British stadiums by Bale,[2] this paper analyses stadiums as a site for the development of the specific disciplinary technologies of the Chinese State. The locations, architecture, and occasions for use of Beijing's stadiums inscribe state power onto space and time. In this paper I will sketch out the history and locations of Beijing's major stadiums from the end of the Qing Dynasty to the present. I will also analyse the relationship between their architectural form and the forms of state power in China as it moved from the Imperial to the Republican to the Communist State.

## Geography of Imperial Beijing

At the end of the Qing Dynasty (1644–1911), the layout of Beijing conformed to the ancient principles dictated by geomancy and cosmology. It was made up of five walled districts, three of which were concentric. The symbolic and literal heart of the city was the Forbidden City where the Emperor and his court lived, surrounded by a wall and a moat. Around the Forbidden City lay the Imperial City where the lesser members of the court lived. Surrounding this was the Inner or Tartar City, where members of the ruling Manchu ethnicity lived. The legation quarter, a small district in the southern part of the Tartar City, was given over to official representatives of foreign countries. Below this series of three boxes was the Chinese City, occupied by the Han Chinese subjects of the Manchu. The entire city was laid out on a north–south axis according to the principles of geomancy, which dictated that north was inauspicious and south auspicious. Thus, there were fewer gates in the

95

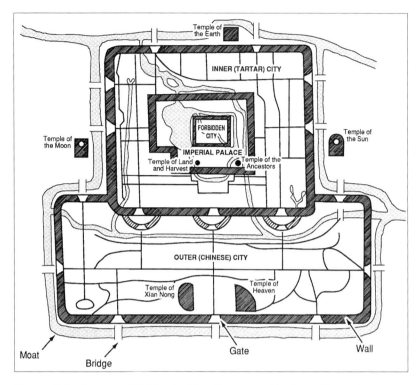

**Figure 6.1** Layout of Beijing in Qing Dynasty, with city walls, major streets and important temples (adapted from an old Chinese map)

north walls and the main gates were in the south walls of each district. Streets did not pass straight through any district because that would make the way easy for evil spirits. The centre was of course the most auspicious location because it was the source of prosperity and fertility. The palace of the Emperor of the Central Kingdom, Son of Heaven, was located there (see Figure 6.1).

Urban landmarks also functioned as a map of the Qing state. The state religion divided official sacrifices into three types: Grand, Middle, and Common. Grand Sacrifice was conducted by the Emperor himself at the temples in the capital and its suburbs. Middle Sacrifice was conducted by the Emperor or delegated officials in the imperial and lower-level capitals. Common Sacrifice was performed by local officials at all capitals.[3] The Grand Sacrifices were most important to the maintenance of the cosmic-social order.

There were four Grand Sacrifices: to Heaven, Earth, the Imperial Ancestors, and the Land and Harvest. The most important ritual was the Emperor's worship of Heaven, which he performed on the winter solstice at the Temple of Heaven in the southern suburb of Beijing. Earth was worshiped on the summer solstice at the Temple of Earth in the northern suburb. The Imperial Ancestors were worshiped on an auspicious day in the first month of each of the four seasons and at the end of the year, in the Temple of the Ancestors within the walls of the Forbidden City. The Land and Harvest were worshiped in the middle month of spring and of autumn at the Temple of Land and Harvest in the western suburb. It is clear that the timing and location of the sacrifices imposed a distinct order onto time and space. Temporally, they marked important moments in the lunar calendar that governed the practice of agriculture. Spatially, the temples structured the land-scape of Beijing, as they still do today, functioning as major landmarks. Blending space and time, the sacrifices moved from south (in the winter, at the Temple of Heaven) to east (in the spring, at the Temple of the Ancestors) and west (in the spring, at the Temple of Land and Harvest) to north (in the summer, at the Temple of Earth) to east and west again (in the fall, at the Temple of the Ancestors and the Temple of Land and Harvest) and back to the south.[4]

A Middle Sacrifice was held at the Temple of Xian Nong, god of agriculture. I mention this because these grounds were the site for a suc-cession of recreational facilities after the fall of the Qing, as we will see.

Sports occupied only a minor role in the religion and architecture of the Imperial State. Kick-ball and polo stadiums had been a standard feature of ancient palaces up until the Song Dynasty (AD 960–1279), but by the Qing they no longer comprised an element of palace archi-tecture. Before the introduction of Western sports, the one large-scale spectator sport seems to have been horse-racing. These races had been an occasion for the Manchu nobility to display their horses and finery before the fall of the Qing Dynasty in 1911. The racecourse was a flat straight, lined on both sides with mat sheds where the spectators could sit and sip tea or eat sunflower seeds. They were not 'races' in our understanding, as the riders merely paraded their horses up and down for the enjoyment of the spectators, occasionally displaying their speed at a gallop.[5] Thus, the race-track was not, as Eichberg calls it, an 'achievement space' like Western sports fields of the time.[6] One course was located near the White Cloud Temple outside the Western Wicket Gate of the old walled city. After the establishment of the Republic of China in 1912, the races were still held to celebrate the temple's yearly temple festival until the 1930s.

A second racecourse was located at a recreation centre in the south of the city, just outside the wall of the Temple of Xian Nong. This site was known as the 'International' racing grounds, and from the 1910s onward, the temple was a major recreation area. In 1918, the South City Amusement Park, a group of concrete buildings with theatres and restaurants, was built in the northeast corner of the temple.[7] In later decades, sports fields and a sports institute were built on the grounds.

A Chinese horse-racing ground also appears near the Temple of the Sun, east of the city, in a map of 1936.[8] Horse-racing seems also to have been the major large-scale spectator sport for the foreigners in Beijing. Several miles west of the city was a Western-style racecourse accessible from a stop on the railroad named the 'Racehorse Track' (*paoma chang*) station. A golf-course was also located nearby. A hand-drawn map from 1936 marks the racetrack with a cartoon drawing of empty liquor bottles and turned-over glasses.[9]

One of the first events of the Boxer siege of 1900–1901, when 'Boxers', trained in martial arts and meditation, surrounded and attacked the foreign legation quarters in Beijing, was their burning of the grandstand at the international horse-racing course six miles west of the city wall. According to the British reporter, Landor, it was with this outrage that 'all the young men of a sporting disposition in Pekin began to realise how serious matters were getting … They could hardly believe that Boxer villainy could reach so far.'[10] The Boxers may have been more conscious of the significance of their act than we might think: surely they were able to recognize the international horse races as events which, like the Manchu races, displayed aristocratic privilege and power. Their attack was no doubt motivated by this recognition, just as the international outrage was.

When troops from the Eight Powers (Great Britain, the USA, Italy, France, Germany, Austria, Japan, Russia) arrived from abroad to relieve the siege, they had their revenge. The Temple of Heaven was occupied by the British relief troops and the Temple of Xian Nong by the American; they bivouacked there 'for want of a better spot' because of the open green areas and the fresh well water.[11] Although the temples were not chosen with the goal of desecrating the sacred sites of the Qing State, once they were inside the troops were quite aware that they had penetrated the *sanctum sanctorum* of the Qing. The temple complexes were looted, furniture destroyed for firewood, grass used for grazing horses. At the Temple of Agriculture the soldiers used the Emperor's throne as a barber's chair until their commanding general took it into his own possession.[12] Sports were common in garrison life and the British instituted regular field hockey, polo, and gymkhana events on the grounds at the Temple of Heaven that drew participants from several of the other Eight Powers.[13] By playing sports on these grounds, the victorious international troops had their revenge on the Boxers and the Qing court which, it was felt, had covertly supported them.

To the best of my knowledge, the occupation of the temples at the end of the Boxer siege was the starting point for the use of these sites as recreational areas. Because Beijing's temples were surrounded by large

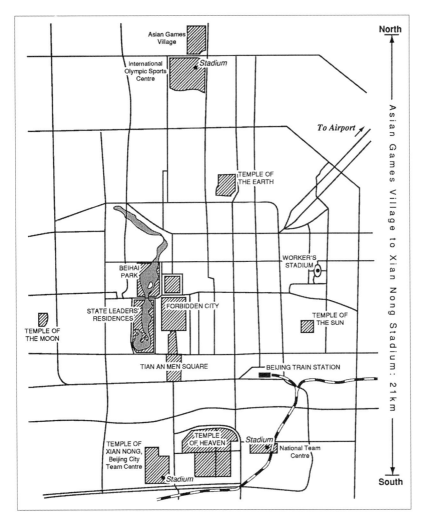

**Figure 6.2** Qing Dynasty temples, major streets and highways, landmarks and stadiums in Beijing (1994)

tracts of land, they were the logical site for sports fields in a densely-populated city. Because Beijing's few parks are landscaped according to traditional principles, with paths winding beneath trees along twisting, man-made lakes and canals, there are not usually many large open fields for sports in these areas. In preparation for the 1990 Asian Games, large gymnasiums were built at the Temple of the Moon and the Temple of Earth, and stadiums are located near the Temple of Heaven and at the Temple of Xian Nong, as discussed below (see Figure 6.2).

## Sports in the Republic (1912–1948)

Western sports were introduced into China through missionary schools and the American YMCA at the turn of the century. The first modern sports meeting, a track and field event, was held in 1890. In 1914, the second Republican National Games in Beijing attracted over 20,000 spectators in two days.[14] They were organized by the YMCA and held at the Temple of Heaven. I have not established whether they were held on the actual temple grounds inside the walls, or outside the walls at the site of the current stadium. In those days the spectators sat in temporary bleachers, even for the two Far Eastern Games held in Shanghai in 1915 and 1921.[15] Even sixteen years later, at the 1933 National Games in Nanjing, the facilities were primitive, and the railing broke when too many people crowded at the finish line, injuring many people and killing two.[16]

The Nationalist Government established its capital in Nanjing from 1928 to 1948 so that Beijing lost its importance as the centre of state power. For the National Games in Shanghai in 1935, the Nanjing Government built what was the first large-scale modern stadium in China, the River Bend (*jiangwan*) stadium. Wang states that it seated nearly 100,000 spectators, but this must be an exaggeration.[17] After the end of the War of Resistance against Japan in 1944, the stadium was utilized as a military barracks and for munitions storage and was badly damaged from an explosion. It was later poorly repaired for the Seventh and last Republican games in 1948, when there were three separate incidents involving collapsed railings, and many people and even athletes were injured.[18]

The first modern stadium in Beijing was built at the Xian Nong Temple in 1937, with a capacity of 10,000, and a dirt soccer field in the centre.[19] From the historical record it is difficult to establish the nature of stadiums because the Chinese language uses the same word (*tiyuchang*) for a simple playing field with one small bank of concrete steps for sitting on, a huge stadium that seats tens of thousands, as well as everything in between. Before the founding of the People's Republic of China in 1949 there were only thirteen stadiums with permanent seating in the entire country.[20]

Let me conclude this brief overview of pre-Communist sports sites by noting the ways in which sporting events marked the transition away from a dynastic empire and towards a modern nation-state. A very interesting point is that many of the important sporting grounds were located on the ancient temple grounds where the major state rituals had been held during the Qing. The 1914 National Games were held near the Temple of Heaven; sports fields, a stadium, and a race-track were located in and near the Temple of Xian Nong; and another race-track was located near the Temple of the Sun. There seem to have been two reasons for this: first, the temples were surrounded by large tracts of open land; second, they fell into disrepair after the establishment of the Republic and the regime seemed uninterested in managing them, much to the consternation of some Westerners who wanted to preserve the dynastic landmarks (even while others looted them). Thus, the land was available for use by Westerners. Still, one can't help but marvel at the implications of Westerners setting up sportsfields on the sacred grounds of the Qing State religion. As discussed by Hevia, the Eight Powers clearly came to perceive their occupation of the Qing sacred sites as a way of demonstrating their superiority over the Qing court and destroying the traditional reverence for the throne; their parade through the Imperial Palace was a calculated display of power.[21] Although we can imagine that the Chinese were distressed by the playing of games on temple grounds, modern Chinese sport histories do not provide any insight on the matter because they are more interested in recording the 'progress' in the development of their sports. The Western occupation of these territories gives a spatial dimension to the transitional power relations that characterized the period after the Imperial State and before the Communist takeover. We now turn to the Communist period.

## The Communist Period (1949–present)

With the establishment of the People's Republic, Beijing became the national capital once more, and the relationship between the stadium and the state became even more transparent. Under the socialist government, funding and planning were centrally administered according to Five Year Plans, and stadiums were constructed as sites for celebrations of the state. Immediately after Liberation, the new Communist State funded the construction of three small stadiums around Beijing. The stadium at Xian Nong Temple was enlarged to a capacity of nearly thirty thousand, lights were added, and the infield was covered with grass. The first large-scale sports event of the PRC, the First National Workers' Games, was held there in 1955.[22] In order to celebrate the tenth anniversary of the PRC in 1959, the Workers' Stadium was built. This remains the Republic's largest stadium. It occupied over seventy thousand square metres and seated eighty thousand people. In 1959 the opening ceremonies of the First National Games of the PRC were held in the Workers' Stadium which was also the site for the opening and closing ceremonies, track and field events, and soccer, for the Games of 1959, 1965, 1975, and 1979. After two absences in 1983 (Shanghai) and 1987 (Guangzhou), they returned in 1993. The Workers' Stadium was also the central site for the Asian Games of 1990. It was refurbished for this event at a cost of 60 million yuan with funds from the national and municipal governments and from stadium revenues. The 1990 Asian Games marked another turning point in the relationship of the stadium and the state: after this event the stadium was expected to support itself and state and city subsidies were ended, except for those needed for large-scale competitions such as the 1993 National Games. Today, the Workers' Stadium relies on revenues from the same sources that many businesses rely on in the wake of the withdrawal of state subsidies. It has its own fleet of taxis, a hotel inside the stadium with over a thousand beds, a karaoke bar, a hair salon, an air travel service, and advertising, food, and furniture companies. With revenue from ticket sales, it basically supports itself. However, it is important to note that it does not support itself on sports alone: it also relies on the very basic human services of moving, feeding, and housing people. Beijing's economy is not so developed that sports alone can generate large revenues.

National Games have taken the place of the Qing Grand Sacrifices as the major events on which state power is represented before the people. It is useful, then, to contrast the roles of space and time in this representation. The Workers' Stadium is not located in a significant space according to the traditional principles of geomancy. It is in the southeast quadrant of the city outside the old city walls. It is interesting, however, that the facilities for the National Team training centre are now located next to the Temple of Heaven, and the facilities for the Beijing City Team are located at the former Temple of Xian Nong. Thus, two important sports stadiums are located on sites where important Qing sacrifices took place. Overall, however, the National Games show very little of the spatio-temporal orientation that governed Qing rituals. The modern state does not place much importance on establishing collective social rhythms of the cyclical, agrarian kind.


## Stadium Architecture as a Mirror of State Power

Consideration of the architecture of Chinese stadiums offers interesting contrasts with what can be said about stadiums and state power in modern Europe. In tracing the territorialization of the British stadium, Bale notes that such developments as the enclosure of stadiums and their segmentation into luxury boxes and individually numbered seats reflect the methods increasingly utilized by the British State and élites to confine and control the unruly masses. He discusses stadium architecture as an example of what Foucault calls 'modern disciplinary technologies'.[23]

Foucault's work itself concerns the architecture of such places as prisons, military barracks, schools, and mental hospitals. In such institutions, the buildings are the physical shells within which operate the entities that have the power of authority to decide, judge, execute, correct, and punish outside the court system.[24] Foucault calls this trend 'the Great Confinement'. While his insights into the confining functions of architecture are useful in analysing sports stadiums, it is important to keep in mind a crucial difference with prisons, barracks, etc. Sports stadiums house periodic performances, not permanent administrative entities that are charged with shaping and reforming individuals to fit the needs of modern industrial society. In analysing stadium architecture, we must also keep in mind the particular characteristics that go along with cultural performances – that is, the characteristics that have to do with symbolic representation. This element is particularly pronounced in the architecture of Chinese stadiums because they are so closely associated with occasions on which state power is represented before the masses. Let me just mention that one such occasion is the public execution, sometimes held in sports stadiums. Unfortunately, very little is known about them outside China.

The most important function of stadiums in China is to serve as an imposing backdrop for ceremonies, and certain architectural features enable them to do so effectively. The opening ceremonies of the National Games constitute the biggest national celebration in China apart from a few National Day festivities. Opening ceremonies of the Chinese National Games consist of the elements that have become common internationally: a parade of athletes, welcoming speeches by state leaders, raising of the flag and playing of the national anthem, athletes' and officials' oaths, and a cultural performance. In China the performance typically consists of mass callisthenics with a placard section as background. Much of this performance is oriented to the state leaders sitting in their own territory in the stadium. Typically, their space is located in the best viewing spot: the centre of one long side of the stadium about halfway up. It consists of several flat areas terraced upwards. Long tables are set up on each area, covered with a white cloth, and provided with hot tea and refreshments. State leaders sit in padded chairs behind these tables. This area is literally called the 'chairman's platform' (*zhuxi tai*), though a better English translation may be 'rostrum' or 'reviewing platform.'

Chairman Mao and Premier Zhou Enlai attended every National Games held during their lifetimes. Though Deng Xiaoping was not present at the 1987 Games, Premier Zhao Ziyang was. Li Peng was present in 1993. Newspaper articles about the Games always begin with a list of the thirty or more state officials, in order of importance, who sat on the rostrum at the opening ceremonies to review the parade of athletes.

When the athletes march onto the field, sometimes shouting slogans as they go, their performance is directed toward the high officials. The

**Figure 6.3**　The 'Chairman's Platform', Haidian Stadium, Beijing (1994)

officials review the performance just as they review the military displays of soldiers. The placard section is located on the opposite side of the stadium so that it is visible to the officials, as if presented for their approval. Spectators on the same side as the placard section cannot, of course, see it. Thus, there is a decided hierarchy, with one side of the stadium much more prestigious than the other. In mid-size stadiums, the lower-status side may not have a roof. All the Chinese stadiums that I photographed have some sort of rostrum. Even in open-air stadiums, the rostrum is still covered, often by a roof supported by high pillars that lend a stately air (see Figure 6.3).

Because the Chinese social order takes on a different shape from the British order discussed by Bale, its spatial manifestation in stadium architecture is also slightly different. If we take the Workers' Stadium as an example, the most striking difference from Western stadiums is the absence of glassed-in luxury boxes. As of yet, Chinese stadiums do not possess luxury boxes; when they first appear (as they undoubtedly will), it will certainly be a sign that the egalitarian ideals of the Revolution are finally dead, and that capitalist class difference has taken their place. But for the moment, high-ranking officials sit on the chairman's platform out in the open air with everyone else (see Figure 6.4). The platform leads back to a large room inside the building with carpeting, paintings on the walls, and padded chairs. The wide staircase that exits this room leads to the stadium entrance that is opposite the main gate to the stadium grounds, thus giving easy access to dignitaries in their limousines.

**Figure 6.4** The 'Chairman's Platform', Beijing Forestry University Stadium, decorated for 1994 Beijing City College Athletics Meeting

For the 1990 Asian Games, fifty glassed-in 'observation booths' were added in a row on either side of the chairman's platform. These booths are used by announcers, security and communications personnel, and some reporters – but not by dignitaries. A more clearly-demarcated social hierarchy was evident in changes made to the seats. The original seating consisted of wooden benches which were very narrow, enabling the stadium to seat eighty thousand people. For the Asian Games, the wooden benches were replaced with individual fibreglass seats, the most desirable of which are on either side of the chairman's platform and have backs. Many of these are occupied by foreigners, who pay almost twice the cost of the most expensive tickets available to the Chinese. The prices of seats decrease the further they are from the chairman's platform. Thus, for an international soccer game in May 1994, I was quoted the following prices: 500 yuan ($US 60) for foreign guests below the chairman's platform; 280 yuan for the seats with back supports near the chairman's platform; 160 yuan for seats with no backs further from the chairman's platform and above it; 120 for the seats further from the centre; 60 yuan for seats on the ends of the stadium and near the players' entrance; 40 yuan for students (see Figure 6.5).

Another feature of stadiums is their exclusivity. They are surrounded by walls and are relatively inaccessible, even to sports teams who want to

**Figure 6.5** The 'Chairman's Platform' and observation booths, Workers' Stadium (1994)

train in them. When I was a member of the Beijing City collegiate track and field team in 1986, the team leaders constantly had to negotiate with the manager of the Xian Nong Temple stadium to get access for us, even though we were backed by the Municipal Education Commission. My coach quoted a Chinese pun, *xianguan buru xianguan*, which literally means 'the county official can't measure up to the person immediately in charge'. This sort of insularity is characteristic of most administrative units in China, and is spatially expressed in the walls that surround them.

At major sporting events, this exclusivity extends to the difficulty in obtaining tickets for the most popular events – the opening and closing ceremonies and the soccer finals. For example, the 1990 Asian Games placard section required that twenty thousand seats be reserved for the local students who held up the cards. The same number were reserved for journalists, distinguished guests, and fund-raising officials.[25] A large area of the stadium, as mentioned, is occupied by high officials. Over twenty thousand seats were sold to foreigners, leaving only ten thousand tickets available for the Chinese. For such major sports events, many of these tickets tend to be allocated through the 'back door': officials, members of the organizing committees, and others with 'connections' obtain tickets for themselves, their families and friends, and their political network, leaving only a small number of tickets to be sold publicly. Many thousands of people may congregate outside the gates to the sports complex on the night of the opening ceremonies hoping to buy scalped tickets. This source of control over access to tickets derives less from the state and more from the diffuse social control of 'connections'. Ultimately it is a result of the fact that large-scale sports events are designed primarily to display state power; earning a profit is a secondary consideration. During a discussion of opening ceremonies with a Chinese sports sociology professor, I commented that one reason we do not have placard sections in the USA is that the ten thousand students involved do not buy tickets; in fact, they are a net drain because they also receive subsidies for lunch and other expenses during the several-month training period. This was of great interest to the professor, who turned to his wife and commented, 'You see, *they* pay attention to economic efficiency.'

In sum, an analysis of the ways in which the disciplinary technologies of the state are expressed in stadium architecture is incomplete because the stadium also serves a representative function. This reveals an important character of state power in China: on public occasions, state rulers represent their power *before* the people rather than *for* the people.[26] This representative public sphere is tied to the personal; it is created by the presence of state leaders.[27] This character of PRC state power contrasts with the impersonal, rationalizing, normalizing disciplinary technologies discussed by Foucault and Bale for the West.

## The Internationalization of Stadiums

In 1990, China held its first Asian Games, thus marking its increased openness to the outside world. The Asian Games were also a prelude to China's bid in 1993 to host the 2000 Olympics, and the facilities were constructed with an eye towards that goal. As has been typical throughout Chinese history, the new stadiums were built in preparation for specific occasions of importance to the state. The Workers' Stadium was renovated, a second 40,000-seat soccer stadium was built at the sports centre in Fengtai just outside of the city, and a new 20,000-seat soccer stadium was built in the National Olympic Sports Centre nine kilometres north of Tian An Men Square. The chief architect of the centre, Ma Guoxin, stated that he attempted to include 'national characteristics' in the design.[28] In recent years, greater attention has been paid to 'Chinese characteristics' as international influence increases and the Chinese try to distinguish themselves from the non-Chinese (see Figure 6.2). This was not important at the time the Workers' Stadium was built in 1959. I remarked to one of the stadium managers that the new Olympic Sports Centre was said to have 'Chinese characteristics', and asked if the Workers' Stadium had any. She replied that it didn't – it was built according to a commonly-used international standard; they didn't pay attention to this

**Figure 6.6** Dragons and cauldron for Asian Games torch, Workers' Stadium (1994)

issue in the 1950s: 'It's not like the Olympic Sports Centre, which has curved roofs that look like an airplane. At least I think it looks like an airplane.' She did note, however, that the cauldron that was added for the Asian Games torch is held up by two large dragons, which are very Chinese (see Figure 6.6). As she thought for a moment, she recalled a final 'Chinese characteristic': the two electronic screens that were added for the Asian Games are the largest in Asia, and were built by a Chinese company. Her comment illustrates the way in which measurable scientific/industrial achievements are taken to represent a nation in the same way that traditional cultural elements do.

The greater internationalization of Chinese sports was reflected in the funds donated by wealthy Chinese from overseas. For the Asian Games, the largest donation from such sources was the sum of $HK 100 million. Singers from Hong Kong and Taiwan also performed benefit concerts. For China's bid to host the 2000 Olympic Games, a Hong Kong developer offered $US 300 million to build the Olympic stadium if it was named after him. I. M. Pei, the American architect, agreed to design it. Beijing lost the bid to Sydney, but it may try again for the 2004 Games. We can be sure that if China hosts an Olympic Games, the design of the stadium will utilize 'Chinese characteristics' to represent a nation with an ancient history that has much to contribute to world culture.

## Conclusions

In sum, the history of stadium-building in China serves as an accurate map of the development of national state power and its relationship with the outside world. The first stadiums were the product of Western influence. The fact that the two most important stadiums in Beijing were located in the grounds of two major Qing temples exemplified the process by which a nation-state inspired by the Western model was superimposed over the ruins of the Qing Dynasty. However, the Western model underwent some changes which are evident if we look at the uses to which the stadiums were put. They have been used as grounds for public executions, but more importantly they are the sites for the opening ceremonies of sports games during which the state hierarchy is displayed. The importance of this display is reflected in the reviewing platform that is built into stadium architecture, from which the officials can review the parade of athletes and the placard backgrounds. Thus, while the surrounding walls, the numbered sections, and the individual seats reflect the 'rationalization of space' that has been typical in Western stadiums, Chinese stadiums also serve a representative function that is not so important in the West. As Chinese sports become increasingly internationalized, we can expect this representative function to expand to include the goal of symbolizing an essential Chineseness to the outside world through stadium architecture with 'Chinese characteristics.'

## Notes

1. M. Foucault, *Discipline and Punishment*, trans. Alan Sheridan (New York, 1977); *Madness and Civilization* (New York, 1965).
2. J. Bale, 'The Spatial Development of the Modern Stadium', *International Review for the Sociology of Sport*, Vol. 28, 2–3 (1993), pp.121–34.
3. S. Feuchtwang, 'School-Temple and City God', in William Skinner (ed.), *The City in Late Imperial China* (Stanford, 1977), pp.585–6.
4. A. R. Zito, 'Re-Presenting Sacrifice: Cosmology and the Editing of Texts', *Ch'ing-shih Wen-t'i*, Vol. 5, 2 (1984), p.59.
5. S. D. Gamble, *Peking: A Social Survey* (New York, 1921), p.29.
6. H. Eichberg, *Leistungsräume: Sport als Umeltproblem* (Achievement spaces: sport as environmental problem) (Münster, 1988).
7. Gamble, *Peking*, p.239.
8. *The Peiping Chronicle*, 'A Bird's-Eye View of Peiping and Environs', 1 October 1936.
9. F. Dorn, Hand drawn map of Peking printed on silk scarf, 1936. New Haven, Yale University Library Map Collections.
10. A. H. S. Landor, *China and the Allies* (New York, 1901), p.19.
11. Ibid., p.253.

12. Ibid., pp.248, 267.
13. R. A. Steel, *Through Peking's Sewer Gate: Relief of the Boxer Siege, 1900–1901*, edited and with introduction by George W. Carrington (New York, 1985), pp.63–7.
14. Wang Zhenya, *Jiu Zhongguo tiyu jianwen* (Information on Sports in Old China) (Beijing, 1987), pp.131–39.
15. Rong Gaotang *et al.* (eds.), *Dangdai Zhongguo tiyu* (Contemporary Chinese Sports) (Beijing, 1984), p.479.
16. Wang Zhenya, *Jiu Zhongguo*, p.159.
17. Ibid., p.161.
18. Rong Gaotang *et al*, *Dangdai*, p.479; Wang Zhenya, *Jiu Zhongguo*, p.184.
19. Rong Gaotang, *Dangdai*, p.479.
20. Ibid., p.480.
21. J. L. Hevia, 'Making China "Perfectly Equal"', *Journal of Historical Sociology*, Vol. 3, 4 (December 1990), pp.379–400.
22. Rong Gaotang, *Dangdai*, p.478; Zhou Yixing (ed.), *Dangdai Zhongguode Beijing* (Contemporary China's Beijing) Vol. 1 (Beijing, 1989), p.260.
23. Bale, 'Spatial Development'.
24. M. Foucault, 'The Great Confinement', in Paul Rabinow (ed.), *The Foucault Reader* (New York, 1984), p.125.
25. *Beijing Review, XI Asian Games: Beijing, 1990* (Beijing, 1990), p.7.
26. J. Habermas, 'The Public Sphere: An Encyclopedia Article' (1964), *New German Critique*, Vol. 1, 3 (1974), p.51.
27. Habermas, 'Public Sphere,' p.51, n. 4.
28. *Beijing Review, XI Asian Games*, p.11.

# 7

# Growth Politics, Urban Development, and Sports Stadium Construction in the United States: A Case Study

*Kimberley S. Schimmel*

## Introduction

> Under the cover of darkness and downpour, the Baltimore Colts galloped to Indianapolis early yesterday in a caravan of Mayflower trucks to end the city's 31-year era in the National Football League.
>
> Reneging on a promise, the team's controversial owner, Robert Irsay, did not even call the mayor to say good-bye.[1]

The National Football League Colts' move from Baltimore, on 29 March 1984, ended eight years of threats from the team's owner, Robert Irsay, to relocate his franchise to another city. However, not until February 1984 did the people of Baltimore genuinely fear they might lose the Colts. The franchise had existed in their city since 1953, and in only a few short years a relationship which Baltimore residents referred to as a 'love affair'[2] ensued between the community and 'its' team. Many times throughout this era the Baltimore Press referred to the franchise/community relationship with nuptial-like analogies. That the Colts would end this 31-year-old marriage and sneak off to a little-known suitor city in the Midwest seemed to Baltimore residents as not only disloyal, but mean-spirited as well. Baltimore's Mayor Donald Schaeffer, whose tearful picture appeared on the front page of the city's newspaper lamented: 'I'm trying to retain what little dignity I have left in this matter. If the Colts had to sneak out of town at night, it degrades a great city ... I hate to see a man cry.'[3] For the Baltimore community, Irsay's clandestine move added insult to injury. Not only did Irsay's disinvestment decision threaten Baltimore's business image but the Colts' fans also charged that the franchise's night-time gallop was intended to 'humiliate and degrade' them. In fact, two Baltimore Colts fans filed a $US 30 million law suit ($US 5 million for compensatory damages and $US 25 million in punitive damages) against Irsay on behalf of all Colts' season-ticket holders. The plaintiffs alleged the Colts' move caused them 'to suffer severe depression, severe physical and emotional disability, severe disturbance of mental and emotional tranquillity and mental distress of a very serious kind'.[4] Irsay's flight, however, was undoubtedly precipitated by more lucrative motivations. Although the research presented in this chapter does not focus on franchise relocations *per se*, it was through an exploration of the issues involved in the movements of professional sports teams that the problematics associated with stadium construction began to be formed.[5]

The Colts' departure from Baltimore captured the attention of the media and sports fans across the nation. The taken-for-granted assumptions held by many sports supporters regarding the sentimental nature of the relationship between professional sports franchises and their host communities began to be more seriously questioned. By their departure, the Colts had deeply violated the 'norms of reciprocity' assumed to exist between franchises and communities.[6] The cities of Baltimore, Indianapolis and Phoenix were in direct competition for the Colts' franchise. It was a competition from which both winners and losers would emerge. It was a competition which dramatized the relationship between the modern sport industry and the modern city – a relationship between capital and community.

The bonds that exist between professional sports franchises and their host communities are not held together by sentiment, loyalty, or tradition. Furthermore, a community's endearment to a professional sports team is not of primary import to franchise owners when they review their location/relocation decisions. When owners consider relocation their dialogue is with city governments or city 'authorities,' not with fans. As Ingham *et al* point out, the ties that exist between professional sports teams and communities have become attenuated by the prevailing economic arrangements of professional sports leagues.[7] These authors tell us that the modern professional sports industry is a capitalistic enterprise that operates in an ongoing quest for capital accumulation. But while invoking the capital logic thesis helps to demystify the sport/community relationship, it oversimplifies (perhaps ignores) the myriad of factors that condition the investment decisions of capitalists – be they owners of manufacturing firms or sports firms. There is much more to the game.

The fact that both Baltimore and Phoenix offered the Colts' owner more lucrative contracts than did Indianapolis indicates that it was not the profit principle alone that wooed Robert Irsay. That the city of Indianapolis had risen from relative obscurity, in terms of a national identity, and successfully corralled the footloose Colts' franchise, suggests some intensive efforts on the part of city leaders in this mid-sized, midwestern town. Judging by the response of Indianapolis civic authorities to the Colts' relocation, it is evident that even a professional football franchise was just part of a much larger civic story. The Mayor of Indianapolis, William Hudnut, wasted no time in publicly framing the Colts' relocation as being an indication that his city was moving in the right direction: 'Yes sir, we're going all the way now. It's a wonderful thing for our community. It's a boost to the city's image nationally and to local morale as a symbol of major league status … We want people to sit up and say "By God, that city has a lot going for it."'[8] Successfully luring the Colts from Baltimore provided tremendous support for a pro-growth campaign that was initiated in Indianapolis in the late 1970s. Robert Irsay's capital investment decision helped to legitimize this strategy. Further, local boosters publicized the strategy's successes in hopes of attracting the attention of future capital investors. Paying less in relation to the other cities' offers helped advocates of growth in Indianapolis to argue that the team's financial impact on the community would be as 'noticeable as the domed stadium'.[9]

Likewise, civic boosters scurried to use the publicity surrounding the Colts' move to advertise the Indianapolis climate to other capital investors. The Indianapolis Project, Inc., a public relations firm hired by growth advocates, sent letters to thirty-three publications explaining that the Colts' move should be included in financial sections and general news stories concerning the growth of Indianapolis.[10] In 1984, four major firms (Purolator Courier, Hudson Institute, Overland Express, and Dana Corporation) moved their national headquarters to Indianapolis. The Hudson Institute received a $US1.5 million grant from the Lilly Endowment, Inc., a $US100,000 state grant and $US700,000 from the business community to defray relocation costs.[11] The Lilly Endowment, Inc. is the philanthropic arm of the Indianapolis-based Eli Lilly and Company, one of the largest pharmaceutical concerns in the world. The endowment's role in the city's growth initiative is a crucial one and will be presented later in this chapter. Overland Express's financial incentives included a $US9.5 million low-interest industrial development bond to assist the construction of a new terminal and office.[12] Interestingly, the Dana Corporation required no financial incentives before relocating to Indianapolis. The firm was attracted to the city by its central location, 'by Indiana's generally good business climate and by Indianapolis' image as progressive, affordable and free of many typical urban problems'.[13] This 'image' was achieved through considerable effort on the part of Indianapolis's growth advocates.

That sport would enhance the city's business image and attract capital was a driving force behind Indianapolis's growth strategy. Building a new domed stadium and acquiring a professional football franchise was only one, albeit significant, item on a lengthy agenda. Prior to its growth strategy, Indianapolis had no distinct identity or 'image' and no natural geographic assets from which it could draw to compete for capital investment; it had no harbours, no major waterways, no mountains, and no lakes; it was not known nationally by a nickname like 'The Blue-chip City', 'The City of Brotherly Love', or 'The Big Apple'. In fact, the only thing Indianapolis was really identified with was its annual 500-mile auto race – an event novelist Kurt Vonnegut, Jun., a native son, said the city woke up for one day and then fell back to sleep for the other 364. Such besmirchments earned the Indiana capital nicknames like 'Naptown' and 'India-no-place'.

If the city was to entice capital investment successfully, civic leaders argued, it would be necessary to build and promote a distinct Indianapolis image. City leaders decided to transform Indianapolis from a sleepy town into a white collar tourist and corporate headquarters centre. They decided to target the nation's expanding service sector economy in an attempt to redevelop the city. Perhaps realizing the city's aesthetic limitations, public officials and private entrepreneurs collaborated in using sport as a foundation on which to build an amenity infrastructure. Turning Indianapolis into 'Sports Capital of the USA' would, argued growth advocates, bring national reputation, capital investments, and jobs. Between 1980 and 1984, over $US 126 million, in public, private, and philanthropic funds, would be invested in the construction of sports facilities that were located in the downtown area.

Although Indianapolis may be distinctive in its explicit and broad-scale attempt to harness the sports industry for its growth strategy, there are a number of other cities in the United States that are building new sports stadiums. In fact, research by Baade and Dye indicates that in 1988 half of the nation's sixty largest metropolitan statistical areas (MSAs) had plans for a new stadium.[14] Nine of the top twenty MSAs had such plans despite the fact that they already had a stadium within their geographical boundaries. Three of these areas, Atlanta, Baltimore and Chicago, were considering plans to build two new stadiums each. Furthermore, as Johnson has shown, new stadium construction is not limited to large metropolitan areas.[15] Many small-to-mid-sized US cities are building new stadiums as inducements to obtain or retain minor league professional baseball franchises.

Currently, the analysis of stadium construction has been dominated by a micro-economic perspective. The focus has been limited to studying issues such as the economic rationale for subsidizing stadiums, the assessment of stadiums as 'wise investments,'[16] and the impact of a new stadium on a local economy (variously operationalized). While these studies are invaluable to understanding the specifics of stadium development and have aided in separating economic myth from reality where stadium impact is concerned, they are insufficient in that they do not always address the *political* economy of urban development of which stadium construction is a part. In short, micro-economic analysis often provides a text that lacks a context. These types of analyses rarely frame for us the larger social, historical, economic, and political issues related to the cities in which these edifices are located.[17] In order to provide this context, a reading of the urban studies literature is necessary.

But here, too, one finds the extant knowledge to be insufficient in fully elucidating the articulation between the urban political economy and the culturally specific manifestation of the United States sports industry. What the urban studies literature does provide is a paradigmatic map with which we may explore this articulation. What it does not provide are details concerning what we might expect to find on our intellectual journey. Comprehending the problematic of urban development and the role that sports facility construction may play in it requires a concern for the logic of capitalist relations *and* a concern for how that logic is experienced, understood and acted upon by individuals and collectivities in the historical period in which events take place. Presently an intellectual gap exists between the narrow specifics of the economics of sports facilities and the broad theorizing about urban political economics. What is called for is connected knowledge which helps us to understand the ways in which capitalist relations can enable and/or constrain the social actions of economic and political actors. For example, Cynthia Horan, in calling for a new research agenda for analysing the coalitions that promote and condition urban growth, points out that the 'connection between the politically active and the economically dominant remains largely unexplored'.[18] Perhaps we may begin to provide connected knowledge by pursuing research questions such as: Who comprises local growth coalitions? In what ways is sport stadium/facility development related to local development strategy? Who finances it? In what ways is the development strategy articulated to the public? And, what factors hinder or facilitate the success of the development strategy? I begin by addressing such questions.

It has become broadly accepted that the impact of urban public policy should be evaluated. Leitner points out that there have been very few detailed analyses of the degree to which development strategies meet the goals of creating jobs and securing a more healthy urban fiscal environment. In Leitner's words:

> … coalitions have been highly successful in propagating a pro-growth ideology and in determining the course of economic development initiatives … the paucity of studies by the local state empirically assessing the impact of these policies and the neglect of academic research critical of urban development strategies, illustrate how the discourse about these policies reflects the relative power of their proponents and critics.[19]

The research presented in the next section responds to the urges and challenges presented by Leitner. It treats as problematic the assertions captured in the ideology that equates private capital investment with the public good. It attempts to elucidate our understanding about growth coalitions and to examine the articulation between urban political and economic realms. In addition, this research attempts to bridge the intellectual gaps that exist between the disciplinary knowledge generated in sports studies and urban sociology by exploring the ways in which the modern sports industry and the building of sports stadiums and arenas have been used in constructing an agenda for urban development. It therefore situates the modern sports industry within the broader context of urban politics – politics which are contoured by inter-city competition for capital investment. In this context, winners and losers emerge both between and within cities.

## Conceptualizing Local Development Policy: Issues of Structure and Agency

In the last two decades, the agenda of US urban politics and planning has been overly dominated by growth-promoting public-sector development policies.[20] In contrast to the local public policies of the 1950s and 1960s that stressed providing social services and public goods, more recent policies have been preoccupied with accelerating growth or reversing decline in local economies in order to create jobs and improve the tax base.[21] Investigating these policies – their creation, their biases, their relationship to global and national restructuring, their efficacy – has become the central theme of urban research. This section of the chapter highlights the theoretical debate between economically-determined (structuralist) versus politically-generated (urban praxis) explanations of local development policy. Both of these schools of thought recognize that local policy is shaped by forces which extend beyond their geographical boundaries; however, they differ dramatically in their ontological and epistemological approach to explaining the processes at work.[22]

*Emphasizing structural constraints: economistic paradigms*

From this perspective, the structure and dynamics of the capitalist system *determine* the policy options available to local governments. Local state development merely reflects broader (i.e., national and global) structural developments. The titles of prominent books reflect their authors' deterministic orientations. For example, *Captive Cities*, *City Limits* and

*The Dependent City* depict a pessimism regarding a local government's ability to invent creative policy.[23] In an attempt to understand the broad, underlying economic forces, the politics of local place are devalued. The focus, from an economistic perspective is on: (a) structure, rather than agency; (b) economics, rather than politics; and (c) global factors, rather than local ones.[24]

The tenets of economism are upheld by both right-wing market-oriented analyses and left-wing structural-Marxist urban scholarship.[25] The most basic of these principles is that urban economic restructuring, population redistribution, and uneven patterns of growth and decline are the products of 'economic processes operating in an autonomous sphere called the economy'.[26] The theoretical traditions of both these perspectives – neo-classical economics on the right and the capital logic school of structural Marxism on the left – are basically determinist and fundamentally functionalist. For example, to devotees of right-wing market capitalism, unevenly developed cities and regions are the inevitable outcome of an economic system that readily adapts to innovation and technological change.[27] This implies that spatial and economic development patterns emerge as natural and immutable products of a system that is progressing toward efficiency. In other words, changes in the form and function of urban areas are viewed as healthy adaptations to new market conditions and to new technologies. Locational choices of people and firms, in the long run, become beneficial to society as a whole by facilitating greater economic efficiency.[28] Government intervention into the forces of the free market are viewed as unnecessary, wasteful, and possibly even harmful to the general welfare of society.[29] For example, Swanstrom points out that the right-wing version of this perspective was incorporated into national urban policy-making in 1980 by President Jimmy Carter's Commission for a National Agenda for the Eighties.[30] This report, *Urban America in the Eighties*, argued that, as a necessary by-product of a national transition from an industrial to a post-industrial economy, many urban areas would experience economic decline. The report recommended that the Federal Government should stop trying to stem urban decline, especially in the cities of the north, because it would only result in encouraging people and businesses to remain in inefficient locations. In other words, market imperatives determine urban development and should drive policy, not vice versa.[31]

Another example of a right-wing economistic perspective to the study of American urbanism is Paul Peterson's *City Limits*.[32] This was the winner of the 1982 Woodrow Wilson Foundation Award for the best book published in the United States on government, politics, or international affairs. It has been so influential that any review of the study of US urban development politics would be remiss to exclude it. The direct scholarly response to Peterson's work comprises a substantial body of literature.[33] Peterson's book is enormously ambitious. Comments about it here will be limited to major points that relate to the current discussion.

Peterson views cities as essentially market entities that 'compete with one another so as to maximise their economic positions.[34] Simplifying Peterson's theory greatly, a city's economic goal is clear because development benefits 'all members of the city'.[35] Policy is an outgrowth of the market-driven competition between localities; policies that make the city more attractive for residents or investors are in the whole city's interest. The local state has little control over the flow of capital and labour, and can show little concern for redistributive policies because they are believed to worsen a city's economic position *vis-à-vis* that of other cities. Redistributive policies would discourage investors and residents who contribute most to the local revenue base causing both to locate elsewhere.[36]

Peterson assumes a neutrally-operating market as well as a neutrally-operating political system.[37] According to him, neither contains either domination or conflict. Business participation in development policy is 'apolitical', support for developmental policy is 'broad and continuous', and political leaders are able to 'give reasoned attention to the longer range interests of the city taken as a whole'. Politics is dismissed because local policy is constrained by market forces leaving little room for choice. Peterson states that 'ordinarily, local politics are … very dull indeed. Because cities have so few policy options open to them, partisan political life becomes one dimensional'.[38] In the final analysis, suggests Swanstrom, what Peterson produces in *City Limits* is a 'market theory of urban politics'.[39]

Leftist-oriented urban political scholars offer a direct challenge to Peterson's consensual model of urban development. Structural Marxists, for example David Harvey, uphold the basic tenets of economism while stressing the conflictual nature of social class struggle for the control and enhancement of conditions of their own existence. Harvey argues that unequal patterns of US urban development result from the internal contradictions of a capitalist economic system.[40] The laws of motion of capitalism are seen to be the basic engines of urban change. Harvey agrees with Peterson that cities must compete with one another for jobs and investment but stresses that this is not a competition between equals. He also argues that power is structured hierarchically within urban areas, resulting in the local state having to assume the role of manager of class conflicts and economic contradictions. Due to the necessity of maintaining capital accumulation, the local state favours the capitalist class. Therefore, class alliances often form (with the local state) which then use their political and economic power to enhance economic growth. According to Harvey's capital logic view, the preoccupation with the growth agenda is a political manifestation of the needs of capital accumulation. The logic of capital accumulation largely circumscribes the relation between the local state and its managers and the structure and dynamics of the economic system. Like Peterson, Harvey argues that there is little autonomy for localities from broader economic structures. Similarly, both Harvey and Peterson imply that a single theory is capable of explaining local state actions in different capitalist cities.[41]

The single-theory approach in analysing the phenomena of urbanism is most heavily emphasized by those economistically-oriented Marxist scholars who focus on global forces in their interpretation of local urban development. These researchers emphasize the effects of global restructuring of the capitalist economy on cities and regions. For example Beauregard argues that capitalism is now a worldwide system 'with a logic independent of the elements that constitute it'.[42] The capitalistic world economy periodically requires global economic restructuring which has an immediate effect on any city's built environment.[43] This is also the perspective of Hill whose research on Detroit highlights the social consequences of uneven urban development stemming from the reorganization of the automobile industry.[44] In a continuation of this research, Hill and Feagin collaborated in an investigation focused on Houston. This was a comparative analysis of the two cities 'in the light of a changing world economy'. Hill and Feagin state:

> Houston … was to experience an economic crisis in the 1980s not unlike the one which began to confront Detroit a decade earlier. Ironically, by the mid-1980s, it was the two cities' similarities, not their differences, that were most obvious … Cities are spatial locations in a globally interdependent system of production and exchange. That global system is in crisis and transition. So the path a city follows in the future will depend on the niche it comes to occupy in a changing international division of labor.[45]

The results of global economic restructuring will not be to make all cities the same. Rather, according to this view, the urban hierarchy will be reshaped with some cities having higher functions than others.[46] But while 'economic restructuring and technological change' are the 'major underlying cause' of the changing structure of American cities,[47] pessimism regarding a city's ability to determine its own economic destiny prevails. The increasing mobility of capital and foreign investment sharply limit cities' 'conscious and concerted efforts to control and direct growth'.[48] The emerging 'international division of labor' results in cities that are less able to deal with their financial problems. Glickman cites Friedmann and Wolf on this topic:

A major loser is the local state. Small, isolated without financial power, and encapsulated within the world economy, it is barely able to provide for even the minimal services its population needs. And yet, instead of seeking alliances with neighbouring cities and organised labour, it leaves the real decisions to the higher powers on which itself is dependent ...[49]

In summary, despite their policy differences, both right-wing market capitalists and left-wing structural Marxists share the view that uneven urban and regional development is a mechanical reflection of the national and global productive system. Cities change as a result of the requirements of economic logic. Urban politics is largely irrelevant to the 'laws of motion' of economic development. 'Politics and society are reduced to "bearers" of inexorable economic and technological forces'.[50] The structural features of the capitalist economic system leave little (or no) room for local agency.

There is, however, an alternative view to that of cities held 'captive' within a determinist economic imperative. The next section of this chapter will highlight this other argument: one that recognizes the influence of broader economic processes but asserts that politics matters in the development of local urban policy. This perspective gives more allowance to local autonomy and places much more emphasis on the need to include 'place-specific' contingencies in the study of local development policy.[51] It is a perspective that attempts to validate the role of economic factors in urban policy development without falling into economic reductionism.

*Emphasizing local agency: regime paradigms*

A number of scholars have emphasized the importance of local politics in their studies of development policy. Whether labeled as 'growth machines',[52] 'growth coalitions',[53] 'governing coalitions',[54] or 'urban regimes',[55] the basic premise about local political groups is similar: local level US policy development is not an inevitable result of broad structural forces; rather, it is produced through the proximate actions of interested actors. As an empirical matter, adherents to this paradigm assert that local development policy has real consequences for cities which may be problematic.[56] Local economic development may produce 'winner' and 'loser' social groups. Thus, contra Peterson, these researchers argue that there is no unitary interest called 'the city' that benefits from economic development. In a direct challenge to Peterson, Stone paraphrases the National Rifle Association to make his point: 'Cities don't make development decisions; people do. And these people have neither uniform material interests in the decisions that are made nor a common understanding of the risks involved in and the probable consequences of those decisions.'[57] While emphasizing the need to examine policy choices in specific places, analysists of urban regimes have also attempted to situate local policy against broader national economic and political struggles.[58] Sanders and Stone state clearly:

> Our aim is not to deny the importance of economic competition among localities. That such competition is mediated through the governing coalition does not mean that it is absent. It means that concrete response to economic competition is shaped by more than one consideration and that participants may well disagree about how best to meet the need for development. All of this suggests to us that causation is manifold.[59]

In other words, politics matters. Cynthia Horan has recently written a description of the urban regime research that emerged in the 1980s. In this description, she points out that development policy is viewed as political in at least three ways. First, it involves choice. Because of the divergent interests that exist within cities, policy often involves compromises. Putting together and maintaining a dominant governing coalition is one of the most important (and distinctly political) objectives of development policy. Second, development policy is influenced by the organization of at least some of the city's economic élite. In so doing, they become political actors. Third, the investment decisions of those willing to contribute capital from the private sector are influenced by public sector policies. This point has been less frequently examined than the first two. Rather, it has been assumed, based on the fact that businesses attempt to influence policy decisions. Presumably businesses would not be involved in policy development if its consequences did not matter to them.[60]

Two of the most influential examples of the politics-driven model of development policy within the United States can be found in the writings of John Mollenkopf and Clarence Stone. Both authors in varying degrees insist on the relative autonomy of local political processes. In *The Contested City*, Mollenkopf reviews the development data of two cities, Boston and San Francisco, and focuses on the influence of 'political entrepreneurs' who put together pro-growth coalitions. He defines a political entrepreneur as 'one who gathers and risks political capital or support in order to reshape politics and create new sources of power by establishing new programs'.[61] Many different kinds of political entrepreneurs have helped forge many versions of pro-growth coalitions. In Boston and San Francisco, four mayors and two public administrators (with assistance from national political entrepreneurs) broke through climates of economic and political stagnation. The result was the construction of huge redevelopment programmes. Without reducing his argument to federalism, Mollenkopf argues that national policy-makers do influence local state action. But he insists that this influence is not uniform. Growth coalitions can be more or less successful, depending on the political skill of their actors.

Stone adopts a position similar to Mollenkopf but places even more emphasis on local political practices and argues for an even greater degree of local political autonomy. In *The Politics of Urban Development*, Stone and his co-authors present evidence that local government officials do make real choices which do not simply follow the imperatives that emanate from the national political economy. Local policy-makers must interpret the national economic situation, apply it to their local conditions, and act on it in a way that does not jeopardize the political arrangements they have built.[62] In this respect, these authors share with Swanstrom the view that: 'No one puts a gun to the heads of local policy makers; there is simply not one 'rational' policy to follow. Policies are always a choice between competing values'.[63] Stone insists that the interests and preferences of the governing coalition determine urban policy formation. Thus, he argues, 'the city's governing coalition is the agent through which conceptions of the interest of the whole community are mediated'.[64] These interests and preferences are not necessarily the interests and preferences of the remaining urban residents. This, of course, is a direct retort to Peterson's conception of a unified city interest.

In this section, I have presented the highlights of an ongoing epistemological debate among urban studies scholars over the ways in which the development policies and actions of the local state are to be conceptualized. Much too simply stated, the debate centres around the scope and extent of local political autonomy from broader economic structures. This discourse arose largely in the 1980s and is exemplified in the US context in the writings of Peterson, Harvey, Mollenkopf, and Stone.[65]

Why was this review necessary? In the United States, the field of critical urban studies is relatively new. In order to understand this subdiscipline it must be viewed as an ongoing project. The intellectual arena is replete with competing interpretations of urban phenomena. Paradigmatic conflicts account for most of this diversity. As Stone reminds us (following Kuhn), paradigms compete not only over which has the best evidence, but also over which has the best questions.[66] An academic discipline develops as scholars respond to the questions which have been raised and the issues they highlight. This chapter, then, is positioned within the nascent subdisciplinary perspective referred to as the urban regime paradigm. Such a perspective grew out of the theoretical debates that occurred in the 1980s. The questions explored in this chapter, relative to the role that stadium construction plays in local development policy, build upon the arguments presented in these earlier analyses and respond to more recent calls for further elaboration of the paradigm.

### Analysing urban regimes in the 1990s

Recently, a number of scholars have revisited the theoretical debate regarding issues of structure and agency that characterized the urban studies literature of the 1980s.[67] According to Leitner, 'the dispute about whether the formation and implementation of urban development policies is determined by "economic necessity", or whether "politics matters"' has not been adequately addressed.[68] Both Leitner and Horan call for a new agenda in critical urban research.[69] They contend that urban regime research of the 1980s tended to over-estimate the importance of local political arrangements in forming development policies. These scholars argue for an expanded conceptualization of the ways in which both political and economic forces contour local development policy. Both scholars place emphasis on issues associated with economic restructuring. Leitner calls for more case-study research that compares local-context variables in order to understand differences in policy outcomes between cities.[70] She provides an example of this comparative method by presenting data on two cities, San Francisco and Minneapolis, highlighting the ways in which their respective local economies influenced the nature of their development policies. Horan, while not specifically advocating comparative case study methods, agrees with Leitner that the nature of the local economy must not be overlooked when analysing local growth politics. She outlines a research strategy for the future.

Urban studies research in the 1990s, says Horan, must continue the challenging task of disentangling the political aspects of economic processes. Recognizing the dialectical relationship between political actors and economic structures, she asserts that the local growth coalition may influence the local economy, and likewise, that economic conditions (both local and non-local) will shape a city's development policy. In her work, Horan presents an alternative to the image of cities captured by the economic imperative (the structuralist position) and calls for a new research agenda that explores this perspective. In Horan's words:

> This alternative view emphasises the diverse politics of local situations, whatever the global forces at work. Thus, as they survey the globe, corporations encounter a variety of local conditions including, but not limited to, governing coalitions with different development agendas and differing abilities to implement those agendas …

Adopting this perspective permits us to analyse whether, and under what circumstances, local responses are effectively organised or whether these differences among localities are irrelevant to the process and outcomes of restructuring.[71]

There are, according to Horan, three strands of variation among cities as they make development policy: (a) the composition and agenda of the local growth coalition; (b) the structure of the local economy; and (c) the institutional resources of the local state. The first strand, the growth coalition's composition, has been discussed throughout this section. Horan, like other urban praxis theorists, asserts that political actors influence economic processes. She calls for a continued examination of the make-up of the growth coalition and a detailed assessment of ways in which the coalition's composition influences the agenda for urban development. It is to these issues that we now turn our attention.

## From Naptown to Sportstown: Urban Development in Indianapolis, Indiana

The research contained in this portion of the chapter is taken from a much larger case study that explores the construction and consequences of growth politics in Indianapolis.[72] In the sections that follow, portions of this larger project are presented. First, the economic and social conditions which concerned local growth advocates were is described. Second, the characteristics of the local growth strategy, and the role that stadium construction played in it, are discussed. Third, highlights of growth agenda implementation are presented.

### A city in search of direction

In the 1970s downtown Indianapolis was dying. The core was dirty and filled with vacant, dilapidated buildings. As in many old, industrial cities, businesses and residents were fleeing from the central business district. When city officials reviewed Indianapolis's development patterns they discovered an almost total mismatch between where development was supposed to occur and where it was in fact occurring. According to the city's 1980 growth policy review, people were moving away from areas where substantial public and private investment (e.g., in the form of schools, thoroughfares, shopping) existed. A population increase had occurred in areas where services, facilities, jobs, and tax bases were limited. This lead the city's Department of Metropolitan Development to conclude: 'The result is the underutilization of developed areas of the county leading to abandonment, isolation of low-income groups, and a reduced tax base'.[73] These circumstances were not unlike those that existed in many other urban areas where capital and middle- and upper-class residents fled from city cores. Referring to this trend, Fainstein and Fainstein observe that central cities had become places where ethnic minorities and low-income whites were encapsulated in 'obsolete sectors of the economy and deteriorating physical environments'.[74] 'Urban crisis' is the term used by urban political scientists to describe the myriad of social and economic problems associated with these conditions. By the mid-1970s, Indianapolis was facing an urban crisis of great proportions.

Reflecting upon this time, Jim Morris, an aide to 1968–74 Indianapolis Mayor Richard Lugar (and later to become a key figure in planning and implementing the growth strategy) stated: 'You had all these dumpy old buildings along Illinois Street, the Atkinson Hotel was virtually history, and bums and winos living in Union Station. The city had a real problem on its hands.'[75] The emptiness of the city led to some rather interesting Sunday afternoon excursions for local Jaycees (escorted by police). Robert N. Kenney, Director of the Indianapolis Department of Metropolitan Development in the late 1970s recounts:

> They were downtown with shotguns and bags, shooting pigeons. If you can imagine a downtown so desolate, there were roving guys with shotguns. We had nothing downtown. If our goal was to create a city nobody wanted to live in, we'd done it. I used to make the comment that the mayor would mortgage his mother-in-law to get jobs in downtown Indianapolis. We couldn't get anything down there. Any project that created jobs got approved.[76]

The Mayor's concerns regarding employment were well founded. Not only was job creation problematic, job retention was difficult as well. Employment loss, particularly in the city's bellwether industries associated with automobiles, was accompanied by population loss and increasing levels of poverty.

Employment data presented in the *Indianapolis News* indicates that in 1970 the Indianapolis MSA's (Marion County plus the seven surrounding counties) economic structure was well diversified with 29.3% of total employment located in the manufacturing sector, 29.2% in services, and 21.6% in trade.[77] However, Indianapolis's manufacturing jobs were generally labour intensive and reliant on the automobile industry. As Robert Kirk, economist at Indiana University-Purdue University at Indianapolis explained, 'As long as the auto industry was doing well, we had our day in the sun. When things started going badly, we became vulnerable because we were a branch town. We didn't control our own destiny.'[78] The 1974–75 national economic recession forced many Marion County residents out of their jobs. In one year, the county's employment rate fell 5% with manufacturing employment declining by almost 11,000 workers. This pattern of unemployment would continue throughout the 1970s as civic and business leaders searched for ways to 'control their own destiny'. From 1978 to 1982, an additional 35,000 private sector jobs were lost in Marion County. Close to 20,000 of those jobs were from the manufacturing sector as the number of firms fell from 17,021 to 16,654. Moreover, the number of large establishments (those employing 1,000 or more workers) dropped from 35 to 25.[79] A study published in the *Indiana Labor Market Letter* (July 1981) shows that 5,000 of the lost manufacturing jobs were located in the automobile and parts industries.

The out-migration patterns of the Indianapolis population would continue throughout the decade. In 1970, the Indianapolis MSA's population was 1,109,882. The vast majority (792,229) resided in Marion County. Marion County is divided into nine townships with appropriately named Center Township representing the area in which the central business district is located. In 1970, Center Township's total population was 273,598. African-American residents comprised 38.8% (106,124) of Center Township's population and 17% of Marion County's population. Comparing these figures to those of 1980 reveals the magnitude of the city's centrifugal migration. For example, from 1970 to 1980, Center Township lost 23% (65,010) and Marion County 3.4% (26,996) of their populations. In Center Township, the percentage of the total population that was made up of African-Americans rose to 40.4% (from 38.8% in 1970) even though the area lost 19,797 of its African-American residents. This is accounted for by the fact that 47,177 Anglo-American residents left the area. Marion County was the only county in the MSA to experience population decline. By far the greatest increase occurred in Hamilton County (Marion's northern neighbour) which experienced 51.1% population growth and, not surprisingly, also contained the MSA's highest median family income ($US 24,407 in 1980). Marion County and Center Township median family income in 1980 was $US 17,400 and $US 14,098 respectively.[80]

A series of studies conducted by the Committee on National Urban Policy, under the auspices of the National Research Council, provides additional insight into the social and economic trends that existed in Indianapolis in the decade of the 1970s. The publication *Inner-City Poverty in the United States*, reports the findings of a study that examined ghetto poverty. In this study, a ghetto was defined as an area in which the overall census tract poverty rate is greater than 40%. The ghetto poor were defined as people of any race or ethnic group who live in such high-poverty census tracts. The data for the Indianapolis MSA indicate that the number of ghetto tracts rose from four to five between 1970 and 1980. The number of ghetto poor increased from 4,885 (3,899 were African-American) in 1970, to 6,483 (5,107 were African-American) in 1980.[81] Because the study does not include the identity of the ghetto tracts listed, it is not possible to know their exact location in the city. However, these data, combined with those reported by the city's Department of Metropolitan Development, indicate that the highest concentration of poverty existed in the neighbourhoods located in the downtown area.

The loss of jobs and population from central Marion County threatened the economic viability of the city's central business district. At the same time, the low-income population that was left behind became increasingly entrapped in a downtown core filled with many structures that were rapidly becoming obsolete. In other words, as Robert Kennedy stated succinctly, 'the richer they are, the farther out they live'.[82] Although the city had many of the institutional mechanisms in place to respond to these conditions and a history of coalition-building with local corporate élites, a clear and aggressive urban development strategy would not emerge until the late 1970s.

*City image problems*

As early as 1947, Indianapolis had been the target of taunts from outsiders. Expressing his perception of the city's appearance and proclivities, John Gunther wrote in *Inside USA*: 'Indianapolis is an unkempt city, unswept, raw, a terrific place for basketball and auto racing, a former pivot of the Ku-Kluxers, and in it you may see the second ugliest monument in the world.'[83] Though the besmirchments would soften over the years, they would not disappear. One of the comments that particularly incensed local leaders occurred during the 1969 passage of Unigov – the name given to Indianapolis's unusual consolidated city-county government structure. A reporter for the *Hartford Times* wrote: 'It seems a little strange that a city like Hartford, with its reputation for progress in so many areas, could be so far behind in its approach to local government. You have to go to some corn pone town like Indianapolis to find innovation in government …'[84] A year later, the corn theme emerged again, this time in an article in *HUD Challenge*:

> Some time ago an urban magazine story on innovation in Indianapolis asked the question, 'Why Indianapolis of all places?' The implication was clear: why should urbanologists and others concerned with the plight of cities turn to Indianapolis, allegedly surrounded by a cornstalk curtain and commonly believed to offer little beyond the Indianapolis 500?[85]

In 1972, the Lilly Endowment, Inc. donated $US 10,000 to the Indianapolis Chamber of Commerce. The purpose of the gift was to hire an industrial consulting firm to analyse the city's appeal to potential capital investors and to suggest improvements. The Fantus Company, from Chicago, was selected and in their presentation to Indianapolis political leaders in 1972, a spokesperson said: 'Gentleman, the good news is your city does not have a bad image. The bad news is it doesn't have a good image. In fact, to many people in the country, Indianapolis has no image at all.'[86]

Business and political leaders point to the Fantus Report as a significant event in the city's history. Civic leaders had grown increasingly defensive about the ways in which others viewed the city. They did not feel complemented when others referred to Indianapolis's 'small town qualities'. Additionally, nicknames such as 'Naptown' and 'India-no-place' drew their ire. These leaders were well aware of the stigma attached to the rural state of Indiana and desperately desired a way to distance themselves from it. The state's image was perhaps best expressed in a study funded by the Indiana Economic Development Council, Inc. (1986):

> The traditional family based, rural value orientation of the state make it attractive and friendly to regional visitors. However, those qualities are sometimes seen as non-cosmopolitan, risk aversive and anti-intellectual to many foreign and business leaders.[87]

The study concluded that the 'fundamentally good values of the hard working rural Hoosier' had a negative effect on the state's economic growth. Not surprisingly, to political and business leaders in Indianapolis 'Hoosier' was a pejorative term applied to 'anybody that resided in Indiana and lived outside of Marion County'.[88]

The Fantus Report confirmed civic leaders' worst fears: that Indianapolis's lack of 'image' was bad for business. According to Sidney Weedman, Vice-president and Director of Governmental Relations, Merchants National Bank & Trust, after the Fantus Report:

> There was a lot of discussion about 'what are we going to be when we grow up?' The City Chamber was trying to figure out how to attack this problem, the Mayor's office was trying to figure it out, the Greater Indianapolis Progress Commission was trying to figure it out and I suppose a half dozen other groups were too. We were discussing how to come up with a strategy.

Addressing Indianapolis's predicament, Weedman continued:

> Sure this is a nice place to raise a family but visiting people from corporations went nuts because there wasn't anything to do except

eat at St. Elmos Steak House ... What could we hang our hat on? We had no seashores, the 500-mile race was almost a stigma, *Sports Illustrated* had come out with an article calling it a 'snakepit' and saying it was a horrible event, filled with crashes, drunkenness, and mayhem. And there was an article that really ticked everyone off about cornfields. That one really drew blood![89]

Creating a 'good image' for the city was to become a crucial aspect of growth politics.

*Economic conditions in the early 1980s*

In 1983, the *Indianapolis Star* published a lengthy article titled 'Area Jobs Becoming More Service Related'.[90] The article, written by the newspaper's business editor, was the second in a series on employment related trends in the city and state. The article presented results of a study conducted by economist Robert J. Kirk showing that from June 1979 to June 1983 the Indianapolis MSA had lost 40,300 jobs from its total employment, 28,000 of them in manufacturing. However, during that same period (which also corresponded to a national recession), the local service division grew by 11,000 jobs. According to the newspaper's business editor: 'Much of the city's political leadership, business community and the public has become convinced that the community must take action to promote economic growth rather than just allow the local economy to take care of itself.'[91] Also according to this article, an Indianapolis consulting firm, Central Research Systems, Inc., had documented the changes taking place in the local economy prompting 'public/private efforts' aimed at retaining, expanding, and attracting firms.

The Central Research Systems Study to which the *Star* referred was a report commissioned by the Department of Metropolitan Development in 1980. The project was assisted by Dan Birch of the Massachusetts Institute of Technology and in its 'Background Briefing for Mayor William H. Hudnut, III' it stated:

> The character of US industry is changing ... our analysis shows that Indianapolis also has been undergoing its own dramatic transition. Within the past twenty-five years, employment shares within manufacturing and service-related sectors have literally exchanged places.[92]

The report recommended that the city emphasize innovative technologies by development of business and industry in such areas as industrial automation, telecommunications, instrumentation, health care, and computer software.

The Greater Indianapolis Progress Commission formed an Industrial Growth Task Force to study the Birch report. In December 1982 it presented 'An Economic Development Proposal' which began:

> Indianapolis and the nation are in the midst of a transition that is every bit as fundamental as those who [sic] followed the introduction of electricity. That change is rapidly gaining momentum. If it has not done so already, it soon will touch every one of our lives. Old industries are being eroded and new ones forged. The metals industries and autos – both important to Indianapolis – are being severely buffeted. The results are obvious. Heavy manufacturing is in a serious structural decline in terms of investments and jobs.[93]

In a discussion regarding Indianapolis's reliance on heavy manufacturing, David Carley (director of the Department of Metropolitan Development from 1982–1989), underscored the significance of these two reports. Carley offered the following insights:

> We were very conscious about the shift to a service economy. There was a great deal of debate in Indiana about whether we should go with that flow or chase smoke stacks. The state chose to chase smoke stacks, the city chose to chase services … In the early 80s when the rest of the country, particularly the Midwest, was so hard hit, we decided we were going to use public money to continue our growth … We got a real jump on other cities. We spent a lot of taxpayer's money. We spent a lot of the [Lilly] Endowment's money, but we kept our progress.[94]

City leaders entered the 1980s with a determination to put Indianapolis 'on the map'. Representatives from planning groups (e.g., Greater Indianapolis Progress Commission, and the Corporate Community Council), the Mayor's office, the Department of Metropolitan Development, and the Lilly Endowment, Inc. met formally and informally to devise an agenda for the city's development. Over the next decade, growth strategies would require large-scale public and private investment. Responding to the coalition's agenda for growth, Harrison Ulman, runner-up in the 1984 Indiana gubernatorial election, said: 'Oh, sure it's all framed in terms of jobs. I suspect that someone will even argue in court one day that the reason they robbed the bank was to create jobs in the justice system.[95]

*The growth strategy*

If the city was successfully to entice capital investment, growth advocates argued, it would be necessary to build and promote an Indianapolis image. Public officials and private entrepreneurs collaborated to advance an urban development campaign with the stated objective of turning Indianapolis into a mecca for tourists and conventioneers. Although the city lacked 'natural' attractions, it was certainly not without geographical assets. First, Indianapolis's location puts it near the geographical centre of the nation. The city is therefore quickly and inexpensively accessible from both coasts. Second, five US Highways and four Interstate Highways converge on the city placing it within a day's drive of 60% of the nation's population. Hence, millions of potential tourists either drove through (or flew over) the city yearly. Finally, because Indianapolis had no seashores, mountains, or large neighbouring cities, it had plenty of land for development. Its downtown area alone covers seven square miles and Marion County covers about four hundred square miles. With these factors in mind, an ambitious growth strategy was initiated to develop an amenity infrastructure aimed at enticing private capital and luring large conventions, affluent tourists, and residents to the downtown area. Concurrent with this growth initiative, Hudnut launched a massive image-making campaign to portray Indianapolis as a gleaming city.

Growth and image-making campaigns proceed hand-in-hand. If successful, they are mutually reinforcing and self-perpetuating; i.e., to stimulate development (growth) the local state (public entrepreneurs) provides incentives (e.g., land, tax abatements, grants, revenue bonds, among others) which ease the financial burden and minimize the financial risk to private capital. By absorbing some of the costs of investment, the local state either increases private capital accumulation (profit) or reduces private capital loss. Image-making campaigns and boosterism strategies are designed to legitimate the actions of growth coalitions by expressing them as being necessary for the betterment of the 'community-as-a-whole.' They also suggest to private capital that the local state is actively seeking to promote the material interests of the dominant class. Thus, boosterism not only symbolically constructs consensus behind the banner of pro-growth, it also markets the local state's business climate to private capital, thereby encouraging future capital investment. When capital investment occurs, especially if it is relocated capital, it fuels boosterism campaigns by suggesting to the public that the local state's actions are in fact working. It also captures the attention of other investors who may be contemplating disinvestment/reinvestment decisions.

Thus, boosterism is a calculated activity – a campaign that not only seeks to promote the interests of the dominant class but also seeks to legitimize political solutions to urban 'problems' by symbolically constructing consensus (i.e., by blurring conflict in the redevelopment process). Civic 'authorities' propagandize their visions of a 'good business climate' and 'quality of life' throughout the population and seek to portray their cities to capital investors as 'clean, orderly, new, and expanding, with lower classes that are hidden, quiescent, and shrinking'.[96] In Indianapolis, the building of new sports facilities, the attempt to lure professional and amateur sports organizations, and the hosting of sports events articulated with these broader strategies of pro-growth and urban redevelopment.

*Implementing a growth agenda*

In 1980 an updated version of an earlier Greater Indianapolis Progress Commission revitalization plan was published. The document (Regional Center Plan), prepared for the Department of Metropolitan Development by Hammer, Siler, George Associates outlined, to the year 2000, the city's revitalization objectives. The three-hundred-page report focuses exclusively on the downtown:

> The image of the downtown area serves as constraint to some market groups. Crime is perceived to be a major problem, as is security of private personal property. Also, the predominance of lower income households in the central area creates an overall *image* [emphasis added] of poverty households living in substandard and overcrowded housing. Most downtown neighborhoods are not safe, pleasant, and attractive neighborhoods that most *new* [emphasis added] home-seekers would consider.[97]

This segment of the Regional Center Plan suggests that problems related to Indianapolis's downtown had to do with the perceptions that outsiders have of it, rather than the reality of life for its residents. Often forgotten in discussions concerning the 'emptiness' of the central business district, is the fact that people *do* live there. In fact, in 1980, a community of 208,624 people lived in Center Township.[98] According to Jim Morris (former Indianapolis mayoral aide who became Vice-president of the Lilly Endowment, Inc. in 1977 and President in 1984), 'the sports strategy was a part of community development, of helping to build an infrastructure for a community'.[99] This type of legitimating argument was not well received by large segments of the city's racial and ethnic minority populations. According to Sam Jones, President of Indianapolis's Urban League: 'Infrastructure for us means sewers, transportation ... I'm not sure that we in the black and minority communities had very much input into the sports strategy ...'[100]

Nevertheless, between 1980 and 1984, over $US126 million was invested in downtown state-of-the-art sports facilities. Among the most expensive were: (a) a $US 21.5 million, 5,000-seat swimming and diving complex, (b) a $US 6 million, 20,000-seat track and field stadium; and (c) a $US 2.5 million, 5,000-seat velodrome. Consistent with the 'partnership' ethic, funding for these projects was provided by public and private sources. The local state provided grants, tax abatements, and industrial revenue bonds. The Lilly Endowment, Inc. contributed $US 10.5 million to the swimming and diving facility, $US 4 to the track, and $US 700,000 to the Velodrome.[101] However, the largest investment (in terms of physical size and financial cost) would come to town through the backdoor.

*The Hoosier Dome*

In 1979, Indianapolis architect James E. Browning and banker William K. McGown, Jun., travelled to Syracuse, New York, to measure the dimensions of the Carrier Dome. On their return they penciled the dimensions onto a map of Indianapolis downtown. As reported by the *Indianapolis News*, Jim Morris paced off the site selected to verify the fit.[102] Deputy Mayor David Frick helped determine the potential for land assembly. Browning's architectural firm was eventually hired to design a domed stadium exactly where he had sketched it, and Frick, as treasurer of the public agency in charge of the stadium project, helped oversee the work. All three men were members of an informal group who met privately to discuss directions for the city's development.

Interestingly, the Indianapolis Hoosier Dome was something of a 'Trojan Horse' sports facility. David Carley explained:

> You see we wanted to [build] a stadium and it met with resounding negativism everywhere. So, about that time we were looking to expand the Convention Center. So we said O.K., we're going to expand the Convention Center, we're going to add 200,000 square feet of meeting space on, and oh, by the way, it's going to have this multi-purpose room attached, which has this inflatable ceiling, seats 60,000 – but the floor can be used for exhibits. And honest to God, we sat around the table at the Mayor's office and took a vow that we would never call it anything but the Convention Center Expansion.[103]

The 'Convention Center Expansion', like Indianapolis's other sports complexes, is a state-of-the-art facility. The 60,300-seat structure is one of only six air-supported domed stadiums in the United States. It contains ninety-nine luxury suites each of which can accommodate up to sixteen guests, and a projection screen with instant replay capabilities. Final costs of construction in 1984 totaled $US 77 million.

On 8 February, Mayor Hudnut announced that the Lilly Endowment, Inc. would contribute $US 25 million and the Krannert Charitable trust another $US 5 million to the stadium/convention centre expansion. Six weeks later the Indiana legislature passed a bill authorizing the City-County Council to enact a 1% food and liquor tax on all restaurants and taverns in Marion County to back the revenue bonds. Announcement of the new tax prompted law suits from local citizens who opposed the stadium project. Their sentiments were expressed by Julia Carson, Center Township trustee:

> I had difficulty supporting a stadium [the Hoosier Dome] when our schools are woefully underfinanced and other city services are inadequate. The mayor and the Lilly Foundation wanted the stadium, so it was built. That's the way things get done here.[104]

The bonds were not offered for another thirteen months (and sold out in five days). By the time they were bought, construction on the stadium had been underway for approximately six months and the law suits had all been either settled or dismissed.[105] Because of the large final price tag, funds ran low near the end of the project. To reduce costs, the 31,000 seats on the lower level were padded, the 29,500 seats on the upper level were not. When converted to an exhibit hall, the 7.25 acre building expands the connecting convention centre's total area to one million square feet.

Not surprisingly, the Hoosier Dome was promoted by Mayor Hudnut as a wise investment for 'the community'. The growth ideology that justified such a conclusion was clearly articulated by him:

> In Indianapolis, we are trying to leverage amenity infrastructure for economic advantage. Our commitment to sports facilities, for example, is not an end in itself. The Hoosier Dome is a job generator. It creates new business opportunities. As a result of its construction, new convention business is coming to town, new restaurants and hotels are opening up, new national organisations are moving to Indianapolis, and new people are interested in investing in our city.[106]

According to Hudnut and other civic boosters, the 'Indiana Convention Center and Hoosier Dome' (its official name) symbolized the rebirth of downtown. Whether or not it and the other downtown amenities would serve as a magnet to 'new people' did not seem much solace to some of the city's established residents. Shadeland Avenue, on the city's east side, where working-class communities once thrived on manufacturing jobs, began to be referred to as 'Memory Lane'. When Chrysler and RCA announced they would be closing Indianapolis branches, 800 people lost their jobs. When Western Electric closed in 1985, 8,000 people were left jobless. On the west side of the city, 2,000 employees at General Motor's Detroit Diesel plant were victims of a 1982 cutback. A former Chrysler employee, who lost his $US28,000 per year forklift job, told Levathes and Felsenthal that, after 24 years with the company, 'it's alarming to think about having to scratch at this point in my life. But I'll think of something'.[107] This worker's optimism was not shared by all. Quoting from Levathes and Felsenthal:

> 'I don't know what I'll do,' said Tim Fout, 33. 'The only thing I know is that I don't want my son working here.'
> To many workers the downtown development is like a mirage in the desert. 'Who are they bringing the city back for? Not for us,' said Ted French, 42, a job setter, 'I pay tax on restaurant food and beverages in the city to help finance the Hoosier Dome, but I've never been in it.'[108]

Presumably, the Hoosier Dome/job generator, would in some way ease these residents' burdens. It is possible that this was the intention of the Lilly Endowment's $US25 million check to 'the community'. Perhaps, a belief that the convention centre's 'expansion' would benefit people in need somehow vindicated the actions of a philanthropic institution whose traditional concerns had been related to education, science, health, religion and social services.

Waldmar A. Neilsen does not think so. In 1985, he published an historical analysis of American philanthropy, in which, in his study of the Lilly Endowment, Inc., he makes the following statement about the Lilly/Hoosier Dome connection:

> In the history of American philanthropy, there has never been a foundation expenditure of equivalent size given on weaker economic justification, more questionable grounds of social benefit, and more dubious distribution of benefits among local politicians, profit-seeking entrepreneurs, and the needier elements of the population.[109]

*Creating an image*

A year after the Hoosier Dome project was announced, Indianapolis increased the intensity of its boosterism strategy by hiring a New York public relations firm to implement a nation-wide image campaign. The firm was called the Indianapolis Project, Inc. It consists of a five-member group whose primary responsibility is to assure national coverage of the city's development successes. According to Bill Carr, the

Project's President in 1984, in addition to writing press releases, the firm functions as a resource centre to give interested people the names of individuals to interview in order to get 'the other side of the story'.[110]

Along with capturing the attention of potential tourists and capital investors, city officials have used the results of the firm's efforts when competing with other cities for capital investment. For example, in 1985 when Indianapolis was vying with Charlotte, North Carolina for the services of an 'unidentified company' that planned to relocate, John Krauss, Deputy Mayor for Indianapolis asked the Nexus Data Bank how many times in the previous two years each city had appeared in the major national media (excluding sports references). As a part of an inducement package, Krauss informed the company's owner of the results: Indianapolis had appeared 797 times; Charlotte, 18.[111]

The impact of Indianapolis's zealous self-promotion campaigns in some cases spurred controversy. For example, a June 1984 article titled 'WHITEWASH' which appeared in the *Indianapolis Star* lambasted the city's Convention and Visitors' Association for its tourism publication. According to the *Indianapolis Star*:

> [the brochure] gives glowing descriptions of the city's culture and other amenities. It talks about the continental cuisine and exotic menu offerings … There are numerous pictures of city residents dining, socializing and enjoying Indianapolis ambiance, none of them black. Only in one picture is there a black person. He is playing basketball.[112]

Also that month the *Star* published an investigative report concerning allegations that city officials were trying to deny the existence of youth gangs in the city. The article, subtitled 'NOT COUNTED IN CITY'S IMAGE,' headlined the newspaper's front page and detailed the location, nick-names, and activities of what the investigator considered to be 'gangs' in the city's low-income neighbourhoods. It emphasized that city officials acknowledged their concern over what appeared to be gang-related crime, but refused to refer to the groups responsible as 'gangs'. Instead, police officials called the groups 'youth groups', 'juveniles with big league criminal records', and 'mobs with names'.[113] The article brought to public attention problems such as unemployment, crime, and lack of social activities in the city's minority neighbourhoods. It underscored one of the main criticisms of the city's growth strategy voiced by community leaders – that city officials were so consumed with efforts to construct facilities that the needs of the downtown residents (particularly minorities) had been neglected. To quote Sam Jones, the executive director of the Indianapolis Urban League:

> I'm not knocking the growth, I can show you relative progress here for blacks. But we have not really been financial recipients from the

massive development that has occurred, and the feeling in the black community is that while we're building a city with bricks and mortar, the inclination is to forget the human side.[114]

*Urban development for whom?*

In the downtown area, the growth scheme branched out from sports facilities to include other types of development to attract middle- and upper-class populations. By 1984, the Department of Metropolitan Development had assembled enough financial incentives to convince developers to break ground on a $US 180 million Circle Center Retail mall. A consortium of three Indianapolis Banks provided $US 32 million in 'favorable terms' to developers to renovate Union Station – (i.e., to turn an under-used structure into a hotel/retail project adjacent to the Hoosier Dome). Moreover, a host of large luxury hotels, including a $US 40 million Convention Center Hotel adjacent to the Hoosier Dome, was either being planned or constructed. From 1980 to 1984, sixteen new restaurants were added to the downtown and a total of $US 1.7 billion was invested in inner-city construction between 1974 and 1984.[115] According to a press release from the Indianapolis Project, Inc., US Census Bureau figures showed that, from 1980 to 1984, Indianapolis had the fastest population growth of any of the ten largest Midwest cities. In fact, Indianapolis (1.4% increase) and Columbus, Ohio (0.2% increase) were the only two cities that exhibited a positive growth rate. Indianapolis's population increased from 700,807 in 1980, to 710,280 in 1984. The Indianapolis Chamber of Commerce suggested that the population increase may have been partially attributed to the nearly 1,000 new businesses and 19,294 new residential units that opened within those four years.[116] Residential growth had been extensive in the downtown area. Bamberger and Parham note: 'Providing housing had become a key focus of the Hudnut administration and the private sector'.[117] The types of housing that were encouraged (and financially supported) command closer investigation.

The vacant downtown structures that were left in the wake of centrifugal migration produced an abundant inventory of buildings suitable for conversion into condominiums and luxury apartments. From 1980 to 1984, nearly 40 buildings totalling over 750 units were purchased for such conversion.[118] In 1981, an ambitious inner-city condominium project sold all of its 120 partially-constructed units in 11 business hours.[119] Public and private entrepreneurs assisted the implementation of luxury apartment, townhouse, and condominium construction projects that proliferated throughout the city. Securing upper-class residents in the downtown area was encouraged to provide support for the local consumer/service economy. Furthermore, upper-class residents assisted civic boosters by enhancing the city's 'quality of life' appearance. Ironically, while upper-class housing was being supported, a programme to assist lower-class home buyers was being denied and public housing was suffering from neglect.

In May 1984, the *Indianapolis Star* revealed that the city was in danger of losing millions of dollars in federal mortgage money because no local bank could be found to loan the mortgages. The funds were available through a nation-wide programme designed to assist low-income residents in buying a house. The programme was backed by $US 100 million through the Federal National Mortgage Association, or Fannie Mae. The National Association of Real Estate Brokers (a trade group whose members are mostly black real estate agents) was co-ordinating the programme through thirty of its chapters. The Indianapolis chapter was represented by a group of predominantly black real estate agents called Realists. According to J. Herbert Williams, the national co-ordinator for the programme, the Indianapolis chapter was the only one of the thirty that was unable to locate an in-state bank to offer the Fannie Mae loans.

Under the proposed programme, residents who qualified would have been granted up to thirty-year mortgages (averaging $US 50,000) at a 9.5% starting interest rate. Rates were guaranteed not to rise more than 5% over the life of the loan. The programme was specifically designed so that it would not compete with existing bank mortgage programmes. The President of the Realist group, Edna L. Johnson, charged that racism was behind the local banks' refusal to co-operate. Without such co-operation, hundreds of inquiring residents were denied the programme's benefits. Johnson stated that when she attempted to involve local banks, she faced a network of resistance focused around feelings that the programme would not look good for Indianapolis.[120] Local bankers gave various reasons for not participating. However, the important point here is that the same financial community that was willing to 'shave their profits' to help fund capital investment projects was unwilling to participate in a non-competitive programme to assist low-income residents.[121]

In June 1984, a federal official for the Department of Housing and Urban Development (HUD) sharply criticized Indianapolis's housing policy, calling their efforts to provide low-income residents with adequate housing 'atrocious.' HUD announced that because of federal budget cuts the Indianapolis Housing Authority's budget would be slashed by approximately 10% because 547 of the city's 2,622 public housing units were standing vacant and being neglected. In what the *Star* called a carrot-and-stick approach to improving lower-class living conditions, HUD offered to award the Housing Authority $US 800,000 if it agreed to a county-wide commitment to provide 'cost-effective, decent, safe and sanitary public housing'. The funds could only be used to construct new housing that was to be operated by a private firm – not by the city Housing Authority.[122] HUD's censure of Indianapolis's public housing efforts unveiled the stark realities of the class-biased attempts at urban rehabilitation.

Finally, on 27 May 1984, the city announced a positive step towards improving the living conditions for some of its lower-class residents. Revitalization efforts were to be extended to a deteriorating downtown residential area, known as Midtown, which had been decimated since the early 1950s. According to the *Indianapolis Star*, directors of the revitalization plan explained that the purpose of the project was to improve housing for existing residents and to change the image of the neighbourhood so new residents would move in. Announcement of the city's plans sparked both hope and scepticism from Midtown residents who had seen whole neighbourhoods removed to make way for urban development projects.

Paving the way for Midtown's revitalization was a study conducted by Indiana University-Purdue University at Indianapolis. The study declared the area 'blighted' after finding seventy-one vacant lots within a six-block area. Once an area has been declared blighted, Indiana state law provided Indianapolis's Department of Metropolitan Development with legal access to the private property contained within it. The city may then proceed with redevelopment plans. Indianapolis's use of the blight label was the source of considerable conflict.[123] Inherent in this conflict was a class struggle for urban territory. Conflict surrounding the blight zone labels centred on three issues: inconsistencies between publicly-stated plans for, and eventual use of, blighted areas; methods used by the city to designate blighted areas; and the city's practice of designating as blighted larger areas than it actually needed for development. For example, in 1974 businesses on an entire block of downtown property were removed when the city announced plans to build a hotel. As of April 1984, the land was being used as a parking lot.

In May 1984, the Metropolitan Development Commission declared a large downtown site a 'redevelopment area' to make room for the Convention Center Hotel. It included the property of business owners who were located blocks away from the approved hotel site. The area had been declared blighted when a study conducted by the city's Division of Housing and Economic Development found 84% of it's buildings to be deficient and substandard. However, a study paid for by the Indianapolis Taxpayers' Association found 84% of the building to be sound. The conflict led to a hearing before the City-County Council in which the President of the Taxpayers' Association recommended nine changes in the law that allowed non-elected officials to designate blighted areas. After the ninety-minute hearing, more studies involving the hotel site were ordered.[124]

The blighted/redevelopment zone argument was played out in the city's newspapers and generated a great deal of controversy. David Carley (former Department of Metropolitan Development director) offered the following illustration:

> The *Indianapolis News* ran an editorial that said '30% of the downtown is a redevelopment [hence blight] zone and that this is unconscionable that it's gotten this far and there ought to be curbs on this kind of growth.' So I said to my staff, 'I want every square foot we have under a redevelopment district measured ... I want to write a letter back to these people.' [My staff] came back and said, 'Mr. Carley, we have 42% of our downtown labeled a redevelopment district.' Oh Geez! Forget the response![125]

City-County Council minutes document that the Council wanted 'to find a way' to accomplish urban development purposes without having to use the 'blight term' because it was 'too emotional'.[126] The Department of Metropolitan Development eventually assembled all the redevelopment powers, except eminent domain, under a new label called 'economic revitalisation'.[127]

By securing representation from the Taxpayers' Association and attracting mass public attention via the local newspapers, the business owners in and around the proposed hotel site were able to mount a resistance to the local regime's redevelopment strategy. This was an extremely rare occasion in Indianapolis. As has been illustrated, the redevelopment strategy up until 1984 was powerfully legitimated and explosively effective. However, by 1984 a number of problem areas arose that, if left unchecked, might have threatened it with a legitimation crisis. The Department of Housing and Urban Development's criticisms and the blight controversy have already been discussed. In addition, despite growth advocates' insistence that development would have a pay-off for everyone, the county found it necessary to adopt a 0.2% local option income tax (with a 0.6% maximum), along with a local property tax increase of up to 5 cents. These taxes, like the Hoosier Dome tax, were imposed without going before the voters.[128] But perhaps none of these problems was as glaringly eye-catching as the empty Hoosier Dome. The mushroom-shaped structure now dominated the Indianapolis skyline. Although litigation aimed at blocking its construction had been terminated, critics abounded. When construction began in 1981, many people in the city had been convinced it would capture an National Football League expansion team. But when the roof was inflated in 1984, neither Indianapolis nor any other city had made great strides towards being awarded a new franchise, and the NFL made no indication that it planned to expand. Indianapolis was thus forced to lure an existing team – it looked to Baltimore.

## Corralling the Colts

Inter-city competition for professional sports franchises produces both winner and loser communities. For winning communities (e.g., Indianapolis) sports franchises are portrayed as being symbols of the community's economic and social health. Losing communities (e.g., Baltimore), on the other hand, are left to assess their damages and plan strategies with which to overcome the economic and political battering.

Growth coalition members in Indianapolis had wanted to obtain a professional football team even before the Hoosier Dome had reached the drafting board. Members of the city's growth coalition met with various National Football League owners to find out what types of things they desired in a domed stadium. Well before the first offers to the Colts' owner, Robert Irsay, were made public, Indianapolis 'authorities' had been negotiating a contract with him. In fact, Irsay had signed a deal with Indianapolis three days prior to making his midnight escape from Baltimore. Mayor Hudnut would be identified by news reporters as the Indianapolis spokesperson during the competition for the Colts. The actual chief negotiator was David Frick, a former Deputy Mayor, Capital Improvements Board treasurer (the Hoosier Dome's authority), city committee member, and confidant of Hudnut.[129]

After Indianapolis's public offer to Irsay on 27 February 1984, a virtual bidding war took place between 'public entrepreneurs'[130] who hoped to lure the football franchise to their respective cities. The headlines of the cities' newspapers revealed the drama of the contest as inducements were offered and then countered. For his part, Irsay remained non-committal throughout the month, encouraging the cities to stay in the battle. Even when presented with offers that met his specific demands, he took time to 'study' the deals or made himself unavailable, giving competitors a chance to counter.

Heading Irsay's list of demands was his insistence that major improvements be made to Baltimore Memorial Stadium, home ground of the Colts. The stadium was built at a cost of $US 6 million (second lowest in the National Football League) and opened in 1954. It is managed by the Baltimore Division of Recreation and Parks and also served as home ground to the Baltimore Orioles major league baseball franchise. Steve Rosenbloom, the son of former Colt owner, Carroll Rosenbloom, told the *Baltimore Sun* that his father had considered the stadium to be a major problem when he owned the Colts in the early 1970s. Said the younger Rosenbloom: 'That stadium was outmoded two years after it was built. My father felt the city, team, and the fans deserved a better place to play'.[131] Using the threat of relocation, Irsay told the Los Angeles press in 1977:

> I like Baltimore and I want to stay there, but when are we going to find out something about the stadium? I'm getting offers from towns like Indianapolis to build me a new stadium and give me other inducements to move there. I don't want to, but I'd like to see some action in Baltimore.[132]

In 1983, both Irsay and Edward Bennett Williams, owner of the Baltimore Orioles baseball franchise, began lease negotiations with the Baltimore City Parks Board. Baltimore Mayor, Donald Schaeffer, had anticipated brief and friendly negotiations, but after months of talks neither owner had signed contracts. In February 1984, Schaeffer gave the Parks Board one more round of talks to reach an agreement with the franchise owners. If none was reached, he planned to change negotiators in hopes of expediting the process. Generally, lengthy stadium lease negotiations are not of grave concern to city officials, but in Baltimore, the case was different. In 1983, the Maryland General Assembly agreed to grant the city $US15 million in state bonds for modernizing Memorial Stadium. The bonds could only be used if both owners signed six-year leases. If only one owner signed, $US7.5 million would be granted. Thus, because the bonds were in danger of expiring, Schaeffer faced a very difficult time element.[133] According to the Baltimore Mayor, his top priority in the legislature in 1984 was going to be aid to education and he could not lobby for an unpopular topic such as extending the stadium bond authority.

The poor condition of the thirty-year old Memorial Stadium was openly acknowledged by Baltimore city officials. The bonds were an attempt by the state to upgrade the stadium environment. But according to Vito Stellino, Baltimore sportswriter, many National Football League people considered Memorial Stadium such a poor football arena that major capital improvements could not be made for $US15 million. One franchise owner made the comment to Stellino that, 'They should use that stadium as a movie set for what an old-time stadium looked like'.[134] Furthermore, in addition to its structural inadequacies, there were other elements that made Memorial Stadium (from Irsay's perspective) a less-than-ideal setting for professional football. For instance, it generated a great deal of controversy by presenting itself as a problem for the citizens who resided in the surrounding neighbourhood. On days of home games, streets were heavily congested and parking space was insufficient. As an editorial in the *Baltimore Sun* described the situation:

Some problems are never going to be solved ... the city should take greater pains to enforce traffic and parking laws, at least to ensure fire and ambulance protection in streets and alleys, and to prevent roughnecks from renting alley parking spaces to which they have no right and harming cars, including those of residents, whose drivers do not pay.

Last year saw record attendance at the stadium. That is fine for folks trying to pay Cal Ripken's salary. It should not have to be a nightmare for those Baltimoreans who happen to have the stadium as a neighbor.[135]

The shortage of parking space forced game-goers to park their cars blocks away from the stadium and walk to their destination. Due in large part to this logistical difficulty, crime was a perennial problem in the stadium area. Assaults, thefts, and larcenies, especially from parked automobiles, threatened unsuspecting out-of-town tourists.

Because most National Football League games are played on Sunday, the congested stadium neighbourhood presented another problem. Church officials and residents of the stadium area believed that game traffic and limited parking space would interfere with church-goers and discourage church attendance. Community leaders argued that residents who drove their cars to church would return home to find their parking places had been filled with Colts fans. Additionally, limited parking space in stadium-area churches was likely to be filled by stadium-goers and not church-goers. As a result, city Blue Laws prohibited sports teams from scheduling home games earlier that 2.00 p.m. on Sundays. Irsay wanted to move the time to 1.00 p.m. so that major television networks could fit Colt games into their regular broadcasting schedules. Then, as now, all network games are at 1.00 p.m. and at 4.00 p.m. (EST). The 2.00 p.m. start inconvenienced networks by forcing them to miss the beginning of a 4.00 p.m. game. Irsay had tried for more than a decade to get the law repealed, but strong opposition between stadium neighbourhood residents had always circumvented his wishes.

The conditions under which Irsay had been operating his franchise in Baltimore prior to 1984 proved vulnerable to attack by rival cities. The Colts paid $US 600,000 annually, directly to the Baltimore city government, in stadium rental, taxes on admission tickets, parking fees, concessions revenues, and scoreboard advertising commissions.[136] Moreover, Irsay's 1980 (Baltimore) Owings Mills training complex placed him under a financial burden, and, at the same time, he was still paying on an 8% interest loan he acquired in 1972 when he bought the Colts, a loan which was due to expire in 1984. On 2 March, it was reported in the *Baltimore Sun* that the key to obtaining the Colts was to meet Irsay's demand of a multimillion dollar replacement loan at the 1972 interest rate (3% below the 1984 prime). Indianapolis had reportedly offered such an inducement in its package of 27 February. Baltimore, on the other hand, had not included a low-interest loan in its lease proposals. When Irsay took time to study the Indianapolis package, Baltimore's Mayor Schaeffer hoped that the city's banks and business executives would come forward to match the new incentive. His hopes, however, did not materialize and on 2 March he told the *Baltimore Sun*, 'It's an amazing thing ... I haven't heard from any banks in Baltimore'.[137]

Two days later the proposal was still not matched by Baltimore and the Indianapolis community anticipated the arrival of the Colts. Public and private entrepreneurs seized the opportunity to legitimate the Hoosier Dome project and advance the pro-growth ideology. The *Indianapolis Star* reported:

> Again and again, Indianapolis city officials point to this financial gain – rather than entertainment value – to justify dishing out tax money to build the Hoosier Dome and lure a franchise.
>
> If Indianapolis lands the Colts or any NFL team, 'It's going to do some amazing things for the city in terms of prestige, economic development, in terms of enticing companies to locate in Indiana-polis,' says Alan J. Armstrong, project director of the Hoosier Dome.[138]

By contrast, two days later, the lead story in the *Baltimore Sun*'s business section addressed how losing the Colts could possibly harm Baltimore's 'business image'. The story also revealed how Baltimore's 'leaders' planned to explain the loss of the Colts. Sam Fulwood wrote:

> ... [losing the Colts might] inflict a painful blow to the city's renais-sance image that could slow economic development. 'Outside of Baltimore, no one knows about the problems with Irsay' says Robert Kunisch, executive vice president of the PHH Group, Inc., a Balti-more firm that assists companies, to relocate its operations and employees. 'All they know is that the Colts left. The question, in their minds, is why?'[139]

A war of inducements between Baltimore, Indianapolis (and eventually Phoenix) would continue throughout the month of March. Although Irsay made no verbal indication that he had reached a decision, on 28 March a fleet of moving vans arrived at the Colts training complex in Owings Mills. The vans remained at the complex all day as rumours of an impending move spread throughout the Baltimore area. Carloads of fans, reporters, and photographers drove to the complex. Police were dispatched to the area to keep order and to keep traffic from blocking the streets. At around midnight on 29 March, Irsay ordered the packed vans to drive to Indianapolis. The *Baltimore Sun*'s morning headline read: 'BALTIMORE'S COLTS ARE GONE: IRSAY ENDS THE 31-YEAR MARRIAGE.'

The day the Colt's relocation was publicly announced, the *Indianapolis Star* published an article that highlighted the financial rewards the Colts would bring the city. According to the *Star*:

> To the business community, news of the Colts coming to Indianapolis ranks with a stock market surge or a cut in corporate taxes. The football team's presence will mean an annual inflow of $US21 million to $US25 million to the city … Businesses large and small will benefit, ranging from the kid who sells pennants outside the Hoosier dome to the radio station that lands the prestigious broadcasting rights.[140]

To reiterate an earlier point, the logic of the pro-growth model equates business interests with the interests of the community as a whole. In Indianapolis, pro-growth advocates wasted no time in using the arrival of the Colts to refine the ideology that contends that private capital accumulation trickles-down to benefit the entire city.

## The Problematic Growth Model

Many local 'officials' in many cities put their images, strategies of boosterism, and business climates against one another to secure sport-related firms and events. Their presence, officials argue, supports strategies of boosterism, other capital investment, real estate development projects, and service sector growth. It is the growth model and its assertion of a trickle-down effect that underlies public and private support for urban redevelopment.[141] Because capital is mobile it can disinvest from a city that does not provide for its specific needs. As they mobilize public incentives in order to compete for private resources, city officials now call themselves 'entrepreneurs in the public interest' and espouse the pro-growth model as beneficial for the community as a whole.[142] According to this model, private investment necessarily produces an increase in tax revenues and jobs, which in turn produces an increased per capita spending that results in less citizen dependency on government funds. The premise that growth is the social tide that lifts all boats has been used in the attempt to co-opt the support of subordinate groups. In the long run, so this ideology proclaims, private capital accumulation will yield benefits for all, especially in the provision of jobs.[143] Such ideologies fuel the 'pro-growth' policies of public officials. Such trickle-down effects of growth, however, often require public subsidy and the residential relocation of the poor. Here, the collective consumption privileges of the middle class are enhanced at the expense of the impoverished or ethnically marginalized.

Smith and Keller have concluded that not only is the efficacy of the growth model questionable, but that growth premised on this model may alter the economic base of a city in such a way as to make life more difficult for low-income residents. Obviously, those residents who are displaced from their homes with no civic plans to reabsorb them will be faced with hardships. But Smith and Keller reject the solace that growth produces jobs which result in raised spending levels and are beneficial for the entire community. This evaluation rests on an argument that the distribution of the costs and benefits of this growth model have regressive effects.[144] Swanstrom also takes issue with the claim, aggressively promulgated by developers, civic boosters and political officials, that this model of growth necessarily benefits the working-class. He points out in his case study of Cleveland's growth politics that civic leaders avoid speaking of growth as useful for profits. Instead, growth advocates iterate the necessity of growth for 'making jobs'. But, says Swanstrom, 'local growth does not, of course, make jobs: It distributes them'.[145] Job quantity, not job quality, often becomes a key rhetorical element in the articulation of a growth agenda. As Beaumont and Harvey express the point, the only underlying economic theory that many economic development policies seem to contain is 'that more jobs are good and less jobs are bad'.[146] While it is difficult to dispute the point that *any* job is better than *no* job, it can be pointed out that policy-making is always decision-making; it always involves choice. That these choices are not trivial, as Stone reminds us, is 'what is meant by the phrase "politics matters"'[147]. The distributive aspects of job creation were addressed by Smith and Keller in their analysis of New Orleans growth strategy. They claim that what usually occurs is an expansion in the service-sector and tourist related economy. These jobs, they lament, are typically low-paying, part-time and often dead-end. Those who benefit from this form of growth usually include finance capitalists and developers. Choosing policies that rely on this type of job creation can exacerbate existing structural problems in the local economy.[148]

**Summary**

The theoretical approach I have employed throughout this chapter is a critical one. The underlying theme has been the interrelatedness of economic, political, and social/cultural aspects of capitalist urban development. Consistent with an urban praxis perspective, I have emphasized the importance of capital accumulation in the shaping of urban areas and highlighted the ways in which human beings, possessing varying amounts of power, intervene in ongoing economic processes. I have also addressed the articulation of class and race relations, and the capital accumulation process, with space that creates uneven patterns of built urban environments. I have drawn attention to the fact that the mobility of capital *vis-à-vis* cities and communities means that cities must compete with one another for capital investment. Finally, I have provided an examination of the ways in which the local state is linked to the capital accumulation process.

It is not to be denied that local governments are dependent, to some degree, on economic growth occurring within their jurisdictional boundaries. Yet, neither the precise nature of that dependency nor the specific growth strategies are generalizable to all geo-historical contexts. As Jonas instructs us, local growth policies and strategies will vary according to local conditions and the political and economic interests in places they are intended to help and reproduce.[149] It will be recalled that Horan identifies three strands of variation among cities as they make development policy, the investigation of which, she explains, could serve as a framework for urban regime research in the 1990s. According to Horan, such research must look more closely at (a) the composition and agenda of the local growth coalition; (b) the institutional resources of the local government; and (c) the structure of the local economy.[150] I have been mindful of Horan's framework in my investigation of Indianapolis's growth politics.

My research, when combined with that of other urban praxis theorists,[151] lends support to the contention that, while broader economic processes influence local development, politics matters in the creation of development policy and implementation. In emphasizing this, I have focused on the activities of Indianapolis's growth coalition and its attempts to direct local development along lines conducive to its own interests. Indianapolis's growth agenda was produced through the proximate actions of interested and powerful local actors. This coalition's actions, while similar to those in some other cities, did not simply emanate from the imperatives of a broader-level (e.g., national or regional) political economy. Rather, those involved interpreted broader trends, applied them to their local conditions, and made real choices concerning how best to pursue local economic growth. In so doing, they became integral to the very processes they were interpreting. In other words, local and national political economies exist in a dialectical relationship – one of ongoing tension where each has the ability to shape the other.

Indianapolis's growth politics emerged out of the historical context of the 1970s. This was a time when, like many old, industrial cities, business and middle-class residents were migrating outward toward suburban areas. The loss of jobs and population from Marion County threatened the economic viability of the city's central business district. At the same time, the low-income population that was left behind became increasingly entrapped in a dirty downtown core. Center Township was rapidly becoming a place where ethnic minorities and low-income whites were relegated to obsolete sectors of the economy in a deteriorating physical environment. The city was faced with a myriad of social and economic problems. The response to this 'crisis' was political: It involved choices which embodied class and racial interests. In other words, as Stone has shown us, the question about how best to pursue growth does not answer itself. The answer, argues Stone, comes out of the city's political arrangements.

Growth politics in Indianapolis emerged and evolved from a long tradition of alliance-building between corporate élites and eminently skilled mayors who were able to combine their financial, bureaucratic, and political resources behind 'big ticket' development projects. Designed to enhance the city's quality of life for middle- and upper-class residents, these projects were presented to the community as job generators – a way out of urban crisis. These public and private élites, fuelled by a desire to shed their small-town image, mobilized behind a banner of pro-growth that not only sought to promote the interests of the dominant class, but also sought to legitimize political solutions to urban problems by symbolically constructing consensus (i.e., by blurring conflict in the redevelopment process). Concerned that Indianapolis's 'Naptown' image put them at a competitive disadvantage for specially-skilled labour and capital investment, corporate élites were highly influential, if not determinant, in fashioning a growth agenda that propagandized their visions of a good business climate and 'quality of life' throughout the population. Thus, the power of the local state and the influence of private capital merged to form political 'solutions' to Indianapolis's urban 'problems'. The building of new sports facilities, the attempt to lure professional and amateur sports organizations, and the hosting of sports events, articulated with these broader strategies of pro-growth and urban development. Given these circumstances, perhaps we can understand the cynicism of Indianapolis's Judson F. Haggerty, former Marion County Democratic Party Chairman: 'If the point is to make a city appear to be beautiful, prosperous, functioning, no matter what the real underlying problems are, then of course the Hoosier Dome and all the other things have been a success.'[152]

A sports strategy for spurring economic growth is not unique to Indianapolis. Many cities across the United States have built new stadiums and arenas in an attempt to lure professional sport franchises, stimulate economic development, and validate the 'big league status' of their communities. Some cities have been successful in their quest, Charlotte comes to mind;[153] others have floundered: St. Petersburg serves as a case in point. Not only is this attempt widespread, it is not new. Research from Lipsitz and from Smith and Keller's show that using sports-facility construction to anchor urban development characterized the renewal strategies of Houston, St. Louis, Los Angeles, and New Orleans in the early 1960s.[154]

However, while the ideology behind such attempts may be similar to that which is explored in this chapter, the financial arrangements behind the building of new stadiums and arenas may be changing. Mihoces contends that the days of leveraging public funds for stadium projects may be nearing their end.[155] For example, after failing to persuade the city of Miami, Florida, to build a replacement for the Orange Bowl, the owner of the Miami Dolphins, Joe Robbie, turned exclusively to private capital. The new $US100 million Joe Robbie Stadium was funded by the sale of ten-year leases on luxury sky boxes and club-level seats. If Mihoces is correct, perhaps some of the concerns that have been raised concerning the 'wise use' of public funds for stadium construction projects, may be beginning to create something of a legitimation crisis for the pro-growth ideology. Or perhaps more specifically, leveraging public investment in professional sport as a primary means of spurring economic growth may no longer be a viable agenda for local states. Rather, it may be that pro-growth coalitions will have to devise different strategies.

Regardless of the economic strategies that will be employed in the future, I think it is safe to project that the spatial and social issues involved in urban redevelopment will remain unresolved if the agenda for redevelopment remains unchanged. If, as the Fainsteins assert, the agenda is to re-establish business and middle-class control of urban territory by bringing back the white middle class while settling lower classes and minorities in peripheral locations, then it does not matter how stadium and arena construction is financed. And if the spatial and social fault lines remain, it is reasonable to assume that the question 'Does a professional sports franchise regenerate a sense of "community as a whole" or is the regeneration a class-biased figment of the local politician's imagination?' will continue to be asked.

## Notes

1. *Baltimore Sun*, 30 March 1984, p.1.
2. *New York Times*, 8 April 1984, p.22.
3. *Baltimore Sun*, 30 March 1984, p.1.
4. *Indianapolis Star*, 3 April 1984, p.35.
5. Portions of this chapter were published in K. S. Schimmel, A. G. Ingham and J. Howell, 'Professional Team Sports and the American City: Urban Politics and Franchise Relocations', in A. G. Ingham and J. Loy (eds), *Sport and social development: Traditions, Transitions, and Transformations* (Champaign, Ill, 1993) pp.211–44. Adapted with permission.

6.  A. G. Ingham and J. Howell and T. S. Schilperoort, 'Professional Sport and Community: A Review and Exegesis', in K. B. Pandolf (ed.), *Exercise and Sport Sciences Review* (New York, 1987).

7.  Ibid.

8.  *New York Times*, 30 March 1984, p.22.

9   *Indianapolis Star*, 30 March 1984, p.31.

10. Ibid., 23 June 1985, p.10.

11. Ibid., 17 May 1984, p.A1.

12. Ibid., 19 May 1984, p.31.

13. R. J. Bamberger and D. M. Parham, 'Indianapolis's Economic Development Strategy', *Urban Land* (November, 1984), p.13.

14. R. A. Baade and R. F. Dye, 'Sports Stadiums and Area Development: A Critical Review', *Economic Development Quarterly*, Vol. 2, 3 (1988), pp.265–75.

15. A. T. Johnson, *Minor League Baseball and Economic Development* (Chicago, 1993).

16. D. V. Baim, 'Sports Stadiums as "Wise Investments": An evaluation', *Heartland Policy Study No. 32* (Chicago, 1990).

17. There are, of course, notable exceptions to the micro-economic research perspective. Specifically, G. Lipsitz, 'Sports Stadia and Urban Development: A Tale of Three Cities', *Journal of Sport and Social Issues*, Vol. 8, 2 (1984); M. P. Smith and M. Keller, 'Managed Growth and the Politics of Uneven Development in New Orleans', in S. S. Fainstein, N. I. Fainstein, R. C. Hill, D. R. Judd and M. P. Smith (eds.), *Restructuring the City: The Political Economy of Urban Development* (New York, 1983), pp.126–66; Ingham *et al.*, 'Professional Sport and Community'; and C. C. Euchner, *Playing the Field: Why Teams Move and Cities Fight to Keep Them* (Baltimore, 1993) present broader perspectives relative to franchise/stadium/city problematics.

18. C. Horan, 'Beyond Governing Coalitions: Analysing Urban Regimes in the 1990s', *Journal of Urban Affairs*, Vol. 13, 2 (1991), pp.119–35.

19. H. Leitner, 'Cities in Pursuit of Economic Growth', *Political Geography Quarterly*, Vol. 9, 2 (1990), pp.146–70.

20. Ibid.

21. M. Gottdiener, *The Decline of Urban Politics* (Beverly Hills, 1987).

22. Leitner, 'Cities in Pursuit of Economic Growth'.

23. M. Harloe, *Captive Cities: Studies in the Political Economy of Cities and Regions* (London, 1977); P. Peterson, *City limits* (Chicago, 1981); P. Kantor and S. David, *The Dependent City: The Changing Political Economy of Urban America* (Glenview, Ill, 1988).

24. T. Swanstrom, 'Beyond economism: Urban political economy and the postmodern challenge', *Journal of Urban Affairs*, 15, 1 (1993), pp.55–78.

25. M. P. Smith, *City, State, and Market: The Political Economy of Urban Society* (New York, 1988); Swanstrom, 'Beyond Economism'.

26. Smith, *City, State, and Market*.

27. M. Gottdiener, *The Social Production of Urban Space* (Austin, Texas, 1985), Ch. 7.

28. Smith, *City, State, and Market*.

29. J. D. Kasarda, 'The Implications of Contemporary Redistributional Trends for National Urban Policy', *Social Science Quarterly*, Vol. 16, 3 and 4 (1980), pp.373–400; J. D. Kasarda, 'The Spatial Redistributional Trends and Public Policy: Prescriptions and Proscriptions', *American Planning Association Journal*, Vol. 47, 3 (1981), pp.340–345.

30. T. Swanstrom, *The Crisis of Growth Politics* (Philadelphia, PA, 1985).

31. J. R. Feagin, *Free Enterprise City: Houston in Political-Economic Perspective* (New Brunswick, 1988); Swanstrom, *Crisis of Growth Politics*.

32. Peterson, *City Limits*.

33. C. N. Stone and H. T. Sanders, *The Politics of Urban Development* (Lawerence, KA, 1987).

34. Peterson, *City Limits*, p.29.

35. Ibid., p.147.

36. Leitner, 'Cities in Pursuit of Economic Growth', p.150.

37. Ibid.

38. Peterson, *City Limits*, pp.109–42.

39. Swanstrom, *Crisis of Growth Politics*, p.16.

40. D. Harvey, *The Urbanization of Capital* (Baltimore, MD, 1985).

41. Leitner, 'Cities in Pursuit of Economic Growth', pp.150–2.

42. R. A. Beauregard (ed.), *Economic Restructuring and Political Response* (Newbury Park, 1989), p.221.

43. Smith, *City, State, and Market*, p.5.

44. R. C. Hill, 'Crisis in the Motor City: The Politics of Economic Development in Detroit', in Fainstein *et al.*, *Restructuring the City*.

45. M. P. Smith and J. R. Feagin, 'Detroit and Houston: Two cities in global perspective', in J. R. Feagin and R. C. Hill (eds.), *The Capitalist City: Global Restructuring and Community Politics* (New York, 1987), pp.155–77.

46. Swanstrom, 'Beyond Economism', pp.55–78.

47. M. Castells, (ed.), *High Technology, Space and Society* (Beverly Hills, 1985), p.32.

48. N. J. Glickman, 'Cities and the International Division of Labor', in M. P. Smith and J. R. Feagin (eds.), *The Capitalist City: Global Restructuring and Community Politics* (New York, 1987), pp.66–86.

49. Cited on p.81 of Glickman, 'Cities and the International Division of Labor', from J. Friedmann and G. Wolf, 'World City Formation: An Agenda for Research and Action', *International Journal of Urban and Regional Research*, Vol. 6 (1982), p.327.

50. Smith, *City, State, and Market*, p.4.

51. Leitner, 'Cities in Pursuit of Economic Growth'.

52. J. R. Logan and H. Molotch, *Urban Fortunes, the Political Economy of Place* (Berkeley, CA, 1987); H. Molotch, 'The City as Growth Machine', *American Journal of Sociology*, Vol. 82 (1976), pp.309–33.

53. J. Mollenkopf, *The Contested City* (Princeton, NJ, 1983); Swanstrom, *Crisis of Growth Politics*.

54. H. T. Stone, 'The Study of the Politics of Urban Development', in Stone and Sanders, *Politics of Urban Development*, pp.3–24.

55. S. L. Elkin, 'Twentieth-Century Urban Regimes', *Journal of Urban*

*Affairs*, Vol. 7, 2 (1985) pp.11–28; S. S. Fainstein and N. I. Fainstein, 'Economic Change, National Policy, and the System of Cities', in Fainstein *et al.*, *Restructuring the City*.

56. H. Molotch, 'The Political Economy of Growth Machines', *Journal of Urban Affairs*, Vol. 15, 1 (1993), pp.29–53.
57. Stone, 'The Study of the Politics of Urban Development'.
58. Horan, 'Beyond Governing Coalitions'.
59. Stone and Sanders, *Politics of Urban Development*, p.550.
60. Horan, 'Beyond Governing Coalitions'.
61. Mollenkopf, *The Contested City*, p.6.
62. Stone and Sanders, *Politics of Urban Development*.
63. Swanstrom, *Crisis of Growth Politics*, p.22.
64. Stone and Sanders, *Politics of Urban Development*, p.6.
65. Peterson, *City Limits*; Harvey, *The Urbanization of Capital*; Mollenkopf, *The Contested City*; Stone and Sanders, *Politics of Urban Development*.
66. T. Kuhn, *The Structure of Scientific Revolutions* (Chicago, 1970).
67. See especially Horan, 'Beyond Governing Coalitions'; Leitner, 'Cities in Pursuit of Economic Growth'; Molotch, 'The Political Economy of Growth Machines'; Swanstrom, 'Beyond Economism'.
68. Leitner, 'Cities in Pursuit of Economic Growth', p.167.
69. Horan, 'Beyond Governing Coalitions'; Leitner, 'Cities in Pursuit of Economic Growth'.
70. Leitner, 'Cities in Pursuit of Economic Growth'.
71. Horan, 'Beyond Governing Coalitions', pp.122–3.
72. K. S. Schimmel, 'From Naptown to Sportstown: Growth Politics, Urban Development, and Economic Change in Indianapolis', unpublished Ph.D. dissertation (Greensboro, North Carolina, 1994).
73. Department of Metropolitan Development, *A Growth Policy for Indianapolis* (Indianapolis, 1980), p.4.
74. S. S. Fainstein and N. I. Fainstein, 'Economic Change, National Policy, and the System of Cities', in Fainstein *et al.*, *Restructuring the City*.
75. *Indianapolis News*, 13 November 1989, p.A7.
76. Ibid.
77. Ibid., 1 May 1982, p.B1.
78. Quoted in L. E. Levathes and S. Felsenthal, 'Indianapolis: City on the Rebound', *National Geographic* (August, 1987), pp.230–59.
79. Bamberger and Parham, 'Indianapolis's Economic Development Strategy'.
80. Department of Metropolitan Development, *Marion County's Black Population from 1970–1980* (Indianapolis, 1981); Department of Metropolitan Development, *Demographic Trends in the Indianapolis SMSA from 1970–1980* (Indianapolis, 1981); Department of Metropolitan Development, *A Decennial Statistical Profile of Indianapolis – Marion County 1960–1970–1980* (Indianapolis, August, 1984).
81. L. E. Lynn and M. G. H. McGeary (eds.), *Inner-City Poverty in the United States* (Washington, DC, 1990), p.61.
82. G. Policinski, 'Indianapolis Outgrows its Small-Town Image', *Planning*, Vol. 44, 4 (1978), pp.13–15.

83. Quoted in C. J. Owen and Y. Wilbern, *Governing Metropolitan Indianapolis: The Politics on Unigov* (Berkeley, CA, 1985) p.1.
84. Ibid., p.2.
85. Ibid.
86. Quoted in the *Cincinnati Enquirer*, 27 July 1993, p.A1.
87. Indiana Economic Development Council, *The Futures of Indiana: Trends affecting economic change 1986–2000* (Indianapolis, 1986), p.51.
88. Personal communication, 20 October 1992.
89. Ibid.
90. *Indianapolis Star*, 22 August 1983, p.B1.
91. Ibid.
92. Department of Metropolitan Development, *A Growth Policy for Indianapolis*.
93. Industrial Growth Task Force, *An Economic development proposal for the Indinanapolis economic growth corporation* (Indianapolis, December, 1982), p.1.
94. Personal communication, 20 October 1992.
95. Personal communication, 24 September 1992.
96. Fainstein and Fainstein, 'Economic Change, National Policy, and the System of Cities', p.252.
97. Department of Metropolitan Development (1980), *A growth policy for Indianapolis*.
98. Department of Metropolitan Development, *A decennial statistical profile of Indianapolis*.
99. *Indianapolis News*, 15 November 1989, p.A12.
100. Personal communication, 30 October 1992.
101. *Indianapolis News*, 13 November 1989, p.A8.
102. Ibid., 14 November, 1989, p.A1.
103. Personal communication, 20 October 1992.
104. Personal communication, 14 September 1992.
105. *Indianapolis Sun*, 16 February 1984, p.A1.
106. W. H. Hudnut III and J. Keene, *Minister/Mayor* (Philadelphia, PA, 1987).
107. Levathes and Felsenthal, 'Indianapolis: City on the Rebound', p.24.
108. Quoted ibid., p.241.
109. W. A. Neilsen, *The Golden Donors* (New York, 1985), p.295.
110. Personal communication, 17 August 1992.
111. *Indianapolis News*, 9 January 1985.
112. *Indianapolis Star*, June 1984, p.C1.
113. Ibid., 2 June 1984, p.1.
114. Personal communication, 30 October 1992.
115. Bamberger and Parham, 'Indianapolis's Economic Development Strategy'; Indianapolis Project, Inc., 8 March 1986.
116. Indianapolis Project, Inc., 20 September 1985.
117. Bamberger and Parham, 'Indianapolis's Economic Development Strategy', p.16.
118. Ibid.
119. Indianapolis Project, Inc.

120. *Indianapolis Star*, 6 May 1984, p.11.
121. Bamberger and Parham, 'Indianapolis's Economic Development Strategy' p.16.
122. *Indianapolis Star*, 16 May 1984, p.1.
123. Bamberger and Parham, 'Indianapolis's Economic Development Strategy'.
124. *Indianapolis Star*, 19 April, 6, 17 May, 8 June 1984.
125. Personal communication, 20 October 1992.
126. Indianapolis–Marion County Council, Proceedings, 1984, p.342.
127. Personal communication, 20 October 1992.
128. Bamberger and Parham, 'Indianapolis's Economic Development Strategy'.
129. *Indianapolis News*, 14 November 1989, p.A5.
130. Hill, 'Crisis in the Motor City'.
131. *Baltimore Sun*, 7 February 1984, p.D5.
132. Ibid., 30 March 1984, p.A14.
133. Ibid., 1 February 1984, p.E2.
134. Ibid., 2 February 1984, p.D1.
135. Ibid., p.A10.
136. Ibid., 6 March 1984, p.C7.
137. Ibid., 2 March 1984, p.A8.
138. *Indianapolis Star*, 4 March 1984, p.2D.
139. *Baltimore Sun*, 6 March 1984, p.C8.
140. *Indianapolis Star*, 30 March 1984, p.31.
141. D. R. Judd and M. Collins, 'The Case of Tourism: Political Coalitions and Redevelopment in Central Cities', in G. Tobin (ed.), *The Changing Structure of the City* (Beverly Hills, 1979), pp.177–99; M. P. Smith, and D. R. Judd, 'Structuralism, Elite Theory, and Urban Policy', *Comparative Urban Research*, Vol. 9, 2 (1982), pp.127–44.
142. Hill, 'Crisis in the Motor City'.
143. Smith and Keller, 'Managed Growth and the Politics of Uneven Development in New Orleans'.
144. Smith and Keller, 'Managed Growth and the Politics of Uneven Development in New Orleans'; Lipsitz, 'Sports Stadia and Urban Development: A Tale of Three Cities'.
145. Swanstrom, *Crisis of Growth Politics*, p.137.
146. Harvey, *The Urbanization of Capital*, p.328.
147. Stone, 'The Study of the Politics of Urban Development', p.6.
148. Smith and Keller, 'Managed Growth and the Politics of Uneven Development in New Orleans'.
149. E. G. Jonas, 'Urban Growth Coalitions and Urban Development Policy: Postwar Growth and the Politics of Annexation in Metropolitan Columbus', *Urban Geography*, Vol. 12, 3 (1991), pp.197–225.
150. Horan, 'Beyond Governing Coalitions'.
151. Fainstein and Fainstein, 'Economic Change, National Policy, and the System of Cities'; Elkin, 'Twentieth-Century Urban Regimes'; Stone, 'The Study of the Politics of Urban Development'; Leitner, 'Cities in Pursuit of Economic Growth'.

152. *Indianapolis News*, 15 November 1989, p.A1.
153. K. S. Schimmel, 'Modernizers Court the NBA: Professional basketball comes to Charlotte, North Carolina', unpublished manuscript (1988).
154. Smith and Keller, 'Managed Growth and the Politics of Uneven Development in New Orleans'; Lipsitz, 'Sports Stadia and Urban Development: A Tale of Three Cities'.
155. *USA Today*, 31 March 1987, p.C7.

# 8

# Copenhagen's Parken:
# A Sacred Place?

*Per Jørgenson*

## The Background

All nations have their sacred places. The football stadium called 'Idræts-parken'[1] which was situated in Østerbro in Copenhagen almost had that kind of status until it was demolished in the autumn of 1990 (see Chapter 4). Idrætsparken was where the national team had played almost all its football matches for about eighty years. The five biggest football clubs in Copenhagen also played their home games there for generations. Numerous boys and men – and some women – have had their greatest football experiences as spectators in this place.

In the early 1980s the number of football spectators declined and it became increasingly common for the big clubs to play their games on smaller local fields. Idrætsparken was only used for international matches and annual cup finals and in the summer for two or three big rock concerts. But even if there were not many spectators for the ordinary club games, there were packed houses for the international matches in this period. As a result, Idrætsparken witnessed the rise of Danish football into the ranks of the best in Europe.

Thus it is understandable why it was such a great shock when plans were suddenly published in the autumn of 1986 for the building of a new national stadium, not to be situated in Copenhagen at all, but in the suburb of Brøndby. The proposal for the new stadium, which was to be called 'Stadion Danmark',[2] led to considerable activity among people who wrote letters to the newspapers; a conflict of opinion existed among opinion formers, leaders of football clubs and also among local politicians in Copenhagen.

## The Course of Events

*'Stadion Danmark' and Dansk Boldspil-Union*

It was Dansk Boldspil-Union (DBU)[3] which started the process, when they unsuccessfully addressed themselves to 'Københavns Idrætspark',[4] (see Chapter 4) several times from the middle of the 1980s in order to get better conditions. According to the information giving by DBU,[5] the first meeting was held in November 1984, and it was the lack of response that provided the impetus for the plans of Stadium Denmark less than two years later.

Københavns Idrætspark was an independent institution governed jointly by sports organizations and the Copenhagen political parties. Its purpose was to administer and organize the leasing and the letting of most of the sports facilities in Copenhagen, one of which was Idræts-parken itself. Basically, what DBU wanted, among other things, was a share of the ever-increasing income to which Københavns Idrætspark was entitled from advertising during international matches. Besides this, DBU wanted improved facilities for the spectators who were outgrow-ing Idrætsparken especially at national matches. In short, DBU wanted a more economic environment and a better image for their product.

According to DBU, Københavns Idrætspark was not very positive, and this led directly to the initiation of the Stadion Danmark project. Behind the plan was a corporation, started by DBU and the local authorities of Brøndby, whose official purpose was to prepare for the building of a modern stadium in Brøndby with 60,000 seats. DBU paid Dkr. 100,000[6] of a share capital of Dkr. 5.1 million. Among the shareholders were the main sponsors of DBU, 'Danske Mejeriers Fælles-organisation'[7] and Brøndby football club.

Several facts gave credibility to the plans of Stadion Danmark and forced the surrounding world to take a stand. First of all, DBU as orga-nizer of international football in Denmark had a powerful team which could attract spectators. Second, Brøndby local authorities owned the area on which the stadium was going to be built and could provide it for nothing. Third, Brøndby football club belongs there and was at that time by far the richest and the most successful Danish club, and they needed a larger home ground.

The plans for Stadion Danmark made Københavns Idrætspark respond immediately. In November 1986, they presented a plan for the recon-struction of Idrætsparken at a price of Dkr. 300 million. The reconstructed stadium would be able to seat 30,400, with room for 14,600 standing; there would also be a sports hotel and an office area included as part of the overall package.

But DBU was not satisfied with this alternative. At the yearly meeting of representatives in March 1987, their chairman announced that FIFA[8] had just told DBU that a stadium with standing room would not be legal for official international matches after 1992. Idrætsparken, even if reconstructed, would not be able to meet these demands. So the Stadion Danmark project remained in place, and an architectural competition was announced with prizes totalling Dkr. 1 million. From the twenty-nine submitted entries, the winning project, a colosseum-like structure, was announced in November 1987. It had an audience capacity of 60,000 seats and would cost about Dkr. 700 million.

The more real the idea of Stadion Danmark became, the more opposition it met among ordinary people and among decision-makers in Copenhagen's local authorities. Would it really be possible to leave Østerbro and all its memories for the concrete jungle of Brøndby? It was a great time for those who enjoyed writing letters to the newspapers! Three weeks later, at the beginning of December, Københavns Idrætspark published its second attack on Stadion Danmark in Brøndby. The plan now was to turn the national field in Østerbro through 90 degrees and to retain the old grandstand. This alteration was expected to take a little more than four years and be finished by the summer of 1992. The audience capacity would now be 50,000 seats; the office area would be 15,000 square metres.

But Københavns Idrætspark had to watch from the sidelines for yet another three or four months. As late as the meeting of representatives of DBU in March 1988, a motion for negotiating for the playing of international matches in a new Idrætsparken was rejected. In other words, DBU remained loyal to Stadion Danmark. But a few days later DBU was freed from this obligation when the Brøndby project was rejected, enabling them to enter negotiations concerning the use of a new Idrætsparken. This meant that Københavns Idrætspark was able to send plans to the Copenhagen local authorities very soon after. Things now began to move quickly. Less than three months later, the plans were given preliminary acceptance by the politicians in the town hall and were submitted to a public hearing.

With the Brøndy project no longer a proposition, it might be interesting to find out what role had really been planned for Stadion Danmark. Had the project ever been thought of as serious by DBU? Or was it used to put pressure on the slow negotiations with Københavns Idrætspark? There can hardly be any doubt that if the project that was suggested at the beginning of 1987 had had any economic foundation, it would have become reality for the following reasons: (a) there had been an competition for the architectural design of the new stadium, the only one in the course of events; (b) the share capital behind Stadion Danmark was no small amount (Dkr. 5 million); (c) it is tempting for any football leader to have a new stadium which can seat 60,000 people; and (d) DBU had been the reason for the project in the first place.[9]

On the other hand, there are several factors which support the theory that the project was initiated expressly in order to exert pressure, at least by DBU. First, DBU only gave Dkr. 100,000 to the project, which amounted to less than 2% of the share capital. In this context it is interesting to look at the role DBU played in relation to the other shareholders in the Stadion Danmark project. It is said[10] that DBU put very strong pressure on their main sponsor 'Danske Mejeriers Fælles-organisation' to make them give Dkr. 1 million to the project and they did the same thing to 'Handelsbanken'.[11] It cannot be denied that DBU appeared to be more interested in using others people's money than their own. Second, the corporation Stadion Danmark was not formed with the specific purpose of building a stadium, but rather to find out what the options were.[12] In other words, it looks as if DBU was only set free from its obligations to the project in Brøndby when Københavns Idrætspark had given a serious and satisfactory offer. The total cost of this manœuvre, including the expenses for the architects' competition, has been estimated at Dkr. 1.5 million, of the original share capital of Dkr. 5.1 million.[13] DBU probably lost no more than Dkr. 30,000. Third, there was always a lot of opposition within DBU itself against the Stadion Danmark project. This opposition was expressed at the meetings of representatives in 1987 and 1988. It was said that, in principle, DBU should not be engaged in the administration of a stadium and that they should only organize football. It was also said that national games should not be taken away from Copenhagen.

*The new 'Idrætsparken' and 'Parken'*

The Københavns Idrætspark/DBU project for a new Idrætsparken was submitted to a public hearing in the autumn of 1988. The nature of the public debate now changed: it was no longer just a matter of modernization but of a completely new stadium. Because of this, the debate was not powered simply by football nostalgia; a building of this kind and size would affect all of Østerbro. Opposition grew and protest groups were formed.

The hearing period was characterized by an extraordinary level of activity on behalf of the population and various institutions and organizations, and also by a number of alternative projects.[14] But protests and alternative suggestions did not help. After the hearing period and the conventional treatment of protests, the plans were finally approved at the town hall.

In the meantime, public attention had increasingly been focused on the economics of the project. Who was going to pay? At the first anniversary of the project in the spring of 1989, the finances for the new Idrætsparken had still not been found and DBU regularly expressed its worries from the sideline. Without a modern stadium, there would be no international football matches. In August the same year, there were rumours sent out by DBU that 'an attractive and central provincial town has got very far with the plans for a stadium seating 30,000 people who can all sit under cover'.[15]

At that time, there were local elections going on all over Denmark. The new Idrætsparken problem had found its way into the local election campaign of Copenhagen which did not make the debate less emotional: a Social Democratic town council candidate stated in a letter to the editor that: 'Idrætsparken cannot be moved. The Romans never moved Forum Romanum either'.

At the same time that the local election campaign entered its last phase in October 1989, another stadium project was launched. This was the one that was finally to be carried through under the name of 'Parken'. In its first version it was a plan to reconstruct Idrætsparken for less than Dkr. 200 million. For an extra Dkr. 90 million, an office area of 12,000 square metres could be built. In this plan, too, the field was to be turned through 90 degrees and there were to be 50,000 seats.

The plan included roughly the same qualities as that for the new Idrætsparken but at half the price. The project created a great stir, not least with Københavns Idrætspark. They quickly recovered, however, and supplied a counter-attack – not a third stadium, but a discount version of the one that had already been decided. For it now turned out that the original plan (at a price of more than Dkr. 600 million) could be made for less money. Now, according to Københavns Idrætspark, it could be built in a slightly cut-price version for Dkr. 400 million. So, in a matter of very few weeks, the projected new Idrætparken became cheaper by Dkr. 200 million. One month later, DBU again put pressure on the authorities to turn the plans for the stadium into reality. FIFA would grant no exemption from the demand for seats. The stadium would have to be finished by 1 July 1992 if Denmark wanted to play international football.

At the beginning of the new year came the greatest breakthrough in the long history of Copenhagen's new stadium. For the first time there was real money involved. Baltica Finans, which is a subsidiary company of Baltica, one of the largest insurance companies in Denmark, agreed to finance this last plan for the stadium. There were now two competing stadium projects: one which was accepted and approved in the town hall, and one that could be financed. A few days later strong powers in the football world[16] put their faith in the new project, which in its final form was going to cost Dkr. 350 million and have 45,000 seats and 15,000 square metres of office area. DBU would carry through the new cheaper project somewhere else in Denmark if nothing happened now.

But DBU did not have to worry any more. In February 1990 Baltica Holding gave a Press conference, at which they introduced the plans for the project that they hoped would become Denmark's new national stadium and which was going to be called Parken.[17] The Press material was filled with spelling mistakes and other errors and had obviously been written in a great hurry. Nevertheless, everything now should have been satisfactory, but a month later there was yet another problem. DBU and Baltica Finans could not agree on the financial conditions and Baltica threatened to withdraw from the project if DBU could not guarantee that the new stadium would be used for the national team.

However, finally the day came. On 6 April, Baltica Finans and DBU signed a contract which guaranteed DBU more money than previously. The final political decision was no more than a formality: a stadium had already been accepted. It did not matter too much that the original plans had changed – there was not a great deal of difference – and the politicians came to an agreement at the beginning of May.

On 14 November 1990, Denmark played a match in the European tournament against Yugoslavia. It was the last match in the old Idrætsparken. The day after, its demolition and the building of Parken started. In December 1990 it was announced that the price of Dkr.365 million on which the budget had been based had become Dkr.450 million. By the inauguration in September 1992, the price had risen to Dkr.500 million.

After the opening match in Parken in September 1992 between the European champions, Denmark, and the world champions, Germany, several hundred seats had to be removed. Furious spectators had pointed out that they could not see the match from their seats because of advertisement signs and television gear. The stadium which was originally planned for 45,000 spectators ended up having room for 40,000 people. It also turned out that the grass of the football field, which had been laid only a few weeks before the opening, could not stand the wear and tear. In addition, the drainage system was inadequate and the field quickly developed into a swamp. Matches and concerts had to be cancelled and the field had to be reconstructed for more than Dkr.20 million. All in all, it was estimated that Parken had cost its builder Dkr.600 million, including the losses resulting from cancelled arrangements and inadequate leasing of the office facilities.

In the meantime, the insurance company Baltica had run into serious economic difficulties and the subsidiary company Baltica Finans, the real owner of Parken, had gone bankrupt. But, so far, any attempt to sell the stadium has been in vain, including an attempt in the spring of 1994 when the municipality of Copenhagen was offered it for Dkr.100 million – but the municipality was not interested.

## The Decision-Making Process

More than eight years had passed since the mid-1980s, when a discussion on improving or reconstructing Idrætsparken had begun, until a completely new stadium, Parken, was finished and inaugurated in September 1992. During this period the decision-makers – the local politicians of Copenhagen, the municipal officers and the institution Københavns Idrætspark – did not take many initiatives. In those eight years, most actions were in response to initiatives from outside.

The politicians of Copenhagen were involved several times. The first time was when the local plan involving the new Idrætsparken was initially discussed in the town council in June 1988. To build a construction as large as a stadium, a comprehensive local plan for the area is needed.[18] From the time when Københavns Idrætspark, in March 1988, officially asked the local authorities to work out a local plan, it took less than three months for it to be finished and approved at the first attempt in the town hall. This is very fast, especially for such an enormous case. An ordinary, smaller case would normally have taken at least six months. Such speed has only one possible explanation. The department for district plans had been told to speed up the treatment of the case. The then Mayor was a Social Democrat. Less than a year later, his job was taken over by a man from the same political party, Jens Kramer Mikkelsen. At the time of the planning, the latter was also assistant chairman of Københavns Idrætspark and group chairman of the Social Democrats at the Copenhagen town hall. As a result, the project was approved, the local district plan was accepted and submitted to the obligatory hearing. And in reality the case was closed.

Investigations have shown that less than 10% of local plans are changed as a consequence of a public hearing, and these are hardly ever important changes. This means that the actual period during which the Copenhagen local authorities made their decision about the project, which was later transformed into Parken, was from 18 March until 16 June 1988. In less than three months, Copenhagen created the framework for the most expensive building in the history of Denmark. Within this short time, the dimensions and the exact situation of the national stadium were decided. There was no architectural competition, and there were no thorough investigations of the effects on the surrounding area before the decision was taken. One may wonder whether it was wise to take such an important decision so quickly, but seen from the point of view of the politicians, it was a good idea. After all, it was a case that had the interest of the public and therefore also the media; and at the time the protests were few and muted. In fact, there was a strong interest in securing Idrætsparken as the place where international football matches were played.

So for most politicians is was a clear case. And the local plan was passed by a great majority. The planned office area, which was necessary for the project to be economically profitable, met with a great deal of opposition, but apart from this, there was no serious initial opposition to the project. What the few opponents said, apart from the problems with the office areas, was that it was too tall and would dominate the surrounding streets; it would take away the sun from the Brumleby housing area, which is a conservation area; it would result in increased traffic; it was ugly. The supporters were pleased that the big football matches would still be in Copenhagen. In this way the city would keep its status as the capital and cultural centre of the country.[19]

However the debate centred on economics. Could the project be financed? How and by whom? Would it be economically sound? Would the municipality of Copenhagen in any way run into financial problems? These questions could not, of course, be answered at the first meeting; the economic possibilities were a question of the future, but – it was argued – they could be investigated during the public hearing period. In fact one of the arguments for the quick treatment of this case was that, with a local plan in hand, it would be easier for Københavns Idrætspark to secure financing of the new Idrætsparken.[20]

The public hearing would finish in November, and then the protests which had come in would be discussed by the administration. What seems surprising, compared to the speed of the treatment so far, is that it now took more than a year for the town council to finish the case. This was not so much because it decided to proceed with the protests with special thoroughness. The background was that there was simply no pressure to hurry. As mentioned above, no economic basis for the project had been secured during or after the public hearing period, so there was no hurry to have the protests treated and the project finished.

But in June 1989, the final discussion started. Forty-one protests, and a number of comments from public authorities, had been submitted. These were sent for discussion in a committee, as is usual. After the summer holidays, the town councillors of Copenhagen, according to the plan, were to look into the district plan for the last time and thus also at the projected new stadium. This happened on 14 September 1989.

At this point, the local election campaign in Denmark was in full swing. The debate at the town hall of Copenhagen took place in the presence of a crowded audience. Everybody knew exactly what the result would be: the local plan would be passed. This had already been stated in the media. After a long debate, the plan was passed with twenty-eight votes for and twenty-two against. A number of parties had changed their minds during the election campaign, but not enough to prevent the plan from being accepted. No new arguments had been used, although the weight of the debate shifted a little and the discussion as such was more emotional than the first time. This may have been caused by the large audience and by the fact that it was in the middle of an election campaign. Besides the known arguments from the initial debate, there were now a lot of questions about the democratic aspect of the process.[21]

At the first discussion the year before, the economy had had a central place in the debate. The opponents at that time wanted to know how the project was going to be financed, while the supporters had simply maintained that a local plan was all that was necessary for Københavns Idrætspark to be able to obtain any kind of financing. At the final discussion, therefore, it was not so much a matter of economics, although this question had not been resolved in any way during the previous year. Opponents still wanted to know how financing was going to happen, but they also realized that they would have no answer. So although there was still no financial backing for the project, the local plan was accepted, and the new Idrætsparken could, in principle, be started. However, it was immediately after this that the alternative Parken project (later guaranteed by Baltica Finans) was launched so the case returned to the town council on 3 May 1990, when the choice had to be made between the two projects.

But this was not a real choice. As noted above, the original project for the new Idrætsparken had been cut to the bone, so that it was almost economically competitive. But still it could not fully compete. The new project, Parken, had watertight economic backing and could be carried through without financial risk for the local authorities. Baltica Finans took the full economic risk. Copenhagen only had to provide Dkr. 2 million Danish krone. for shared management, which would be in charge of the day-by-day running of the place. Baltica undertook the building of a stadium with 45,000 seats and 15,000 square metres of office area at a fixed price of Dkr. 365 million.

But the local authorities of Copenhagen had almost to give away the area, whose estimated value was Dkr. 49 million, on which Baltica was to build. This took place at a transaction at which it seemed that a bag of money was being passed round the table. Baltica Finans started by buying the land where Idrætsparken was situated for Dkr. 30 million from Københavns Idrætspark. Københavns Idrætspark then had to pay this money to the Copenhagen local authorities to cover old debts. But Copenhagen then had to pay Baltica exactly Dkr. 30 million for the administration of Parken during the building period, so the bag of money returned to its starting point.

One may wonder why Parken, which in effect was a completely new project, did not require a new local plan and a new public hearing. But it did not. According to the law, if the revised project stuck to the intentions of the district plan, which had already been accepted, no new local plan would be needed. The town councillors agreed that this was the case. In addition most of them thought that the new construction was more attractive than the old, though there was very little excitement about the architectural design. The difference was not very great and the city architect was probably correct in his estimation of the two projects which he was legally obliged to give: 'Both projects have fine features, but do not answer the architectural demands which one must make for a project with this special content, of this size, and in this place. Which, can mainly be ascribed to the complex circumstances.'[22] This statement can be translated, when you know his way of expressing himself, into more direct language: 'What a mess'.

*Protests from the public hearing*

The public hearing is an important democratic element in the process of decision-making, when new local plans are going to be passed. During the hearing period, which usually lasts two months, the citizens, organizations, institutions, associations, etc. may protest and try to have the project in question changed or refused. The protests are sent to the town hall of Copenhagen, where the municipal officers go through them. At the final decision, the politicians take protests as well as answers into consideration, at least in principle.

As mentioned before, forty-one protests were submitted during the hearing period, none of which produced any changes in the project. Usually, the protests have no important influence on the decisions. Only very rarely is anything essential changed in a project after its first discussion in the town hall.

In the debates in the town hall before the final decision, the politicians do talk about the protests that have come in; the protests are a part of the democratic procedure and also contain the pros and cons that the politicians themselves are aware off. But the protests that the politicians use as a basis for their arguments are not in their original form. Instead almost all of them make do with a summary made by the municipal officers. It is obvious that the finer details are lost in this process. The nearest neighbour of Parken is the Brumleby housing area which would have the thirty-five-metre high stadium placed at a distance of about thirty-five metres (see Figure 8.1). The Tenants' Association of Brumleby therefore sent a four-page protest. But in the official summary, this only took up seventeen lines. Such editing was in no way unusual. Another neighbour had his ten page protest reduced even more.[23]

The comments of the municipal officers to the summarized protests are made after each individual protest. But as protests are often against the same thing, the officers always refer to previous answers as if the problem in question had been mentioned earlier. So in the case of the protest from Brumleby the response of the officials aggregate various comments (given earlier) together in a one-line answer. The comments of the municipal officers are meant to refute the protests, not to oblige them. The project in question always has a political majority behind it

**Figure 8.1** Idrætsparken in 1955. Note the large area of open space between the stadium and Brumleby in the bottom right of the photograph. This was to disappear with the re-alignment of the stadium (see Figure 4.4)

when it is sent out to a public hearing, otherwise it would never have been submitted. So the officials are tied; they have to defend the project against the protests and as a result their comments almost invariably support the majority.

Politics in general is about deciding or determining development. In a democratic system, of course, you can only do this if you have the majority behind you, or at least not against you, and it is necessary to argue the case, otherwise everything ends in a show of strength supported by a language of power. The majority has to argue for, or at least make it seem probable that they are doing, the right thing. The municipal officers help them with this. Usually, this is no great problem. In most cases, such as the placing of buildings, the size, the architecture and prices, arguments on the basis of emotion, attitude, or economic reality can combine with very flexible political possibilities of dispensation. This is quite a normal political way of arguing. It is more difficult for a majority when there are technical arguments against them, arguments which are highly objective and which cannot be refuted straightaway. It is very interesting to look at how arguments are presented in such a case.

When piles of material about a specific case like this are examined, a picture arises of a way of arguing, which can be difficult to see in the individual case, but which is striking when you read a whole process. This debating technique consists in transforming technical, objective argument into political argument based on personal attitudes.[24] At this transformation, the supporters of a project, in this case the new Idræts-parken, structure the discussion as if it were a question of attitudes and of statement versus statement. When both arguments appear equally good, based on belief you choose your own.

An example can throw light on the technique. In the protest from Brumleby, it was said at the beginning of the summary made by the municipal officers that residents gave three arguments: these concerned the shadows, the traffic and the car parking. In the original four-page protest from Brumleby, these three problems are in three separate paragraphs. In the seventeen-line summary made by the municipal officers they are all placed together.

The technical argument in the protest concerning the effects of the big shadow on the neighbours, even in the middle of the summer, was not answered. The well-documented connection between the number of office jobs and increased traffic was related to a previous answer which didn't cover the question. Both arguments were treated together with the third and undocumentable argument of the protest. This was the theory that even with the same number of spectators, the traffic would be increased because of the new stadium. And that argument was, of course, a matter of belief and was, in fact, the only one of the three to be really answered. By responding to that specific argument and pretend-ing that all three protests were being addressed, the validity of the whole protest could be questioned. The town hall did this by referring to possible contracts with the public transport system and the establish-ment of extra parking space.[25]

The opponents of the project in the town hall, however, did follow up the fact that there were no answers to the shadow effects on Brumleby. This resulted in the technicians looking into the problem, but they found that the shadow effect was of no importance. However, their mea-surements were so obviously unreasonable and incorrect, that another protest was mounted. The local authorities did now admit that the shadow effect would be great, even in the middle of the summer. However, they also demonstrated that there were several big trees in Brumleby, which cast shadows just as much as the new stadium would. After having compared shadows from a building with those from trees, the majority at the town hall concluded that the total effect on Brumleby would largely be unchanged.[26]

The documentation which is not produced is often as interesting as that which is. The closer one is to political power, the less technical documentation is needed, it seems. So power defines reality, more than it analyses and documents it. The opponents of the project often asked for, but never effected, neutral thorough estimations.[27] Instead the sup-porters made estimations which were based on a set of criteria that were geared in advance for the solution they wanted and which accentuated the advantages of that solution, while the disadvantages were stressed when it came to the alternatives. The result of such estimation was given in advance, and it served as a way of rationalizing a political decision which had already been made. Several alternative solutions and possibilities were suggested over the years. Objectively-founded estimation of such alternatives would involve an argued evaluation of advantages and disadvantages. Such arguments were never produced.

In the demands made by the law relating to the size of a local area plan, there are also many possibilities for rejection of criticism. The word 'local' is taken very literally. Many of the forty-one protests demonstrated that the construction, by its mere size, would dominate and destroy the public preserved area of Fælledparken, in which the new stadium would be situated. The local authorities gave the same response to this every time. It was that the local plan did not involve the green areas of Fælledparken which were already being used for sports purposes.[28] This meant that even if the new construction, like the old, was to be placed in Fælledparken and would thus really be part of the same park, the ethics of its situation and effects could not be discussed. By sticking to the local area plan in its narrowest sense, every discussion about the placing and the dominance of Parken could be stopped by resorting to the letter of the law.

Most protests expressed some degree of misgiving on behalf of Brumleby. But all criticism relating to the height of the stadium and its distance from the Brumleby houses was refuted by the local authorities who argued that they were going to construct a wind break and also that the height and the distance were in accordance with building laws.[29] In this case, the majority refrained from discussing attitudes and ethics, and instead used a more convenient argument. The real effect of a building of 200 by 150 by 35 metres, placed at a distance of 35 metres from a preserved housing area, was not discussed. Instead, the argument was reduced to a mathematical formula.

## Conclusions

If Stadion Danmark had been based on economic realities it would probably have been built. But if we look back at the process as a whole, we might get the impression that DBU was using this project especially in order to make Københavns Idrætspark act. The federation certainly showed a great talent for lobbying over the years. On the other hand, throughout the eight years that the process took, politicians at the town hall of Copenhagen almost exclusively reacted to initiatives coming from outside. They did not take initiatives themselves.

**Figure 8.2** One of the most expensive buildings in Denmark

The plans for the new stadium were politically helped by the fact that there were Social Democrats both in the leadership of Københavns Idrætspark and in the town hall. In a matter of three months, from March until June 1988, it was decided what was going to be built, where it was going to be placed, and, to a certain extent, what it was going to look like. During those three months, no thorough investigations of the effects that such a stadium would have on the surrounding area were made. What ended up becoming the most expensive building in Denmark so far, did not come into existence as the result of any kind of architectural competition (see Figure 8.2). The only such competition had been in connection with Stadion Danmark.

The stadium which was accepted, for which the local plan was approved, was never actually built. But Parken, which looked similar and which also fulfilled the local plan, was. The only real reason for choosing Parken and not another project was economic. Parken was the only one of all the planned stadiums which could be financed.

The protests which were submitted against the projects were never taken into account in any real terms. Opponents came up with objective technical arguments but they were ignored, or the discussion was structured so as to diffuse the argument. This was done by transforming the technical objective argument into a political one based on an individual point of view.

If a political majority feels very strongly for a case such as the Parken project, it can get the decision through the legal system very quickly within the frame of the law. If the finances are in place, the goal can be reached.

In this case, the decision to build one of Denmark's most expensive buildings was made in less than three months. This can not be called a thorough way of making decisions. It took eighteen months to find the money – and that was for a different stadium. The economic facts decided the structure of the building. The decision was popular when it was first made, but later it became a controversial issue. None of the many protests – from the public hearing alone there were forty-one – was taken into account.

## Perspectives

All in all, without judging the architecture, the situation or the effect that Parken would have on its surroundings, the following facts are clear: that the decision was made in a hurry; that it was not part of an overall plan for Østerbro and Copenhagen; that all protests against the views of the political majority were only a nuisance; that the citizens and politicians of Copenhagen had no influence on the way the building looked. So how can a thorough and democratic – and not simply a legal – procedure be ensured next time? It will always be difficult, especially when the subject is extremely popular, when it attracts regular media attention and, in its final phase, when it coincides with an election campaign.

First, it could be made obligatory that a huge building must be subject to an architectural competition, thus ensuring there would be a choice and the chance to formulate precise demands (apart from those pertaining to the plan for the local area) in the conditions set for such a competition. Second, it could be made obligatory that the effects of such a building on the physical and the mental environment were made the subject of a far more thorough investigation. This must take more time than the three months (or less) that the decision over Parken took especially when it is recognised that once the building has been built, it may stand for a hundred years. Requirements for investigations when big buildings are planned have been questioned recently, but they can still hardly be called thorough.

Third, the overall planning could be much stricter and more specific. Which surroundings and contexts do we want for our preserved areas, our parks, housing areas and buildings? What will happen to our town if we are too often concerned with a narrow local plan and not with the town as a whole? These questions will be very important in the years to come, when there will be developments in the harbour area of Copenhagen. Will that also be a step-by-step development, or will we have an overall plan?

171

# Notes

1. 'Idræt' is an old Nordic word. Nowadays it is used synonymously with sport. 'Park' in this connection means 'stadium'. Normally 'park' means 'park'.
2. 'Stadion Danmark' means 'Stadium Denmark'.
3. 'Dansk Boldspil-Union' (in short 'DBU') means 'Danish Football-Association'. In 1993 the association had 260,000 members. It is by far the biggest member of 'Danmarks Idræts-Forbund' ('Denmark's Sports-Federation') which has 1.5 million members.
4. The institution, 'Københavns Idrætspark' ('Copenhagen Sportspark') in 1993 changed its name to 'Københavns Idrætsanlæg' ('Copenhagen Sportsgrounds'). However, the purpose of the organization is the same.
5. Chairman Carl Nielsen on the representative meeting, 7 March 1987.
6. Danish krone. In 1992 when the building of the stadium was finished Dkr. 10 was worth about £1 or $US 1.5.
7. 'Danske Mejeriers Fællesorganisation'. An organization which takes care of the interests of the Danish dairies.
8. FIFA is the international football organization. Every country has to be a member if it wants to play international football.
9. See note 5.
10. Representative meeting of DBU, 5 May 1988.
11. 'Handelsbanken' was one of the biggest Danish banks. It was later amalgamated with two other banks and is now called 'Den Danske Bank' ('The Danish Bank').
12. On 18 March 1988 DBU was set free from its obligations to the project in Brøndby, and was allowed to negotiate with Københavns Idrætspark. This was made known in a letter from the limited company behind the Stadion Danmark project:
    Stadion Danmark's finest task is to contribute to the building of a modern stadium for the international matches of DBU. Regarding the opinion which has been expressed lately, it is our understanding that it is appropriate that DBU starts negotiations with Københavns Idrætspark to estimate the implementation of the new project (i.e. the new Idrætsparken).
13. *Dansk Boldsport*, 2 (1988), p.34 (official periodical of DBU).
14. In the hearing period there were a lot of articles and letters to the editors of the two local papers. But the big national papers also often mentioned the project. During the hearing period at least three new stadiums were suggested instead of the new Idrætsparken. One of these, a so-called 'Multistadion', received a lot of public attention (*BT*, 2–14 September 1988).
15. *Berlingske Tidende*, 9 August 1989.
16. *Politiken*, 7 February 1990.
17. 14 February 1990.
18. When a new building is going to be constructed, local planning suggestions are made by the municipal officers in the town hall. They estimate the consequences on district and environmental planning

172

(traffic, etc.) and they make statements relating to the legislation for city-planning. After that, the local plan is presented to the politicians in the town hall, examined, debated and sent to a public hearing.

19. 'BRs forhandlinger' (the uncensored negotiations from city-hall meetings) (1988), pp.710 and 755.
20. Ibid., p.755.
21. 'BRs forhandlinger' (1989), p.1131.
22. Ibid., pp.244–5 and 649.
23. 'Tenants' association of Olufsvej'.
24. This technique is found and described by Bent Flyvbjerg, *Rationalitet og Magt* (Copenhagen 1991), in which he analyses the city-planning in Aalborg, the fourth biggest town in Denmark.
25. The municipal officers refer to a recommendation from the chief mayor dated 24 May 1988.
26. Søren Nagbøl, 'Enlivening and Deadening Shadows', *International Review for the Sociology of Sport*, Vol. 28, 2 (1993), pp.265–79.
27. Not only ordinary opponents, such as the public and the opposition in the town-hall, objected to the project, but also several institutions, e.g. Ministry of Ecclesiastical Affairs, The Royal Building Control Department, Denmark's Nature Conservation Association, The Academy of the Fine Arts, to mention but a few.
28. 'BRs forhandlinger' (1989), p.936.
29. Ibid., p.935.

# 9

# Toronto's SkyDome: The World's Greatest Entertainment Centre

*Bruce Kidd*

Toronto, Canada's largest city, with a metropolitan population of more than four million, stretches along the north shore of Lake Ontario.[1] The major focal point of public life is City Hall and the large open-air plaza on which it stands, Nathan Phillips Square. Public debates on the issues of the day in the council chambers are sometimes well attended, while thousands of Torontonians greet the New Year and celebrate other holidays in the Square. It is space for both state-sanctioned and popular, even oppositional initiatives: multi-cultural festivals and political assertions, ranging from the annual International Women's Day rally to anti-war and environmental demonstrations, are just as likely to be found on a visit as Remembrance Day services, and educational, health and welfare campaign kick-offs. A pool-sized fountain is a favourite spot for impromptu lunch-hour picnics during warmer weather and late-night skates during the winter. In a tradition which dates from the nineteenth century, athletes who have been successful in major competitions like the Olympics are honoured there, usually after a triumphal parade north from the waterfront, about a kilometre away.

But recently, that sporting tradition has been reversed and City Hall overshadowed by a new venue, the SkyDome. After the Toronto Blue Jays won the Major League Baseball (MLB) championship (the World Series) in October 1992 – and again in 1993 – the team paraded south, completely bypassing City Hall, to be honoured in SkyDome, the provincially owned stadium where they play. Certainly, the covered stadium offered fans and city boosters more comfortable accommodation than the Square, including ready access to well-designed washrooms, an important consideration during the blustery, cold winds of October. It afforded everyone a clear sightline, and enabled spectators to see the players, speech-makers, as well as themselves in close-up on the stadium's gigantic (10 x 35 metre) Jumbotron screen. But locating public celebration within an enclosed stadium subtly changes the dynamic of power relations in the life of the city. Nathan Phillips Square invites people to participate as citizens on a roughly equal footing (see Figure 9.1). It can be

**Figure 9.1**  Nathan Phillips Square permits undifferentiated, fluid mingling

entered by anyone at any point and time, and permits undifferentiated, fluid, serendipitous mingling. By comparison, both access to and location within SkyDome are controlled. When events are not taking place, visitors pay $C 8 for a guided tour. When the stadium is in operation, the frequent audience close-ups on the Jumbotron encourage the crowd to contribute to its own surveillance.[2] The dedication of the facility to male sports, the seating arrangements, which prominently elevate two tiers of private boxholders and give 'club' seatholders privileged access to restaurants, and the ever-present commercial messages testifying to the power and status of national and transnational corporations, sustain and extend social hierarchy. Even though no admission was charged during the Jays' victory ceremonies, the concessionaires did booming business. SkyDome invites people to participate as consumers. To be sure, it affords room for alternative readings, even alternative forms of expression. But if the stadium has become the cathedral of the late twentieth century, as Michael Novak suggests,[3] it is no less heavily ideological nor patriarchal.

This chapter will examine the development of Toronto's SkyDome, the political economy which led the Ontario government to assume responsibility for its construction and operation, and the role which it plays in the life of Toronto and region. I will also share the thinking which went into the public authority's decision in 1991, just two years after it was opened, to sell SkyDome to the private sector. My perspective is that of an outsider on the inside. I spent almost twenty years in active opposition to the construction of a covered stadium in Toronto using public funds. I felt then, as I do now, that tax dollars ought first be spent on extending opportunities for active physical activity and important social needs like child care, education, housing, and health. Wealthy corporations have no need for subsidization.[4] After the fight was lost, with a change in provincial government in 1990, I was appointed to the stadium board. 'Sometimes poachers make the best gamekeepers', Ontario Treasurer Floyd Laughren explained at the time.

## From Private to Public Entrepreneurship

The modern North American professional sports team has retained very little organic connection to the cities it claims to represent.[5] Players no longer develop in local clubs and leagues, but are purchased and traded in a globalized labour market. Only one of the victorious Blue Jays learned his baseball in Toronto, and only a handful have done so in the club's seventeen-year history. The rest are well-paid migrant labourers: they come from all over North America, principally the United States and the Spanish-speaking Caribbean, and return at the end of each season. In many respects, the sports franchise is not unlike its counterparts in the fast food or clothing industries; it sells nationally and internationally known brands in a protected market. If the owners deem location inadequate for its expectations of profit, they simply move to another city, no matter how much they disappoint the fans in their former area of operation. Despite these familiar practices, the North American sports franchise has been remarkably successful in mystifying its 'bottom line' economics and inventing or refashioning 'communities' of team identification. Owners have exploited team loyalties to win concessions from local governments that would never be granted to capitalists in other ventures. In fact, in the period since World War II, as cities have become more vulnerable to the global mobility of capital, including sports franchises, the degree of public subsidization has increased. The most obvious form of subsidization has been the provision of facilities.[6] The practice began in earnest in 1956 when Walter O'Malley, the owner of the Brooklyn Dodgers MLB franchise, persuaded the city of Los Angeles to give him 315 acres of land intended for low-cost housing and other benefits to move his team across the continent.[7] Virtually every single North American sports facility built since has either been constructed or heavily subsidized by a public body. James Quirk and Rodney Fort estimate that the annual stadium subsidy effect in the United States is $US 500 million.[8]

**Table 9.1** From private to public ownership: commercial sports facility development in Toronto

| Facility | Opened | Major tenant | Ownership |
|----------|--------|--------------|-----------|
| Sunlight Stadium | 1890 | Prof. baseball | Private |
| Island Stadium | 1907 | Prof. baseball | Private |
| Arena Gardens | 1912 | Amateur hockey | Private |
| Maple Leaf Stadium | 1926 | Prof. baseball | Private; but reverted to public authority when unable to pay taxes |
| Maple Leaf Gardens | 1931 | Prof. hockey | Private |
| Exhibition Stadium | 1949 | Amateur sports | Public; renovated for professional baseball and football in 1975 |
| SkyDome | 1989 | Prof. sports | Public authority; in partnership with private consortium; sold to consortium in 1994 |

These advantages, and the spatial arrangements which they have effected, have not been won without vigorous politics. In Toronto, the construction of SkyDome by a public authority represented the reversal of a long-standing expectation that spectator sports facilities – even those intended for amateur sports – be built by entrepreneurs or autonomous bodies like the University of Toronto. As Table 9.1 illustrates, the local state only assumed responsibility for the provision of commercial sports facilities, first during the depression when the Toronto Harbour Commission assumed control of Maple Leaf Stadium (where the International Baseball League franchise played) in lieu of unpaid taxes, and then in 1958 when the Toronto Argonauts (Canadian-rules) Football Club moved from the University of Toronto's Varsity Stadium to the new facility on the Canadian National Exhibition grounds. The idea of a completely covered stadium, initially proposed as part of unsuccessful Toronto bids for the 1960 and 1976 Olympics, was stalled for many years. In 1969, when a suburban alderman sought to develop a dome, he found neither public nor private appetite for the huge investment required. A few years later, when Paul Godfrey, the powerful Chairman of Metropolitan Toronto, the regional government, tested the waters for a publicly-financed dome to attract Major League Baseball, he aroused a vocal opposition of ratepayers and amateur sports groups. While the sports columnists and business interests pleaded for a better facility, Godfrey was forced to settle for a renovated Exhibition Stadium. To assuage amateur sports enthusiasts displaced by the renovated field configuration, Metro was persuaded to construct a new track and field facility. It took the domed-stadium faction another decade of energetic trying, and the direct intervention of an even more powerful politician, Ontario Premier William Davis, to create the SkyDome.

It was a significantly different situation in 1985 when Davis announced the establishment of the Stadium Corporation of Ontario (Stadco), the provincial crown corporation which constructed and managed SkyDome until the sale. The citizens' movement was in decline, with leading opponents of mega-projects out of office, in part because the success of its earlier efforts to preserve inner-city neighbourhoods took the anger out of its middle-class base. With the 1976 Montreal Olympics a fading memory, the amateur sports groups enjoyed far less political appeal. Widespread criticism of professional sport which accompanied the youth radicalization of the previous decade had subsided, and the growing fitness movement was increasingly drawn into the web of corporate discourse.[9] Ironically, liberal feminist campaigns to break down the last bastions of male-exclusive sports with well-publicized court challenges (such as Justine Blainey's successful suit against the Ontario Hockey Association) aroused the curiosity of women who had once scorned sports.

While the critical currents which had buoyed up the opposition to the earlier stadium proposals ebbed, the neo-conservative tide was rolling in. With the waning of the Fordist economy, as David Harvey observes, cities have been transformed from centres of production to focal points of consumption organized around an immense 'accumulation of spectacles'.[10] Within this context, the Toronto élites aspired to achieve a 'world class city' with cultural activities and special events similar to those found in other metropolitan centres. These desires were fed by the tremendous expansion of American commercial culture into Canada, in the context of the global concentration of the communications industries.[11] In particular, the spectacular growth of televised sports gave leagues like Major League Baseball new currency. Both public and private Canadian media are interlinked with the sports industry[12] and the stadium proposals enjoyed their full support. With three daily newspapers, seven independent television stations and several mass circulation weeklies, Toronto is a highly competitive market, but on this issue, all sportswriters and editorialists were of one voice. Uncritically equating the desires of their own industry with the needs of the 'community', they endlessly decried the deficiencies of the renovated Exhibition Stadium, where the Jays played, as a public embarrassment while touting the benefits of tourism for the region as a whole. Toronto's and Canada's honour and economy, they argued, required the dome.

**Table 9.2** The campaign for a covered stadium in Toronto, 1954–1984

| Date | Advocate | Proposed ownership | Outcome |
| --- | --- | --- | --- |
| 1954 | Local politician | Public; planned as major stadium for 1960 Olympics | Unsuccessful; Rome got the Games |
| 1967 | Regional government | Public; planned as major stadium for 1976 Olympics | Unsuccessful; Montreal got the Games |
| 1969 | Local politician | Private | Unsuccessful; private capital said it wasn't profitable |
| 1971 | Regional politician | Public | Unsuccessful; citizen's coalition defeated it; Exhibition Stadium renovated as alternative |
| 1984 | Provincial politician | Public/private partnership | Successful |

Unlike the municipal politicians who had to steer their proposals through unruly 'weak-mayor' councils which could vote any way at any time, William Davis enjoyed the relatively unchallenged power of majority government with an effective parliamentary whip. In Canada, provinces have the constitutional power to impose their will upon municipalities. Nevertheless, Davis was hesitant to subsidize a domed stadium until he had obtained the promise of private capital contributions. His principal backer was Trevor Eyton, a corporate lawyer whose strategy of aggressive leveraged take-overs had made Brascan, the holding company of which he was chief executive, one of Canada's most powerful conglomerates.[13] Brascan held the controlling interest in Labatt's, the beer and food company which owns the Blue Jays, as well as The Sports Network, the cable network which telecasts many of the team's games. Eyton and the London, Ontario based Labatt's had close ties with Davis's Conservative Party.[14] Eyton recruited fourteen companies, each of which agreed to contribute $C5 million towards the costs of construction, in exchange for a box, parking privileges, first supplier rights, and first refusal rights to advertising.[15] Along with the provincial contribution of $C30 million from lottery funds, and another $C30 million from the Municipality of Metropolitan Toronto, the offer of the Eyton group, Dome Stadium Inc. (DCI), meant that $C130 million was

**Table 9.3**    'The Best Laid Plans' (all amounts in $C millions)

| | Cost | Government | DCI | Boxes | Debt |
|---|---|---|---|---|---|
| Original plan (January 1985) | 150 | 60 | 70 | | 20 |
| Construction* | 580 | 60 | 150 | 60 | 310 |

Annual cash profit/losses (not including depreciation)

| | | | |
|---|---|---|---|
| 1990 | (21.9) | | 321 |
| 1991 | (13.9) | | 361 |
| 1992 | (3.7) | | 374 |
| 1993 | 4.1 | | 398+ |

\* Whereas SkyDome opened on 3 June 1989, construction continued well into 1990.

+ As of 31 December 1993. Includes $C 30 million in litigation settlements.

available to build the stadium. With that much in hand, Davis confidently predicted that the stadium would not burden the taxpayers.[16]

Eyton also convinced Davis to depart from the widespread practice of locating new stadiums in the suburbs. The committee Davis appointed to choose a site recommended a little-used federal airport in North York, with a subway and an expressway nearby, an idea which was enthusiastically supported by suburban boosters and entrepreneurs. Instead, Davis chose the abandoned railway shunting-yards, not far from the downtown commercial core. There, the stadium could serve multiple purposes. The railway lands were close to an expressway, subway and commuter systems, and most important, adjacent to a provincially owned convention centre. Like the locations of all earlier baseball stadiums, the site was near the lake (see Figures 9.2 and 9.3).

The previous decade of neighbourhood politics had made inner-city Toronto attractive for investment in entertainment and tourism. Upscale condominiums, shopping, restaurants, and theatres, along with their more artistically adventurous low-rent competitors, had sprung up around several new publicly developed residential areas. Davis himself had contributed significantly to this process by stopping an unnecessary expressway planned to slice through the inner city. One of the most important new neighbourhoods was Harbourfront, the renovated docklands just south of the railway lands. Eyton, whose holdings included a trust company and who was a major developer, articulated the dream,

**Figure 9.2** The Toronto downtown and waterfront; the site of the SkyDome was occupied by railway land to the right of the photograph, taken in the late 1950s. Note the Maple Leaf Stadium, bottom left

for many of his class, of a major commercial development on the railway lands, with the domed stadium among its important amenities. It represented a new phase in the city's long history of waterfront redevelopment.[17] The federal government's railway company, Canadian National, came to share the dream and agreed to contribute the land.[18]

### 'The World's Greatest Entertainment Centre'

Designed by local architect Rod Robbie, SkyDome was constructed between 1986 and 1989.[19] The Blue Jays and Argonauts moved in as soon as it was ready. The final design included a hotel with seventy rooms overlooking the field, seven restaurants and bars, a private fitness club, and five hundred underground parking spaces. There is capacity for fifty thousand spectators for baseball, fifty-three for football and sixty-seven for rock concerts. The hotel and restaurants had the effect of significantly reducing the number of inexpensive 'bleacher' seats which traditionally have been wrapped around the outfield. Despite the pleas of Olympic leaders and the Ontario Ministry of Tourism and Recreation, proposals for an aquatics centre and a field configuration which would allow for Olympic track and field were not considered. SkyDome claims

**Figure 9.3**  The SkyDome and the CN tower

the world's first fully retractable roof, which can open and close in fifteen minutes; the remarkable Jumbotron, the largest video display board in the world; a 'Skytent', a large acoustical curtain which creates a more 'intimate' space for ten to twenty thousand spectators; and $C4 million of sculptures, decorative banners, and water fountains (see Figures 9.4 and 9.5).

Astute management and the Jays' success have turned many of the original sceptics and critics, including this one, into admirers. Though the symmetrical, synthetically-carpeted field has little of the idiosyncratic,

**Table 9.4** The burden of the debt on SkyDome finances

|  | 1990 | 1991 | 1992 | 1993 |
|---|---|---|---|---|
| *Events* | | | | |
| Number | 165 | 187 | 237 | 256 |
| Attendance | 5.2m | 5.5m | 5.9m | 5.7m |
| *Financial results (in $C millions)* | | | | |
| Revenue | 44.2 | 45.6 | 47.9 | 47.3 |
| Expenses | 16.7 | 15.7 | 13.9 | 12.3 |
| Operating surplus | 27.5 | 29.8 | 34.0 | 35.0 |
| *Less* | | | | |
| Interest | 39.2 | 34.0 | 27.0 | 20.7 |
| Taxes | 10.2 | 9.7 | 10.7 | 10.3 |
| *Annual cash* | | | | |
| Surplus (losses) | (14.0) | (21.9) | (13.9) | 4.1 |
| *Less* | | | | |
| Depreciation | 17.3 | 17.9 | 18.0 | 18.3 |
| Net loss | (39.2) | (31.8) | (21.7) | (14.2) |

pastoral charm prized by baseball traditionalists,[20] entrances, seats, concourses and washrooms[21] are well designed, and the staff are courteous and supportive. For many, SkyDome has become the preferred venue not only for sports, but for musical entertainment, circuses, family and trade shows. The number of event days has been increased from 165 in 1990, the first full year of operation, to 256 in 1993. Almost six million admissions have been paid each year; more than one third of patrons come from outside Metropolitan Toronto; the Jays are sold out for virtually every game. Despite the limited parking under the stadium, traffic congestion before and after games has not proved to be a problem, because a majority of patrons uses public transport, or cycle or walk to and from events. The location has proved a great boon to the restaurants and bars in the area, and along with several theatres and the city's premier concert hall has contributed to a lively year-round entertainment district. During 1993, the stadium's popularity was further enhanced by several 'free' events, when hockey and baseball fans were invited to watch their teams play out-of-town play-off games on the Jumbotron screen. (These are nevertheless profitable occasions: Stadco receives 38% of concessionaires' gross revenues.) Audience surveys indicate a high degree of satisfaction. National Access Awareness, an advocacy group for persons

**Figure 9.4** The SkyDome hosting the Toronto Blue Jays baseball team; note the retractable roof and the flexible seating arrangements

**Figure 9.5** The 'Jumbotron' at work as the SkyDome awaits the Toronto Argonauts football team

with disabilities, has judged SkyDome the 'most barrier free' facility in Canada. The Ontario Liquor Control Board has honoured it for a 'commendably low incidence of alcohol-related incidents'. With these accomplishments, the industry has added its own praise: for each of the last four years, the US *Performance Magazine* has declared it the 'Stadium of the Year'. SkyDome presents itself as much more than a sports facility; it unabashedly calls itself 'the World's Greatest Entertainment Centre'.

## Dealing with the Debt

Despite its unprecedented success, SkyDome had grave financial problems, stemming from construction overruns of more than $C 300 million. Whether Davis, his colleagues and advisors ever believed the original estimates is a moot point, because the Conservatives were out of office when construction actually began, defeated by David Peterson's Liberals. (Davis himself retired shortly before his party's collapse; he was appointed to the Stadco board.) The Peterson Government showed little interest in controlling costs, perhaps believing, during the frenzied spending of the mid-1980s, that economic growth would continue unabated. In such an environment, the 'fast track' design process, the last-minute addition of the hotel, restaurants and the fitness club, the decision to use 'top-of-the-line' materials and furnishings, and the undertaking to open on schedule, no matter how much overtime was necessary, contributed to rapidly escalating costs. When it became clear that the initial investment was insufficient, Eyton recruited another sixteen firms with another $C 80 million. The advance leasing of private boxes and 'club' seats raised another $C 60 million.[22] But that was still not enough. When the stadium opened on 3 June 1989, the total cost had soared to $C 562.8 million, the overrun to almost $C 300 million. Putting the finishing touches on construction continued well into the following year, pushing the final cost to $C 580 million (see Table 9.3). In addition, SkyDome faced an estimated $C 70 million in legal claims and costs in construction-related disputes. As these were settled (eventually for about $C 30 million), the amounts were added to the tab. Such an enormous debt meant that, despite record revenues and a tight rein on operating expenses, which combined to produce sizable annual operating surpluses, interest charges, depreciation and taxes put the annual totals into the red. In 1993, for example, there was an operating surplus of $C 35 million, but interest, depreciation and taxes turned that into a loss of $C 14 million (see Table 9.4). In the first four full years of operation, the 'Stadium of the Year' lost $C 107 million.[23] On 31 December 1993, the debt stood at $C 398 million.

When Stadco and DCI contemplated the stadium in operation, they envisioned a public-private partnership which would manage it along business lines. The draft agreement gave the DCI member corporations the lion's share of any profits, but required both the Province and the DCI members to contribute to any losses, with a formula for loss of equity and privileges if any of them refused to pay. The partnership was to go into effect on the day the stadium opened. But DCI gave themselves an escape clause: if the debt rose above $C 165 million, they could pull out of the partnership with Stadco. When it turned out to be more than twice that amount, DCI refused to sign, leaving the crown corporation solely responsible for the mounting debt, while they enjoyed their boxes and first supplier monopolies. The chief beneficiaries of the ensuing subsidies were the Blue Jays. Originally purchased for $C 7 million in 1977, the Jays are now worth an estimated $C 180 million, and *Financial World* recently ranked it as the third most valuable sports franchise in North America, behind the Dallas Cowboys of the National Football League and MLB's New York Yankees. Other partners – and the capitalist class as a whole – gain advertising and legitimation benefits. Boxholders gain a fashionable place to do their business with clients. They are doubly subsidized, because they can also deduct 50% of their costs as a business expense.[24]

The Peterson Government was unexpectedly defeated at the polls in September 1990 by the social democratic New Democratic Party (NDP) led by Bob Rae. One of the first riddles the new government had to solve was Stadco's runaway debt. With interest rates at 14%, the debt charges for that year were $C 39 million. Despite record attendance for the Jays and other events, which after expenses brought SkyDome $C 27.5 million, interest, depreciation and taxes produced a loss for the year of $C 39.2 million. With the capitalization of these annual losses, Stadco faced the frightening prospect of a spiral of debt, a difficult burden for any government, but an extremely onerous one at a time of deepening recession. It was at this time that I was appointed to the Stadco board, along with Bob White, a successful labour leader and negotiator. (White was President of the Canadian Auto Workers; he now heads the Canadian Labour Congress.) Ontario Treasurer Laughren also appointed a five-man negotiation committee (chaired by White, and including me, two other members of the board, businessmen Paul Morton and Ron Fournier, and SkyDome President Richard Peddie) to meet with DCI to find a solution.

Essentially, we had three options: (1) retain and operate SkyDome as a public corporation; (2) force the partnership with DCI; or (3) sell it outright. Those who felt SkyDome to be an unquestioned benefit advised us to get the Province to pay off the debt with a lump sum and keep the stadium, arguing that the NDP would earn political credit for the operating surpluses which could be expected in good years. But that option was simply not acceptable to the Government or to us. It would have meant spending funds that it hoped to invest in social programmes and capitulating to the socialization of risk and the privatization of profit. Even if the Treasurer had paid off Stadco's debt, he would have had to borrow to do so, so the Provincial obligations would not have been reduced. We did explore the option of forcing the partnership, but received legal advice that this would almost certainly not be feasible without first bringing the debt down to below the $C 165 million ceiling, which would have required $C 203 million. Even then, SkyDome would have been encumbered with a debt which the expected operating revenues could not service, let alone discharge. So we tried for a sale, which had the advantages of generating some private funds to reduce the Treasurer's problems, and stopping the haemorrhaging once and for all.

After protracted negotiations with DCI and consideration of bids from other entrepreneurs, in November 1991 we reached an agreement to sell SkyDome to Eyton and a smaller grouping of corporations (which became Stadium Acquisitions Inc or SAI)[25] and recommended this to the Treasurer. Because of the complex multi-party legal structure which underlay the stadium, more than two years of further negotiations were needed to implement the sale.[26] The deal was finally closed in March 1994.[27] Under its terms, the Province received a $C 151 in cash, and various provisions to protect it against a quick flip. The sale enabled the Province to walk away from SkyDome at a cost to taxpayers of approximately $C 263 million (not including the original $C 60 million in public contributions). Since the Blue Jays are closely tied to the purchasers, it will have the added benefit of providing some disincentive against franchise flight if the team becomes less profitable in the future. To the best of my knowledge, it is the only 'privatization' of a money-losing stadium and its financial risks in North America.

## The Dilemma of Public Ownership

As a 'Schedule II' provincial corporation, SkyDome was planned and managed from the beginning as a revenue-maximizing 'business'. While board members and senior management were sensitive to public issues and trends, nothing was allowed to interfere with the 'bottom line'. Although it started to accommodate high school, college and community events and to fund raise for charities, Stadco had no policy to attract and support non-profit groups; on the contrary, it gave privileges to its most frequent corporate customers, such as the Blue Jays, and turned away community organizations with risky ventures. The senior management was paid according to industry rather than civil service standards. In the first heady days of the new NDP Government and my appointment to the Stadco board, some friends and I wondered about whether and how we could subvert this logic, to transform the 'corporate culture factory' into the 'people's pleasure palace'. We dreamed about booking events by Toronto artists and athletes, especially women's sports teams; using the Jumbotron to celebrate Ontario amateur athletes and to provide a public outlet for fans' voices; allowing fans to bring in their own food (so that they would be not held captive by the DCI monopolists); developing a more democratic allocation of tickets, and giving community groups access to SkyDome's broad concourses. But our mandate of reducing the debt forced me to bite my tongue lest Stadco scare away the corporations which provide the bulk of its revenue, and risk incurring even heavier losses.

The dilemma confounding any populist strategy is that Stadco's revenues were highly dependent upon the activities of the corporations and the sustained satisfaction of the élite groups which it subsidized. Rental and concession income (about 32% of revenue) depended upon the ability of the Jays, TSN, Labatts, McDonalds, Bitoves, Coca Cola and the other partners to produce and sell their spectacles and associated products. Advertising on the Jumbotron and elsewhere within the stadium (another 20% of revenue) depended on the presence of an affluent audience with the demographics that advertisers sought to reach. Attracting and retaining an affluent audience was crucial for still another reason: the 'club' seatholders and corporate boxholders contributed a whopping 40% of revenue through their seat and box rentals. (The remaining 8% of revenue came from the hotel, the fitness club, and parking.) In short, any effort to check the activities of the corporations and reduce the privileges of the élites would have seriously jeopardized revenue flows.

It was not just the debt that led some of us to pursue the 'privatization' option. The fundamental logic of the stadium requires the economic and ideological reproduction of the national and transnational corporations, while enhancing the consumption of the élites who work within and with them. Although we were not in a position to overturn this logic, we did not wish to legitimate it any further through the continued ownership of a social democratic government. A sale would not only put the stadium into the hands of those with the best chance of making it a success; it would clarify the questions of benefit and control. As engaging as it may be for many, SkyDome markets a carefully controlled, masculinist, consumerist culture, with a highly artificial sense of belonging and place. The ads, the fillers, the electronic cheerleading and the sound effects are similar, if not identical, to what one sees and hears in other stadiums and arenas across the continent. The result is not only the 'corporate takeover of public expression', as Herbert Schiller has argued in another context,[28] but the silencing of indigenous voices. Defenders of the subsidy claim that SkyDome is not unlike the publicly-owned and operated Art Gallery of Ontario, Roy Thomson (Concert) Hall and the St Lawrence Centre (for the Performing Arts). Certainly, SkyDome provides a stage for enormously popular cultural forms. But there is a key difference between it and these other institutions: despite their own fascination for 'world-class', touring exhibits and performers, they actively contribute to the identification and nurturing of Toronto and Ontario artists and provide for the exhibition and performance of their work, much of which explores the particularity of the experiences of those who live here. While SkyDome engages the best of the continental name-brand entertainments, it largely ignores – and thereby marginalizes – the development of the athletes and artists of Ontario.

In gender terms, 'what the province has done is kick in $C 300 million exclusively for men's pro sport', Ann Peel of the (Toronto) Women's Sport Network has argued. The WSN is demanding that an equal amount be spent on women's sport.[29] The uncritical reproduction and celebration of male sports also contributes to what sociologist George Gerbner calls the 'symbolic annihilation' of women.[30] I am a devoted Jays fan myself. But I cannot ignore that the uninterrupted display of male prowess ideologically reinforces the power and privilege of men, and the corresponding marginalization of women, while leaving the gendered nature of sports unexamined. Women as well as men are capable of difficult, dramatic, and pleasing feats of grace, agility, strength, and teamwork, but we are encouraged to forget this in SkyDome. I think of it as the 'men's cultural centre'.[31] Perhaps it is utopian to dream of alternatives, but I still believe that public investments should contribute to a more equitable, democratic, and interesting public culture.

Of course, SkyDome enthusiasts point to economic benefits. The Metropolitan Toronto Convention and Visitors' Association estimates that the stadium (including the hotel) generates $C 352 million in annual direct spending, including $C 70 million in provincial taxes – considerably more than the annual deficit.[32] But as Robert Baade has argued in this volume (see Chapter 13), such estimates are methodologically flawed. They ignore any decline in entertainment spending elsewhere in the region and discount the 'leakage' experienced when beneficiaries spend their earnings outside the local economy. Baade's method has been to examine overall economic growth rates before and after the stadium is constructed. In particular, he seeks to determine the extent to which public stadium investments generate (a) 'export' earnings (expenditures by individuals and businesses from outside the region and (b) import substitution (a reduction in entertainment purchases outside the region). He also considers their opportunity cost (the likely benefits from alternative investments). After investigating the experience of forty-seven American cities, he concluded that 'public funding of professional sports, particularly as it relates to stadiums, is not a sound civic economic investment. If opportunity costs are included, … [it] may well exhibit negative returns' by encouraging low-wage industries.

In a study of seven small municipalities in the region of Dallas-Fort Worth, Texas, Mark Rosentraub found that the cities which had invested in stadiums experienced a substantial increase in debt without a commensurate increase in revenue or services. This result led him to conclude:

> It almost appears that the middle and lower classes are being asked, through their elected officials and governments, to reduce the risks of investment for individuals and corporations whose income and wealth are but dreams for the millions who pay their local property taxes … With the returns on investments in professional sports as substantial as they are, it is time the élites involved took the capitalist risks they are so fond of recommending for others and stopped using the collective financial strength of cities to minimize their risks.[33]

In Fort Wayne, Indiana, a decision *not* to invest in a minor-league stadium seems to have spurred economic growth.[34] The evidence seems conclusive that subsidizing the sports industry is not in the public interest.

## The Need for Alternatives

Yet the entrepreneurs' appetite for public subsidy shows no sign of abating. Such is the celebrity of professional sport that there are still politicians and boosters eager to feed it. At the time of writing, four National Hockey League franchise ownerships are demanding further concessions from the Canadian cities in whose arenas they play, and the local and provincial political leaderships are scrambling to satisfy them. In Winnipeg, the owners want a $C 200 million new arena, and they threaten to take the team elsewhere if not satisfied.[35] The National Basketball Association has just wrung tax concessions from the provinces of Ontario and British Columbia as a condition for locating franchises in their principal cities, Toronto and Vancouver.[36] As Alan Ingham has written, 'when capital confronts community, it is capital that wins the day'.[37] Obviously, new strategies are necessary.

For a municipality, however, there are very few options. To the extent that sports teams contribute to 'a sense of continuity and unity in a discontinuous and increasingly atomized society'[38] and are valued for the identification and cultural dramas they provide, a majority of citizens may well decide that the investment in sports teams is worthwhile. But those decisions should be made by a broad, democratic process. Cities should expect equity and publicly accountable management of any subsidized franchise, and perhaps establish tourist-targeted taxes to capture some of the subsidy-induced growth. (The SkyDome's Richard Peddie suggests a surcharge on hotels, restaurants and car rentals for this purpose). On the other hand, the tremendous costs involved may well produce the discipline necessary to break the dependence upon the drug of 'world-class' culture and end the subsidies. If subsidies were simply not granted, and money-losing stadiums were demolished, it would force the sports franchise to construct its own production facility, operate on a more realistic budget or locate elsewhere. Although extremely disappointing for the dedicated fan, the loss of a sports franchise is hardly the cultural end of the world. (Saskatoon, without an NHL team, is just as interesting a city as Winnipeg, which owns shares in one.) It would probably mean that more public funds would become available for local sports and the arts.

Yet the economic unit of commercial sport is the league, not the franchise. League-wide policies, such as the presence or absence of revenue sharing, can intensify the franchise pressures upon cities, especially in the so-called 'small market' areas. Leagues will continue to play one city off against another unless co-ordinated national and continental strategies are developed and implemented. In this regard, there is a growing number of useful proposals being considered. For example, municipalities could join together to bargain collectively with the leagues for a fairer share of the monopoly created revenues.[39] National governments could regulate the leagues, all of which operate as monopolies, like other utilities,[40] or levy a special surtax on professional sports, as Ontario once did through the Ontario Athletic Commission, using the proceeds to provide grassroots opportunities for a broad range of physical activities and recreation.

Or, since state intervention goes against the reigning political orthodoxy, national governments could simply break up the monopolies, by prohibiting or regulating the franchise fee, thereby drastically reducing the barriers to entry and the ability of franchise-owners to bargain with cities. Andrew Zimbalist believes that many of the current inequities could be overcome by making sports franchises available to all those cities which wanted them.[41] Any of these strategies would have a profound effect upon the sports industry. It might well mean that profits and salaries would drop considerably. But given the revenues involved, there is more than enough for the industry to pay its full costs of production and its fair share of taxes, and still end up in the black. I have no doubt that commercial sports – and fans' pleasures – will survive.

Such joint strategies will be difficult to implement. They will require both citizens and elected officials to recover from the illusion that commercial sport uncategorically serves the broad public interest, no doubt an heroic task given the ideological power of the sports media complex. But the result could unleash a much more critical examination of the spatial and cultural needs of the city. That in itself would be worth the effort.

## Acknowledgements

I am grateful to Richard Peddie, David Garrick, James MacArthur and other members of the SkyDome staff for information, and to Phyllis Berck, Jon Caulfield, Tim Hutton, David Kidd, Jim Lemon, George Sage, David Whitson, and the participants in the 'The Stadium and the City' conference in Gothenburg, Sweden, 15–17 November 1993, for many helpful comments on earlier versions of this paper. Of course, the views expressed, and any errors or omissions are my own. I should also acknowledge my debt to the friends who contributed in so many ways to my thinking on SkyDome.

## Notes

1. M. Careless, *Toronto to 1918* (Toronto, 1984); and J. Lemon, *Toronto since 1918* (Toronto, 1985), provide comprehensive histories.
2. Ioan Davies, in a Foucaultian echo, calls SkyDome the 'entertainment arena as panopticon'. Personal communication, 2 February 1993.
3. Michael Novak, *The Joy of Sports: End Zones, Bases, Baskets, Balls and the Consecration of the American Spirit* (New York, 1976), p.126. For a useful discussion of the development of enclosed stadia, see J. Bale, 'The Spatial Development of the Modern Stadium', *International Review of the Sociology of Sport*, Vol. 28 (1993), pp.121–34. The provision of open space is not sufficient to facilitate undifferentiated mingling; for a comparison of the spatial basis for 'festival' at three Olympic Games, see J. MacAloon, 'Festival, Ritual and Television', in R. Jackson and T. McPhail (eds), *The Olympic Movement and the Mass Media* (Calgary, 1989), pp.VI–7–20.
4. Bruce Kidd, 'Bruce Kidd Turns Thumbs Down', *City Hall*, 1 (1971), pp.114–15; 'No to the Domed Stadium', Land Use Committee, City Council, City of Toronto, 23 April 1985; and 'Safeguarding the Public Interest in the Domed Stadium', Public Accounts Committee, Legislature of Ontario, 18 September 1985.
5. C. Euchner, *Playing the Field: Why Sports Teams Move and Cities Fight to Keep Them* (Baltimore, 1993); R. Gruneau and D. Whitson, *Hockey Night in Canada* (Toronto, 1993); A. G. Ingham, J. W. Howell and

T. S. Schilperoort, 'Professional Sports and Community: a Review and Exegesis', in K. Pandolf (ed.), *Exercise and Sport Science Reviews*, Vol. 15 (1989), pp.427–65; and G. Sage, 'Stealing Home: Political, Economic and Media Power and a Publicly-Funded Baseball Stadium in Denver', *Journal of Sport and Social Issues*, Vol. 17 (1992), pp.110–24.

6. Another significant form is tax subsidy, especially the owners' depreciation of players and businesses' deduction of tickets and boxes as expenses. In addition, state-supported schools, colleges, universities and national sports organizations train athletes for careers in the industry, while socializing non-athletes to become paying spectators. In the USA, the Supreme Court has exempted Major League Baseball's monopoly from anti-trust legislation, while Congress has sanctioned the National Football League's monopoly through the 1966 Football Merger Act.

7. G. Lipsitz, 'Sport Stadiums and Urban Development', *Journal of Sport and Social Issues*, Vol. 8 (1984), pp.1–17.

8. J. Quirk and R. D. Fort, *Pay Dirt: the Business of Professional Team Sports* (Princeton, 1992), p.171.

9. A. Ingham, 'From Public Issue to Personal Trouble: Well-Being and the Fiscal Crisis of the State', *Sociology of Sport Journal*, Vol. 2 (1985), pp.43–55; and P. Brodeur, 'Employee Fitness: Doctrines and Issues', in J. Harvey and H. Cantelon, *Not Just A Game: Essays in Canadian Sport Sociology* (Ottawa, 1988), pp.247–66.

10. David Harvey, 'Flexible Accumulation through Urbanization: Reflections upon "Post-Modernism" in the American City', *Antipode*, Vol. 19 (1987), p.35.

11. J. Nelson, *The Perfect Machine: TV in the Nuclear Age* (Toronto, 1987); and H. E. Hudson, 'Satellite Communications in Canada', in R. Negrine (ed.), *Satellite Broadcasting: The Politics and Implications of the New Media* (London, 1988), pp.234–48.

12. S. Jhally, 'The Spectacle of Accumulation: Material and Cultural Forces in the Evolution of the Sport-Media Complex', *Insurgent Sociologist*, Vol. 12 (1984), pp.41–61.

13. P. Best and A. Shortell, *The Brass Ring: Power and Influence in the Brascan Empire* (Toronto, 1988).

14. In 1990, Conservative Prime Minister Brian Mulroney appointed Eyton to the Federal Senate.

15. The $C 5 million gave them these rights for ten years, but they also got the right to renew them in 1999 for $C 100,000 for another 89 years.

16. H. Macaulay, W. Bremner and L. H. Schipper, *The Stadium Study Committee Report* (Toronto, 1985).

17. G. Desfor, M. Goldrick, and R. Merrens, 'A Political Economy of the Water-Frontier: Planning and Development in Toronto', *Geoform*, Vol. 20 (1989), pp.487–501.

18. In exchange for the right to transfer density from the stadium lands to its other holdings. The stadium and its grounds occupy 15 acres of the approximately 105 acres of CN lands slated for redevelopment. The

plans for redevelopment have been the subject of perhaps the most protracted political battles in the city's recent history, as CN sought to maximize the amount of commercial and institutional office space they could build, while a broad coalition of residents, labour and public interest groups wanted residential neighbourhoods. In 1986, CN won approval for a 5.1 million square feet of commercial and 5.1 million square feet of residential development. But the subsequent recession exposed millions of square feet of unrented office space, so the development has not begun. At the time of writing, CN is seeking an official plan amendment to permit 5.5 million square ft of residential, while scaling down the commercial to 4.4 million square ft.

19. Mike Filey, *Like No Other in the World: The Story of Toronto's SkyDome* (Toronto, 1989).

20. P. Bess, 'City Baseball Magic: Plain Talk and Uncommon Sense about Cities and Baseball Parks', *Minneapolis Review of Baseball* (1989), pp.1–48.

21. To reduce frustrating queues, almost twice as many toilet facilities were installed for women as for men, a feature which has contributed to rising attendance by women. In 1993, females comprised 49% of the Jay's 4.1 million patrons.

22. The DCI members were: Ainsworth Electric, BCE, Bitove, Canadian Airlines, Canadian Imperial Bank of Commerce, Canadian National, Coca-Cola, Cogan, Controlled Media, Crupi Group, Degasperis-Muzzo, Ford, HiramWælker, Imasco, Imperial Oil, McDonalds, Merrill Lynch, Nabisco, Nestle, Olympia and York, The Sports Network, Blue Jays, Toronto Sun, Trilon, George Weston and Xerox. In addition, three breweries, Labatt, Molson and Carling-O'Keefe (subsequently acquired by Molson) each contributed $C5 million. The boxes cost from $C100,000 to $C250,000 per year, depending upon location; the 'club' seats from $C2,000 to $C4,000, plus an annual subscription. Both were leased for ten years.

23. Robert Baade recounts that in 1990 he was flown into Toronto to advise SkyDome on how it could become profitable. 'All you'll need is 450 paying dates a year', he wryly noted.

24. Prior to June 1993 for provincial taxes and February 1994 for federal taxes, the deductibility was 80%. That continues to be the rate for unincorporated businesses. The Ontario Fair Tax Commission, *Fair Taxation in a Changing World* (Toronto), p.239, recommends that entertainment deduction be abolished altogether. If implemented, this proposal would have a significant dampening effect upon commercial sports.

25. The members are the Canadian Imperial Bank of Commerce, Coca-Cola, Controlled Media Corporation, Ford, TSN, and the Toronto Sun from DCI, plus a group of private pension funds, Penfold Capital.

26. The deal became an 'annuity for lawyers'; the transaction costs for both parties came to more than $C11 million.

27. M. Mittelstaedt, 'Ontario unloads Dome at a loss', *Globe and Mail*, 17 March 1994.

28.  H. Schiller, *Culture Inc.: The Corporate Takeover of Public Expression* (New York, 1989).

29.  J. Christie, 'Women's Place is in the Dome', *Globe and Mail*, 1 November 1990.

30.  George Gerbner, 'The Dynamics of Cultural Resistance', in G. Tuchman, A. K. Daniels and J. Benet (eds), *Hearth and Home: Images of Women in the Mass Media* (New York, 1978), p.44.

31.  Bruce Kidd, 'The men's cultural centre: sports and the dynamic of women's oppression/men's repression', in M. A. Messner and D. F. Sabo, *Sport, Men and the Gender Order* (Champaign, 1990), pp.31–44.

32.  'Economic impact analysis: SkyDome and activities', Metropolitan Toronto Convention and Visitors' Association (Toronto, 1993). Of course, the different levels of government will continue to enjoy tax revenue from the privately owned SkyDome.

33.  Mark Rosentraub, 'Public Investment in Private Businesses; the Professional Sports Mania', in S. Cummings (ed.), *Business Elites and Urban Development* (New York, 1988), pp.94–95.

34.  M. Rosentraub and D. Swindell, 'Fort Wayne, Indiana', in A. T. Johnson (ed.), *Minor League Baseball and Local Economic Development* (Chicago, 1993), pp.35–53.

35.  W. Houston and D. Shoalts, 'Canadian Cities Play on Thin Ice', *Globe and Mail*, 4, 5, 6 and 7 January 1994.

36.  C. McInnes, 'Big-league Basketball Coming to Toronto', *Globe and Mail*, 11 February 1994.

37.  Ingham *et al*.,'Professional Sports and Community', p.437.

38.  Ibid., p.461.

39.  Euchner, *Playing the Field*, pp.179–82.

40.  Cf C. Gray, 'Keeping the Home Team at Home', *California Law Review*, Vol. 74 (1986), pp.1329–72; and S. F. Ross, 'Monopoly Sports Leagues', *Minnesota Law Review*, Vol. 73 (1989), pp.643–761.

41.  A. Zimbalist, *Baseball and Billions* (New York, 1992), pp.167–86.

# 10

# Scales and Values in Stadium Development: A Tale of Two Ullevis

*Olof Moen*

## Introduction

The industrial city's division of time and space, work and play, is reflected in contemporary culture and leisure activities. These leisure activities differ between nations and time periods, but when a national structure is established, it tends to persist. In Sweden, at the turn of the century and during the following decades, recreational physical activity in general was strictly regulated, carried on by few, observed by the masses and forced by the urban environment to a special place, 'the stadium',which at this time began competing with other types of land use. The scale and the values behind the physical structure of the stadium, reflect the magnitude of sport as part of a city's culture.

The British historian, Stephen G. Jones, points out that central to the interpretation of working-class sport is the complex association between dominant sporting culture and working-class aspirations.[1] In a Swedish context, these aspirations have developed in the form of large, municipally-owned stadiums. Since sport in modern industrial society is interrelated with the political process, and to a large extent represents a question of public sports provision, the stadium has become the symbol of sport in the city. Through the high degree of national urbanization and the development of its large factories, Gothenburg, on the Swedish west coast, became the hotbed for sport as a cultural activity. The masses who imigrated there were far from the peace and quiet of the countryside, where young and old participated on the landscape's green carpet, the hayfield. Sport, and in particular soccer, became the substitute. It met the necessary requirements for creating a culture that produced soccer stars and gave them idol status. In Gothenburg, the industrial heart of Sweden, sport, and in particular soccer, has been synonymous with working-class aspirations in the society for the whole of the twentieth century.

## The Roots of Physical Activity

There has been a modest but lengthy tradition of physical activity at the Swedish universities in Lund and Uppsala. As early as the seventeenth century, Chancellor Axel Oxenstierna commanded that young men from the privileged nobility who studied at these universities be trained in chivalrous sports such as equestrianism, fencing and dance, in order to 'culture' them sufficiently to be presentable in foreign courts. These formal physical activities came from the social geometry that characterized the Renaissance.[2] The job of 'exercise-master' was created and 'exercise-houses' (drill-houses) were built, which can be compared with today's sports facilities. In 1663, an exercise-house was built at the University of Uppsala, where the courtyard outside functioned as a training field.[3] Of the activities included in sport today, fencing, equestrianism, gymnastic vaulting and the pommel horse, all started in the house or courtyard. As a result of organized training and practice, fencing experienced a period of glory during the 1700s when the Porath brothers were the exercise-masters, bringing fame in Europe for the Uppsala students.[4]

At the beginning of the eighteenth century a radical change in the goals of physical activity occurred in Sweden. From training in chivalric sports, the emphasis by the early 1800s had developed into physical activity with military benefits, and subsequently to exercise for the improvement of one's health.[5] The person responsible for this shift was the exercise-master at the University of Lund, Per Henrik Ling. Ling moved to the Swedish capital Stockholm in 1813, founding the Central Gymnastics Institute. Ling gymnastics were systematized during the 1860s by his son, Hjalmar Ling, through detailed written instructions describing the concept of the exercise, i.e., gymnastic drills done in groups. This became standard in the Swedish school system and gained popularity in Europe and North America as 'Swedish Gymnastics'.[6] Official school gymnastics done in the Ling method were questioned by Fritholf Holmgren, a professor of physiology, who started the Uppsala Student Body Gymnastic Club in 1874. Holmgren insisted that no boundary between gymnastics and sport was necessary and recommended free physical activity as well as apparatus gymnastics including rowing, ice-skating, javelin-throwing, cross-country skiing and ball-kicking.[7]

Viktor Balck, a Swedish officer and teacher at the Central Gymnastics Institute from 1868, was inspired by Holmgren, and from the beginning was associated with the idea of gymnastics as the basis of physical activity. Balck travelled with a group of Swedes to southern England and Belgium in 1880 where he came in contact with what was later called in Sweden, 'English sports'. Viktor Balck is commonly recognized as the 'father' of Swedish sport – on his return he organized competitions among the military, both in Stockholm and Örebro, similar to those he had encountered on his travels.[8] It was not long before the idea was mooted of having the incipient sports movement organized as a national federation. However, such a step was delayed by the antagonism which existed between Stockholm and Gothenburg and the severe conflict with Ling gymnasts. Finally, at the turn of the century, unity was achieved and a national federation of gymnastic and athletic associations was formed in 1903, with Viktor Balck as its President.

## Gothenburg and Stockholm: Ideological and Geographic Differences

The decades around the turn of the century witnessed a number of battles fought in the area of physical activity, resulting from major social changes. The basic conflict was between Swedish Ling gymnastics and the English sports. Ling gymnastics were based upon a polite and rigid pattern of movement with roots in the old Nordic poetic ideal, a romantic infatuation of 'Göticism' (the Old Norse culture), and a strong emphasis on body culture in the form of vigorous manliness associated with the ancient Norsemen.[9] So-called English sports, on the other hand, had their roots in the scientific and technological developments in Britain during the 1700s which led to the industrial revolution and urbanization.[10]

Apart from the ideological differences between the 'Lingists' and the 'English Sporters' there were geographical differences within the sports movement itself. In Gothenburg, English sports, despite being intro-duced within the upper classes, became established alongside industrialism and production. Soccer in particular became a working-class activity, openly competitive, with Gothenburg as the 'point of diffusion' to the rest of the country. Gothenburg, situated on the west coast and with traditional ties to England and Scotland, was able to assimilate cultural impulses much faster than Stockholm.[11] In sports, it was short-term workers from England and Scotland who contributed to this spread.[12] In 1892, Örgryte Sport Society introduced the modern form of 'associ-ation football' with the help of six Scottish textile workers on the team. Four years later, the team from Örgryte won the first Swedish Cham-pionship with players who were all from Gothenburg.[13]

In a national context Gothenburg is regarded as the model for sports activities. One of the reasons for the differences between Gothenburg and Stockholm lies in the personal traits which resulted from the social differences between these rival cities. In Stockholm, the leadership was mainly upper class, with public officials, university graduates and the military, Viktor Balck being the most influential. There were not many such figures in Gothenburg.[14] There, the middle class was excessively represented, with merchants and clerks recruiting athletes from the working class. These differences symbolically represent the distinction between body and soul, between worker and official, between English sport and Ling gymnastics. However, it is important to remember that the organization of sport in Gothenburg during the 1890s was opposed to Balck and the hegemony of Stockholm. The rapid success and independent attitude of the representatives of the sports movement in Gothenburg was one of the driving factors behind Viktor Balck's emancipation from the Central Gymnastics Institute and, on the national level, the organization of modern sport in Sweden.[15]

The diversification of sports in Gothenburg coincided with the social differentiation that took place in society, with the majority of new clubs in the 1890s being in working-class neighbourhoods.[16] The clubs can be seen as an attempt by the working classes to create and define an identity of their own. This was not the case in smaller cities, such as Uppsala and Borås, where the expansion of clubs was initiated by the upper classes and later spread into the working class, mainly due to the increase in leisure time caused by shorter working hours.[17] The Swedish labour party, the Social Democrats, had long been opposed to the sports movement with its bourgeois and upper-class leadership, headed by the royal family. However, Hjalmar Branting, the great leader of the labour movement, gradually brought about a change in attitude, having noted the extensive support given to sport by manual workers. One result of Branting's reformism was that, unlike the other Nordic countries, Sweden never had a strong separate workers' sports movement, even though ideas were presented, in particular in Gothenburg around 1910.[18]

## Gothenburg's Social Pattern

In Gothenburg, the formation of public space has been influenced by industrialization. Heavy industry was concentrated in Gothenburg, including Volvo, the SKF factories, and the shipyards. The city's stronghold as the sport capital is exemplified by the fact that the finals of the World Soccer Championships in 1958 and the European Soccer Championships in 1992 were both played at Nya Ullevi Stadium in Gothenburg and not in the national stadium in Stockholm. There is a strong resemblance between the relationship between Stockholm and Gothenburg and that of Madrid and Barcelona in Spain, where the industrial powerhouses attract capital city status in certain situations. Sport has generated the situation whereby Gothenburg and Barcelona, because they fielded, respectively, such mega-events as the World Championships in track and field in 1995 and the 1992 Olympic Games, project themselves as the national face of their respective countries. However, there are and have been, strong internal differences within the social life of Gothenburg as well. If the social pattern of the city during this century is studied, a clear social segregation can be identified between the owners of capital on the one hand and the workers on the other. Sports such as soccer, European handball and ice hockey, have tended to be synonymous with the working classes, while high culture in Gothenburg has always been associated with the bourgeoisie, industrialists, shipowners and merchants, who, in the form of patrons, financed the city's cultural arenas – e.g., the City Theatre, Gothenburg Art Gallery and the Opera House. Sport versus high culture represents an 'us and them' mentality as a result of the 'either/or' traditions in the social pattern which have traditionally existed.

This chapter will describe how these values and the social situation from the turn of the century have been major factors in the re-building and renovation of the Old Ullevi stadium in Gothenburg in 1992 – the city's traditional stadium which was built in 1916 but abandoned in 1958 for the modern, futuristic creation of New Ullevi – as the city's major soccer stadium. Though far from post-modern in its architectonic conception, participatory involvement in the move was based on a 'workers' ethics', and resulted in action of a post-modern kind.[19] Niels Kayser Nielsen describes the situation of the two Ullevis as a reaction to a mass consumption-oriented experience of the spectators (see Chapter 2). The modern, the new, and the practical were abandoned for an inner experience among equals in an oasis of nostalgia, in distinct contrast to the urban modernism and high-tech jungle of steel, glass and concrete at New Ullevi.

## Old Ullevi

Brickmakers' Field (Tegelbruksängen) was the name of an area of land east of Gothenburg town centre used for ice-skating during the winter, when water was pumped up from the nearby river. In 1896 a velodrome with a sloping track was built by the city's Bicycle Club, enclosed by a soccer field and a primitive running track (see Figure 10.1). The following year, the riders had total control of the area and cycling dominated among sports activities, with strong influences from the United States. Around the turn of the century, cycling was very popular in the USA with ten million bicycles and indoor professional racing which drew crowds of up to ten thousand.[20] Membership of the Gothenburg Bicycle Club was reserved for the upper classes, not just as a result of social segregation but because the cost of a bicycle was equivalent to half a year's salary of an unskilled labourer. But as time went by, the facilities

**Figure 10.1**   The first athletic ground, on the site of the Old Ullevi stadium, was built in 1896. The velodrome enclosed the soccer field. The building on the left is a tennis hall. (Source: R. Jeneryd, *Hur Idrottan kom till stan; Göteborgs idrottshistoria 1800–1950*, Gothenburg, 1981)

built mainly for cycling were seen as substandard. There was no main lawn and as the velodrome had suffered from subsidence, it could no longer be used for riding.

Örgryte Sports Society built the Valhalla sports ground in 1908 after Balders Green, the first athletic ground in Gothenburg, had been laid out in 1888.[21] Örgryte was the city's first large soccer club with a middle-class orientation and because it had its own field most athletes found their way there. There was a great need for new facilities as the two other large clubs in Gothenburg, IFK and GAIS, could only use the enclosed land at the velodrome at Brickmakers' Field. The Gothenburg Sports Association, with subdivisions in cycling, track and field, speed-skating and tennis, started a company together with the Gothenburg Soccer Union and the soccer club IFK, to build a new arena – Ulle(r)vi, as it was initially called. The shares in the company amounted to Skr. 90,000, the total cost being Skr. 160,000 with the city contributing the balance.

As the board was most interested in soccer, the new arena became a soccer stadium (see Figure 10.2). Both riders and marksmen were also promised space but when the blueprints were finished, the architect had been unable to fit them in.[22] The soccer field, however, met the

**Figure 10.2**   The Old Ullevi Stadium, 29 May 1949. The area was enclosed by a three-metre high wooden fence. (Source: B. Johansson and B. G. Nilsson, *Gamla Ullevi*, Gotheburg, 1992)

international regulations of 105 x 68 metres. The main stands accommodated six hundred seated spectators and standing room around the field gave an overall capacity of around twelve thousand. Two additional fields were used for different activities during the winter. General Viktor Balck, the most prominent man in Swedish sport, opened the arena on 17 September 1916. Old Ullevi was a traditional type of facility in the sense that it was only used for soccer, following the English pattern. Track and field facilities, which later became a standard feature of municipal stadiums in the Nordic countries, were not included.[23] The stands consisted of two long sets of steps along the sides, one with seats and one for standing. At the ends of the field there were steps to stand on. Spectator facilities were improved following the increase in popularity that soccer experienced and the stadium was completed in 1935 when a new grandstand was opened with decent dressing rooms and showers, amenities which had been minimal in the earlier building.

## New Ullevi

By the end of the 1940s it was the opinion of many that Old Ullevi was too old and too small. Prestige was at stake; the sporting capital of Sweden should have a more representative arena. In November 1953 the municipal board of the city decided to move the arena to the east, a decision which was not made without controversy and resistance. The deciding factor was the fact that Sweden was to host the 1958 Soccer World Championships, an argument used in the final debate. It was not public opinion that was the problem but the municipal authorities which regulated sport. The sporting movement reasoned 'Now or never! If we are ever going to get all the permits we need and the funding to build a modern stadium, it will have to be for the hosting of the World Championships.'[24] New Ullevi was designed as a multi-purpose stadium. It was planned to include a soccer field and a running track, which could also be used for speedway which meant that the bends were more gentle than Olympic stadium standard. In winter there would be an ice rink for hockey and figure-skating and a speed-skating track. Under the stands there would be two large halls for gymnastics, ball sports and fencing as well as training facilities for boxing, wrestling, weight-lifting, a bowling alley, shooting range and a six hundred metre tunnel for indoor running. The capacity was estimated at 52,000 spectators – the record figure for a soccer match was 52,614 on 5 June 1959.

Ullevi has been used for three separate world championships: soccer in 1958; speed-skating in 1969; and speedway in 1974. In 1995 the fifth Track and Field Championships will be hosted which will give New Ullevi four world championships, a record for one stadium which is unlikely to be beaten. The change from Old Ullevi was dramatic: from an old wooden grandstand to a futuristic creation, architectonically and structurally ahead of its time; a monument in steel, glass and concrete, a symbol for modern society and in glaring contrast to Old Ullevi (see Figure 10.3). During the 1980s the use of New Ullevi was expanded to include rock concerts which attracted more people than did the sporting events. The mega-concerts, which started with the Rolling Stones in 1982, culminated with two Bruce Springsteen concerts in 1985 which brought in a total of 126,856 paying spectators. The second Springsteen event put a stop to future concerts as the public's rhythmic stamping to 'Born in the USA' brought such vibrations that the main stand was in danger of collapsing (see Figure 10.4).

Both the Ullevi stadiums lie on the 60 to 80 metre-deep clay bed that was once the delta of the Göta river. New Ullevi 'floated' on the clay without any anchoring in the rock beneath. The concert was a signal that it was time to renovate the arena and strengthen the foundations. The first attempt at stabilization was a failure but the second, involving the

**Figure 10.3** The New Ullevi Stadium as it was perceived in the 1950s; a futuristic creation of steel, glass and concrete

**Figure 10.4** New Ullevi; the stadium tenses its muscles during a Bruce Springsteen concert in 1985, an event which literally 'rocked' the stadium. (Source: courtesy of *Göteborgs Posten*)

building of a car park beneath the arena directly on the rock, appears to have been successful. In connection with the reinforcement work, the stadium was remodelled by glazing the upper standing-room areas and converting them into luxury lounges. The final change is a new higher east stand with room for nine thousand spectators, paid for by the International Amateur Athletic Federation which will still make money on it through the tickets sold for the World Championships.

## The Move

The idea of moving soccer back to Old Ullevi arose during the summer of 1989 when the municipal council's unanimous vote of placing the new opera house at Old Ullevi floundered because of lack of finance. The Chairman of the city council, the Social Democrat Göran Johannson, was quick to say that 'it is boring watching soccer with 1,000 spectators when the arena is built for 45,000; Old Ullevi would be much better'. A month after this comment, which the conservative politicians did not take at all seriously (regarding it as 'science fiction' from an economic point of view), the socialists presented an alternative proposition. Why not place the new opera house at the harbour instead of at Old Ullevi? The alliance clubs fell for the idea and the Chairman of IFK Göteborg, Gunnar Larsson, another leading Social Democrat politician – with deep roots in the sports movement, having been a vendor at Old Ullevi in the 1950s – was the one who pushed hardest for a take-over. The three clubs of the alliance, IFK, ÖIS and GAIS, worked quietly on plans for the necessary repairs for the virtually condemned old stadium.

From the outside, the initiative of the alliance looked like a consequence of the falling popularity of soccer and fewer spectators (see Figure 10.5). It was hoped that the negative trend could be broken by playing matches at a smaller, more cosy arena. When the plans were published in Gothenburg's largest newspaper in October 1990, they gained massive public support. However, the Recreation Board, was getting worried. If the clubs left for Old Ullevi what would become of New Ullevi where so much had just been invested in improving and stabilizing the foundations as well as in the creation of the new lounges? The city's economy was already shaken in 1990 and the politicians on the Recreation Board were against a move, even though the clubs themselves were to finance the necessary renovation of the decrepit Old Ullevi.

Old Ullevi lies on one of the most attractive pieces of undeveloped property in central Gothenburg. 'Tear down the grandstand and sell the property to the highest bidder' was the proposal from the Recreation Board on the very day that the alliance clubs presented their plans regarding Old Ullevi. The Board claimed 'if the public must come

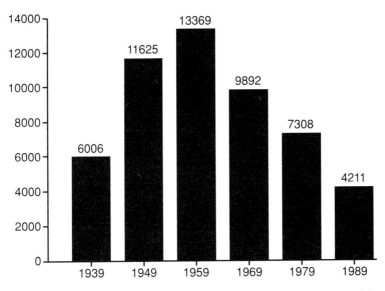

**Figure 10.5** Average size of crowds attending soccer matches, Division 1, Sweden, 1939–1989. (Source: Swedish Football Association)

closer to the game there are other arenas available'. It was also argued that soccer's needs were well met when compared to other sports and recreational activities run by the city. This was indeed true. However, these arguments were not good enough. The move back to Old Ullevi was a symbolic deed in which the full social-psychological consequences were not clearly visible for any of the involved parties, but an avalanche had started. The thought of Old Ullevi as a new 'old' arena was actually utopian in a nostalgic way – bringing back a social way of life that had vanished. Those who wanted to move longed for club feeling and tradition, which depended on a close knowledge of players and an intimacy with the sport. On the other hand, those who argued for New Ullevi and the necessary adaptations for new events (such as the Track and Field World Championships of 1995) were generally influenced by market forces. They no longer regarded football as the primary competitive event. The move back to Old Ullevi can be seen as a post-modern (or perhaps trans-modern) action, the desire for a return to a workers' ethic in the sports movement, as it was in the 'old days'. It involved a return to a unique sense of place.[25] Prior to the move, Skr. 20 million was invested by the alliance clubs for the renovation. The grandstand at Old Ullevi, as stated earlier, was condemned because of the fire risk. It was literally rotting away. The supporter clubs, with twenty thousand members representing the three clubs, worked sixty thousand voluntary hours, while business sponsors paid for materials. Unions assisted and the whole affair was undertaken by 'the Gothenburg soccer family'. The alliance signed a twenty-year lease with the city to cover all costs without public support; soccer is safe at Old Ullevi until the year 2012. There is already talk of a centenary celebration in the year 2016.

## The Official Explanation

In both moves, away from and back to Old Ullevi, the public was used as the official argument for the action. In the first move, Old Ullevi was not big enough, in the second, New Ullevi was too big. Even with the doubling of Gothenburg's population between 1916 and 1958 when New Ullevi opened, it was the increase in spectators that justified the building of the new stadium, as well as the World Soccer Championships. In the third largest city in Sweden, Malmö, the same thing happened. The stadium used for soccer was built in the traditional English style in 1923. Its replacement, designed by the same architects who had drafted the plans for Ullevi, Samuelsson and Jaenecke, gave the Malmö stadium the same futuristic design, though on a smaller scale.[26] As seen in Figure 10.5, soccer popularity reached its peak in 1959, but a spectator average of 13,000 per match hardly requires a stadium that takes four times that amount. Although a loss of spectators has been used as the primary reason for the return to Old Ullevi, there are strong arguments to support the view that, in practice, this was not the deciding factor.

That soccer as the national sport in Sweden has lost ground is beyond all doubt. In Sweden, soccer is called 'the chess of the green field', but technical and tactical ability, elegance and inventiveness, have been replaced by superior conditioning and defensive thinking – hardly the showmanship needed to draw the public. During much of the twentieth century soccer has been Sweden's most popular spectator sport but during the 1980s live spectating has been replaced by televised games from England, Germany and Italy. Furthermore, with few spectators present, the empty soccer arenas have not been able to offer an equivalent to the hockey rink's tight gladiatorial battle between aggressive combatants. Ice hockey has taken the lead in spectator popularity. During the 1960s the erstwhile national sport lost ground and was overtaken in the 1980s by the most popular winter sport – 'King Soccer' was forced off the throne.[27]

## Changes in the Configuration of Space

It can be argued that the primary reason behind the move from New Ullevi can instead be found in what Henning Eichberg describes as

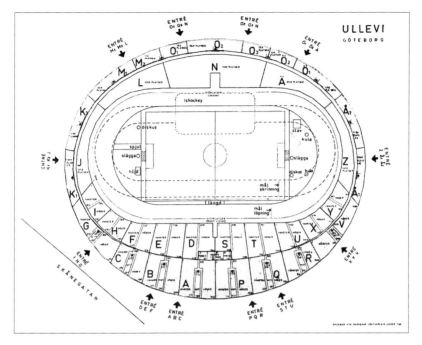

**Figure 10.6** The spatial organization of the New Ullevi. (Source: N. Holmberg, *Från Exercisheden till Nya Ullevi*, Göteborgs Stadskollegium, 1959)

changes in the configuration of sport, due to changes in values and ideas. Eichberg's examples are stretched over a much longer time period[28] but his conceptual framework can be used to show differences in contemporary thinking about the reality behind decision-making. Three distinct phases can be identified. In the case of Old Ullevi, the attitude and ambitions of the leadership in the early twentieth century were to build a soccer stadium meeting the requirements of a modern, but in comparison with the later creation of New Ullevi, a rather traditional English soccer stadium. New Ullevi, at its opening in 1958, was a more true example of the modern, developing as it did an assembly line production of sports space. As a futuristic creation, New Ullevi illustrates the 'crisis of container architecture'.[29] The move back to Old Ullevi is a postmodern action. It is an attempt to re-create the unique, a place for social sport where interpersonal relationships can be cultivated without anti-hooligan devices such as unclimbable riot fences, barbed wire and the ever-present video cameras. In the 1958 move from Old Ullevi to New Ullevi, a new form of spatial organizaton emerged. Actually, New Ullevi can be seen as twelve stadiums in one. Figure 10.6 shows the twelve

209

**Figure 10.7** Crowds queuing to enter the turnstiles, the 'node' in the spectators' time path, at Old Ullevi in the late 1950s. (Source: Johansson and Nilsson, *Gamla Ullevi*)

entrances each one of which leads to a section containing its own group of spectators, self-supported with sanitation and services. The sections are price-differentiated in proportion to the level of seating and the ability to view the sports action. By increasing the number of entrances and creating infrastructural support areas (gathering areas) outside, space was well organized. In comparison, there were no such areas outside Old Ullevi. Instead there were long queues of spectators waiting for hours. The gate opened two hours before kick-off and the line moved slowly but surely forward (see Figure 10.7).

The modernistic design of New Ullevi made it possible to fill and empty the arena of spectators quickly. The large infrastructural support areas were needed so that spectators could gather outside each gate relatively quickly, a need that increased continually along with the tempo in society. Time came to play a major role not because there was a lack of it, but because, as Kevin Lynch noted, 'while city time seems crowded, its scarcity is not the critical problem, the more severe strains accompany time ordering'.[30] What occurs is alienation resulting from the modernistic influences in stadium development where space is ordered to enable optimal effectiveness and economic profit. A perception of placelessness results and city time seems crowded. Scale in stadium development led to a division of space which gives a sameness in the eye of the beholder, a 'placelessness'.[31] Scale is thus an integral part of modernity and becomes a very important detail in the study of stadium development in an historical-geographical analysis.[32] The desire to return to Old Ullevi expresses a longing for a more human, playful period in soccer's history. But there are more factors involved than simply soccer history. One cannot disregard the fact that it was the Social

Democratic party that supported and even pushed the move. The dream of Old Ullevi returned after what is called in Sweden 'the happy 80s money merry-go-round' and 'the age of the yuppies', a living illustration of a workers' movement in crisis. The Social Democrats were in power during this time and by the deregulation of banking laws and a shift in financial policy, played an important role in the financial crisis that has shaken the nation. For the leadership of the workers' movement, the remodelling of New Ullevi symbolized the beginning of a new class society where the negative element is to be controlled by barbed-wire fences and riot police and where the new class of the 1980s buy good seating, comfort and protection in special lounges. But caged people tend to act as animals. This prophecy was fulfilled during the 1992 European Soccer Championships when rival supporter groups were separated from one another while sponsors enjoyed themselves in the lounges. During the 1940s and 1950s when the standard of living was rising, and the masses started to attend events, there was no violence or planned destruction. If anything did happen, the public would take matters into its own hands and teach the instigators a lesson. The arrival of New Ullevi and Malmö stadium represented a change in development, and a reaction against 'container architecture' followed. New Ullevi is therefore a good example of what went wrong in the Social Democratic attempt to manage Swedish society. The dream of a return to Old Ullevi represents a kind of political regression. In Gothenburg class conflict influenced the formation of public space. The important cultural institutions of the city lie along the main street, the Avenue – City Theatre, the Art Gallery, Concert Hall, the Opera House – as monumental reminders of the economic ruling classe's culture. From the early twentieth century, the soccer arena was one of the few places where capital and workers met in peace. The symbolism of the stadium as a meeting point cannot be neglected.


## A Time-Space Model

Predominant values reflecting contemporary society run through the hundred-year time span of the provision of sport at the site of the Ullevi stadiums. Henning Eichberg has pointed out that 'the configuration of sportive modernity is in question', arguing that 'the interest of economic and technological development is pushing in the direction of the small scale and regionalization, which under the dominance of industrial modernity, once had been regarded as "archaic"'.[33] This is exactly what is seen in the move from New to Old Ullevi in 1992. If the configurations of space (and the values behind them) are analysed, one can see that the relation between scale and values differ for different time periods. These changes can be mapped in the basic time-space path of the spectator – using the conceptual framework of time-geography[34] – where six spatial concepts can be identified and where corresponding values of time have clearly affected the design and scale of the stadium.

In Sweden, the first stadiums were simply fields for soccer and track and field events, initially without seating. After the development of a national sports federation in 1903, seating was introduced in the 1910s and 1920s.[35] Old Ullevi is one of those stadiums that was built on land that was already being used for sport. The design was in the style of the traditional English stadium. The location was at the time relatively peripheral due to the impediment caused by the land in the Göta Älv delta. However, as the city grew, the location became more central. When New Ullevi was built, it became the epitome of the modern stadium, futuristically shaped in 'modern materials' and planned for efficiency; an assembly-line production of sports space. Finally, the return to Old Ullevi in 1992 has been a move back to 'missing time', an attempt to reinstate what has been lost to sport through television and hooliganism – what in Eichberg's terms can be called a post-modern action.[36] Of the six concepts of space, movement, node and site, are common geographic terms which can be applied to the individual's own experience in the time-space path of sports consumption. The other three – service, sanitation and formation – identify important factors in the configuration of space in the situations of the two Ullevis. The time-space path of the spectator is shown in Figure 10.8.

*Movement*

In modern society there is a constant move towards rationalization and greater effectiveness. Movement from place to place has changed from walking in the 1910s to public transport and the automobile – now the primary mode of transport. Parking has always been a problem at New Ullevi and one solution is the new garage under the turf with room for 650 cars. At Old Ullevi, parking just outside the arena was planned after its renovation, as a bait to get people to go to the soccer games.

*Formation*

There was no 'gathering area' outside Old Ullevi between 1916 and 1957, as shown in Figure 10.7. There were long queues outside the four gates and spectators waited patiently for the stadium to open. It was not uncommon to get in line three hours in advance in order to be among the first when the gates opened. New Ullevi's twelve gates and large

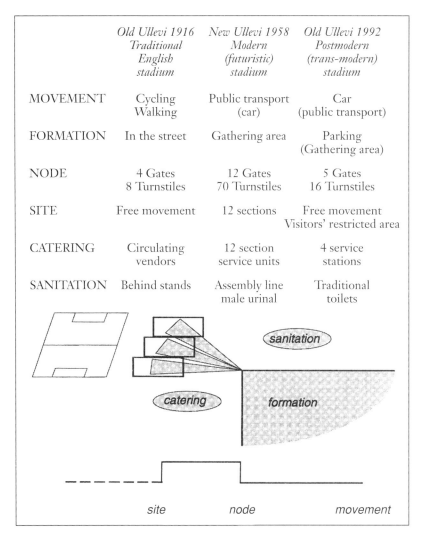

| | Old Ullevi 1916 *Traditional English stadium* | New Ullevi 1958 *Modern (futuristic) stadium* | Old Ullevi 1992 *Postmodern (trans-modern) stadium* |
|---|---|---|---|
| MOVEMENT | Cycling Walking | Public transport (car) | Car (public transport) |
| FORMATION | In the street | Gathering area | Parking (Gathering area) |
| NODE | 4 Gates 8 Turnstiles | 12 Gates 70 Turnstiles | 5 Gates 16 Turnstiles |
| SITE | Free movement | 12 sections | Free movement Visitors' restricted area |
| CATERING | Circulating vendors | 12 section service units | 4 service stations |
| SANITATION | Behind stands | Assembly line male urinal | Traditional toilets |

**Figure 10.8** Time-space path and six concepts of stadium space

gathering area made it possible for spectators quickly to find 'their' gate and section. The time necessary to attend an event was radically short-ened as it became possible to fill or empty the stadium in thirty minutes. With the return to Old Ullevi, the ambition was to allow the public to experience the 'old days' by coming earlier to participate and experience intimacy and fellowship. But this did not happen. In the '90s, soccer fans go out and eat before the game or come straight from home in their cars. Before matches, long queues appeared once more at Old Ullevi, even with spectator numbers of four to five thousand.

*Node*

The turnstile is the nodal point that spectators have to pass in order to enter the stadium. At Old Ullevi there were only four gates with two turnstiles each. This infrastructural deficiency was the prime reason for the long queues in the street. At New Ullevi the twelve gates and seventy turnstiles vouch for efficiency and speed when the stadium is used for large events. Upon the return to Old Ullevi, one new gate had to be built and the number of turnstiles was increased from eight to sixteen.

*Site*

In Old Ullevi it was possible to roam free within the arena. When the attendance record was set in 1957 all available space was used, right up to the field's boundary line, an impossibility today. The differences between Old and New Ullevi were as night and day. New Ullevi was highly segmented and built in a manner which created 'twelve stadiums in one'. Each section was self-sufficient with its own services in the form of refreshments and toilet facilities. In recent years the sectioning has become even stricter for purposes of riot control. At Old Ullevi there has been a return to free movement, but it has been necessary to cage-in opposition supporters in a restricted area in order to prevent fights and vandalism. Supporters (hooligans) from Stockholm actually tore apart the stand surrounding the standing area after the third match in the stadium in the spring of 1992.

*Catering*

Old Ullevi had a system of circulating vendors serving the spectators coffee, ice cream, candy, etc. The vendors – up to forty at big games – were boys in their early teens, usually connected to a sports club whose prime objective was to make some extra money. The situation at New Ullevi was 'modern'. Each section was self-sufficient with its own catering units, one for coffee and candy and one for food, to minimize queues and meet the needs at the busy periods before, at half-time and after the game. Upon the return to Old Ullevi, four catering stations were installed. However, both service-stations and the gates were undersized and long queues became a problem. The clubs of the alliance have been forced to change the initial concept of nostalgia, and the post-modernistic aspirations of a return to 'missing time', in order to keep the audience happy. The capacity of services and entrances have been raised substantially by integrating modern devices to improve efficiency in response to the demand and the changed lifestyle of the soccer-fans of the 1990s.

There were only four toilets at Old Ullevi and the public usually urinated under the stands, which also indicates the gender composition of the spectators. This is of course an impossibility at New Ullevi. The predominately male public was channelled into 'assembly-line urinals' where needs were met one after another along one wall and hands washed in sinks along the next wall. That the stadium was built for men became clearly evident when it was opened for rock concerts. The lack of women's facilities was a great problem. At Old Ullevi after 1992 the six toilets which had been installed were insufficient. The male public again urinated under and behind the stands and, as in the case of services and entrances, a new urinal had to be built to meet the needs and the standards of the 1990's soccer crowd.

## Conclusion

Despite being a small country in terms of population, Sweden has been one of the leading industrial nations in the world with Gothenburg at its industrial heart. Here, property prices and a willingness to develop are far greater than in cities of equivalent size around the world. What is interesting is that the city has been able to save the vast and central areas of land used for sport. In addition to the large area of New and Old Ullevi, there is also the sports area of 'Heden', with five regulation soccer fields and four smaller ones. Figure 10.9 shows the layout of sports grounds in central Gothenburg just east of the main street, the Avenue. It is at Heden – the large area one block from the Avenue – that the 'mobile athletes village' will be built for the 1995 Track and Field Championships, housing 2,700 athletes and it is the main reason why Gothenburg won the bid. Accessibility had become a primary consideration when voting for where the mega-sports event was to be held. The IAAF did not want to repeat the 1991 Tokyo situation, with well over an hour spent in transportation between the athletes' village and the stadium. In Gothenburg, that distance will be a walk of three to four minutes in glazed sky-walks giving athletes and VIPs superb accessibility, due to the unusual land layout of downtown Gothenburg.

In the early 1800s, Heden's exercise-ground was placed next door to the main street, as the town's economic élite wanted a military presence near the town centre for protection from the radical element in the rising workers' movement.[37] That Heden has been preserved for soccer use as well as Old Ullevi being recommissioned as a sports facility, has been an obstacle in the path of those conservative politicians who want to sell the attractive land to the highest bidder. However, in Gothenburg

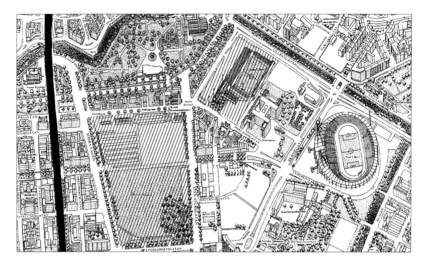

**Figure 10.9** The sports land use of downtown Gothenburg (shaded). The main street, the Avenue, is shaded in black (left). New Ullevi (*Nya Ullevi*) is centre right, with Old Ullevi (*Gamla Ullevi*) immediately to the north west. Some of the original sports area is used for parking

the sports movement is so firmly established in society that the Chairman of the Board in ÖIS – Vice-director of Sweden's largest shipping emporium and as such apparently a representative of capital and the bourgeois – summed up the tensions involved in social construction policies in these words: 'If we have lived above our means and put ourselves in a precarious situation do we have the right to sell attractive property to save our own skin? Shouldn't we wait and let the coming generation make the decision as of what to do with the city's resources of attractive land.'[38] To stand against this market-oriented temptation as described by Örgryte's Chairman is not common among conservative politicians anywhere in Sweden in the 1990s, except in Gothenburg where the Social Democrats and the Conservatives, who came to power in 1991, together developed 'the Gothenburg spirit of understanding'. It is clear that the question is one of ideology as the land on which Old Ullevi stands represented a value of Skr. 600–700 million in 1989–90 for any type of construction, a fantasy figure in regard to the Skr. 20 million used to renovate the stadium (the estimated price of the property, mentioned in the media debate).

The example of Old and New Ullevi confirms the thesis that a national sports structure tends to persist. In Sweden, the differences between Stockholm and Gothenburg have persisted where the latter, as in the case of Spain and the 1992 Barcelona Olympics, has maintained the upper edge as the capital city of sport. Of primary importance is, of

216

course, the feat of winning the bid for the 1995 World Championships in Track and Field. But, in addition, the leading politicians of Gothenburg, whether Social Democrats or Conservatives, are still recruited with the underlying notion that body culture (sport/soccer) is more important then high culture for the majority of the citizens. The two Ullevis are symbols of the symbiosis of the integration of the needs of the working class for its own monument, and the understanding of the bourgeoisie that it is necessary for peace and development.

## Notes

1. S. Jones, *Sport, Politics and the Working Class. Organised Labour and Sport in Inter-War Britain* (Manchester, 1989).
2. H. Eichberg, 'The Enclosure of the body – on the Historical Relativity of Health, Nature and Sports Environment', *Journal of Contemporary History*, Vol. 21, 2 (1986), pp.99–121.
3. Busser, 'Utkast till beskrivfning av Upsala' (Uppsala University Library, 1769).
4. A. Bergmark, 'Ur Uppsala-idrottens historia', *Uppsala stads historia*, VI, 3 (1983).
5. H. Sandblad, *Från Olympia till Valhalla. Idéhistoriska aspekter av den moderna idrottsrörelsen främväxt* (Stockholm, 1985).
6. J. Lindroth, *Från sportfåneri till massidrott. Den svenska idrottsrörelsens utveckling 1869–1939* (Stockholm, 1988).
7. Bergmark, 'Ur Uppsala-idrottens historia'.
8. Sandblad, *Från Olympia till Valhalla*.
9. Ibid.
10. G. Patriksson, *Idrott – Tävling – Samhälle* (Örebro, 1982).
11. J. Lindroth, 'Idrottens väg till folkrörelse. Studier i svensk idrottsrörelse till 1915', *Studia historica Upsaliensia*, Vol. 60 (1974).
12. B. Schelin, 'Den ojämnlika idrotten. Om idrottsstratifiering, idrottspreferens och val av idrott', *Lunds Studies in Sociology*, Vol. 67 (1985).
13. N. Holmberg, 'Från Exercisheden till Nya Ullevi', *Göteborgs stadskollegium* (1959).
14. Sandblad, *Från Olympia till Valhalla*.
15. Ibid.
16. B. Janzon, 'Manshettyrke, idrott och hälsa. Studier kring idrottsrörelsen i Sverige, särskilt Göteborg, intill 1900', *Meddelande från Historika Institutionen i Göteborg*, Vol. 14 (1978).
17. O. Moen, *Idrottsanläggningar och idrottens rumsliga utveckling i svenskt stadsbyggande under 1900-talet. Med exempel frän Borås och Uppsala* (Gothenburg, 1990).
18. Lindroth, 'Idrottens väg till folkrörelse'.
19. H. Eichberg, 'A revolution in body culture? Traditional games on the way from modernization to postmodernity', in J. Barreau and G. Jaoun (eds), *Eclipse et renaissance des jeux populaires* (Rennes, 1991), pp.101–29.

20. S. Reiss, *City Games. The Evolution of American Urban Society and the Rise of Sports* (Illinois, 1989).
21. R. Jernereyd, *Hur idrotten kom till stan. Göteborgs idrottshistoria 1800–1950* (Göteborg, 1981).
22. B. Johansson and B. G. Nilsson, *Gamla Ullevi* (Göteborg, 1992).
23. O. Moen, *Från bollplan till sportscentrum* (Stockholm, 1992).
24. Holmberg, 'Från Exercisheden till Nya Ullevi'.
25. J. Bale, *Sport, Space and the City* (London, 1992).
26. Holmberg, 'Från Exercisheden till Nya Ullevi'.
27. O. Moen, 'Spectator Sports', in H. Aldskogius (ed.), *Recreation, Cultural Life and Tourismen*, The Swedish National Atlas, Vol. 9 (Stockholm, 1993), pp.62–3.
28. H. Eichberg, 'Stopwatch, horizontal bar, gymnasium: the technologizing of sports in the 18th and 19th centuries', *Journal of the Philosophy of Sport*, Vol. 9 (1982), pp.43–59.
29. Eichberg, 'A revolution in body culture?'
30. K. Lynch, *What Time is This Place* (Cambridge, Mass., 1972).
31. E. Relph, *Place and Placelessness* (London, 1976).
32. J. Bale, 'Cartographic Fetishism to Geographical Humansim', *Innovation*, Vol. 5, 4 (1993), pp.71–88.
33. Eichberg, 'A revolution in body culture?'
34. T. Hägerstrand, 'Survival and arena: on the life-history of individuals in relation to their geographical environment', in T. Carlstein, D. Parkes and N. Thrift (eds), *Timing Space and Spacing Time*, Vol. 2 (1978), pp.122–45.
35. Moen, *Idrottsanläggningar och idrottens rumsliga utveckling i svenskt stadsbyggande under 1900-talet*.
36. Eichberg, 'A revolution in body culture?'
37. Janzon, 'Manshettyrke, idrott och hälsa'.
38. Johansson and Nilsson, *Gamal Ullevi*.

# 11
# English Football Stadiums after Hillsborough

*John Williams*

## Introduction

In this chapter I want to try to say something about the changing material and cultural parameters of football in England in the 1990s and, more specifically, about the recent 'modernizing' spurt in the provision of spectator facilities at football, particularly during the period following the Hillsborough Stadium spectator disaster of 1989. I also want to look, briefly, at the interpretation and experience of such changes within the context of wider debates about leisure and consumption in Britain and of the accelerating development of a 'globalized' market for football.

Of course, most football spectators in Europe, if not those around the world, know that 96 soccer fans, followers of Liverpool Football Club, lost their lives at the Hillsborough Stadium in Sheffield on 15 April 1989. National and international knowledge about the causes of the disaster tend to be rather partial. In the United States in 1994, for example, in the build-up to the World Cup Finals to be held in that country, learned journals persisted in describing the Sheffield incidents, wrongly, as being the consequence of spectator hooliganism.[1] In the same year, in England, five years after the tragedy, some commentators were still insisting that the behaviour of 'drunken yobs' lay behind the deaths.[2] In fact, they occurred due to what the official inquiry on the disaster described as police 'operational errors'[3] after a central penned section of terracing at the Leppings Lane end of the Hillsborough ground became fatally overcrowded during the early minutes of the FA Cup semi-final fixture between Liverpool and Nottingham Forest. Most of those who died were crushed to death or were asphyxiated in a fenced enclosure from which it was virtually impossible to escape.

What may also be less well known is that an important aspect of the events at Hillsborough is that they occurred as part of a rather long tradition of spectator tragedies at English football; a tradition in which an aggressive passion for the game among fans, inadequate facilities, poor crowd management, or a combination of all three of these, have

219

claimed the lives of at least 281 fans since the turn of the century in 27 separate incidents in which a further 3,500 fans have been injured. Since the Second World War there have been 186 deaths at Football League matches from a massive total of 1.2 billion spectator admissions.[4] Spectator tragedies have occurred, of course, in countries other than England, though some of those which have occurred elsewhere in Europe have also involved English spectators. Some English commentators might argue – and with at least some justification – that the spectator fatalities which occurred before the European Cup Final between Liverpool and Juventus at the Heysel Stadium in May 1985 owed at least something to lax crowd management and the poor condition of that arena. But few, surely, would contest the view that the tragedy that night, in which 39, mainly Italian, fans lost their lives in a panic caused by crowd violence, owed more to the violent xenophobia and racism of young English spectators than it did to the state of fencing and perimeter walls and the policing at one of Belgium's most historic sports venues.[5]

To my knowledge, the rather unenviable record of the English concerning spectator tragedies at football is unequalled anywhere in the so-called 'developed' world. (I am aware, of course, of spectator tragedies at football stadiums in the former Soviet Union and in South America which, because of the scale of the events concerned and the generally poor facilities and rescue services on offer, have claimed many more victims.[6]) Such a record might suggest there is something specifically different, for example, about the character of English football fans or about the way they watch the game. Certainly, there is still recent evidence to suggest that spectator hooliganism of the kind which so encouraged the British State and football clubs to pen spectators, as at Hillsborough, remains a distinctive and serious aspect of domestic spectator culture (it is worth noting that the England team was not in the USA for 1994 World Cup and, predictably, there was no hooliganism). For these reasons it is difficult to oppose the view that the need to control spectator hooliganism in England from the late 1960s onwards was at least part of the reason why stadiums there remained peculiarly spartan and under-resourced and why they had also become increasingly and crudely carcereal.

Such a poor record might also suggest, however, a long-established relative lack of regard for public provision and for public safety in England's largely privately-owned and privately-maintained football stadiums housing professional clubs. This point was made especially starkly in 1985 when a fire, started accidentally, in a decrepit and dangerous wooden stand during a match at Bradford City's Valley Parade stadium, claimed 56 lives. Perhaps predictably, the official inquiry which followed did little to focus attention on the crucial issue of the parlous finances and poor administration of many of the then Football League's

92 professional clubs.[7] As this last example painfully illustrates, English football had not generally enjoyed the benefits of the football stadium-building modernization programmes more common on the continent, and elsewhere, in the period between 1930 and 1960 (see Table 11.1).

**Table 11.1**  Average age of top division soccer stadiums

| | |
|---|---|
| England | 88 years |
| Germany | 48 years |
| USA* | 43 years |
| Italy | 37 years |

\* Stadiums used for 1994 World Cup Finals.
Source: Adapted from *The Economist*, 18 April 1993.

More municipal ownership or the greater public financing for sports stadiums abroad is clearly a factor here, of course.[8] Stretching this point somewhat, the British sociologist, Ian Taylor, has also recently argued that the tragic events at Hillsborough must be socially and politically contextualized, as just one of a sequence of life-taking disasters which occurred in public facilities of various kinds in Britain during the 1980s and early 1990s.[9] Public awareness of such disasters and of the worsening condition of public spaces, apparently as a matter of policy during the neo-liberal Thatcher administration, are key issues, he contends, in properly 'making the connection' between economic organization and the moral character of social life in Britain of the 1980s.

## Some History

The social effects of recent free-market policies on British football stadiums and on their audiences stands in rather marked contrast, for example, to that of the late-Victorian era when most existing British stadiums where first built. Between 1889 and 1910, fifty-eight Football League clubs moved into the stadiums that most of them continue to occupy today.[10] Black and Lloyd have pointed to the complexity of planning issues associated with the siting of a football stadium in Britain in the 1990s.[11] In contrast to the strong local opposition which is increasingly common among planners and residents to the siting of new stadiums today, the new professional football industry had become so powerful and popular, and the positioning of a new ground so prestigious to a local municipality, that clubs have been able to monopolize some of the prime open land which might otherwise have remained or become private property. As Simon Inglis points out: 'A football ground was in many ways as much part of a burgeoning corporation as a public library, town hall and law courts, and was certainly used by more people. Furthermore, a football ground was often the only place in a town outsiders would visit.'[12]

The civic pride invested in early professional English football clubs and their stadiums was cemented, in the main, by highly localized forms of funding and control and by local sponsorship.[13] Even in the 1950s and 1960s, images of the British football stadium remained replete with accounts of 'advertising boards above the stands, telling of pork pies, ales, whisky, cigarettes and other delights of Saturday night'.[14] These contrast, quite starkly of course, with the TV-regulated 'global' advertising at major football stadiums today in Britain and elsewhere. This highly localized financing and control helped, at the match, to regulate and contain the 'rough' behavioural ethic of working-class male milieux within a social structure increasingly characterized by the virtues of self-restraint and respectability, and by the sorts of 'spiritual' provision – 'free' municipal baths; libraries; playing fields; museums and art galleries – which local capital regarded as its civic duty to provide towards sustaining moral and social cohesion.[15]

As Bale has pointed out, in contrast to the *ad hoc* and idiosyncratic unitary development of local private stadiums in Britain to house largely working-class audiences, by the mid-1930s many cities in continental Europe possessed their own classically-designed publicly-funded 'sports parks', aimed at a rather wider class base.[16] As the German observer of British sport, Rudolf Kircher, noted, 'it has never occurred to the English mind that the state, town council or anyone else could provide them with a sports ground offering them everything their hearts desired from a swimming bath to football'.[17] English soccer crowds, largely made up of working-class men, were also mainly standing crowds, of course. They were often tightly-packed and could frequently be seen to be wildly swaying on ill-finished terraces. When, in the 1930s, English soccer crowds continued to grow and the formal regulation and control of them was minimal, individual fatalities as a result of crushing were probably not uncommon.[18] But, in the main, English soccer crowds of this time seem to have been remarkably well ordered and well behaved and, by modern standards, they were unusually alert to the dangers posed to themselves and to their fellow supporters by their sheer weight of numbers, shoehorned as they were into poorly-appointed and little-regulated spectator facilities.

The immediate post-Second World War era of political consensus and promises of broadly collectivist policies for wealth creation and of 'one nation' welfarist social policies in Britain had already grown distant and hazy by the late 1960s. In the Britain of the 1980s, earlier consensuses around notions of local and regional 'civic pride', and around a sense of collective 'social cohesion', seemed to have been substantially dislodged as policy aims, by national government strategies which lay a more profound stress on the importance of ownership and choice in the private sphere and on individual striving for personal success of the kind most closely associated with Thatcherite social and economic policies.[19]

It would be a grave mistake, of course, to exaggerate the privatized element in contemporary neighbourhood relations in Britain,[20] or to try to contrast an alleged 'solidaristic' past with a 'privatized' present in a way which understates the complexities of local social relations in Britain today.[21] Nevertheless, in the case of the urban-disadvantaged in Britain in the 1980s and early 1990s, there seems little doubt that opportunities for participation in public life have been substantially limited by falling wages, rising unemployment, de-skilling, the erosion of the value of welfare benefits and by the experience and fear of crime[22] as well as by the effective segregation and privatization of formerly public spaces, a fact marked by the proliferation of security-managed private 'public' zones – new shopping malls, for example – seeking customers who best conform to the moral codes of well-ordered consumption.[23] Such pressures, and the associated greater colonization and control of local spaces by men, have also had disproportionate and very different effects on the experiences of women, especially poor women.[24]

If, under these twin pressures of commodification and privatization in Britain, 'a narrower range of 'strangers' are met in public space, and, increasingly, experiences of public life are with a more homogeneous group of others',[25] then these developments really do suggest a theoretical and socio-political connection between recent disasters in public places in England of a kind little made in press coverage of Hillsborough or in the report of the official inquiry into the disaster, chaired by Lord Justice Taylor (the Taylor Report). In this sense, according to Ian Taylor, such disasters – on public ferries, on the railways, in the London Underground, etc. – are:

> [C]learly an expression of a kind of careless inefficiency and neglect for the public interest which characterises the British service industry in general. The Hillsborough disaster was the product of a quite consistent and ongoing lack of interest on the part of the owners and directors of English league clubs in the comfort, well being and safety of their paying spectators: this particular failure within football that I am condemning is a generalised problem in English culture – the lack of regard by authority (and thereby what we now call 'service providers') for the provision of well-being and security of others.[26]

## Football Crowds and Official Policy in Post-Hillsborough Britain

While the media and popular coverage in Britain of the Hillsborough tragedy lacked an incisive socio-political focus of the kind suggested above, at the level of the personal it did have the effect of displacing, or at least disrupting, prevailing stereotypes in England of 'football fans as hooligans', substituting discourses focused through a sense of 'family' and 'belonging'.[27] The victims of Hillsborough were not, in these accounts, the tabloid press's uncivilized 'beasts' or alienated 'savages', descriptions common in media accounts of young hooligan fans, but rather ordinary people, men and women, with homes, jobs and relatives, drawn from ordinary backgrounds. The public mourning in Liverpool, and that which joined football fans from around the world, suggested nothing less than a deepfelt family loss which was experienced by the international community of football followers. It seems reasonable to assume, too, that descriptions of the so-called typical English football audience which emerged out of the Hillsborough catastrophe have done much to shift wider popular perceptions about the sport which had largely been dominated in England by discourses concerning 'the hooligan crisis'. As Rogan Taylor has argued, 'Hooliganism was the word that many, perhaps most, people associated with football fans before the Hillsborough disaster. Fans were always seen as the perpetrators; never the victims of violence'.[28] Moreover, the liberal and progressive report produced by the official inquiry into the Hillsborough disaster, under the chairmanship of Lord Justice Taylor bucked tradition by refusing to confine itself to dealing only with the technical aspects of the disaster or, simply, with administrative concerns about the management and safety of spectators. Instead, its critique of the governance of the sport and its recommendations for, 'A totally new approach across the whole field of football [requiring] higher standards both in bricks and in human relationships',[29] at least promised a programme, an agenda for future development in the British game, beyond the 'crisis management' which had been characteristic of its recent past.

As well as providing a blueprint and a timetable for changes in spectator provision and stadium design, there was also recognition by Taylor, almost for the first time in an official inquiry of this kind, of some of the cultural resonances of the sport and of its national significance.[30] Taylor, for example, sanctioned representation at his inquiry for football supporters in the shape of the high profile and influential national Football Supporters Association (FSA) which had been launched by fans on Merseyside following the débâcle at Heysel in 1985.[31] Taylor found favour with the FSA and other supporter organizations by rejecting as ill-advised and dangerous British Government proposals outlined in the Football Spectators Act of 1989 for the establishment of a national 'members' (registration or identity) scheme for football spectators. His critique of stadium facilities, where 'inside the grounds decay and dilapidation are often extensive', and where 'the safety and comfort of those on the terraces has not been regarded as a priority'[32] was received, however, with rather more equivocation. Relph has identified well how analytic and rational methods of planning can have the paradoxical effect of 'dehumanizing' landscapes; how such places are often described as 'inauthentic', 'placeless' or 'Disneyfied', and how modernism in design and location can lead to 'place destruction' or topicide.[33] Taylor's main proposals, that all major football stadiums in England, Scotland and Wales become all-seated by 1994/95 and, by implication, that some clubs should re-locate into new, purpose-built modern facilities, raised spectres, for some, of the sport increasingly becoming distanced, socially and spatially, from its 'traditional' audience and being played in soulless, 'production-line' concrete bowls in front of passive and affluent consumers (not supporters). In this sense, as Bale points out,[34] his assertion that, 'sitting for the duration of the match is more comfortable than standing' is by no means 'obvious'.[35] Indeed, as the FSA has argued:

> Many traditional and highly enjoyable outdoor recreations involve discomfort, dirt and exposure to the elements and these factors are often recognised as contributing something to the atmosphere of, say, hunting or angling, motor cross, horse racing or even building snowmen. Why should going to football be seen as different? It may not be a popular clarion call, but the right to be uncomfortable should not be taken for granted.[36]

I want to return later to a discussion of the debate over the wider social effects of the Taylor recommendations, but first I want to spend a little time looking at the implementation of his main proposals and at the post-Hillsborough climate in and around English football stadia.


## Implementing and Financing Taylor

Predictably, perhaps, football club owners and the game's administrators in Britain complained about the costs of implementing Taylor's main proposals. (Initially, Taylor had recommended that all ninety-two Football League clubs and all Scottish Premier League clubs convert to all-seated facilities by 1999, but in 1992 the British Government ruled that only larger clubs should dispose of terraces, but by the original 1994/95 deadline.) New seats, it was argued, given conditions of the winter climate in Britain, also meant expensive new roofing, though it was little noted that most modern facilities in the USA – often held as a model for Britain to follow – had little or no covering for seated spectators in cheaper seats. Total costs for refurbishment of the top English clubs soared, according to some estimates, to over £600 million. Escalating player salaries and falling crowds had also meant that by the mid-1980s English football was an industry in which most of its established professional outlets were regular loss-makers and large numbers of clubs were quite seriously in debt.[37] Realistically, there were four possible sources of finance for this mass stadium conversion in England: firstly, the individual personal wealth of club patrons; secondly, the provision of public funds for redevelopment, a substantially new departure for Britain; thirdly, a radical restructuring and refinancing of professional football itself; and, fourthly, money raised directly from football supporters or members of the public.

*Club patrons*

On the first potential source of funding, club patrons, it should be said that football clubs in England are not generally owned by stupendously wealthy benefactors as is often the case for sporting franchises in the USA, nor are they attached to major corporate interests as is the case for some large continental clubs. Also, annual turnover at the largest continental football clubs exceeds that of its English equivalents by five- or six-fold. Table 11.2 lists the eight richest backers of English League clubs in May 1992. Of these, only two, Walker and Thompson, are, in international terms, fabulously wealthy. Two on this list have contributed directly and substantially to the stadium rebuild. Most notable in this connection are Jack Walker at Blackburn and Jack Hayward at Wolverhampton, who have reportedly contributed in excess of £15 million and £10 million, respectively, towards the complete reconstruction of their own club's grounds. Other new club chairmen (Moores at Liverpool, Hall at Newcastle, Pickering at Derby) have also dipped into their own pockets to offset costs of rebuilding. At the time this list was compiled (May 1992) a further seventeen (46%) of the top thirty-seven League clubs in England suggested they had some resources available from reserves and club backers for ploughing into stadium redevelopment while eighteen (49%) claimed they did not. Three clubs, Crystal Palace, Barnsley and Nottingham Forest, warned that costs of redevelopment would take them dangerously into further debt.[38] It seems clear that simply drawing on existing resources alone, or relying on rich owners to fund stadium work would be quite inadequate to help most clubs meet the Taylor requirements.

**Table 11.2**  Eight richest backers of Premier League and Football League clubs, 1992

| Name | Club | Estimated fortune (£m) |
|------|------|------------------------|
| Jack Walker | Blackburn Rovers | 360 |
| David Thompson | Queen's Park Rangers | 350 |
| Alan Sugar | Tottenham Hotspur | 80 |
| Owen Oyston | Blackpool | 50 |
| Leslie Silver | Leeds United | 40 |
| John Madejski | Reading | 25 |
| David Dein | Arsenal | 23 |
| Sir Jack Hayward | Wolverhampton | 20 |

Source: *Independent*, 15 May 1992.


*Public funds*

There were some positive early signs, however, from our second possible source of finance for ground redevelopment, namely public funds. A very small number of clubs in England are already substantially supported by local public funds, but national government had seemed spectacularly hostile both to the game and, indeed, to local government itself in Britain throughout the 1980s. However, in 1990, the Conservative British Government, apparently reversing its transparent disregard for the sport under Mrs Thatcher, and now led by an enthusiastically football-supporting Prime Minister, John Major, announced a 2.5% reduction in betting levy duties imposed on the game in order to allow £100 million over five years to be re-directed from the Treasury into funds for the redevelopment of football stadiums and to be allocated to clubs by the semi-independent 'quango', the Football Trust. The Government later confirmed its promise of an additional £100 million from the same source from 1995 onwards to aid further with the major stadium rebuild. In effect, this means that the Trust, with its additional funds from a tax levied on the pools companies, now has a budget of just over £32 million per year over 10 years to assist around 120 English and Scottish clubs with safety and improvement work. Top clubs were eligible for grants of up to £2 million.

Despite relaxations on the initial requirement that smaller clubs have seats, recent patterns of promotion and relegation in the Football League suggest that up to seventy major grounds in England and Wales may be required to become all-seated over the next twenty years. This represents an unparalleled and, for many people, a long overdue period of stadium redevelopment for the British game, and one which, uniquely for Britain, would be at least partly financed from funds released from Treasury coffers. The limitations involved here were also clear, however. Despite Trust support for new and imaginative innovations in stadium design and for partnerships between clubs, an offer of £4 million for clubs prepared to share a new venue was hardly likely to be lucrative (Briefly, for example, in 1990 Liverpool and Everton considered a move to a shared new stadium in Kirkby on Merseyside: the projected cost of the venture was a cool £125 million.) In October 1992, the Trust announced that no further grants would be available to Premier League clubs for major projects and it increased maximum grants for Division One clubs from £1 million to £2 million. By December 1993, the Trust had allocated grant aid of £89.68 million against total project costs in excess of £300 million.

*Restructuring the game*

Thirdly, the costs and other implications of stadium redevelopment, particularly for the larger clubs in England, hastened, rather than produced, in 1992, a significant restructuring of the English game. Taylor's comments on the game's lack of leadership at the top level characterized by its uneasy 'dual' control, exercised by the Football Association (FA) and the Football League (FL) provoked the offer of a power-sharing partnership proposed by the FL, and summarily rejected by the FA. The FA, instead, established a new breakaway league, the FA Premier League, which is formally led by the FA, but effectively controlled by its chief executive and club chairmen and is made up of the twenty-two (soon to be twenty) top clubs in England. Significantly, an early proposal from the organizers of the new League, bitterly opposed by fans and later relaxed, was that entry into it should depend in part on the nature and quality of stadium facilities offered by applicants, thus breaking automatic links of promotion and relegation.

The main public rationale for the break up of the 104-year-old Football League was to aid the national team by reducing the numbers of matches played by top players. It quickly became clear, however, that the major incentive for top clubs in their new affiliation was the promise of annual sponsorships for the new league of an estimated £112 per season to be shared exclusively by this small élite, and the establishment of the new League as a branch of the culture and entertainment industry with retailing and corporate projects to match; 'a small private corporation producing one product for the culture industry (Premier League football) but connected up to the larger multi-product networks of the culture industry (particularly in retail and television)'.[39]

Three years on, this sponsorship figure of £112 million still seems overblown, but Rupert Murdoch's Sky Sports satellite-TV channel, intriguingly supported by the BBC, soon closed a five-year TV deal with the FA Premier League reputed to be worth some £304 million.[40] This arrangement was far from widely popular among Premier League club fans.[41] But, coupled with individual club sponsorships, burgeoning merchandizing at large clubs and the sponsorship of the League itself by a brewing company, Carling (£12 million over four years), it was clear that Premier League clubs were aided by the split and by what Taylor has called the 'marketization' of the Premier League,[42] in their successful financing of stadium redevelopment and in establishing something of a financial chasm between themselves and the 70 remaining members of the old Football League. Promotion to the Premier League in the 1990s is generally assumed to be immediately worth £2-3 million to successful clubs.

*Drawing from the fan well*

The fourth major potential source of financing for change, and in many ways the most controversial, is direct funding by club supporters. Rogan Taylor has outlined the long history of voluntary fund raising by football fans in England to finance stadium improvements.[43] As relationships between fans and clubs became more 'commercialized' in the 1970s, traditional supporters' clubs were squeezed out by new, more aggressive forms of marketing. By the 1990s, the 'organic' links between fans and clubs had substantially been replaced by formalized memberships mediated by patterns of spectator consumption in and around the club. In this new relationship, money was increasingly raised from, rather than by, supporters. So it has largely been with the Taylor redevelopments.

The most obvious and easiest way to raise finance from fans is, simply, to raise ticket prices. This is explained by clubs, of course, in terms of the provision of improved facilities (refreshments, toilets, etc) and the (forced) substitution of a traditionally more expensive seat for a standing place. Seats also usually mean a reduction in overall capacity, hence the need to raise more income per spectator. This is especially true during the period of redevelopment, of course, when the capacities of some major English grounds was reduced by almost 30% (prices seldom fall again once redevelopment is complete). Finally, stadium improvements also offer some opportunities for clubs to move permanently up-market by targeting themselves more explicitly to more affluent, and possibly more orderly, customers. Such a trajectory has already been pretty clearly recommended by the Henley Centre for Forecasting to the FA in the latter's own Blueprint for Football published in 1991.[44] This last issue

**Table 11.3**  Stadium capacities: clubs in the FA Premier League 1992/93

| Club | Record attendances | Pre-Taylor capacity | Capacity 1994/95 | Projected all-seated capacity |
|---|---|---|---|---|
| Manchester United | 76,962 | 51,000 | 44,411 | 44,411 |
| Tottenham Hotspur | 75,038 | 35,000 | 24,500 | 40,000 |
| Arsenal | 73,295 | 45,000 | 37,500 | 37,500 |
| Chelsea | 82,905 | 44,000 | 28,945 | 42,000 |
| Liverpool | 61,905 | 40,000 | 40,000 | 40,000 |
| Everton | 78,299 | 41,000 | 40,500 | 40,500 |
| Leeds United | 57,892 | 32,000 | 40,000 | 40,000 |
| Queen's Park Rangers | 35,353 | 23,000 | 18,500 | 18,500 |
| Crystal Palace | 51,482 | 31,000 | 17,000 | 26,000 |
| Oldham Athletic | 47,671 | 19,000 | 12,260 | 20,000 |
| Sheffield Wednesday | 72,841 | 38,000 | 36,000 | 36,000 |
| Middlesbrough | 53,596 | 27,000 | 22,000 | 44,000 |
| Nottingham Forest | 49,945 | 32,000 | 22,500 | 30,501 |
| Wimbledon | 30,115 | 14,000 | 17,000 | 26,000 |
| Blackburn Rovers | 61,783 | 19,000 | 30,000 | 30,000 |
| Aston Villa | 76,588 | 40,000 | 40,530 | 40,530 |
| Norwich City | 43,984 | 26,800 | 21,272 | 21,272 |
| Ipswich Town | 38,010 | 31,000 | 22,260 | 22,260 |
| Sheffield United | 68,287 | 32,000 | 23,000 | 30,388 |
| Southampton | 31,044 | 22,000 | 16,000 | 16,000 |
| Coventry City | 51,455 | 26,000 | 22,600 | 22,600 |
| Manchester City | 84,569 | 44,000 | 21,357 | 36,000 |
| Totals | | 712,800 | 598,135 | 704,462 |

Source: Adapted from *Independent*, 15 April 1994.

has much exercised opponents to the football stadium modernization programme *per se*, as we shall see.

In fact, projected stadium capacities at top clubs in England fall not much short of pre-Taylor crowd limits (see Table 11.3) though, iron-ically, the recent popular revival in live support for football in England has meant that at some top clubs (Manchester United, Newcastle United) projected capacities already seem too small, and further building is being considered. In a country traditionally hostile to shared public facilities, it is difficult for any single major club to sustain a 70,000-plus stadium. In the meantime, substantially higher prices and increased pressures on fans to become season-ticket holders or club members during a period when price inflation has been in single figures, and as match attendances have been rising is argued to be excluding some traditional working-

**Table 11.4**  Average admission receipts per spectator, 1988/89–1992/93, for clubs in the Premier League in 1992/93 (£)

| Club | 1988/89 | 1992/93 | % increase |
|---|---|---|---|
| Manchester United | 4.32 | 13.95 | 222.9 |
| Tottenham Hotspur | 6.15 | 11.32 | 84.0 |
| Arsenal | 5.52 | 10.64 | 92.7 |
| Chelsea | 6.43 | 9.73 | 51.3 |
| Liverpool | 4.66 | 9.00 | 93.1 |
| Everton | 4.09 | 8.86 | 116.6 |
| Leeds United | 3.67 | 8.76 | 138.7 |
| Queen's Park Rangers | 5.49 | 8.64 | 57.4 |
| Crystal Palace | 4.10 | 8.43 | 105.6 |
| Oldham Athletic | 3.16 | 8.19 | 159.2 |
| Sheffield Wednesday | 3.95 | 8.02 | 103.0 |
| Middlesbrough | 3.91 | 7.84 | 100.5 |
| Nottingham Forest | 4.70 | 7.62 | 62.1 |
| Wimbledon | 5.16 | 7.59 | 47.1 |
| Blackburn Rovers | 3.29 | 7.56 | 129.8 |
| Aston Villa | 4.33 | 7.53 | 73.9 |
| Norwich City | 5.00 | 7.45 | 49.0 |
| Ipswich Town | 3.43 | 7.44 | 116.9 |
| Sheffield United | 3.21 | 7.12 | 121.8 |
| Southampton | 4.49 | 6.88 | 53.2 |
| Coventry City | 4.85 | 6.70 | 38.1 |
| Manchester City | 3.04 | 6.33 | 108.2 |

Source: Adapted from Digest of Football Statistics, Football Trust.

class fans from football's new future. Prices at Premier League grounds, and especially at larger corporate clubs such as Manchester United, have climbed most since 1988/89 (see Table 11.4 and Figure 11.1). Half have more than doubled in five years. It is hard to disagree with the twenty British MPs, who signed a Commons motion on the subject in October 1992, that some clubs have used the costs of redevelopment as an excuse to hike up prices further. By 1994/95, attendance at a League match for away fans at a moderate Premier League club such as Crystal Palace could cost £20, with no price reductions for young fans. Tickets at larger London clubs now routinely cost over £20. Tickets to stand at spruce small venues in the Third Division can now retail at £8. These are prices quite unprecedented in Britain.

At some larger English clubs, limited-rights issues (Liverpool, Millwall) and public-share issues (Tottenham, Manchester United, Millwall and Newcastle United) have also been used in order to raise capital from fans and investors, with very variable results (the Newcastle share issue

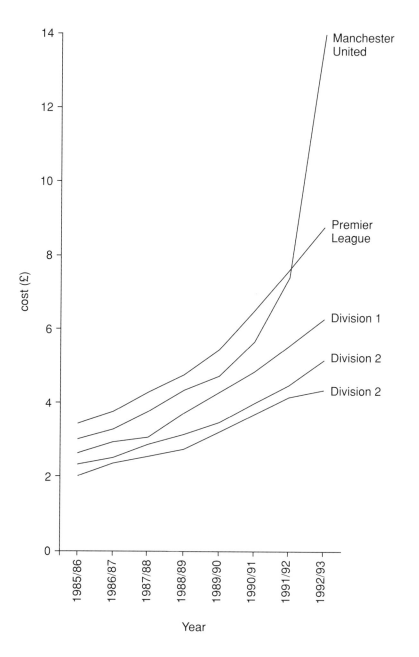

**Figure 11.1**  Average admissions receipts, Football League and FA Premier League 1985/86–1992/93

in December 1990 collapsed in disarray). At two London clubs, Arsenal and West Ham United, attempts to raise capital from fans took on an even more direct approach. The troubled public share flotation at near-neighbours Tottenham Hotspur prompted Arsenal to opt, instead, for a 'bond' scheme to raise capital for the £15 million conversion of the club's North Bank terrace. The scheme invited 12,120 fans to commit either £1500 or £1100 (more in instalments) to the club. In return a bond-holder was guaranteed: an option for ten years to buy a season ticket at a competitive price; a name on a seat in the new stand; a bond certificate; and membership of an obscurely defined 'Bondholders Club'.

At West Ham, the 'Hammers Bond' was aimed at 19,301 potential bond-holders to raise £15.1 million, with bonds priced from £500 to £975. Benefits on offer here were very similar to those at Arsenal. By 4 April 1992, according to the *Independent*, the Arsenal Vice-chairman, David Dein, was claiming that 'over one third' of the Arsenal bonds had been sold, still well short of the club's target figure. On 14 March of that year Arsenal and West Ham fans had organized an unprecedented joint demonstration at the match between the two clubs and Independent Supporter Associations set up at the clubs confirmed their angry opposition to 'a system which will effectively exclude the traditional football supporter and his/her family from all major League grounds before the end of the century'.[45] On 1 March 1993 the *Evening Standard* announced that only 576 West Ham bonds had been sold up to 31 July 1992, raising net revenue of just over £52,000 with additional launch costs to the club of £1.4 million. Match boycotts by home fans had contributed to a loss on the year of more than £2 million. According to the national fanzine, *When Saturday Comes*, in April 1993 the West Ham board 'were defeated because of a well run, vigorous campaign by the people who care most about the club – the fans'.

Elsewhere, the principle of the bond scheme has, interestingly, not been rejected outright. At Leeds United, for example, club research among season-ticket holders helped to assess likely responses of fans to proposals for a £500 bond which would pay them a £700 payback in terms of a £100 annual price reduction for season-ticket holders over seven years. 83% of fans surveyed thought the scheme to be 'a good idea', especially for its practical financial benefits for fans, and it proved a resounding success. Similarly, a modest scheme at Charlton Athletic (minimum bond £25), which also offered a bond-holder's representative on the club board, soon reached £995,000 of a target figure of £1.5 million.[46] Moreover, successful public flotations, as at Manchester United, have introduced something of a democratizing influence on club decision-making, if only on a minor scale. Shareholders' meetings in Manchester have, for example, affected club policy on stadium facilities and on important symbolic issues (for fans) such as the naming of stands.

**Should I Stay or Should I Go?**

Despite major initial fears about financing the Taylor recommendations, clubs, with support from the Football Trust, private sponsors, local agencies, a growing and high-paying fan base, and the new monies coming into the game from TV and merchandizing, have effected a dramatic transformation, mainly of their home sites. Clubs and their sponsors and partners have raised around 73% of the total cost of redevelopment so far. Cost and resistance to change among fans and club administrators has, however, curtailed interest in establishing entirely new venues (One club, Charlton Athletic, successfully campaigned to return to the club's old home in Greenwich.) At some clubs all four sides of the home stadium will gradually be rebuilt on the same site. (The rebuilt stadium at Blackburn stands, quite incongrously, wedged between Victorian factories and cramped terraced houses.) The passage of time and a subterranean campaign by fans, administrators and politicians aimed at retaining some seats, has also mellowed initial enthusiasm among those keen to be a 'lead' club in the post-Hillsborough transformation. A Royal Town Planning Institute (RTPI) survey in 1990 found forty-two League clubs to be seriously considering a move or to have moved; by 1991 that figure was down to thirty-four;[47] by August 1994, just six English and Scottish clubs were in new (post-1989) stadiums, the largest of these holding 20,000 fans; a further two clubs are soon to take up new residences. In addition, five major English clubs were granted extensions on the 1994 deadline for seats because of plans to relocate, and around five or six smaller clubs have similar plans in the pipeline. Only one club, Newcastle United, was granted an extension and has no plans to move. Planning obstructions have severely damaged and delayed the relocation ambitions of a number of clubs and city councils, especially when greenfield sites are involved, including those at Southampton, Portsmouth and Sunderland.[48] By the turn of the century there will be perhaps fifteen new football venues built in Britain since 1989. Only two of these, in Sunderland and at Middlesbrough, are likely to be of international standard in size (over 40,000 capacity) and facilities.

For those 'traditionalists' intent on conserving stadiums and opposed to a new national profile for the game there is perhaps some comfort here. For those promoting change at a faster pace, this picture is, on the other hand, something of a disappointment, revealing a lack of vision and imagination among those charged with leading the sport into the twenty-first century. It also provokes fears that money – up to one third of it public money – has sometimes been spent quickly and badly in patching up older venues, often simply laying seats on existing terracing, with scant attention paid to sight lines and recommended spacing between seats. The Football Stadium Advisory Design Council (FSADC) was set up at a miserly cost of £200,000 over three years, following a recommendation by Taylor, to advise clubs on design matters, including access and facilities for the disabled, but has since had its funding inexplicably, but predictably, withdrawn by the football authorities. The national Football Licensing Authority (FLA), which was used after the Taylor report to operate a licensing scheme for grounds and to monitor the discharge of local authority functions under the 1975 Safety of Sports Ground Act, at least ensures some national consistency on matters of safety, but examples of cheap 'container' architecture using low-cost materials – Chester City; Walsall, Scunthorpe United – with little attention to local identities or aesthetics, abound in the new generation of British stadiums and stands.

The exceptions are obvious, perhaps painfully so. Some richer clubs, Glasgow Rangers, Arsenal and Leeds United, for example, have produced unashamedly modern (and expensive) new developments of real substance and style. The exposed steelwork and enamelled cladding at more modest Wolverhampton Wanderers, Nottingham Forest and Millwall also stand out for representing an adventurous and stylish approach. The New Den at Millwall is especially interesting, as the first new, medium-sized stadium built in Britain for more than seventy years; and this from a club whose supporters are notoriously parochial and allegedly wedded to the old Cold Blow Lane site (on the chaotic last day at the 'old' Den in May 1993 fans invaded the pitch and attacked the Directors' box). In fact, active resistance to the new stadium in SE London has been extremely muted; the idea of building a new ground was sold and interpreted locally as a sign of the club's ambition to return to the Premier League, with guaranteed reasonable ticket prices (£10) and community facilities. Funded from the sale of the nearby old site, a rights issue, a grant from the Football Trust and one from Lewisham Council, and £1 million from the New York-based Ogden Entertainment Services management company which runs the venue, the New Den is both a symbol of the multi-use future of new developments and, perhaps, their trans-global management. Ogdens manages some 115 entertainment venues across the USA and their business is based on such venues. Frank Russo, VP International Operations, told the *Financial Times* on 8 March 1993 that English soccer 'focused on the pitch instead of the customer. There should be value going to the venue, regardless of the event'. For stadium architect, Rod Sheard, of the influential Lobb Partnership, new stadiums are, similarly, 'multi-activity townships' which should house their own 'customer-care centres'. On lavish concourses, the 'stadium streets', the 'emotional cycle' of fans, 'treated as a spending force … can be channelled by stadium owners to make the best use of spectators'.[50] Property journalist, Allan Herman, recently commented in similar vein that 'the buzzword in sports club board rooms these days is 'spectation'; which means that people can enjoy a good day out in a superstadium, while waiting for the main event of the day, whether that is a football match or a firework display'.[51]

The notion that it is the stadium itself which is the product is now widespread in the age of independent stadium management, shared ownership and multiple-event use. (The new Manchester United first team shirt has a large imprint of the Old Trafford stadium integrated into the shirt design.) The New Den is, certainly, invested with something like the civic pride more usually found in relation to sports stadiums on the continent (local fans at the opening match at the stadium sang, proudly, 'Is this Wembley in disguise?'). But the ownership and use of the stadium is profoundly 'privatized' and profit-focused. The facility is licensed for seventy non-football events a year, but it is, in fact, too poorly located to attract major events and it also has considerable access problems, bound as it is by a railway line and by problem housing estates; the kind of 'post-apocalyptic setting … with its scrapyards and building scars' which is immediately threatening to high spending event 'customers'.[52] (Hopes of staging home games of the American Football team, the London Monarchs, recently disappeared when the Monarchs, unsurprisingly, opted for use of the redeveloped White Hart Lane ground.) The stadium also lacks the Millwall 'branding', given its need to attract other events, a fact which goes down badly with local fans who want, specifically, a football stadium clearly identified as such (Ominously, Ogdens soon brought in the London Monarchs' American cheerleaders, The Crown Jewels, to give Millwall home matches that special 'visitor experience'.) But with its improved spectator services, close-to-the-action design, lack of perimeter fencing and its generally more open format, the stadium is also much less of the forbidding prospect for visiting (and home) fans than that provided by its run down and hemmed-in predecessor.

The sorts of partnerships across the private and public sectors established at Millwall have also been necessarily apparent elsewhere. Many of the major new developments involve some public finance, dedicated stadium management teams and, more infrequently, the involvement of local communities and organizations in matters of stadium usage and even design, almost for the first time. By far the most ambitious and imaginative so far of these new projects is the Alfred McAlpine Stadium in Huddersfield, designed by the Lobb Partnership to house both Huddersfield Town and Huddersfield RLFC and used for the first time in August 1994. (Stadiums no longer advertise an exact location in their names, but tend instead to act as signifiers – billboards – for paying sponsors. Huddersfield's old ground was known, simply, as Leeds Road.) The unique 'banana-truss' roof design at Huddersfield gives the new stadium an authentically modern and continental look and feel, 'one of

**Figure 11.2** New grounds for old. Grey and leaky Leeds Road, Huddersfield, struggles to catch the eye as the 'banana trusses' of the new McAlpine Stadium emerge nearby (Source: courtesy of Kirklees Stadium Development Ltd.)

the most innovative designs in Europe' according to Inglis.[53] 'By going for something totally different', says Stadium Administrator, George Binns, 'I feel we've acknowledged the spirit of Taylor rather than just complying with the letter by sticking seats on on the old terraces'.[54] The new stadium is funded mainly by money from the old site; from cash from Huddersfield RLFC and from Kirklees Council; and by grants from the Football Trust and the Foundation for Sports and the Arts. Because it is part publicly funded, and because Kirklees now owns 40% of the stadium equity, the stadium is at least part of an integrated approach to urban leisure planning. Despite its promotion as a football ground the new stadium is also likely to be the central focus for the centenary celebrations of the Rugby League in 1995 and may yet host a national Rugby League museum.

Initial plans at Huddersfield were for a 25,000-seated stadium, far in excess of the club's current requirements, but once again a signal locally of the club's ambitions to return to its glory days of the 1920s – ambitions reined in by the Football Trust's insistence that the initial development is more commensurate to current local requirements. Thus, only three sides of the stadium have yet been built with a projected capacity of 20,000. Nevertheless, it is a thrilling sight in an otherwise architecturally featureless vista. It also boasts all the by now familiar trappings of an ad-speak 'major venue', with a 450-capacity banqueting suite, conference facilities, plans for a golf driving range and facilities for hosting the ubiquitous pop concerts. On-site executive catering is a costly long way from football's traditional 'Bovril culture'; it is provided by Ring and Brymer, no less, caterers for Royal Ascot, Wimbledon, Henley and many state occasions.

The Kirklees 'ground share' may be another sign for the future of football clubs with ambitions on stadium partnerships with local authorities. Ambition, by the way, is everywhere and everything in football, perhaps especially at these times of flux when higher divisions and leagues are able to demand 'improved' facilities from candidates for promotion (clubs achieving promotion to the First Division of the Football League are currently given three seasons to convert to all-seating facilities). Post-manufacturing towns in 'heritage' Britain can also be quietly seduced by plans for service and leisure complexes wrapped around football stadiums, and boasting the usual hotels, banqueting and conference facilities. Holding a commercial seminar at the local football club is only the latest strategy, of course, for creating an interface between the 'heroic' dual domains of business and sport (Liverpool's corporate clients, for example, like many elsewhere, are urged to see executive box hire as 'a unique opportunity to become part of the Liverpool legend'). Candidate cities are already jostling for position to tender for a proposed new national stadium for football in the north of England, reputed to be likely to cost £200 million.[55]

Examples such as the Jack Walker-funded rapid material and playing transformation of a 'lost' northern giant such as Blackburn Rovers inevitably suggests to other fans, councillors and sponsors that clubs (and towns) can, indeed buy back their more successful past with the help of a passing millionaire or even an extravagant redevelopment or relocation proposal. At nearby Blackpool, which was an irresistible club in the late 1940s and early 1950s but which, like the town, has long been in decline, an impossibly(?) ambitious £200 million proposed entertainment complex with stadium and 'wrap-around' hotel, more suited to Chicago than the Lancashire coast, is being mooted at a site which currently has average attendances closer to 5,000 than 25,000 spectators. Talk of the creation of 3,000 local jobs and an annual injection of £100 million into local businesses has spiced regional interest in the project.[56] A water-colour painting hangs, optimistically, in the Blackpool club offices showing the large, futuristic stadium heaving with local fans. In the centre a huge video screen carries the score: Blackpool 3, Liverpool 0.


**What's in It for 'the Lads'?**

Arguably, the general improvement in spectator facilities and, more specifically, the move from terracing to seats in larger English football

238

stadiums constitutes an important material and symbolic shift away from the recent disorderly traditions of support for the national game in England.[57] Critics of the Taylor report have often conveniently misinterpreted his main recommendations as constituting an attack on hooliganism, though Taylor does concede that seating, 'has distinct advantages in achieving crowd control'.[58] Academic[59] and popular discourses on architectural determinism 'read off' human social behaviour from their surrounding built environment. In footballing terms, this usually produces variants on the 'treat 'em like animals, they'll act like animals' theme which informed many post-Hillsborough journalistic accounts of the need to modernize. Certainly, hooligan sub-cultures in England were buoyed in the 1970s, for example, by the appearance of forbidding perimeter fencing inside stadiums, but the role of such measures in actually causing hooligan rivalries is strictly limited.[60] After all, even early on, the best hooligan fights were taking place away from the stadium, after which they moved, ironically in some grounds, into the better-served and unsegregated seated areas. Also, it is worth making the point that as far as general stadium facilities are concerned, English Rugby League fans – not usually noted for their violence – suffered at least as badly as their footballing equivalents before Hillsborough.

Taylor was surely correct, however, to point to the specific combined effects at football in England of poor facilities, military-style police operations, and fencing and segregation, on the experiences and perceptions of hooligan and non-hooligan fans alike.[61] Undoubtedly, for Taylor, the provision of seating is seen as the major means of uncoupling these stifling and cumulative influences and of propelling the English game out of its long-term negative cycle of spectator crises and management by containment. Has the strategy worked? What can be said in this respect is that changes in crowd management and in stadium design following Hillsborough have been accompanied by rising crowds at football in England and falling numbers of arrests. We can say, too, that the experiences of supporters and of the police bears out the impression that hooliganism in and around English stadiums has, indeed, been reducing since 1989. Let us look, briefly, at the evidence here.

Attendances at League matches in England have been rising consistently since the trough following the Heysel disaster. Far from deterring fans, the policy response to Hillsborough seems further to have encouraged English football spectators to attend matches in greater numbers. In 1992–3, crowds were up by almost 30% compared to 1985–6 and rose once more in 1993–4 for the eighth consecutive season. Since the last season before the Taylor report (1988–9), arrests at football matches have also fallen substantially (by more than 20%) (see Figure 11.3). This fall was only interrupted in 1991–2, possibly partly as a consequence of the introduction of a new Football Offences Act (1991) which, among

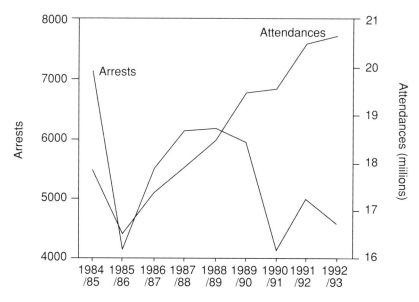

**Figure 11.3** Arrests and attendances at Football League (1984/5–1991/2) matches and FA Premier League and Football League matches (1992–3)

other things, criminalizes encroachment onto the playing area or surrounds, and which accounted for 7.1% of all arrests in 1991–2.[62] The new offences were introduced as a *quid pro quo* for the major, immediate stadium-design consequence of Hillsborough: the removal at most major British football stadiums of perimeter fences for purposes of crowd control. Video surveillance cameras now also monitor streets, crowds and pitch areas for reasons of safety and crowd management – a sporting analogue, for some, of Foucault's panopticon[63] – 'this enclosed, segmented space, observed at every point, in which the individuals are inserted in a fixed place in which the slightest movements are supervised, in which all events are recorded'.[64] At the same time, clubs in England have been judiciously reducing their reliance on the police for crowd management in favour of stewards and private security personnel (see Table 11.5). Some smaller clubs now stage matches with no police presence at all, and larger ones do so with only a fraction of the police manpower used in the 1980s. In short, at a time of widespread and radical stadium reconstruction, when crowds have been increasing in size, policing has been scaled down, perimeter fencing has been removed, and new offences have been introduced, official rates of hooliganism are actually in quite sharp decline.

This 'official' picture of more orderly, modern, stadiums is strongly borne out by recent research on policing football fans in England. In spectator surveys conducted in England in 1992, for example, almost 50% of fans questioned thought that hooliganism had declined 'a lot' since Hillsborough.[65] A national survey of the Police Match Commanders, who have responsibility for policing the ninety-two professional clubs in England and Wales, showed that 47% thought hooliganism inside stadiums had diminished 'a lot' in that time, and 31% that disorder outside stadiums had declined to a similar extent. Very few of these senior officers thought spectator problems had worsened; some felt they had no real problem at all. An extraordinary 89% of Match Commanders agreed that, in the context of other public-order duties, policing football in England was not a serious problem. Six out of ten home fans and one third of travelling fans detected improvements in the quality of football policing since 1989.[66] This may be connected, of course, to the fact that fans are actually seeing fewer police officers at matches. But it is also likely to signal recognition of a de-emphasis on policies of containment (fences, police escorts, rigid segregation, etc.) in favour of a new mode of positional policing, and of a general greater concern at football in promoting safety cultures rather than, simply, cultures of control.[67] And, finally, nine out of ten Match Commanders regarded the removal of perimeter fencing at stadiums to have been a success.[68] In 1993, only two (out of ninety-two) Premier and Football League clubs still had perimeter fencing on all four sides of the ground. Forty-six clubs had no such fencing at all. Larger stadiums have the least fencing and, uniquely, have no deep moats or other major barriers between themselves and the players.

Mapping out cause and effect is difficult here, of course. The influence of the media, for example, in shaping perceptions about, and experiences of, hooliganism should not be understated.[69] Although some accounts of alleged media distortions of the hooligan phenomenon remain hopelessly idealized,[70] in the age of Murdoch satellite-TV deals with football it is surely not too conspiratorial to expect little interest in today's hooliganism, at least from the Murdoch-owned press? There is, undoubtedly, a displacement factor at work here, too, with some serious hooligan incidents now occurring well away from stadium sites. Video surveillance is a powerful disincentive to disorder in and around stadium, especially when offenders are hounded sometimes weeks after the event.[71] Although the new stadiums no longer feel like a natural site for hooligan activity, in England we are frequently and rudely reminded that the 'lads' are still about and can still be a danger to be reckoned with in unprotected venues – there were serious disturbances and attacks on players at the bright New Den, for example, in May 1994. But, the routinized ritual of large-scale male confrontations at football does seem, at least in the short term, to have been punctured in England.

**Table 11.5**  Total police manpower for football policing operations: 'typical' weekends in 1985 and 1993

|  | Total number of officers deployed | Total attendance | Ratio |
|---|---|---|---|
| *1985 Total* | 4,457 | 329,000 | 1:74 |
| *1993 Total* | 3,780 | 500,248 | 1:132 |
| *1993* |  |  |  |
| Premier League | 1,574 | 253,034 | 1:161 |
| Division One | 1,177 | 127,743 | 1:109 |
| Division Two | 593 | 76,473 | 1:129 |
| Division Three | 436 | 42,998 | 1:99 |

Source:  N. Middleham and J. Williams, 'Policing football fans in the nineties' (Leicester, 1993), p.111.

Often reinforcing and being reinforced by changes in stadium facilities and design and refinements in crowd management, there has also been considerable 'cultural contestation' around the game in England, especially over the past five years, which has displaced hooliganism as the prism through which being a fan was widely viewed. This has produced, for example, a stunning revival in popular serious writing about the sport to complement the thriving spectator fanzine scene;[72] a significant new football/music/drugs interrelationship which stresses the non-violent, carnivalesque aspects of football;[73] and a new fashionable concern with the game's aesthetics and with eroticizing its new young stars.[74] There is also more than a mythologized suggestion that intellectuals, the so-called 'chattering classes', have begun to colonize seats in *de rigueur* new stands and concourse cocktail bars (as in the new North Stand at Arsenal) and to dominate debates about the game's meaning and its future direction (Opera North even commissioned and, in 1994, performed an opera about English football, while highbrow composer, Michael Nyman, also wrote a musical tribute, broadcast on British TV, to his footballing hero, QPR's Stan Bowles). This leads me nicely, in fact, into my final section which deals, briefly, with the current struggle over the 'soul' of the English game.

## Looking for a New England? Stadium Modernization and the Future of Football

In a recent social history of English football, Fishwick argues that the fortunes of the game can be seen to run broadly parallel to those of the

British Labour Party, and that 'social change may have affected the Labour Party and the game in comparable ways'.[75] In many ways, in fact, recent debates about the modernization of football in England mirror those around the 'new' Labour Party, which is led by a young, media conscious and self-confessed modernizer, Tony Blair. Recent opinion polls (August, 1994) showing the new 'realism' of the Labour leadership, appealing favourably to women and the middle classes in the prosperous south-east of England, have been matched by new research on football fans in England which shows women and more affluent fans well represented among Premier League club supporters.[76] Both Labour Party and football traditionalists are almost bound to be sceptical of such obvious shifts in favour.

Tom Nairn has recently captured well the masculine 'personal style' and the 'exaggerated workerism' of the traditional British Labour movement and the 'hanging together instinct [which] gave loyalty a quasi-religious dimension reminiscent of the wilder strains of nationalism', which bound together the 'blood ethos' of labourism against the (potential) democracy (women, middle classes, people of colour, etc.) of the present.[77] It is not too difficult to identify a similar kind of spectator vanguard in English football which has thrived on its offer of the most basic amenities. Walvin, for example, is critical of English football clubs and fans for opposing democratizing change, for 'clinging to the wreckage of tradition, that refusal to contemplate alternatives to old habits' and for their blind determination to, 'Remain faithful to the familiar'.[78] Hornby also warns of the 'conservative and and almost neurotically sentimental attachments' of male fans to old stadia and terraces,[79] while Ian Taylor argues that fans' objections to change connect with the 'inert, reactionary nostalgia', of club officials, a nostalgia which produces an image of terrace culture at odds with the 'rampant racism, crudely sexist banter and ... aggravation conducted by groups of young white males of little education and even less wit'.[80]

One does not have to share entirely Taylor's fiercely bleak account of contemporary terrace culture – after all, some women and older men like watching from the terraces[81] – to see the force of arguments such as these in relation to current developments. Against them, Duke contests the view that seating is safer or more secure than terracing, and argues that football modernization in England has produced 'functional but characterless grounds' and 'has led the élite clubs to seek a new kind of football spectator. Executive boxes and expensive seating are cultivated at the expense of traditional cheaper prices'.[82] Such opposition, with some reason as we have seen, also cites increased costs of admission and the alleged plans of the game's administrators to convert football into a television-controlled 'integrated leisure package' for middle class, family consumers as key points of contention.[83] It also laments the likely loss of the strongly partisan atmosphere at English stadiums and the traditional masculine camaraderie of the terraces.

There are a number of points to take up here. Certainly, flicking through the glossy prospectuses of English clubs launching new stands, the onus seems very much to be on commercial diversity and flexibility, on selling corporate and executives hospitality and on marketing and business opportunities rather than on new facilities for ordinary fans. One medium-sized club, Leicester City, for example, has developed an aggressive and diverse marketing profile which involves selling services to business (design and printing; fund-raising; database marketing) and the successful production and retailing of an extensive range of leisure products under the 'Fox Leisure' rubric. Leicester calls its own impressive new arena, 'The business stadium', describes it to corporate clients as 'a purpose-built hotel without bedrooms', and publishes a newsletter, *City Extra*, described as 'the official business to business publication' of the club (see Figures 11.4 and 11.5). Other clubs – Wolverhampton Wanderers, for example – now sport American corporation-style mission statements on customer care in plush stadium foyers, and no major new facility is built any longer on the basis 'that the staging of sport is the prime function'.[84]

These commercial impetuses towards flexible accumulation which are at the heart of stadium redevelopment in England mean, as Ian Taylor has pointed out,[85] that the utopian aspirations momentarily voiced in the Taylor report and elsewhere about creative partnerships at local level between clubs, fans and local authorities are unlikely to take off at most major football venues. Alternatives to the commercial model, available in a limited sense abroad, are also likely to remain unexplored in England.[86] Instead, the Premier League has instigated supporter (consumer) panels at all clubs for 1994–5 and is intent on more (market) research on Premier League fans; initiatives which, in themselves, have at least the potential to be progressive and which mark out a new era of relations between fans and the game's administrators. More disturbingly, however, the new marketing ideologies inside the game seem determined to contest the traditionally creative and independent role of supporter cultures. As Manchester United claimed their first League title for more than a quarter of a century at the rebuilt Old Trafford stadium in 1993, for example, the global sports anthem, 'We will rock you', blared loud on the PA system, drowning out the spontaneous celebrations of frustrated United fans. (Fans at Cup Finals in Germany will already be quite familiar with this kind of event (mis)management and orchestration.) Similarly, the marketing gurus at Aston Villa, quite misreading the nature of the occasion, hired an on-pitch host and dancers to conduct fans on the Holte End in a scripted farewell to the revered old terrace on the last day of the football season in May 1994. The host was

**Figure 11.4** Leicester City's new Carling Stand: 'a purpose built hotel without bedrooms'. (Source: courtesy of Raymond's Press Agency)

**Figure 11.5** Carling Stand conference and banqueting suite, Leicester City: an ode to the 'common man'?

spiritedly booed and abused by Villa standing fans for his trouble. Projects such as Tom Watt's extraordinary fans' oral history of Arsenal's North Bank terrace[87] surely provide a much more fitting epitaph than any marketing man's whim to these 'privileged places of working class communion', as Hopcraft memorably described the great English goal end terraces of the 1960s.[88]

However, it must be said that defending tradition, even in English football, is not always a guarantee of popular appeal, as the large sales of wild new football-strip designs in England loudly testify. In a further telling example, Leicester City, again, have also 'repackaged' reserve-team football in 1994, based around local newspaper promotions and the attractive facilities of their large new stand. Monday reserves-match nights in Leicester now offer children's membership clubs, face-painting, games, music and mascots to accompany games involving young hopefuls and club veterans which were previously watched by just a couple of hundred club die-hards. The resulting new Family Night Football has attracted parents and their kids from the city in their thousands, creating new community networks around the club and bringing with them the much sought-after associated patterns of consumption in and around a previously 'dead' Monday stadium.

As expectations about spectator consumption now routinely shape the way larger clubs connect with their communities – club community schemes, for example, seem, increasingly, to be incorporated into club marketing strategies – the future for traditional fans, effectively excluded by high prices and the new marketing strategies, remains unclear. Meanwhile, debates about tradition and change in the English game continue to be rehearsed among fans, particularly in the pages of spectator fanzines. In a recent survey, jointly undertaken by the national fanzine *When Saturday Comes* and the Sir Norman Chester Centre, 55% of fanzine readers 'generally approved' of structural changes to stadiums since 1989. However, a more hefty 80% of those asked approved of work undertaken at their own club's ground.[89] Fans, showing general approval for changes, spoke of facilities now being fit for human use; improved stadium design; the need to look to the future and not the past; the less intimidatory feel to modernized stadiums; and the opening-up of football to a wider public. The less-approving fans complained about the loss of atmosphere at matches; the inconvenience and price of seats; the ugliness of new stands; and the irrevocable damage done to the traditions of the game by the banning of terracing. A number of respondents described new stands as being products of Legoland. These differing positions were nicely summed up in two letters to *When Saturday Comes*, written in response to complaints from a Newcastle United fan, Ken Sproat, that the new, improved St James' Park, minus the raucous Gallowgate standing terrace, now lacked the necessary edge needed for a real football ground.[90] Signed, delightfully, 'The Justified Ancients of Man U'., the first letter agreed with Sproat's complaints, giving an account of the 'damage' recently inflicted on Manchester United's Old Trafford stadium:

> For Newcastle United read Manchester United. Ken's musings are an identikit picture of modern day Old Trafford. Nice ground, no heart. Old Trafford, 1994. It's a family affair. It's face paint paradise. It's Martin Edward's Terracotta Army. It's a tourist attraction, daytripper theme park. It's Alton Towers. It's Blackpool Pleasure Beach. It's Disneyland. It's football, Sir Matt [Busby] but not as you know it. The changing face of football coming to a Premier League ground near you. Ho, hum.

The second letter, taking quite a different tack, condemns Sproat as being from, 'a self-proclaimed élite of the Geordie faithful', who shout, 'where were you when we were shite?', at fans in the new Leazes End stand. The letter continues:

> In some ways they seem to resent a good side, an impressive stadium and packed crowds. Give them the familiar certainties of mediocrity and a slum of a terrace. [The article] is drenched in the sort of terrace sentimentality which is selective in memory and simultaneously contradictory. The Gallowgate End was open to the elements … [and] it housed some of the more Neanderthal elements of my club's support who brought shame on NUFC with their racist chanting during the '70s and the '80s. The Gallowgate End was an open toilet …

Charting some kind of middle course between these two visions of football's 'authentic' future, against the backdrop of a troubled past and a fast-changing present, is difficult in a culture which makes a virtue – in football as in politics – of painting modernizers and traditionalists into easily-identified, self-contained and self-evidently antagonistic camps. Could the latter letter writer, for example, properly lament the historic loss of leaky Leeds Road, Huddersfield? Can the former see any of the presence and beauty of the new McAlpine Stadium? If football's past is ugly and little mourned for some, inevitably the future is rampantly and dangerously disconnected and unregulated for others. The Scottish fanzine, *The Absolute Game*, eloquently sketched out the contradictions involved in questions of continuity and change in the British game in a recent review of a strident new account by marketing experts Fynn and Guest of football's past failings and future opportunities:

> On the one hand there will be those , including me, who cling to the old ways and traditions and, perhaps, have an over-romantised notion of what football means both personally and in terms of community.

On the other hand, there will be those who see football purely as a commodity which has hitherto been underselling itself, but which has the capacity to go super-nova. The first group, including me, are currently represented in the corridors of power by a collection of half-mad old duffers, crazed by gin, fumbling around in the dark, but at least their hearts are (in the main) in the right place and there is a modicum of democracy propping them up. Fynn and Guest call for a revolution to replace them by ruthless steely-eyed marketing men armed with clip boards, flow charts and plans for world domination, unfettered by any rules other than those of the 'free' market.[91]

Establishing tolerable continuities between the community sentiments of football's fumbling past and the more commercialized possibilities of its marketized and de-localized future remains one of the key issues, of course, for fans in the post-Hillsborough fall out. Predictably, most of the voices yet raised in this tortured debate in England are, like the one above, the voices of football men, and mostly young men at that. Football space in England is perhaps peculiarly highly gendered; it has been contoured, largely, by men's passions and their collective rivalries – and by their sexism and violence.[92] Especially since Hillsborough, access for women as football spectators has almost certainly improved. Some Premier League clubs may have as many as one-fifth of their audience now made up of women.[93] Perhaps it is significant, then, that female voices, still little heard, seem among the most consistent in their perspectives on the new generation of English stadiums. Julie Welch, for example, returning to write newspaper match reports on football after an eight-year absence, confessed herself to be 'gobsmacked' by the transformation which greeted her: 'I thought I was going to hate these new stands but I love them. All that football and a Ladies loo, too'.[94] Fellow football writer, Cynthia Bateman, commenting on a recent visit to 'theme-park' Old Trafford, and clearly aware of, though less traumatized than others by the contradictions she found there, reported:

> It was not like an English Saturday afternoon at football at all. For a start it was neither freezing cold nor raining. But there was more to it than that. Something had changed. The convivial jostling crowds in their players' shirts – 'Cantona 7' was most popular, 'Dieu 7' most original – and the families with tots on their shoulders wearing inflatable 'Fred the Red Devil' horns made the atmosphere more Disney World than Nightmare on Soccer Street. Where had all the nasties and nastiness gone? There was something uncannily wholesome about it all.[95]

In England's secure and distinctive – and gendered – system of class and leisure closures, the above account, and others like it, are easily and testily dismissed by the terrace cognoscente as the limp unknowing reflections of a *Guardian* liberal – in Labour party terms, one of those 'champagne socialists' who don't have, cannot hold, the 'true faith'. In other words, as Hornby might ask, 'Just where is a real fan's suffering in all this?'[96] Nevertheless, it is surely the case that changes in the game, in its audience and in its stadium will necessarily reflect aspects of the shifting contours of class, occupational and gender identities in Britain, and also the influences of the increasingly global market place for football and its various leisure products. Some women and some families are likely to become more important players here; less so, almost certainly, the less affluent, the long-term unemployed and the employment-less male youth. The reverberations of this fact of their effective exclusion may yet be felt way beyond the confines of football and its various markets. The signs of violent male detachment and alienation, and of domestic struggles over space and territory, are already apparent on many public housing estates in Britain.[97] Meanwhile, at the 'new' football, as committed fan, Tessa Davies points out[98] – and undoubtedly this still cheers many football men – the involvement of many female fans in English football's new future remains pointedly conditional:

> The absence of child care facilities in football grounds, the dearth of any decent toilets and refreshment facilities for adults and children alike, (means) many women are clearly unable to experience live football – the supposed life blood of the genuine supporter. Plans for the installation of American-style facilities are often dismissed by purists as attempts to hijack the traditional game as part of the conspiracy to hype, market and package. Presumably, football wouldn't be football without someone peeing on your head. Well, lads, if that's what you want you can keep it. I'll just stick to my TV.

## Acknowledgements

I would like to thank Alex Fynn, Phil Lee and Stephen Hopkins for their helpful comments on an earlier draft of this chapter.

## Notes

1. See, *Criminal Justice International*, Vol. 10, 2 (1992).
2. 'Stop Whingeing, Start Swingeing, Taylor', *Daily Express*, 30 June 1994.
3. P. Taylor, *The Hillsborough Stadium Disaster (15 April 1989): Final Report* (London, 1990), p.5, para. 25.
4. S. Inglis, 'Sitting pretty', *The Face* (1993), pp.117–19.

5. J. Williams 'White Riots', in A. Tomlinson and G. Whannel (eds), *Off the Ball* (London, 1986), pp.4–16.
6. J. Williams, E. Dunning and P. Murphy, *Hooligans Abroad* (London, 1989).
7. O. Popplewell, *Inquiry into Crowd Safety and Control at Sports Grounds*, Cmnd. 9710 (London, 1986).
8. S. Inglis, *The Football Grounds of Great Britain* (London, 1991).
9. I. Taylor, 'Hillsborough, 15 April 1989: Some Personal Contemplations', *New Left Review*, 177 (1989), pp.89–110.
10. Inglis, *Football Grounds of Great Britain*, p.10.
11. J. S. Black and M. G. Lloyd, 'Football Stadia Development', *Town Planning Review*, 61, 1 (1994), pp.1–18; J. S. Black and M. G. Lloyd, 'Football Stadia Development in England and Wales: a Research Note', *Planning Practice and Research*, Vol. 9, 2 (1994), pp.129–34.
12. Inglis, *Football Grounds of Great Britain*, p.12.
13. A. Clarke, 'Figuring a Better Future', in E. Dunning and C. Rojek, *Sport and Leisure in the Civilising Process* (London, 1992), pp.201–20.
14. Alan Sillito, quoted in D. Canter, M. Comber and D. Uzzell, *Football in its Place* (London, 1989), p.140.
15. J. Richards, 'The Savage Face of Britain', *Sunday Telegraph*, 6 May 1990.
16. J. Bale, *Sport, Space and the City* (London, 1993), p.20.
17. R. Kircher, *The Games of Merrie England* (London, 1928).
18. T. Watt, *The End: 80 Years of Life on Arsenal's North Bank* (London, 1993), pp.55–6.
19. A. Walker, 'The Strategy of Inequality: Poverty and Income Distribution in Britain, 1979–1989', in I. Taylor (ed.), *The Social Effects of Free Market Policies* (Hemel Hempstead, 1990).
20. L. Proctor, 'The Privatisation of Working-Class Life: a Dissenting View', *British Journal of Sociology*, Vol. 41, 2 (1990), pp.157–80.
21. L. Johnston, *The Rebirth of Private Policing* (London, 1992), p.155.
22. J. Lea and J. Young, *What Is To Be Done About Law and Order?* (London, 1993).
23. F. Bianchini and H. Swengel, 'Re-imagining the City', in J. Corner and S. Harvey, *Enterprise and Heritage: Crosscurrents of National Culture* (1991), pp.212–34.
24. B. Campbell, *Goliath: Britain's Dangerous Places* (London, 1993).
25. Brill, 'An Ontology for Exploring Urban Public Life Today', *Places*, Autumn (1989), p.30.
26. I. Taylor, 'English Football in the 1990s: Taking Hillsborough Seriously', in J. Williams and S. Wagg (eds), *British Football and Social Change* (London, 1991), p.12.
27. R. Brunt, 'Raising One Voice', *Marxism Today*, September 1989, p.23.
28. *Independent*, 15 April 1994.
29. Taylor, *Hillsborough Stadium Disaster*, para. 138.
30. Ibid., Chap. 1.
31. J. Williams and T. Bucke, 'Football Fans after Hillsborough: a Survey of Members of the Football Supporters Association' (Sir Norman Chester Centre for Football Research, University of Leicester 1989).

32. E. Relph, *Rational Landscapes and Humanistic Geography* (London, 1981).
33. Bale, *Sport, Space and the City*, pp.40–1.
34. Ibid., p.83.
35. Taylor, *Hillsborough Stadium Disaster*, p.12.
36. Football Supporters' Association, 'The Preservation of Standing Accommodation at Football Grounds'; a submission to Roy Hattersley MP (1992), p.10.
37. Jordans Informations Services, *A Survey of Football League Clubs* (London, 1988).
38. *Independent*, 17 May 1992.
39. I. Taylor, '"It's a Whole New Ball Game" – Sports Television, the Cultural Industries and the Condition of English Football in 1993'. Paper presented to the Centre for the Study of Sport and Society, University of Leicester, 18 June 1993, pp.16–17.
40. J. Williams, 'The Local and the Global in English Football and the Rise of Satellite Television', *Sociology of Sport Journal* (forthcoming).
41. A. Langford and R. Hunt, 'Own Goals and Late Winners' (unpublished report, 1993).
42. Taylor, 'It's a Whole New Ball Game', p.20.
43. R. Taylor, *Football and its Fans* (London, 1992).
44. Football Association, *Blueprint for Football* (London, 1991), pp.5–16.
45. *The Gooner*, Issue 28, August 1991.
46. *Evening Standard*, 23 April 1993.
47. C. Shepley, 'Planning and Football League Grounds', *The Planner*, 76 (September 1990), pp.15–17; C. Shepley and A. Barratt, 'Football League Grounds – Update', *The Planner*, 77 (May 1991), pp.8–9.
48. Black and Lloyd, 'Football stadia development'.
49. V. Duke, 'The Drive to Modernisation and the Supermarket Imperative: Who Needs a New Football Stadium?', in R. Giulianotti and J. Williams (eds), *Game Without Frontiers: Football, Identity and Modernity* (Aldershot, 1994).
50. R. Sheard, 'Going to Town on the Extras', *Panstadia International* (1993), pp.44–6.
51. *Western Morning News*, 3 November 1993.
52. *Observer*, 15 August 1993.
53. Inglis, 'Sitting Pretty', p.119.
54. *Independent*, 15 April 1994.
55. *Sunday Telegraph*, 21 August 1994.
56. Ibid., 17 October 1993.
57. Taylor, 'English Football in the 1990s'.
58. Taylor, *Hillsborough Stadium Disaster*, p.12.
59. Canter *et al.*, *Football in its Place*.
60. E. Dunning, P. Murphy and J. Williams, *The Roots of Football Hooliganism* (London, 1988).
61. Taylor, *Hillsborough Stadium Disaster*, pp.6–8.
62. N. Middleham and J. Williams, 'Policing Football Fans in the Nineties' (Sir Norman Chester Centre for Football Research, University of Leicester, 1993), pp.13–14.

63. J. Bale, *Landscapes of Modern Sport* (London, 1994), pp.82–3.
64. M. Foucault, *Madness and Civilization* (New York, 1988), p.197.
65. Middleham and Williams, 'Policing Football Fans in the Nineties', p.16.
66. Ibid., pp.18, 19, Chap. 2.
67. S. Frosdick, 'Public Safety Risk Management in Stadia and Sporting Venues: an Holistic Approach' (M.Sc. dissertation, Cranfield School of Management, 1993).
68. Middleham and Williams, 'Policing Football Fans in the Nineties', p.139.
69. E. Dunning, 'The Social Roots of Football Hooliganism: a Reply to the Critics of the Leicester School', in R. Giulianotti, N. Bonney and H. M. Hepworth (eds), *Football Violence and Social Identity* (London, 1994).
70. R. Haynes, 'Marching on Together', in S. Redhead (ed.), *The Passion and the Fashion* (Aldershot, 1993).
71. See G. Armstrong and D. Hobbs, 'Tackled from Behind' in Giulianotti *et al.*, *Football Violence and Social Identity*.
72. D. Bull (ed.), *We'll Support You Evermore: Keeping Faith in Football* (London, 1992); N. Hornby, *Fever Pitch: a Fan's Life* (London, 1992); D. Campbell and A. Shields, *Soccer City: the Future of Football in London* (London, 1993); I. Hamilton, 'Gazza agonistes', in *Granta* (Harmondsworth, 1993).
73. S. Redhead, *Football with Attitude* (Manchester, 1991); A. Brown, '"Ratfink reds": Montpellier and Rotterdam, 1991', in S. Redhead (ed.), *The Passion and the Fashion* (Aldershot, 1993).
74. See *The Face*, No. 20 (May 1990), pp.38–49; No. 48 (September 1992), pp.106–15 and *passim*.
75. N. Fishwick, *English Football and Society, 1910–1950* (Manchester, 1989), p.150.
76. J. Williams, 'The Carling Fan Survey: General Report' (Sir Norman Chester Centre for Football Research, University of Leicester, 1994).
77. *Guardian*, 25 August 1994.
78. J. Walvin, *The People's Game* (London, 1994), p.191.
79. Hornby, *Fever Pitch*, p.221.
80. Taylor, 'English Football in the 1990s', pp.14–15.
81. J. Woodhouse, 'A National Survey of Female Football Fans' (Sir Norman Chester Centre for Football Research, University of Leicester, 1991).
82. Duke, 'The Drive to Modernisation and the Supermarket Imperative', p.7.
83. Williams, 'The Local and the Global in English Football'; 'The Final Whistle', *Time Out*, 29 April–6 May 1992, pp.12–13.
84. S. Inglis, 'Making a Stand', Building Centre Trust, London, p.3.
85. Taylor, 'It's a Whole New Ball Game', pp.19–20.
86. A. Spillius, 'Club Class', *Fhm Magazine* (April 1994), pp.86–90.
87. Watt, *The End*.
88. A. Hopcraft, *The Football Man* (Harmondsworth, 1971), p.161.

89. *When Saturday Comes*, 90 (August 1994), pp.20–1.
90. Ibid., 89 (July 1994).
91. *The Absolute Game* (March/April 1994), p.14; A. Fynn and L. Guest, *Out of Time: Why Football Isn't Working* (London, 1994).
92. Woodhouse, 'A National Survey of Female Football Fans'.
93. Williams, 'The Carling Fan Survey'.
94. *Independent on Sunday*, 28 August 1994.
95. *Guardian*, 22 August 1994.
96. Hornby, *Fever Pitch*.
97. Campbell, *Goliath: Britain's Dangerous Places*.
98. T. Davies, 'Why Can't a Woman, be More Like a Fan?' in D. Bull (ed.), *We'll Support You Evermore: Keeping Faith in Football* (London, 1992), p.175.

# 12
# Where Sports and Money Meet: The Economic Geography of an Ice Hockey Stadium

*Hans Aldskogius*

I suspect that to many people the phrase 'The stadium and the city' suggests a rather substantial sports facility in a reasonably large place. However, stadiums come in many different sizes and can be located in places both large and small. In this chapter I will examine a stadium that is a far cry from the Wembleys and SkyDomes of this world, and which is located in a place that, in terms of the size of its population, must be described as microscopic when compared with the metropolises where these stadiums are situated. Such disparities notwithstanding, there are basic similarities between stadiums of varying size and different types, and smallness does not in itself rule out the possibility of illuminating general characteristics of the organization and functioning of stadium facilities. And it may well be that the linkages between stadium, sport and place are more easily distinguished when the context is that of a relatively small community.

Leksand is a municipality in central Sweden with some 15,000 inhabitants – 6,000 of them live in the town of the same name, the rest are dispersed in a few larger and several scores of small villages. However, in Sweden, Leksand is quite well known. It is situated in a district that has long been a major tourist destination – and it has a great ice hockey team. This small place is the home of the hockey club that has the longest series of consecutive seasons in the first division in the whole country – almost an anomaly in this very competitive and capital-intensive sport, which today leads all Swedish team sports in terms of the number of spectators. The Leksand team has now played in the first division for forty-five seasons in a row, it has won the league several times, and it occupies a rather special place in the Swedish hockey world – as a David among Goliaths. 'The stadium and the city' – well, there is a stadium in Leksand, an ice stadium, but there is certainly not much of a city. Before I turn to the main theme of this chapter, let me present a rough sketch of the historical and geographical context of the ice stadium.[1]

255

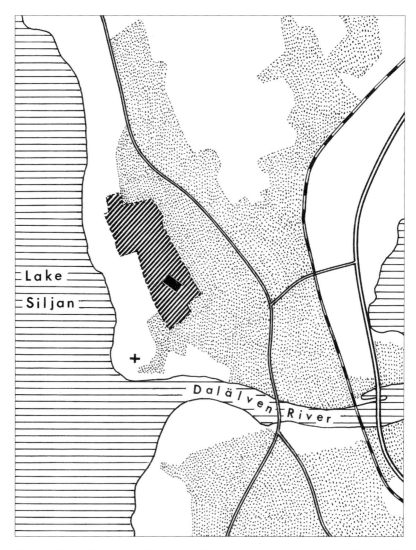

**Figure 12.1**　The town of Leksand. The map shows built-up areas (stippled), the sports area (line shading), the ice stadium (black rectangle) and the church

There is an expression in Swedish, the meaning of which is that what is important should be placed at the centre of things – 'to put the church in the middle of the village'. In the case of the church in Leksand, this is not literally the case. The magnificent medieval church is actually situated on the outskirts of the old village, on a beautiful site, a promontory overlooking an arm of Lake Siljan and the wide river as it leaves the lake.

**Figure 12.2**  View across the snow-covered track and field arena of part of Leksand's sports landscape, with the ice stadium (centre), field house and indoor swimming pool (right) and indoor tennis courts (left)

In this secular age and time, some people would claim that ice hockey has replaced the old faith as the major religious movement in Leksand. Be that as it may, neither is the ice stadium situated in the centre of the small town that Leksand is today. It is in fact located fairly close to the church, though not in nearly so beautiful a position. The ice stadium is part of a small sports complex that spreads over a sandy area with the lake not very far off on one side and a pine forest on the other. In this sports landscape ensemble we find a combined field house and indoor swimming pool, the soccer and track and field arena, baseball, softball and more soccer fields, indoor and outdoor tennis courts, a curling rink, illuminated jogging and skiing tracks – and the ice stadium (see Figure 12.1). The exterior of the ice stadium hardly suggests that it might be a major place of worship. Nor is it an architectural masterpiece. It is a drab, greyish, low structure – the first impression is one of a large work-shop of corrugated iron; 'ice barn' is a Swedish term that seems rather appropriate (see Figure 12.2). However, to people in Leksand the ice stadium is impregnated with local history.

When ice hockey was first played in Leksand, in the late 1930s, it was on a rather primitive outdoor rink. As the club climbed up through the league system, and spectator crowds grew, the arena was expanded, and eventually a new and bigger outdoor stadium was built and soon upgraded with an artificial ice-making system. This was in 1956, twenty years after the first hockey game had been played in Leksand. Around 1960 some

257

phenomenal spectator figures were recorded – phenomenal, that is, considering the small local population. In 1959 between thirteen and fourteen thousand people were jammed into the arena and some instant carpentry work was needed to prop up some of the swaying temporary stands that had been erected for the occasion – the final championship play-off game. However, such crowds are a thing of the past. In 1965 Leksand got its indoor ice stadium which today has a capacity of around 6,500 spectators. The story of ice hockey facilities is not just an appendix to the chronicle of club successes on the ice. It has provided much material for what one is tempted to call the mythology that surrounds ice hockey in Leksand: the first rink with sideboards nailed together from planks bought from a local saw-mill for five pounds; the fund-raising campaign to get the first artificial ice installation, a campaign that was initiated by one of the club's legendary player-heroes; and above all the building of the indoor stadium. A season-long fund-raising campaign turned into a veritable explosion of activities – bazaars, auctions, lotteries, box collections, village charity dances, and, to top it all, 'the roof nights', a series of outdoor fiestas which clinched the campaign that would help 'put a roof over the rink'. And it did. Enough money was raised to match the grant and loan that the municipality put up for the building of the stadium.

There are still people around who can tell these tales. They have perhaps become somewhat embellished over time, but they still bear witness to a remarkable mobilization of local resources for the cause of ice hockey in the past. Times have changed, the pioneer days are over and perhaps with them some of that district-wide enthusiasm that accompanied the rise of Leksand to the top of Swedish ice hockey. Still, ice hockey is, without doubt, the leading sport in Leksand today; it dwarfs all other sports in terms of economic turnover, impact on the local economy, spectator interest and media attention. And there is broad popular support for ice hockey in Leksand.


**The Ice Stadium**

Let me take you on a quick tour through the stadium on a match day. When we approach the building from the town – it is pretty well hidden behind the field house – we come right up against the main entrance, which is actually a wire fence with a dozen gates through which different categories of spectators are processed. The central gate area is capped by a rather unobtrusive sign – ISSTADION (ice stadium). Along the front gable are the club offices, half a dozen rooms in a row. As we proceed into the interior of the stadium, and buy the match programme from a hockey youngster, we pass a big board with small plaques which bear the names and logos of the members of the Elite Sponsor Club. On our left we see a line of booths where volunteers from the supporters' club, the youth section and also the local orienteering club are busy getting ready to sell souvenirs, coffee and soft drinks, popcorn, sweets, hamburgers and hot dogs, and to rent out cushions to those who have experienced the hard wooden benches on one side of the rink too many times.

We can peep through a door on one side of the hall for a quick look into the 'VIP tent', which is just that – a not very large plastic tent attached to the building, where sponsors and other guests are entertained with beer and sandwiches, coffee and cakes, during the intermissions between the three game periods. We guess, correctly, that at the far end of the building, but hidden away from us, are dressing rooms and other facilities for the home and visiting team, and a place where the game officials can recuperate between periods.

The ice-machine is making its last few swings around the rink, music blares through the loudspeakers, interrupted by messages about coming attractions and about cars left with their lights on in the parking lot. The stadium fills up quickly while the big clock above the rink ticks away towards game start. There is a feeling of expectation in the air. Soon the two teams will skate onto the ice, the home team in its white-and-blue star-studded uniforms, and line up for the national anthem. The game can start.


## The Economic Micro-Geography of the Stadium

A stadium is a place that has to be spatially organized in order to function properly, and it is in that sense that we might speak of a geography of the stadium. In the context of geographic studies in general, the stadium is a small space, and it is appropriate to indicate this by the prefix micro. The geography of the stadium, its spatial structure, is determined by a number of different principles and forces which, in some way or other, result in differentiation and segregation of areas within the hall. Some of the factors behind the spatial organization are well known, rather trivial, and to some extent standardized. The rink itself, the sports area proper, is regulated by standards set up by international and national ice hockey organizations, the number, dimensions and location of passageways and exits are controlled by fire security regulations, etc.


*The spectator areas*

In other respects, however, circumstances can vary a great deal. In Leksand's ice stadium, for instance, capacity is about evenly divided between

259

seated and standing spectators, but this relationship varies considerably between the arenas of the top-division clubs, from 100% seated down to 25%. Stadium owners, whether municipalities or clubs, can obviously make strategic decisions with respect to this relationship, and, as in other arena sports, the general trend has been to increase seating capacity at the expense of standing-room capacity, in order to attract spectators by increased comfort, to increase revenues from ticket sales, and sadly enough, for reasons of crowd control. This last motive, however, has so far not been a factor in Leksand. The spatial differentiation of spectator areas reflects the operation of economic factors which are obvious and familiar to anyone who has bought tickets for sports or cultural events. The best places are the most expensive ones, in the case of a hockey stadium those from which you have the best view of the action on the ice. The higher-priced seating sections are alongside the length of the rink. Beyond and above these sections there is standing room for a few hundred people, but almost all standing-room capacity is actually located on the tiers at the end sides of the rink (see Figure 12.3). In Leksands's ice stadium about 55% of the 3,300 seats are sold as season tickets or are VIP tickets – included as part of 'sponsor packages'. In addition to these two categories of pre-booked tickets, roughly equal in numbers, a small number of seats is held for club functionaries, media people, special guests, etc.

Ticket prices are actually not very differentiated in the ice stadium – normally Skr. 110 for a seat and Skr. 80 for standing room, with an additional charge of Skr. 20 at some of the most popular 'derby' games, play-off games, etc. The seating sections on one side of the rink are equipped with individual plastic chairs, while those on the other side just have wooden benches, but this difference in the degree of comfort that can be enjoyed is not reflected in ticket prices.

We find, thus, an expected and predictable, but not highly-differentiated spatial pattern of the spectator areas in the stadium, broadly determined by ticket prices. It is perhaps possible to detect some correlates of this economic stratification with respect to behavioural patterns in different sections – the more measured reactions in the sedate seating sections, and a bit more folksy rowdiness in the stands. But these are just impressionistic observations during a few games. At least if things are going well for the local lads on the ice, enthusiasm is ubiquitous in seating sections and stands alike. And most people join in to 'do the wave' – in section after section they rise from their seats and raise their arms to help produce the moving wave that sweeps around the arena – one of the recent innovations in crowd behaviour at sports events.

There are a few additional elements in the spatial organization of spectator areas. The club 'claque' is located in the stands at one end of the rink. There is a rather strong tradition of organized cheering in Swedish

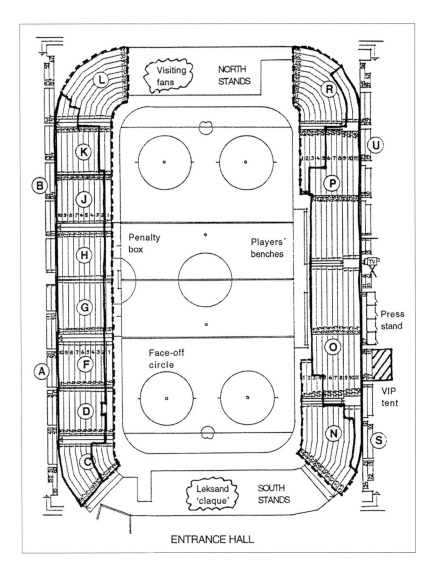

**Figure 12.3** The socio-economic differentiation of spectator areas in Leksand's Ice Stadium. Areas enclosed by solid lines are seating sections, with reserved VIP and season tickets for the 1993–4 season. Areas enclosed by broken lines are seating sections where tickets for individual games are sold. In addition to the stands at the north and south ends, there is limited standing room in sections A, B, S and U

261

sports. This can take different forms but a common one is that chants and rhymes are performed by a more-or-less well-rehearsed chorus of fans. In Leksand, the club, in co-operation with the schools, has tried to form a 'positive claque' of youngsters, as part of its youth programme and in the hope that this would raise the standards of cheering at home games. The fans travelling with the visiting team usually congregate in the stands at the opposite end of the stadium. When an invasion of more rowdy groups is expected they might be herded to this section by police and club functionaries. At best, this division of the turf can result in an entertaining antiphony of cheering and chanting during the game, at least as long as the hopes of a win have not been definitively squashed on either side.

### The geography of 'advertising space' in the stadium

In the words of its manager, Leksand Ice Hockey Club is not just a sports club, it is a branch of the local economy. The club has, in fact, an annual turnover that is exceeded by no more than fifteen to twenty businesses in the municipality. The club is typical of the Swedish sports movement in the sense that it is an association that grew out of sports as a popular movement, that it has a broad membership base (around 2,000 members, and 1,500 in the supporters' club), and no owner interests (see Chapter 10). In broad terms, ticket sales account for 25% of total revenues, sponsor-support for about one third, while the rest comes mainly from player transfers, from the popular summer hockey school, and from sales in kiosks in the ice stadium. Sponsor-support is thus of vital importance for the club's economy and can take several forms. One option is to join the Elite Sponsor Club by buying one of several packages which offer different combinations of promotional articles, season tickets, parking space with engine pre-heater, and a number of special VIP offers. With few exceptions, the sponsor packages are bought by firms and organizations, and the range of differently-priced alternatives means that even a small firm can easily afford to become involved.

There is, of course, a certain amount of flux in the population of sponsors, particularly between seasons, when contracts with the large core of rather permanent sponsors have to be renegotiated and great efforts are made to recruit new sponsors. A reasonable estimate is that, in recent years, the total number of sponsoring firms, institutions and organizations has been about three hundred. Some only buy one of the sponsor packages, some also buy additional advertising, others just advertising in some form. Even the least expensive sponsor package includes a minute element of publicity in the form of a small plaque on the Elite Sponsor Club signboard in the entrance hall of the stadium.

But it is the opportunity to buy advertising space in more prominent and eye-catching places that attracts the bigger sponsors and generates the bulk of sponsor revenues for the club. Advertisement space is sold in several forms – inside the hockey arena, on the player uniforms, in match programmes, club newsletters, etc. In addition, there is the option to become a 'game sponsor' – the sponsoring firm or organization is presented over the loudspeaker system, flyers can be distributed in the arena, the products of the firm might be demonstrated on the ice in the breaks between periods if that is feasible, and the sponsor nominates and awards the trophies to the players. There are other ways as well in which the club can offer something in terms of publicity value – players can take part in sales campaigns, the club can contribute to school acti-vities, and so forth. However, advertising within the stadium is clearly the most important commodity that the club can sell, and it is in this domaine that the economic micro-geography of the stadium becomes particularly expressive. Here, we move into a world that is familiar to visitors to many types of sports facilities – the world of signboards around arenas.

For the sake of simplicity one might say that most advertising space in Leksand's ice stadium is sold as 'boards' or 'signs', and priced on the basis of two principles: the size of the individual signboard (in running or square metres), and visibility. Obviously, one has to pay more for a large board than for a small one in a similar position. It is the 'visibility' factor, however, that creates the quite elaborate segmentation of adver-tising space in the stadium. It is the action on the ice that catches the eye during most of the game, and the most expensive advertising space is actually not any fixed place in the arena itself, but the players' uniforms. These are particularly valuable, of course, because not only can the messages be seen in the home stadium but they travel with the team all around the country – and abroad as well, for that matter.

Advertising on the players' uniforms is almost entirely monopolized by the club's biggest sponsor, STORA, one of the larger industrial groups in Sweden, with its base in wood processing, and its head office in the city of Falun, some forty kilometres away from Leksand. Today, the group is a truly international enterprise and employs considerably more people abroad than in Sweden – and very few in Leksand. Nevertheless, there are subtle historical ties between the company and its traditional home base in the province, which partly explains its long-standing fin-ancial support of the Leksand team. The name STORA appears on the helmet, across the shoulders, on both arms of the jersey, on both trouser legs and around the leggings – in several of these places in large bold letters. A couple of other sponsors are also represented on the uniforms. In the 1993–4 season, the logo of Mitsubishi, the Japanese firm, appeared on the uniforms of all the first-division teams, and yet another firm is

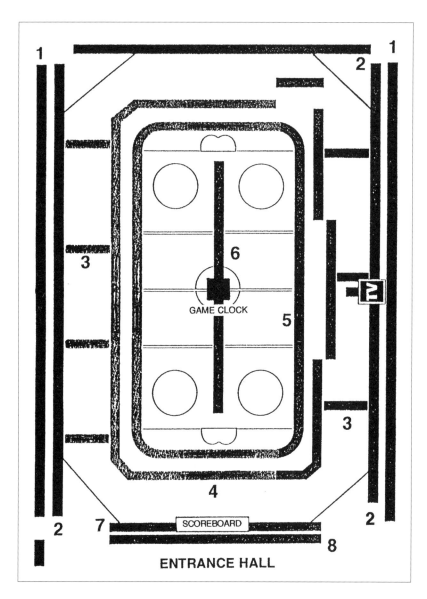

**Figure 12.4** Advertisement space in Leksand's Ice Stadium. 1 – aisles; 2 – panels above spectator areas; 3 – stairways; 4 – outer sideboards; 5 – inner sideboards; 6 – above rink, on and around the game clock; 7 – scoreboard panel; 8 – boards. Areas in grey are exposed when games are televised

represented on the helmets – in both cases as a result of a joint league advertising contract. However, it is the STORA message that dominates very emphatically on the uniforms of the Leksand team.

Advertising space is also sold on the ice itself, again by way of joint hockey league contracts. The four corner face-off circles are bought by the Swedish national trotting tote, and the mid-rink circle by a Swedish telecommunications group. Broadly speaking, the price of advertising space around the rink peaks along the inner sideboards and then drops as one moves away and upwards from the ice – away from the eye-catching action (see Figure 12.4). There is no need to go into details, but a few examples and comparisons might be illuminating. Space along the aisles is relatively inexpensive; signboards around the match clock above the rink and on the panels above the seating sections and the stands are about twice as much. For signs on the outer sideboards one has to pay another two-thirds of that price, and space on the inner sideboards and the scoreboard is roughly four to five times as expensive.

But it is not only the eyes of the spectators that follow the action – so does the television camera. The situation is this. Commercial television is a very recent thing in Sweden, and the televising of ice hockey league games is still mainly within the realm of the public service TV sector (commercial TV channels have, however, outbid the public service company in the case of some international championship tournaments, and is also beginning to televise league games). Telecasts from league games in public service television are thus not interrupted by advertisements – but advertising signs in the arena are allowed. Even though normally only glimpses from a relatively limited number of home games are shown on national television during a season, the possibility of television exposure is a powerful sales argument on the part of the club. The position of advertising signs relative to the eye of the TV camera is reflected in the 'cost map', as it were, of advertising space. As shown in Figure 12.4, the lower parts of a little more than half of the arena can be seen from the television camera position, and here advertising space is roughly 70–80% more expensive than in the corresponding 'dark side' positions.

There is, then, a considerable degree of price differentiation within the ice stadium with respect to advertising space. The shrewd buyer of advertising space might consider additional aspects. Some parts of the rink are 'hotter' than others, and attract special attention from spectators and TV cameras alike. The area around the goals, of course, where the scoring of goals or spectacular saves might also be shown in instant replay sequences on television; the rink corners, where a bunch of players often fight over the puck for quite some time; the face-off circles where teams slowly line up many times during the game; the penalty boxes, towards which more or less repentant sinners reluctantly navigate, and

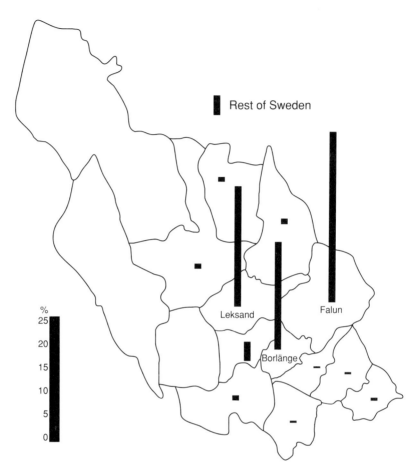

**Figure 12.5** Leksand Ice Hockey Club's sponsor and advertising revenues in 1992; percentage figures by municipality of origin

where lengthy palavers between referees and team captains take place. In short, it matters where along the sideboards the advertising sign is placed, and some canny buyers of signboard space will pay a visit to the TV camera box before they decide where they want to place their advertisement.

*Local, regional and national linkages in stadium advertising*

A look at the map of the geographic distribution of sponsor-support highlights the strong dominance of a core area of three municipalities

266

**Figure 12.6** A view of the interior of the ice stadium (at a not so well-attended youth hockey game!). Across the rink one can see the advertising signs on the inner and outer sideboards, on the panels above the seating sections, around the match clock, and next to the scoreboard at the far end

(see Figure 12.5). Leksand itself accounts for about one quarter of total sponsor revenues, roughly the same proportion as of home game spectators. Falun and Borlänge, which are the two largest towns in the province and are both situated some forty kilometres away from Leksand, together make up around 60% of sponsor revenues. This is in fact considerably more than their one third share of home game spectators, largely due to the contribution by the club's major sponsor in Falun. The rather broad regional support for the Leksand hockey team – in terms of both spectator and sponsor interest – indicates that it has become something of a flagship for sports in the province.

Relatively speaking, the number of sponsoring firms and organizations is greater in Leksand itself than in other municipalities in the sponsor core area, and there are more rather small sponsors here than elsewhere. This is not surprising. Charity begins at home, as it were, and, although most sponsors regard their contributions to ice hockey in Leksand, not as charity but as business-motivated investments in marketing and in place resources, it is obviously easier to drum up support for the team in its own backyard than further away. Also, Leksand is a typical small-industry community and there is only a handful of businesses that are able to give more substantial sponsor support.

If there are differences between the profiles of local sponsors, that is sponsors from Leksand, and sponsors from the wider surrounding region, and perhaps also sponsors from farther away, might such differences, then, be reflected in the pattern of signboard advertising in the ice stadium? A preliminary hypothesis might be that paying power would determine, at least in a broad sense, where sponsors try to buy advertising space. However, this hypothesis is a little too pat. In the first place, there is the possibility that advertisers would opt for more, and cheaper, signboard space rather than less space in a better but more expensive location. Second, there might be differences between advertisers with respect to how they value the opportunity for TV exposure. For a business that essentially operates on a local or regional market, TV exposure might not be of particular significance. Indeed, interviews with sponsors in this category indicate that the motive for advertising in the ice stadium is often simply to show the firm's or organization's presence at and support of the 'Leksand ice-hockey system'. One does not necessarily believe that such advertising will result in more jobs or increased sales, and none of the advertising sponsors which were interviewed had in fact made any attempt to evaluate possible effects of that kind. Conversely, firms that sell up towards 90% of their products on the international market cannot really expect to promote sales through advertising signboards in the ice stadium in Leksand, TV exposure or not.

In fact, most major sponsors look upon advertising as just one element of a 'marketing mix', amongst a variety of other considerations. To sponsor ice hockey in Leksand is an investment in place resources that gives the firm goodwill and helps provide good entertainment during a long season for employees and other people in the region alike. And, almost unanimously, the interviewed sponsors emphasized the very useful role that ice hockey plays for their relations with customers and other business contacts. A meeting, supper, and then a home game in the ice stadium is a successful formula that many sponsors have adopted in their relations with customers, their own sales representatives, etc.

Nevertheless, sales of advertising space in the ice stadium is the form in which much of the sponsor-support is channeled to the club. Given the reservations about the original hypothesis put forward above, perhaps a more cautious and tentative formulation is called for. A reasonable assumption might be that the more expensive signboard locations are bought primarily by 'big' sponsors and particularly those which may be interested in having their message exposed to a national audience through telecasts, for instance because they make consumer products and operate on a national market.

Figure 12.7 shows the distribution of the signboards within the ice stadium, classified according to the geographical provenance of the advertisers – they have been rather crudely grouped into three categories:

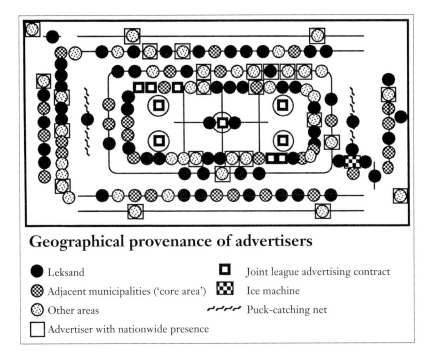

## Geographical provenance of advertisers

● Leksand

⊗ Adjacent municipalities ('core area')

◉ Other areas

☐ Advertiser with nationwide presence

☐ Joint league advertising contract

▨ Ice machine

⌁⌁⌁ Puck-catching net

**Figure 12.7** Distribution of signboards in Leksand's Ice Stadium, autumn, 1993, by geographical provenance of advertisers. The plan is slightly distorted in its proportions, but with few exceptions it reproduces all the different areas for advertising shown in Figure 12.4. The stairways have been excluded; on the front of the 'light side' steps are stickers with the name of the local grocery store. Not shown on Figure 12.4, but here, are some signboards on the walls and the nets which protect spectators in the end stands from wild pucks; stitched into the nets are five transparent logo signs for a local construction firm

local (Leksand), 'core area' (adjacent municipalities), and others. At first glance, the pattern may seem rather random. Signboards of firms and organizations from Leksand are numerous and appear everywhere within the stadium, and so do the signboards of advertisers from the 'core area' of adjacent municipalities, as well as those of firms and organizations from the rest of the province and from other parts of the country. However, it is possible to detect some patterns that lend some support to the hypothesis stated above.

On the sections of the inner and outer sideboards that are seen by the television camera (the 'light side' in club parlance), Leksand advertisers account for 40% of the signboards, the 'core area' for 24% and the rest for 36%. It should be added that the club tries to sell packages of signboard space on both the 'light' and the 'dark' side of the rink, at a discount, and to some extent the dark side is therefore a mirror of the light side signboard pattern. Roughly 25% of the space on the light side is sold to firms and organizations that can be characterized as having a national presence, in the sense that they are nationwide organizations, and to that figure one can add the eight places where the names or logos of the general league sponsors can be seen, including the five face-off circles.

A rough estimate suggests that about 60% of the advertisers in the TV-exposed areas can be regarded as firms and organizations with a national presence or a national market – this classification consequently includes some local or regional businesses which are oriented towards a nationwide market. Banks, insurance companies, construction firms, food producers, a local mail-order company and a resort hotel are examples of this broad and diversified group of advertisers. A comparison with the panels above the seating sections, which are not seen on television, is illuminating. Here, Leksand advertisers account for 53%, those from the 'core region' for 27% and others for 20% of total signboard space, but only two or three of the advertisers can be said to have a national presence or to be oriented towards a national market for their products. The local and regional firms dominate very markedly. If we turn to the cheapest spaces, the aisles, where signboards are seen only by passers-by, the club has hardly been able to sell any space at all.

It would be possible to add more detail to this discussion of the map of advertising around the stadium, but a few general observations may suffice. It is hardly surprising, of course, to find that the major sponsors are well represented in the more expensive advertising spots – including the players' uniforms. Also, advertisers with an interest in national exposure are over-represented in the most visible places on the 'light', TV-exposed, side of the arena. It is also very obvious that, in relation to their share of the club's total sponsor and advertising revenues, advertisers located outside Leksand and the adjacent core area are greatly over-represented in the more expensive signboard areas. They seek an advertising outlet whereas the local and core area sponsors are more actively involved in the hockey itself, and are more likely to buy sponsor packages with VIP season tickets, and go to the games.

There is thus some support for the hypothesis advanced above. In themselves, these findings are quite trivial – we would not really expect buyers of advertising space to behave in any other way. Nevertheless, the sketch map in Figure 12.7, in all its simplicity, is a document that illustrates that a top-level sports club can serve different interests in its function as a medium for advertising and public relations. To support the club – as a provider of entertainment as well as of sports for the young Leksanders – to get goodwill in the community and among employees as a sponsor of the pride of Leksand sports, to be able to capitalize upon customers' and other business contacts' interest in ice hockey, to reach now and then a nationwide television audience: these are some of the motives for sponsoring ice hockey in Leksand, and to some extent these different interests are accommodated through the price differentiation of advertising space within the ice stadium, and are reflected in the pattern of its allocation to different groups of sponsors.

## The Ice Stadium – A Link between Club and Municipality

What I have called the economic micro-geography of the ice stadium tells parts of the story about the links between the hockey club and the local and regional business community that helps to sustain top-level ice hockey in Leksand through its financial contributions. But the ice stadium is also an incarnation of the economic relationships between the club and the municipality. Today, ice hockey in Leksand is a profitable activity for the municipality. It generates tax revenues, directly through income tax on the club's salaried personnel – functionaries as well as players – and indirectly through the turnover in the local economy that the club's own purchases, as well as those of the home game spectators, generate. Municipal revenues from ice hockey activities exceed municipal costs by a substantial margin. And the financial situation of the club is quite satisfactory.

However, this has not always been the case. From the late 1970s, the club had persistent economic problems, and repeatedly submitted requests that the municipality should help to cover its operating deficits. The club attributed the problems primarily to the high running costs for the ice stadium, although escalating player costs was clearly another significant factor. In 1981 the municipality bought the stadium from the club in order to ease its economic problems, but during the next few years the municipality had several times to step in with direct subsidies and loan guarantees before the club's finances were stabilized. A massive effort on the part of the club to increase sponsor revenues was equally important in this process of financial reorganization.

For a number of years the hockey club's financial problems became something of a serial story in local politics. The debate was at times heated, the majorities behind the decisions to grant the club financial support were by no means overwhelming, and there are still bitter memories of these controversies in some political quarters. In essence, the debate concerned what should be regarded as legitimate reasons for municipal involvement in sports activities. In the view of those who opposed some of the municipal rescue operations, the youth hockey programme, for instance, was a useful activity and one that should be supported by tax money, as should other sports and recreational activities for the resident population at large. Professional or semi-professional élite sports, however, were regarded as something that the municipal budget should not be burdened with; this was something that should be the concern of the business community.

Today, the direct economic relations between the club and the municipality are almost exclusively tied to the ice stadium. The municipality owns the stadium, but has relinquished all advertising rights in the stadium to the club. However, through a separate sponsor contract, the municipality has, at a modest cost, secured the right to make use of the stadium and the club for various public activities. Another contract regulates the rent that the club pays for its use of the ice stadium. For a number of years the operating costs for the stadium have shown a deficit – as have most other sports and recreational facilities in the municipality – and in the last few years the rent that the club pays has amounted to about one third of this deficit. Since the hockey club uses up most of the ice time, those opposed to the sport argue that the rent is too low and is in fact a form of municipal subsidy. Members of the pro-hockey lobby predictably wave that argument aside, and point to the social benefits of the hockey youth programme, to the substantial tax revenues that accrue to the municipality through top-level ice hockey, and particularly to the difficult-to-measure, but, in their opinion, price-less publicity that Leksand can enjoy thanks to its hockey team. Be that as it may, the ice stadium stands there as the visible symbol of the invisible threads that link ice hockey and the municipality together. A rather unpretentious building, to be sure, but it houses what, in the context of the local economy, must be regarded as quite an impressive economic enterprise. To quote again the words of the club manager: 'ice hockey in Leksand is not just a sport, it is a branch of the local economy'.

## Concluding Remarks

Let me add a brief 'progress report' on the current plans of the club. The ice stadium is actually the only rink with artificial ice in the whole municipality, which may seem a bit surprising in view of the long tradition and dominant role of the sport in Leksand. The stadium is very intensively used. There is ice for ten months of the year, and during most of that time it is booked from eight in the morning till eleven o'clock at night. One would perhaps expect that, if the club contemplated any kind of expansion of its facilities, an additional artificial ice rink would be at the top of the list. But of course, even a simple training rink in the form of an extension of the existing facility would be a relatively costly project.

However, the immediate plans of the club concern something else. It is perhaps a telling illustration of the importance of customer relations that what is planned is an upgrading of the VIP facilities – the replacement of the present rather prosaic VIP tent with a more spacious and hospitable lounge, cafeteria facilities and so forth. Also, the club has proposed that a national ice hockey museum be established in conjunction with the stadium – another example of how activities around the hockey games themselves steadily become more varied – for the benefit of sponsors as well as for the hockey fans in general. An application for financial support for the planned museum has been favourably received by the provincial government.

With some 120,000 home game spectators each season, one might well say that the Leksand Ice Hockey Club is a major power in the local and regional entertainment business. In terms of its formal relations with the municipality, the club falls under the Committee for Leisure Affairs, which administrates the ice stadium. With reference to the magnitude and local importance of ice hockey in Leksand, the club management, headed by the manager, a former municipal commissioner and presently the Chairman of the municipal council, has recently proposed that the ice stadium be separated out from this organizational structure, to become instead an administrative unit directly subordinated to the municipal executive committee. This is certainly an innovative as well as a controversial idea, and the pro- and con-hockey forces are again bracing themselves for a power play in the arena of local politics where, through the years, representatives of the hockey club have often been powerful actors.

In this chapter, I have focused, rather narrowly, upon the ways in which Leksand's ice stadium can be interpreted as a concrete manifestation of economic linkages and relations between the hockey club and its environment. This perspective is important – in turnover terms the club's A-team, the Premier Division team, dominates club activities, and top-level ice hockey today is big business. Nevertheless, élite activities are not the only things that count in ice hockey in Leksand, and it is perhaps appropriate to conclude on a different note.

The club has retained its original character of an association with a broad membership base, no owner interests, and a tradition of basing élite activities on a platform of mass participation. In the case of ice hockey, the latter means a youth programme, and, in addition to its two junior teams, the club has around three hundred youngsters engaged in this programme, and a dozen teams in regular league play in the 8–16 age group. Very few of those will eventually become top-level hockey players, in Leksand or anywhere else – as do other clubs, Leksand has for many years recruited players at a national and even international level. To watch a game between the 4–7 year olds in the Bear League is both a rewarding and a thought-provoking experience, and not only because the entertainment value is in some ways even greater than at some first-division games played on the same rink – the frantic stumbling around of the miniature hockey gladiators in a 'score-or-die, tactics-all-forgotten' spirit can offer some wonderful examples of ice hockey at its best and worst. The tiny tots in the Bear League are also a reminder of the fact that one essential feature of Swedish club hockey is kept alive in Leksand – the combination of a broad base and excellence at the top.

'Money makes the world go around', so the song says, and this is certainly true of the hockey world as well. An overwhelmingly large share of the money that meets sports in and around the ice stadium circulates around the A-team. Indirectly, revenues from that level will help keep other activities in the club going, and the youth programme is largely financed through sales in the ice stadium – of programmes, in the kiosks, for instance – but also through other activities which are organized and carried out by the youngsters themselves, their parents, and other voluntary workers. Money alone would not make the Leksand hockey system go around; without a good deal of unpaid, idealistic work by parents, club members and supporters, parts of the system would grind to a halt.

Leksand and its ice hockey is not a unique phenomenon, but it is perhaps an unusual one in today's top-level team sport in Sweden. The ice stadium itself is not unusual, but rather a commonplace example of what Swedish hockey arenas look like and how they are used today. And in many respects what has been discussed in this chapter are well-known phenomena in other arena sports and in other places. Perhaps this chapter should be characterized as a study of 'the stadium and the region', rather than of 'the stadium and the city'. Since there is no city in the real sense of that word, and since after all the scale of the activities is relatively limited, in terms of attendance (an average of around 5,000 spectators per game) and traffic, questions about the physical or nuisance impact of stadium activities on the local community are not particularly relevant. To my mind, it is the role of the ice stadium as a focal point for regional networks, social and economic, that is particularly significant in the case of Leksand.

I have not yet heard anyone from Leksand speak in endearing terms of the ice stadium as such, either as a revered landmark or an asset to the cultural landscape. For most of the time it just functions as a busy sports facility, as a workhorse used by the ice hockey club, a few other local lower-division teams, schools, the figure-skating club, and, very marginally, by the general public. But it is when this drab, grey, rather charmless structure is filled with action, spectators and sound that it really comes to life as a place of meaning and importance to people in the community and in the surrounding region. At least once a week it becomes a place of joy and despair. When the home team scores, a jubilant song ('Olé, olé, olé') blares through the loudspeakers; when the opponents score, the first four notes from Beethoven's 'Destiny symphony' thunder through the stadium. On their way to the penalty box, players from the visiting team are accompanied by a catchy tune ('That's life, so full of falseness'), while sinners from the home team are followed by a cute little song about the innocent pranks of children. Folk-music tunes alternate with current pop-music hits in the intermissions; there is chanting and cheering from the claque; the crowd roars or groans as the play sways back and forth across the rink.

For a sizable fraction of the local population, and for many more loyal fans from the rest of the province, this is a familiar scene and one to which they return many times from late September to early April. For the large majority of people in Leksand who seldom attend a game, ice hockey is nevertheless an ever-present part of local life during a long season. And for many years the name of Leksand has been drummed into the heads of people around the country through the messages intoned by reporters on the radio, on television and on the sports pages of the Press with the words 'in Leksand's ice stadium'.

## Notes

Most of the data for this chapter comes from the Leksand Ice Hockey Club, from the Board for Leisure Affairs in the municipality of Leksand, and from interviews with a sample of sponsors. A more extensive study of the role of ice hockey in Leksand is H. Aldskogius, *Leksand, Leksand, Leksand! En studie av ishockeyns betydelse för en bygd* (Hedemora, 1993), which includes a documentation of the sources and literature used for that study, as well as for this chapter, which is also based on additional information, specifically on the ice stadium, collected from the club. An abbreviated version in English of parts of the above-mentioned study can be found in H. Aldskogius, 'Ice Hockey and "place": A great club in a small town', in John Bale (ed.), *Community, Landscape and Identity: Horizons in a Geography of Sport*, Department of Geography, Keele University, Occasional Paper 20 (1994), pp.33–53.

With respect to general, and in particular to geographic or spatial aspects of stadium development and stadium use, I have profited greatly from the following two works: J. Bale, *Sports Geography* (London, 1989) and J. Bale, *Sport, Space and the City* (London, 1993). Both books include extensive bibliographies.

# 13

# Stadiums, Professional Sports, and City Economies: An Analysis of the United States Experience

*Robert A. Baade*

To some people, professional sport is the transcendent experience in contemporary Western culture. As such, sport is inextricably bound to myth. While some might debate the transcendental character of the sports experience in total, few would disagree that the economics of professional sport has surpassed the ordinary. Many would also agree that, increasingly, economics has become the focus of professional sport. The growing intimacy between professional sport and economics has spawned myths about the economics of sport. Beliefs about certain aspects of the economics of professional sport are uncritically accepted and advanced by those whose self-interest is served by them. For example, in seeking public subsidies for the construction of stadiums and arenas, sports boosters have described professional sport as a significant catalyst for economic growth. To what extent does professional sport represent a civic economic investment? The purpose of this chapter is to separate myth from reality in assessing the contribution of professional sport to urban economic development in the United States.

The chapter consists of five parts. In the first, the literature on professional sport and urban development is briefly reviewed. Theory about the subject is identified and analysed in section two. In part three, methods for testing the relationship between sports and development are presented. The results of the tests are recorded and analysed in section four, and in the final portion of the chapter, conclusions are drawn and the implications for policymakers are discussed.

## Review of the Literature

Critical assessments of the contributions of professional sport to urban economic development in the United States are a relatively recent phenomenon. A number of factors have conspired to heighten scholarly interest in the subject. Arguably the most conspicuous and compelling reasons for the nascent scholarship are the ongoing American urban fiscal crisis and the extraordinary financial privilege enjoyed by professional sports owners and players. In this era of growing popular resistance to government largess, it is difficult to rationalize public subsidies for infrastructure improvements for the very profitable professional sports business. In the face of opposition, apologists for professional sports have rationalized subsidies as civic investments. Sports-facilities supporters have rejected the notion that choices have to be made between, for example, schools, sewers, streets, and stadiums, by portraying the stadium as a 'cash cow'. Rather than forcing painful trade-offs, these boosters envision the stadium expanding the economy and thus enabling public investment in critical areas. Such logic is seductive, and has proved successful in convincing some cities to assume the considerable financial risk posed by stadium construction and operation. The conspicuous failure of some stadiums to provide for the promised economic expansion has galvanized popular resistance to public stadium subsidies in cities throughout the United States and Canada. What does scholarship conclude about the efficacy of professional sports as a development tool?

Benjamin Okner elevated the debate to a national level in a 1974 article in which he examined stadiums across the USA, and concluded that most produced revenues insufficient to cover their costs.[1] If the history of stadiums has been written in red ink, logically how could stadium activities fund other public projects?

For the booster bent on proving that stadium subsidy is a sound civic investment, there is no necessary inconsistency between a losing private enterprise and a profitable public activity. In fact, the booster would argue that it is precisely the public benefit which cannot be appropriated by the private stadium enterprise that justifies, indeed mandates, public financial support. Thus, an assessment of the worthiness of a stadium project requires a comparison of the social, as opposed to private, benefits and costs. Not surprisingly, rare is the team-commissioned study that identifies stadium social costs in excess of stadium social benefits. In fact, in reviewing many studies commissioned by teams, a city could be sued for financial malfeasance for not subsidizing sports infrastructure.

Recognizing the importance of the social dimension, scholars have sought to find ways to measure stadium externalities or the indirect benefits accruing from stadium activities. Research has produced widely divergent results. For example, a 1983 study by a University of Pennsylvania researcher estimated that Philadelphia's professional sports teams accounted for more than $US 500 million of economic activity.[2] More recently, New York City's Mayor described plans to build a publicly-funded, $US 400 million stadium for the Yankees in response to George Steinbrenner's threat to move them across the Hudson. The Mayor rationalized the proposal by asserting that the Yankees should contribute $US 200 million annually to the city's economy.[3] By contrast, a Baltimore study estimated that the NFL Colts (now the Indianapolis Colts) generated a mere $US 200,000 in additional economic activity.[4] These sharply different results were compelled by sharply different assumptions. It is also worth noting that the Philadelphia study was funded by a consortium of the city's professional teams, while the Baltimore study was completed shortly after the Colts had bolted for the greener pastures of Indianapolis.

Since assessments of a stadium's estimated economic contribution are critically dependent on the model employed, it is essential to develop theory not identified with any particular interest. Richard Dye and I together constructed a model that sought to determine whether stadiums or the presence of professional sports teams correlated with higher levels of economic activity.[5] The results of our research indicated that, in the majority of cities analysed, stadiums and teams contributed nothing of statistical significance to the metropolitan economy. The difficulty inherent in the regression technique which we employed relates to isolating the stadium and/or team from other factors that account for changes in urban economic activity. Despite this non-trivial issue, a comparison of urban economic profiles before and after the stadium construction or team adoption offers the most potential for an objective assessment of how stadiums and teams influence metropolitan economic activity. The theoretical portion of this chapter offers a justification for this approach.


## Theoretical Issues in Assessing the Correlation between Stadiums and Urban Economic Growth

Debate surrounding the benefits created by stadiums occurs on at least three levels: direct expenditures; indirect expenditures; psychological and other non-quantifiable benefits. In the realm of direct expenditures, the construction phase of the stadium project must be distinguished from the operational phase. The focus in this chapter is on expenditures associated with stadium and team operations. James Quirk and Rodney Fort define the procedure commonly used to define direct expenditures.

The procedure that is used to estimate the economic benefits provided by a team or a facility is first to estimate the direct expenditures by the team for goods and services in the city, and then to add to this expenditures by fans on goods and services (other than game tickets)

purchased in the city, together with expenditures by players on purchases of goods and services in the city. The resulting sum is the amount
of direct expenditure benefits to the city provided by the team.[6]

Businesses and their employees derive income from direct expenditures and spend a fraction of those incomes on goods and services within
the metropolitan area. Spending derived from direct expenditures constitute indirect expenditures. Their very existence depends on the direct
expenditures undertaken. Since direct expenditures translate into income
for those providing goods and services, the effect of direct spending on
economic activity must be multiplied to estimate the total economic
impact of direct expenditures. The size of this multiplier depends on the
amount of additional income and spending induced by direct expenditures within the city's geographic area. In reviewing studies supporting
stadium subsidies, multipliers greater than three have been estimated.[7]
However, the recent norm for stadium multipliers is two or less.[8]

If stadium subsidies cannot be justified on the grounds of direct and
indirect expenditures, apologists for subsidies cite several benefits that
are not easily quantifiable. Some have suggested that the presence
of professional sport encourages businesses to locate. The theoretical
underpinnings for such an assertion are rarely specified, but, perhaps,
a professional sports presence suggests a vitality that correlates with
heightened business activity. However, there is no evidence to suggest
that professional sport is an important location factor. For example,
Baade and Dye found no connection between professional sport and
manufacturing activity in approximately 90% of the tests conducted for
a number of cities in the United States.[9] Certainly it is reasonable to
expect that other factors, such as the tax environment and the existence
of a skilled labour force, determine business location to a far greater
extent than professional sport.

Some welfare gains attributed to the stadium and professional sports
teams are virtually impossible to quantify. Stadium boosters have cited
the psychic benefits associated with the enhanced quality of life imparted
by the presence of professional sports. Others have ascribed value to the
appearance of a city's name each day in sports pages across the nation
and the world. In this, the deep space of the stadium debate, any value
can be assigned to psychic gains to justify the stadium project on rational
grounds. However, there is the possibility that feeling better about
ourselves through a professional sports presence translates into measurable economic benefit. At any rate, given the complex nature of the
relationship between the stadium and professional sports teams and
metropolitan economic activity, to assess their economic impact requires
contrasting the urban economic landscapes before and after the introduction of a stadium or team to the city's economy.

Total economic benefits imparted by the stadium and team emanate from the change in a city's direct expenditures attributable to the change in the professional sports environment. Given the critical role of direct expenditures, it is necessary to elaborate on their source. In the standard development models, local growth comes from increased export sales – net inflows of spending from outside the area. The multiplier then follows the new spending with expansion of locally-produced secondary activities. The other way for a local area to grow is through import substitution – if the twenty dollars spent by a local resident on a sports ticket would have been used to buy goods outside the area, then net local spending will increase.

The size of the multiplier following any net increase in area spending depends similarly on the locus of the re-spending. If all the new income is re-spent on locally-produced goods, then the multiplier will be substantial. If, however, the highly-paid athletes or executives maintain their residences outside the area or if the concessionaires import their semi-finished goods from outside, then the multiplier will be small.

The impact of a stadium depends, therefore, on the details of where each dollar is spent and would be spent – on imports, on exports, or on local production. This information is extremely difficult to obtain (especially since it requires both the factual and the counterfactual) and the common technique is to proceed by making assumptions about the sources and uses of spending. Not surprisingly, those who estimate the greatest impact of stadiums on local economies assume that all the direct spending represents a net increase in local spending (implicitly they are saying that all the spending is either export sales or import substitutions) and that all the re-spending stays inside the area.

Without knowledge of the origins of direct expenditures, the orthodox impact study methodology which treats all direct spending on sports as net new spending, the stadium or team contribution to the urban economy may be vastly overstated. Indeed, since the indirect expenditures are derived as a multiple of direct expenditures, errors in estimating net direct expenditure increases are compounded in defining increases in spending overall. In defending the treatment of all sports expenditures as net new expenditures, some authors of impact studies have opined that the infeasibility of identifying that spending, for which professional sports substitutes, leaves no alternative. While admitting to the complexity of identifying the origins of sports spending and its net contribution to spending, empirical evidence on the net increase in spending due to sports can be obtained. Once again the method involves comparing the city's economic profiles before and after the stadium is built or the team is adopted.

Any economic analysis of the impact of a stadium or professional sports team would not be complete without considering the opportunities a city forgoes in subsidizing the team. The question should not be whether a new stadium would have any net impact on area development, but rather, if it has the largest impact on the area from the set of alternative development projects. The local development authority has limited time and budgets: tax-exempt industrial development bonds are now restricted and rationed;[10] tax receipts from gambling and lotteries, a popular new technique for financing stadiums, are not available for schools or public transportation. In general, the political capital to sell projects to those who pay the taxes, or who lose from the redistribution of economic activity, is limited. Scarce development subsidy resources might better be targeted to industries which are more clearly engaged in export sales or import substitution. The attention of those who allocate development resources should be devoted to the types of jobs which are being created in alternative development products.

It may well be true that public support for high-visibility development projects like stadiums does come more easily than for some alternatives. However, if such support comes only from the perception of substantial development flowing from the project, bolstered by the assumption-compelled impact studies, then this is not much of an argument.

Since a stadium or sports-based development strategy may change the structure of the local economy, the long-run impact is not necessarily amenable to prediction with the direct expenditure-multiplier approach. Indeed, when opportunity cost is included, stadium costs may well exceed benefits. The types of jobs induced by stadium activity are low-wage and seasonal: ticket takers, ushers, vendors, restaurant and bar workers, taxi drivers, etc. An area-development strategy which concentrates on these types of jobs could lead to a situation where the city gains a comparative advantage in unskilled and seasonal labour. Compared to other areas (with their comparative advantage in high-wage, high-skilled labour) future growth in sports towns will be concentrated in low-income jobs.

It is conceivable that the economic outcome of public subsidies for professional sports may differ substantially from the benefits projected by their advocates. Given the cost to a city of building or refurbishing a stadium, the economic impact of professional sport requires empirical examination. To supplement the sports impact studies, an alternative methodology which provides after-the-fact audits of the contributions of professional sports to metropolitan economies, needs to be devised. The evaluative technique should be designed to serve at least two functions. First, the model needs to provide evidence on whether sport induces increased economic activity or simply realigns it within the metropolitan area. Second, the model needs to provide evidence on the efficacy of a sports-development strategy relative to some alternative means for inspiring growth. The manner through which these demands are met by the model employed in this study are discussed in the next section of the paper.

## The Model

The economic impact of sport has been estimated using a variety of techniques. One method involves regressing data on metropolitan economic performance on city characteristics before and after a stadium is built or a team is adopted. As noted earlier in the paper, this technique has theoretical appeal, but implementing it is not without complications. Most prominent among the difficulties is a need to model precisely the economy of each city to ensure that the contribution of sport is accurately estimated. When change occurs in the professional sports industry, other changes, such as a modification of the state personal income tax, are occurring simultaneously. If important changes affecting economic performance are excluded from the model, the contribution attributed to alterations in the sport sector may well be misrepresented.

Modelling an urban economy with precision is a formidable task, and before undertaking it, it is logical to determine first whether the economic contribution of sport is statistically significant, i.e., is the economic impact of professional sport on a city demonstrably greater than zero? A model to test this proposition can be constructed without specifying all the variables that have shaped the time path of urban economic activity. In this regard, it is useful to recognize that the pattern of economic activity for cities considered individually mimics national, regional, and state trends at various points in time, as well as following a trend line that is peculiar to that city through time. Once these fixed effects have been factored out or accounted for in explaining changes in a city's economic activity, all that remains is the change inspired by factors unique to a city at various points in its history. Through the use of this 'fixed-effects' model, we simplify our conceptual task by dispensing with the need to include those variables explaining economic trends. This enables us to focus attention on how new stadiums or teams differentiate one city's economic performance from others, as well as describing how sports affects the city's economic performance over time. This fixed-effects approach distinguishes this study from its predecessors.

Changes in a city's professional sports industry, as defined by changes in the number of franchises or stadiums, represent unique city events. Do these sports developments explain a portion of the observed changes in municipal economic activity not accounted for by trends? Our first task is to use our model to answer this question. Equation 13.1 embodies the technique used in addressing this issue.

**Equation 13.1**

$$(y_{i,t} - \sum_{j=1}^{k} \frac{y_{j,t}}{k}) - (y_{i,t-1} - \sum_{j=1}^{k} \frac{y_{j,t-1}}{k}) = \beta_0 + \beta_1 NT_{i,t} + \beta_2 NS_{i,t} + e_t$$

*where*

$y_{i,t}$ = real per capita personal income in city i at time t

k = number of cities in the sample

n = number of years in the sample

$NS_{i,t}$ = number of stadiums less than ten years old in city i at time t[11]

$NT_{i,t}$ = number of professional sports franchises (baseball, football, basketball, and hockey) in city i at time t

$e_t$ = stochastic error

Operationally, equation 13.1 allows for an estimation of the extent to which changes in a city's per capita income from one year to the next, adjusted for trends in economic activity, are explained by changes in either the number of new stadiums or professional sports franchises that a city acquires.[12] Since the professional sport industry is small relative to a large city's economy,[13] finding a city in which professional sports is statistically significant in determining per capita income is arguably unlikely if the dependent variable is city total real personal income. However, to establish that professional sport contributes positively to city economies, the method employed here requires only that sport be significant in determining changes in city per capita income not explained by trends. It is reasonable to conclude that, in the absence of a statistically significant relationship between professional sports and that portion of changes in per capita income not explained by trend, professional sport is of little consequence to the conduct of an urban economy.

If, through the empirical application of equation 13.1, it is determined that professional sport is of little or no economic consequence to a city, an explanation is required. After all, sports-spectating involves spending, and it is axiomatic that one person's spending is another person's income. In the example cited earlier in the paper, the New York Yankees' threat to move across the Hudson to the New Jersey Meadowlands has inspired New York State and city officials to consider funding a new $US 400 million stadium for the team in New York City. This civic largess has been rationalized on the grounds that the Yankees annually contribute $US 200 million to the New York City economy through the spending generated by fans.[14] As explained previously, estimates of this magnitude tacitly assume that spending in conjunction with sports spectating represents spending that would not otherwise occur. Such an assumption is not realistic. Spectating at a sporting event is but one option with regard to the use of leisure time and money. If aggregate spending does not increase with a city's acquisition of a new stadium or professional sports franchise, it may well be because sports expenditures replace spending on other leisure pursuits. If equation 13.1 fails to confirm a connection between professional sports and city per capita income, it may well be because sports spending substitutes for other forms of leisure-spending.

Amusement and recreation spending could conceivably increase with an expansion of a city's professional sports offerings for two reasons. First, spending increases if a new stadium or team induces increased spending by fans from outside the city (increased exportation of professional sport services). Second, spending increases if residents of the city expanding its professional sports offerings spend money at home on professional sports-spectating rather than in other cities (professional sport import substitution). On the other hand, spending on sports-spectating could substitute for other kinds of leisure-spending. Therefore, spending on amusement and recreation in a city expanding its professional sports activities could increase, decrease, or remain the same.

What ultimately happens to amusement and recreation-spending within a city overall depends on the magnitude and nature of the spending substitutions identified here. Professional sport effects a city's personal income not only through its impact on spending overall, but an expanding or contracting sports industry may effect the composition of the metropolitan economy. A city that subsidizes its sports sector may gain a comparative advantage in sport in considering trade with other cities in the state, region, or nation, and this is not without consequences. Professional sport creates certain kinds of jobs, which in turn modify the distribution of income and spending. What happens to city personal income overall through a change in the professional sports environment is a complex question. In short, it is an empirical question, that will be answered through an application of equation 13.1.


## Empirical Results and Analysis

The results of the empirical tests based on equation 13.1 are recorded in Tables 13.1 and 13.2. The sample used to run the tests consisted of the experience of forty-eight cities in the United States from 1959 through 1987. Every city that hosted a professional team in one of the four major team sports (baseball, football, basketball, and hockey) over this time period has been represented in the sample. In addition to ensure a broader, more representative sample, cities that have not hosted a prof-essional team, ostensibly because of their size, were included. A list of the cities comprising the sample is included in the appendix at the end of this chapter. Tests were conducted for individual cities as well as for all the cities in the sample. Results are recorded in Table 13.1 of the extent to which adding a new stadium or changing the number of teams effected real, per capita, personal income in cities taken individually and together.

The information recorded in Table 13.1 overwhelmingly indicates that professional sport is not statistically significant in determining real, personal income per capita. Thirty-five cities that hosted professional sports over the sample period were tested, and not a single one exhibited a positive stadium effect on real income. Logically, the data suggest that stadium benefits are appropriated not by society as a whole, but rather by team owners and professional athletes. In two cases, Washington, DC and Oakland-San Francisco, stadiums contributed negatively to real personal income. It is noteworthy that both Washington, DC and the Bay Area have rather high per capita incomes, relatively speaking. In light of this, these results may be attributable to jobs created by sports in these areas that pay below the metropolitan norms. Furthermore, it is noteworthy that the majority of cities, more than 61% percent of those sampled, exhibited a negative stadium coefficient. In other words, the tendency appears to be for stadiums to push rates of economic growth below the average defined by trend lines for cities nationally. These results support a conclusion relating to economic growth and profes-sional sport subsidies reached by Baade and Dye in 1990:

The impact of stadium construction or renovation on the metro-politan area's share of regional income is negative and significant. This result is consistent with the kind of economic activity that sta-diums and professional sport spawn. Professional sports and stadiums divert economic development toward labour-intensive, relatively unskilled (low-wage) activities. To the extent that this developmental path diverges from less labour-intensive, more highly skilled labour (high-wage) characteristic of other economies within the region, it would be expected that the sports-minded area would experience a falling share of regional income.[15]

Given the rather substantial amounts of public money required to build stadiums, these results fail to provide an economic rationale for public subsidization of stadium construction. Professional sport does not appear to create a flow of funds from which cities can finance public projects that had been foregone to permit stadium construction or some other form of professional sport subsidization. Furthermore, if the costs of

**Table 13.1** Changes in real per capita income as it relates to new professional sports stadiums and franchises for selected US cities, 1959–1987

| City | $\beta_1$ | $\beta_2$ | $\beta_3$ | $R^2$ | Durbin-Watson[a] |
|---|---|---|---|---|---|
| | Statistic | | | | |
| Atlanta | −115.85 | 76.51 | −117.71 | 0.03 | 1.94 |
| | (−0.17) | (0.32) | (−1.34) | | |
| Baltimore | 318.78[c] | −129.56[c] | N.A. | 0.27 | 1.89 |
| | (3.09) | (−2.79) | | | |
| Boston | 199.14[c] | N.A. | −196.69 | 0.32 | 1.86 |
| | (2.08) | | (−1.44) | | |
| Buffalo | 41.06 | −23.2 | −68.0 | 0.08 | 1.85 |
| | (0.54) | (−0.62) | (−1.32) | | |
| Charlotte | −28.38 | 2.99 | N.A. | 0.09 | 1.99 |
| | (−0.53) | (0.02) | | | |
| Chicago | −311.26 | 56.17 | N.A. | −0.07 | 1.95 |
| | (−0.43) | (0.38) | | | |
| Cincinnati | −24.31 | 2.10 | −24.86 | 0.01 | 1.90 |
| | (−0.17) | (0.03) | (−0.50) | | |
| Cleveland | 448.98 | −180.93 | 62.19 | −0.01 | 1.79 |
| | (1.15) | (−1.28) | (0.58) | | |
| Dallas | −89.21 | −8.15 | 158.40 | 0.31 | 1.63 |
| | (−1.30) | (−0.06) | (1.29) | | |
| Denver | −99.42 | 39.23 | 98.77 | 0.04 | 1.23 |
| | (−0.53) | (0.48) | (0.87) | | |
| Detroit | 31.33 | N.A. | −82.81 | 0.04 | 1.16 |
| | (0.19) | | (−0.63) | | |
| Green Bay | 16.65 | N.A. | 12.85 | 0.06 | 1.92 |
| | (−0.40) | | (0.08) | | |
| Hartford | −42.16 | 247.24 | −95.86 | 0.02 | 1.67 |
| | (−0.27) | (1.46) | (−0.70) | | |
| Houston | 292.3 | −148.2 | 140.1 | 0.22 | 1.73 |
| | (0.33) | (−0.52) | (0.49) | | |
| Indianapolis | −208.29[c] | 142.76[c] | −39.32 | 0.12 | 1.86 |
| | (−2.73) | (2.15) | (−0.59) | | |
| Kansas City | 44.77 | −44.59 | 21.23 | 0.04 | 1.93 |
| | (0.40) | (−0.91) | (0.57) | | |
| Los Angeles | 195.92 | −33.81 | −47.43 | −0.02 | 1.88 |
| | (0.50) | (−0.52) | (−1.20) | | |
| Miami | −79.27 | 39.94 | 49.8 | −0.06 | 1.93 |
| | (−0.26) | (0.15) | (0.28) | | |
| Milwaukee | −82.19 | 18.67 | −11.53 | −0.09 | 1.92 |
| | (−0.80) | (0.33) | (−0.10) | | |
| Minneapolis | 448.72 | −119.14 | −133.86 | 0.04 | 1.98 |
| | (0.71) | (−0.54) | (−1.32) | | |

*Table 13.1, continued*

| City | Statistic $\beta_1$ | $\beta_2$ | $\beta_3$ | $R^2$ | Durbin-Watson[a] |
|---|---|---|---|---|---|
| New Orleans | −176.36 (−1.16) | 99.88 (0.93) | −84.28 (−0.67) | −0.04 | 1.82 |
| New York | −846.31 (−1.41) | 93.90 (1.21) | 43.39 (0.83) | 0.04 | 1.99 |
| Orlando | 29.41 (0.28) | −123.22 (−0.44) | N.A. | 0.14 | 1.86 |
| Philadelphia | 12.48 (0.01) | 6.79 (0.02) | −17.94 (−0.18) | 0.09 | 2.00 |
| Phoenix | 35.4 (0.135) | −85.83 (−0.42) | 148.03 (0.73) | 0.10 | 1.77 |
| Pittsburgh | −188.87 (−0.45) | 39.37 (0.28) | 62.58 (1.23) | −0.02 | 1.91 |
| Portland | e | e | e | e | e |
| Sacramento | −50.58 (−0.69) | 176.22 (0.98) | −193.35 (−0.79) | 0.03 | 1.75 |
| Saint Louis | −220.45 (−1.28) | 84.34 (1.41) | −101.1[c] (−3.14) | 0.26 | 1.95 |
| Salt Lake City | −65.86 (−1.71) | −89.69 (−1.59) | N.A. | 0.03 | 1.88 |
| San Antonio | 89.13 (0.66) | −200.16 (−1.50) | 22.82 (0.19) | 0.13 | 1.92 |
| San Diego | 26.09 (0.13) | 1.77 (0.02) | −54.07 (−0.52) | −0.08 | 1.97 |
| San Francisco-Oakland | −18.48 (−0.06) | 49.63 (0.60) | −132.19[c] (−1.94) | 0.16 | 1.85 |
| Seattle | 497.81[c] (1.99) | −132.24 (−1.34) | −227.84 (−1.61) | 0.33 | 1.64 |
| Tampa-Bay | 28.03 (0.16) | 48.54 (0.27) | −57.27 (−0.34) | 0.07 | 1.85 |
| Washington DC | 479.26[c] (1.93) | −76.79 (−0.93) | −204.44[c] (−2.11) | 0.08 | 1.98 |
| ALL[d] | 4.17 (0.31) | 4.24 (0.69) | −22.28 (−1.36) | 0.00 | N.A. |

* t-statistics are in parentheses; a, After Cochrane-Orcutt adjustment; b, Charlotte Hornets and their stadium came on line the same year 1988; c, Significant at least at the 5% level; d, All 48 cities in sample except Portland, Des Moines, and Waco; e, Not possible to transpose the matrix for Portland given the array of data for Portland's teams and stadiums.

**Table 13.2**  The impact of new stadiums and professional sports teams on regional, real, per capita personal income for the eight major regions in the continental United States, 1959–1987

| Region | $\beta_1$ | $\beta_2$ | $\beta_3$ | $R^2$ |
|---|---|---|---|---|
| | | *Statistic* | | |
| Far West | 89.82[a] | –4.23 | –67.54[a] | 0.04 |
| | (3.03) | (–0.37) | (–2.37) | |
| Rocky Mountains | –45.98 | –14.86 | 171.83[a] | 0.04 |
| | (–1.50) | (–0.50) | (2.07) | |
| South West | –55.33 | –32.73 | 168.39[a] | 0.05 |
| | (–1.29) | (–1.22) | (2.88) | |
| Plains | –48.44[a] | 17.63 | –39.23 | 0.00 |
| | (–2.26) | (1.18) | (–1.04) | |
| Great Lakes | –39.39 | 3.86 | –31.57 | –0.01 |
| | (–1.28) | (0.35) | (–0.93) | |
| New England | 128.59 | 18.83 | –141.75[a] | 0.04 |
| | (1.76) | (0.81) | (–1.82) | |
| Mid East | –1.79 | 5.38 | –20.56 | 0.00 |
| | (–0.14) | (0.90) | (–1.28) | |
| South East | –3.61 | 8.08 | –31.66 | –0.01 |
| | (–0.14) | (0.34) | (–0.68) | |

* t-statistics are in parentheses
a, Significant at least at the 5% level

professional sport subsidization include opportunity costs, a public invest-ment in professional sport may be consistent with a negative economic return. Indeed, since public expenditures fail to correlate with per capita changes in real personal income, other things unique to cities, to include other public expenditures, must account for positive changes in real per capita income.

The statistics recorded in Table 13.1 indicate that professional sports teams have little impact on a city's economy. Only in the case of India-napolis did teams exert a statistically-significant, positive impact on the metropolitan economy. This may be attributable to a combination of things to include the relatively small size of the Indianapolis economy and the Hoosier State's tradition for sports involvement, i.e. the Colts and Pacers may have a stronger state following than is usual relative to national standards.

Although individual cities fail to exhibit a statistically-significant impact, it may be that professional sport has a positive effect when a number of cities within a region are considered. It may be, for example, that New

York, Philadelphia, and other large cities in the eastern part of the United States, collectively export stadium services or professional sports to other regions of the country. Large conventions that utilize stadiums and arenas and super-station and cable television broadcasts of games nationally increase the likelihood that stadiums and teams are successfully marketed nationally. Results for tests conducted on the impact that stadiums and teams have on regions defined for the continental USA are recorded in Table 13.2.

The results recorded in Table 13.2 suggest several things worthy of note. First, there is not a statistically-significant relationship between professional sports teams and regional, per capita, real personal income. It does not appear that professional teams export their services beyond the region to an extent that matters economically. Dallas is not yet America's team.

Second, the services of stadiums and arenas are exported or imported on a national basis. In particular, the Rocky Mountains and Southwest regions are net exporters of stadium services, while the Far West and New England regions are net importers of stadium and arena services. Third, after accounting for national trends, neither teams nor stadiums explain much of the remaining variation in regional, real, personal income. Technically speaking, none of the adjusted correlation coefficients exceed 5%. Therefore, there is little benefit to be derived from state governments within a region developing plans to exploit their stadium advantage or to ameliorate their stadium disadvantage.

## Conclusions

Sport is filled with myths. Myths are not without purpose. Professional sport and economics have become inextricably bound. Economic myths have become a part of professional sports. The coupling of dollars and sport has social implications of sufficient scope to warrant research that can assist in separating economic myth from reality. The purpose of this chapter has been to determine the extent to which the economic investment rationale that has been used to support public subsidization of professional sports is a myth. The evidence compiled here indicates that public funding of professional sports, particularly as it relates to stadiums, is not a sound civic economic investment. If opportunity costs are included in the cost-benefit calculus, public investments in stadiums may well exhibit negative returns.

For commercial sport to contribute significantly to the local economy, it must induce increases in spending. The myth is that it does. The reality is that sport very probably does not expand spending, but only serves to realign it. Spending on sports spectating is likely to be

290

financed in part through reduced spending on other forms of amusement and recreation. Individual spending is constrained by time and money. Sports-spectating precludes spending time and money on alternative recreational pursuits. Only an after-the-fact audit on the overall impact of professional sports on spending can inform us about how sport effects the local economy.

The public should view promises about the economic impact of professional sports with a healthy scepticism. Responding to public pressure, officials have sought to fund professional sports stadiums through seemingly innocuous means such as lotteries and taxes on gambling receipts. However, the public should understand that lottery and gambling revenues are scarce, and using these funds for stadiums precludes their use in some other projects that might better stimulate the local economy.

Finally, building stadiums to increase attendance, as suggested by Yankees owner George Steinbrenner, is a short-term solution to an attendance problem. Research indicates that while there is a stadium novelty effect, it erodes after approximately seven years. My research indicates that the on-field competitiveness of the team is critical in determining attendance. Cities should recognize that building stadiums for mediocre teams will add little to fan support beyond the short run.

## Appendix A: Cities in the sample

| | | |
|---|---|---|
| Anchorage | Los Angeles | Savannah |
| Atlanta | Miami | Seattle |
| Baltimore | Milwaukee | Springfield, IL |
| Boise | Minneapolis | Springfield, MO |
| Boston | New Orleans | Tampa-Bay |
| Buffalo | New York | Waco |
| Charlotte | Orlando | Washington D.C. |
| Chicago | Philadelphia | Wichita |
| Cincinnati | Phoenix | |
| Cleveland | Pittsburgh | |
| Dallas | Portland | |
| Denver | Roanoke | |
| Des Moines | Sacramento | |
| Detroit | Saint Louis | |
| Duluth | Salt Lake | |
| Green Bay | San Antonio | |
| Hartford | San Diego | |
| Houston | San Francisco | |
| Indianapolis | San Jose | |
| Kansas City | Santa Barbara | |

## Appendix B: Cities by region

| Region | Cities included in the region |
| --- | --- |
| Alaska | Anchorage |
| Far West | Los Angeles<br>Portland<br>Sacramento<br>San Diego<br>San Francisco-Oakland<br>San Jose<br>Santa Barbara<br>Seattle |
| Great Lakes | Chicago<br>Cincinnati<br>Cleveland<br>Detroit<br>Green Bay<br>Indianapolis<br>Milwaukee<br>Springfield, Illinois |
| Mid East | Baltimore<br>Buffalo<br>New York<br>Philadelphia<br>Pittsburgh<br>Washington, D.C. |
| New England | Boston<br>Hartford |
| Plains | Des Moines<br>Duluth<br>Kansas City<br>Minneapolis<br>St. Louis<br>Springfield, Missouri<br>Wichita |
| Rocky Mountains | Boise<br>Denver<br>Phoenix<br>Salt Lake |

| South East | Atlanta |
| | Charlotte |
| | Miami |
| | New Orleans |
| | Orlando |
| | Roanoke |
| | Savannah |
| | Tampa Bay |
| South West | Dallas |
| | Houston |
| | San Antonio |
| | Waco |

## Acknowledgements

This paper could not have been completed without the help of my research assistants and colleagues. I am very grateful to Sheila Somers, my resourceful and tireless senior research assistant, and colleagues, Professors Jeffrey Sundberg, Richard Dye, and Nader Nazmi. Of course, all errors and omissions in this paper are solely my responsibility.

## Notes

1. Roger G. Noll, 'Attendance and Price Setting', in R. G. Noll (ed.), *Government and the Sports Business* (Washington DC, 1974), pp.115–57.
2. Edward Shils, 'Report to the Philadelphia Professional Sports Consortium on its Contribution to the Economy of Philadelphia', Mimeograph, 17 June 1985.
3. Kenneth R. Clark, 'Threat to Move Yanks Angers NY', *Chicago Tribune*, 18 July 1993.
4. Hal Lancaster, 'Tale of Two Cities: Why Football Mesmerizes Baltimore and Indianapolis', *Wall Street Journal*, 24 January 1986.
5. Richard A. Baade and Richard F. Dye, 'The Impact of Stadiums and Professional Sports on Metropolitan Area Development', *Growth and Change*, Spring 1990.
6. James Quirk and Rodney Fort, *Playdirt* (Princeton, 1992), p.172.
7. See, for example, John E. Peck, 'An Economic Impact Analysis of South Bend's Proposed Class A Baseball Stadium', in *Bureau of Business and Economic Research* (Indiana 1985); and 'The Economic Impact of a Major League Baseball Team on the Local Economy', Mimeograph (Chicago, April 1986).
8. It should be noted that the multiplier will vary directly with the size of the geographic area analysed. The multiplier for the State of Illinois should be larger than the multiplier for the City of Chicago.

9.   Richard A. Baade and Richard F. Dye, 'Sports Stadiums and Area Development: A Critical Review', *Economic Development Quarterly*, Vol. 2 (August 1988), pp.265–75.

10.  Tax exempt bonds for stadium construction in the United States expired on 31 December 1992.

11.  In *Government and the Sports Business*, Noll determined that there is a new stadium novelty effect in determining baseball attendance that lasted somewhere between seven and eleven years.

12.  First differences for real, per capita personal incomes for individual cities were used to capture more completely the change in a city's economic activity induced by a stadium or team. Had an average of city real, per capita personal income over the sample time period been deducted from the observed level of city economic activity in year t, the impact of a sports change in the initial year of that change would have been muted. Using an average would have reduced the likelihood that a sports-induced change would have been found, since the economic impact of a team or stadium in its first year would have been averaged over the stadium or team history. Therefore, the model represented by equation 13.1 maximizes the likelihood of statistically-significant coefficients for the stadium and team variables. The sources for these analyses were: Mike Meserole (ed.), 'Teams and Ball Parks', *The 1992 Sports Almanac* (Boston, 1992); US Department of Commerce, Bureau of the Census, *Census of Business, Selected Services Area Statistics*, Washington DC, US Government Printing Office, various years; Idem, *Census of Service Industries, Geographic Area Series*, various years; US Department of Commerce, Bureau of Economic Analysis, *Local Area Personal Income*, Washington DC, US Government Printing Office, various years; US Department of Labor, Bureau of Labor Statistics, *Handbook of Labor Statistics*, Washington DC, US Government Printing Office, August 1989.

13.  Roger Noll, a Stanford University economics professor, noted that 'a typical stadium's economic impact can be compared to that of a good-sized department store'. See Chris Kraul, 'Fields of Dreams', *Los Angeles Times*, 11 July 1993, p.D1.

14.  See, for example, Clark, 'Threat to Move Yanks Angers NY', Section 1, p.17.

15.  Baade and Dye, 'Sports Stadiums and Area Development', p.12.

# 14

# The Economic Impact of Stadium Events: Taking the Spectator's Point of View

*Tommy D. Andersson*

Economics is the art of making the most out of our resources. To create pleasure and utility in an economically efficient way implies that we should try to do so by using as small an amount of resources as possible. In economic language, the output of a stadium event is the value of the pleasure and utility created at the event whereas the input is the value of the resources used for the event. Economic efficiency is then about maximizing the value of output per value unit of input used. It is therefore impossible to assess the economic impact of a stadium event without assessing the value of the pleasure and utility created by the event. The concept of 'economic impact studies' is, however, often misunderstood and misused. Information on revenue, profit and expenditures of vendors and performers at the event, employee pay records, and gate receipts, becomes the focus of attention and a successful event is characterized as one where these figures are as high as possible. Economically speaking, such criteria are completely wrong. Vendor revenue and employee pay records indicate costs of an event, i.e. resources used for the event, and costs should preferably be as low as possible and certainly not maximized.

From a political and moral point of view, criteria such as maximizing vendor sales may also be deceitful since the implication will be that we should try to make visitors spend as much as possible. Raising entrance fees, prices of hotel rooms and restaurant meals will be in line with such a policy. Multiplier effects, which describe total effects on turnover figures of the regional industry, become the prime concern instead of the quality of the event as such. 'Multiplier values are used as the basis for public sector decision making'[1] and the policy implication will, as, for example, in the tourism policy of Gibraltar, be 'to encourage higher spending excursionists and longer staying tourists.'[2] In practice, such a policy may justify, for example, that in distributing scarce tickets to a sold-out soccer cup final, priority should be given to spectators coming from far-away places and spending a night or two in town, whereas local fans would be given a lower priority. Economically speaking, such a priority

295

would be absurd. The economic result is not equal to the profit figures of the travel industry and the local hospitality industry but to the difference between the value of created pleasure and the value of utilized resources.

It may be argued that the evaluation of pleasure is outside economic territory. The responses to this argument are, first, that if a truly economic impact study is to be made, this difficulty cannot be avoided. Second, assessing cost is far from trivial and not necessarily easier than assessing the value of pleasure. An 'economic impact study' focusing only on expenses is far from exact science[3] but may easily give an impression of being just that – which makes things even worse. The major objective of this chapter is to argue for, and propose, a model for economic impact studies of stadium events where the value of an event is derived from the pleasure and utility of the spectators attending the event. In economic terms, this value constitutes the output of the event whereas the value of all resources used by the spectators and for the spectators in relation to the event constitute the input to the event.

## A Definition and Typology of Events

Being a fairly wide concept, there is a need for a definition of events as well as a relevant classification of the concept. In defining the concept, it seems preferable to keep the definition fairly wide and pick out particular types of event by a detailed classification scheme. The following general definition is suggested: 'An event is characterized by a programme and a time-scheduled termination of the event. There is an organizer as well as participants and an audience.' This definition thus comprises sports, festivals and TV-watching, as well as fairs and professional conferences but excludes permanent attractions such as natural scenery, amusement parks and permanent exhibitions (for example at museums).

By making a distinction between leisure events and professional events we end up with two broad categories which seem relevant from the point of view that stadium events concern leisure activities. More important from the economic point of view is the duration of the event. Many sports events, for example, are of a short duration. Visitors come to town for a couple of hours and may experience an intensive, thrilling game which gives them a lot of excitement and pleasure without having to spend much money in the regional hospitality industry. On the other hand, visitors to, for example, a nine-day long World Championship in athletics may have a more long-lasting and strong impression of the games, and, in addition, a varied, touristic experience from the city and the country where the games take place. Normally, such visitors will also

**Table 14.1**   A classification of stadium events related to an analysis of economic effects

| Duration of the event | Frequency of the event | |
|---|---|---|
| | *Less than once a year* | *More than once a year* |
| More than one day | World Championships in Athletics | A Cricket Game |
| Less than one day | A World Cup Final in Speedway | Soccer League Matches |

spend considerably more in the hospitality industry and show a much more diversified spending pattern.

Whereas the duration of an event is important for the value of the pleasure and the utility of visitors, as well as visitors' spending patterns, the frequency and regularity of an event is important in terms of the value of utilized resources and the cost of the event. An infrequent event (e.g. a yearly event) has the opportunity, if wisely planned and time-scheduled, to use otherwise unemployed capacity and idle resources in the region. It will thus keep opportunity costs at a minimum. This implies that the economic result of an infrequent event may turn out to be quite impressive. Frequent events, on the other hand, normally require fixed resources in terms of, for example, staff and buildings. Thus, for example, the New Ullevi Stadium in the centre of Gothenburg is not only a well-equipped building occupying attractive land, as Moen indicates in Chapter 10, but is also employing administrative and maintenance staff at the arena. The economic effects of these permanent amenities must be that considerable amounts of fixed costs will be distributed on frequent events such as the regular soccer games in the league. To sum up, Table 14.1 describes a classification of stadium events which I believe is relevant for an analysis of economic effects.

## A Descriptive Model of Economic Effects

This model is based on a view of the output of an event, i.e. the pleasure and utility of spectators, as being the benefit of an event. Costs of an event are related to the value of all resources utilized at the event. Evaluation of benefit as well as cost is often a breathtaking act of simplification, which we will discuss in this section both in relation to benefit, cost, surplus, and distribution effects.

297

*Benefit of a stadium event*

The primary beneficiary of an event is the audience. The basic force underpinning an event is the attraction it has on an audience consisting of people living within a region as well as people living outside the region. The value that the audience attaches to an event is decisive not only for the economic result but also for the future prospects of the event. This value of the spectators' pleasure and utility is related to the satisfaction of complex needs. The stadium may, for some spectators, be almost a 'sacred place' satisfying religious needs[4] and it often invokes home-like emotions as indicated in Chapter 2. Popular sports stars have the ability to add extra value to their performance by adding a 'theatrical' touch. 'In football and other sports, "gesturing" or "display" has become common among carnivalistic (or "clown-like") characters such as the post-modern footballer Paul Gascoigne or the tennis player John MacEnroe.'[5] Music also adds value to sports events, and football-related songs in particular constitute an important part of the spectators' pleasure of the total experience of football culture during a game.

The benefit may, however, also be offset by adverse feelings and negative values related to attending an event. Fear and anxiety of stadium violence may reduce the total value of the event. As Williams indicates in Chapter 11, massive investments in safer football stadiums have recently been made in the UK. The size of these investments is a reflection of the negative value attached to spectators' anxiety over violence and disasters. The dilemma of an economist is to reduce this complex of pleasure, fear, utility and satisfaction into one dimension, i.e. the monetary dimension. Since the cost of utilized resources (the input) is measured in monetary units, a discussion of economic efficiency can only be meaningful if output, i.e. the pleasure, fear, and utility of the spectators, is also measured in monetary units.

The most convenient way, from an empirical point of view, is to assess the audience's value of an event through a measurement of the willingness-to-pay – the WTP – for attending the event.[6] This willingness to pay for an event hypothetically covers the pleasure and utility derived from all economic transactions in relation to the event, such as participation fees, lodging, meals, transportation, etc. The audience, being the primary beneficiary, could thus calculate its surplus from attending the event as the difference in value between the total willingness to pay and actual outlays during the event (and related to the event). This primary surplus of the event will be similar to total consumer surplus from the event. Since part of the audience lives in the region, only those outlays which are directly related to participation in the event should be included, i.e. only incremental expenses are relevant. Costs such as normal rent, normal meals, etc. are excluded from the analysis, whereas extra outlays, such as the cost of going to the pub before or after the event, are included in the analysis.

Thus the secondary benefit from the event for secondary beneficiaries includes all outlays that visitors have in the region in relation to the event plus those extra outlays that inhabitants in the region have in relation to the event. These outlays in the region determine the benefit for secondary beneficiaries such as the organizer, the hotels, the restaurants, transport companies and the shops in the region. All secondary benefit is, however, not a surplus since secondary beneficiaries also have costs to cover. Cost of inputs, such as food and beverage purchases made by restaurants, will increase. Salary costs will go up for the organizer as well as for restaurants and hotels. It is the difference in value between revenues from output and costs for inputs that determines the secondary surplus or business accounting profit for secondary beneficiaries.

This is not the end of economic effects however, since costs for secondary beneficiaries imply revenues for tertiary beneficiaries such as employees, owners, tax authorities, social insurance, etc. But not even these economic transactions will be the final ones. Employees will spend a part of their salary increases in the region; regional taxes will be invested or consumed in the regional economy; regional suppliers will have to cover their costs partly within the region, etc. *ad infinitum*.

The final effects of this 'infinite' sequence of transactions can be calculated by input-output analysis and multiplier effects.[7] Final effects can be classified into three categories: direct, indirect and induced effects and into eight tertiary beneficiaries:

| | |
|---|---|
| Employees: | Net increase in salaries (employment) |
| Owners: | Net increase in owners' received payments |
| Investors: | Increased industrial investments in the region |
| Social insurance: | Increased fees for social insurance |
| Government tax: | Increased Government taxes |
| Local tax authorities: | Increased regional taxes |
| Other regions: | 'National' exports |
| | (i.e. to other regions within the country) |
| Other countries: | 'International' exports |

The total amount of payments to these beneficiaries from secondary beneficiaries (e.g. shops, hotels, restaurants, etc.) represents income for tertiary beneficiaries, i.e. tertiary benefit.

*Costs of a stadium event*

Tertiary benefit (equal to secondary cost) will be distributed among some major groups of economic players such as employees, owners, tax authorities, social insurance, etc. In order to determine tertiary cost, we should assess for each one of the eight tertiary beneficiaries, what the opportunity cost amounted to of all resources utilized during the event. The opportunity cost is determined by the benefit that would be achieved if resources had not been used for the event but instead had been used in the best possible alternative way. Consider the following example: if of the 2,380 hotel rooms that were rented by spectators, only 30% would otherwise have been occupied (i.e. 714 rooms rented), then the opportunity cost of 2,380 rooms is the benefit that the hotel would have had from 714 rooms (e.g. if the 'average rate' is £42, then the opportunity cost is $714 \times £42$ = £29,988). Another example would be if salaries increased due to an event and to the fact that employees worked an extra 4,800 hours, then the opportunity cost is the value that the employees attach to 4,800 hours spent in the best alternative way, be it at another job, with the family, or on cultural activities. This value constitutes the opportunity cost and thus the tertiary cost of labour.

In determining tertiary cost of an event, we also determine its final cost. The point raised earlier, that assessing the cost is not necessarily easier than assessing the benefit, may gain some weight from the examples above. In an economic evaluation, we can't avoid the issue of assessing the value of pleasure and utility, neither regarding benefit nor regarding opportunity cost, for the simple reason that the satisfaction of complex human needs is the ultimate goal of economic activities. Another important tertiary cost is the value of the spectators' time. The opportunity cost of this utilized resource is determined by the value that the spectators attach to the best alternative way of spending their time apart from going to the event.

The assessment of tertiary cost equal to opportunity cost of utilized resources brings forward the time aspect of cost assessment. We may talk about short-run tertiary cost as being determined by the best alternative action during the days when the event actually took place. Long-run tertiary cost is determined by the value of the best alternative action taken in a longer perspective, when structural changes in the economy have been taken into account. This distinction can be exemplified by the hotel rooms discussed above where the short-run tertiary cost was £29,988. The long-run tertiary cost would be higher and would have to include the value of capital and labour better used in other sectors of the economy after a structural change.

Taking into consideration the temporal dimension, short-run tertiary cost seems justifiable when we compare opportunity cost to direct payments from the spectators. Long-run tertiary cost, on the other hand, seems to be relevant in comparison to indirect and induced payments derived from input-output analysis.

Chapter 13 presented an interesting study of the long-term economic effects of investments in stadiums, and indicated that resources utilized for stadium events do not seem to generate any additional surplus in the regional economy. These results thus seem to indicate that the long-run tertiary cost equals secondary benefit and that in the long-run, investments in stadiums do not give more secondary + tertiary surplus than investments in other sectors do. Differences in primary surplus as well as differences in distribution effects among primary, secondary, and tertiary beneficiaries, however, are likely to occur, but these issues were not investigated.

*Surplus of a stadium event*

The model describes three types of surplus:

*Primary surplus* remains with the spectators and is determined by the difference between the total value of the event and the expenses that spectators have in relation to attending the event.

*Secondary surplus* is equal to total business (accounting) profit related to the event and is calculated as the difference between direct payments from the spectators and the accounted expenses related to the production of goods and services for the event.

*Tertiary surplus* accrues to eight groups of beneficiaries (including employees, owners, tax authorities, etc.) and is calculated as the difference between indirect (and induced) payments related to the event and the opportunity cost of resources utilized for the event.

Total surplus of the event is then the sum of primary, secondary, and tertiary surplus which is (primary benefit minus primary cost) plus (primary cost [= secondary benefit] minus secondary cost) plus (tertiary benefit [= secondary cost] minus tertiary cost [= opportunity cost]). This is equal to (primary benefit minus opportunity cost) which is also the final economic result based on the difference in economic value between output and input of the event.

*Distribution effects from a stadium event*

Distribution effects occur between the groups of primary, secondary and tertiary beneficiaries as well as within these groups. Depending on political and economic motives behind an analysis, different foci on distribution effects may be relevant. If a football event is organized by a football club, the focus may be on the size of the primary surplus and to what extent club members and local fans enjoy that surplus. On the other hand, if the local industry has organized and/or sponsored a tennis tournament, focus may (and quite rightly so) be on secondary surplus, and on what sectors of the local business (hotels, restaurants, shops, etc.) obtained the major part of the secondary benefit (i.e. sales) and secondary surplus. The local government should focus on all distribution effects, particularly if public funds are used for the arena and/or the organization of the event. An interesting conflict may occur between maximizing secondary surplus by arranging events that attract visitors coming from far away which would satisfy the local industry and, on the other hand, maximizing primary surplus of the local residents by events that are of interest primarily to local people. Figure 14.1 summarizes the descriptive model of regional economic effects from an event.

## Input Data for the Model

The assessment of primary benefit and primary cost can be administered through a survey of a randomly-selected sample of participants at the event. Primary benefit will then be determined by the willingness-to-pay, assessed through questions like: 'What is the maximum amount of money you would be prepared to pay for attending this event (all-inclusive: lodging, tickets, meals, transports etc.)?' Similarly, primary costs can be assessed from questions like: 'How much do you actually spend in this region on a) tickets, b) lodging, c) meals, etc?' Answers to these questions also describe secondary benefit, i.e. revenue for the organizer and incremental revenues for hotels, restaurants, shops and other parts of the regional economy.

Secondary costs are, however, more difficult to assess. Very few regions, if any, have data on the cost-structure of regional industries. A specific survey of average effects of an event at the business level would not be infeasible but it would be complicated and costly to perform. An alternative, more handy, albeit less precise, way to get hold of these estimates is to take advantage of the input-output data prepared on a regional level (preferably) or on a national level which most developed countries have. By using input-output data for these later stages of the analysis, we will also be in a position to use input-output techniques for estimating tertiary effects i.e. the indirect and induced incremental regional benefit classified into the eight categories described above.

## An Empirical Test of the Model

Gothenburg is a city with approximately 500,000 inhabitants situated on the Swedish west coast. In the centre of the city there are several tourist-amenities such as a large fairground, an amusement park and

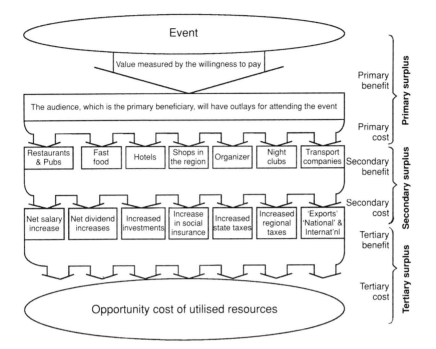

**Figure 14.1** A descriptive model of how economic effects from an event ripple through a regional economy

a stadium with a capacity to accommodate 40,000 spectators. The stadium, called New Ullevi, has, during the last ten years, been a venue for three major types of events: football (soccer), pop concerts, and motorcycle races (speedway and motor cross). Three separate surveys of spectators have been conducted with the intention of describing regional economic effects from the three types of events:

- A random sample of 1,015 spectators at a Bruce Springsteen pop concert in 1985;
- A random sample of 418 spectators at an International Cup Winners' Cup Final in soccer in 1990 between Sampdoria from Italy and Anderlecht from Belgium;
- A random sample of 374 spectators at the 1991 World Cup Final in speedway.

The questionnaire used was almost identical for all three surveys and the data collected thus make it possible to compare the economic impact of the three events.

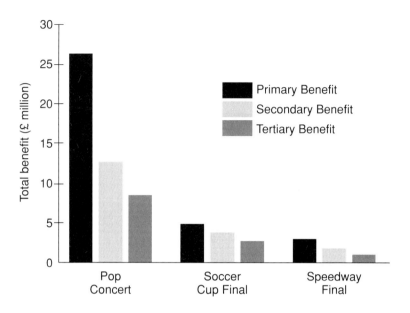

**Figure 14.2** Primary, secondary and tertiary benefit from three types of events

## Empirical Results

The three investigated events differed in size, i.e. in the number of spectators attending the event. Bruce Springsteen was by far the most popular artist and attracted in total 126,000 spectators, during two days, which is still today the all-time record attendance for arena events in Sweden. The soccer Cup Final attracted some 20,000 spectators who were, to a large extent, international visitors since the match was played by a Belgian and an Italian team. The World Cup Final in speedway attracted some 24,000 spectators including a good number of international visitors primarily from neighbouring countries. The size of an event, in terms of number of spectators, has, of course, a considerable influence on primary, secondary as well as tertiary benefit which is clearly brought out by Figure 14.2. (Monetary values are calculated in 1992 year values. Effects of inflation have been considered and the exchange rate used is Skr. 10.10 = £1.) A closer look at how secondary benefit is distributed among secondary beneficiaries certainly brings out the effect of the size of the event but also indicates certain differences in the distribution of benefit which is shown in Figure 14.3.

By continuing the analysis in terms of per capita figures, we will to a large extent eliminate the size component of the event which over-

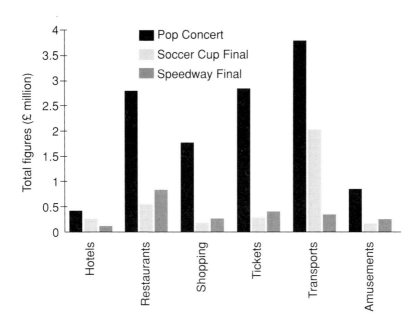

**Figure 14.3** The distribution of benefit among secondary beneficiaries at three types of events

shadowed the analysis in Figures 14.2 and 14.3. Figure 14.4 illustrates differences between the three types of events. The attraction of the event in terms of primary benefit measured by the WTP differs between the three types of spectators. The arena was sold out for the pop concerts but only half full for the soccer and motor events which may explain the somewhat higher primary benefit for the pop concert. The Soccer Cup Final attracted a large number of international visitors who travelled a long way. This high involvement is also reflected in a high primary benefit from attending the event. Figure 14.4 also brings out higher secondary and tertiary benefit which is equal to high costs for the spectators. A closer look at how these secondary benefits are distributed among secondary beneficiaries is brought out by Figure 14.5.

It is interesting to note the low per capita secondary benefit for hotels, restaurants and amusements from pop concert spectators. This may be partly explained by the fact that Gothenburg is not able to accommodate such a large number of visitors. Hotels, restaurants and night clubs were full and many prospective customers had to be turned away. It is therefore worth noting the negative effect of 'oversizing' an event. Not being able to accommodate visitors reduces not only secondary (and thus tertiary) benefit, but also primary benefit since visitors of course have negative feelings about being turned away from, e.g., a restaurant

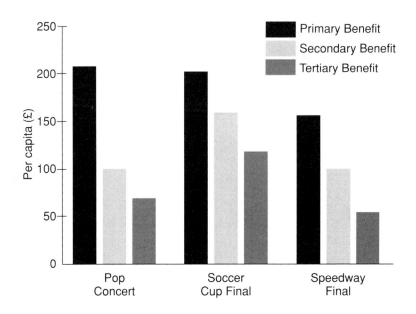

**Figure 14.4** Primary, secondary and tertiary benefit per capita from three types of events

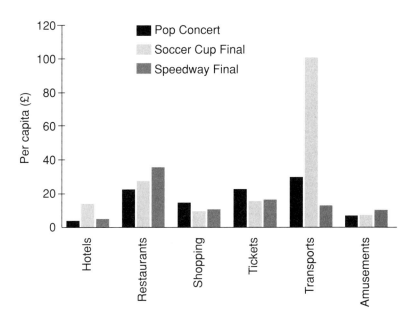

**Figure 14.5** The distribution of secondary benefit per capita for three types of events

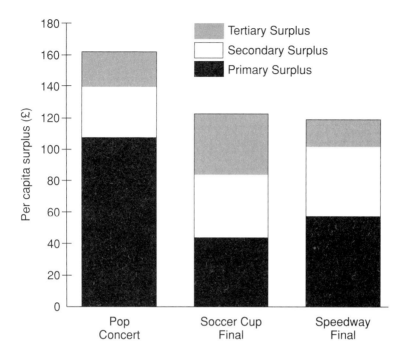

**Figure 14.6** Primary, secondary and tertiary surplus per capita from three events

or a night club. A conclusion of this is that too an large event (i.e. too large for the capacity of the regional hospitality industry) is economically inefficient and unable to realize the potential total benefit. It also reduces the per capita primary, secondary, as well as tertiary benefit.

It is also evident from Figure 14.5 that the cost of transport explains the high costs and high secondary benefit from the Soccer Cup Final which attracted a high proportion of international visitors. The economic effect is that the primary benefit is to a large degree spent on costs for attending the event and the primary surplus is thus reduced. This situation with a low primary surplus and a high secondary surplus reflects the economic effect of playing a Cup Final between an Italian team and a Belgian team in Sweden. This is an ample illustration of the effects of a 'multiplier-driven tourism policy' or, to put it more bluntly, a 'rip-off' approach. Arranging the Cup Final in Sweden (which is about as far away as possible for the Italian and the Belgian fans) boosts the secondary surplus as well as the tertiary surplus at the same time as the fans are effectively exploited. Figure 14.6 reveals the results from the three events in terms of total surplus = primary + secondary + tertiary surplus. Thus the Soccer Cup Final forced the spectators to spend money on travelling, thereby reducing primary surplus and increasing secondary surplus. The pop concert, on the other hand, increased primary surplus and reduced secondary surplus because the spectators could not be provided with what they needed since they were too numerous for the capacity of the hospitality industry in Gothenburg. Neither situation is desirable since primary and secondary surplus are of equal economic value and it is inefficient to sacrifice one for another.

## Conclusions

Regional tourism planning should carefully consider the effects of stadium events. Three aspects are relevant from the point of view of economic efficiency. First, high benefit in terms of a satisfied audience reflected by a high willingness-to-pay must be the primary objective for long-run success in the stadium events. Second, low cost achieved primarily through utilizing resources when opportunity cost is low, i.e. when resources would otherwise have been unused or under-utilized. Third, the distribution of benefits and surplus should also be considered in an economic evaluation of events. A description of distribution effects should then be matched against desired distribution effects which of course, and rightfully so, varies with different economic actors. A discussion of desired versus actually achieved distribution effects is particularly important when public funds are involved.

By the application of the proposed model to evaluations of events the three aspects will be assessed. First, the model determines primary benefit by the willingness-to-pay which gives a clear indication of the value of various events both at an individual level (the average visitor) and at a total level. Second, the model clearly describes which sectors of the regional economy (e.g. hotels, restaurants, shops etc.) will be utilized, and to what extent, for various types of events. This will facilitate regional planning and time-scheduling of events to those periods when the most important sectors are less than fully utilized. Third, the model describes distribution effects in terms of primary surplus, secondary surplus, and tertiary surplus. These three concepts describe a delicate interdependency, i.e. an increased secondary surplus may (*ceteris paribus*) decrease primary (i.e. consumer) surplus but then also boost turnover figures in the regional (hospitality) industry and tertiary surplus. A high primary benefit, i.e. a satisfied audience, is, however, a prerequisite for primary as well as secondary surplus, particularly so in the long run.

Another aspect of distribution effects regards the distribution of secondary surplus: what sectors of the regional economy get most turnover increases out of an event? Is it hotels or camping grounds, fine or fast-food restaurants? etc. Similarly, who, among the group of primary beneficiaries, gets the larger share of the primary surplus? Is it old people or young people? Parents or singles? Rugby or soccer fans? Opera lovers or pop music fans, etc. This awareness gives a different and interesting slant to the concept of social justice. Politicians may give rise to considerable feelings of injustice if they consistently give priority to one type of activity over another, thereby introducing new social dimensions different from, but maybe sometimes just as important as, traditional dimensions such as economic status, education, and social class.

By applying the model to a number of economic impact surveys it is possible to get enough historical data for a fairly good prediction of the future. The model could then become a rather precise instrument for planning and predicting the effects of various tourism strategies aimed at developing tourism through stadium events. To further our understanding of tourism, which has been acclaimed as one of the fastest growing industries in the world, has been given a high political priority in most economies. One of the most effective ways of stimulating tourism in a region seems to be through the creation of public events. 'Probably the fastest growing form of visitor activity is festivals and events'[8] and recently there has been an increased awareness of the value of regional events and the importance of planning, marketing and evaluating events.[9]

The main thrust of this chapter has been to argue for a tourism policy which focuses on visitors' satisfaction. The tourism industry, like, for example, the restaurant and the hotel industries, is a caring industry and the moment it starts to regard visitors, not as visitors, but as income-generating creatures, a process of declining economic effects is set in motion.

## Acknowledgements

The author gratefully acknowledges the support granted for this research by Fritid Göteborg.

## Notes

1.  J. E. Fletcher and B. H. Archer, 'The Development and Application of Multiplier Analysis', *Progress in Tourism, Recreation and Hospitality Management*, Vol. 3 (1991).
2.  J. Seekings, 'Gibraltar: Developing Tourism in a Political Impasse', *Tourism Management*, Vol. 14, 1 (1993).
3.  See P. J. Sheldon, 'A Review of Tourism Expenditure Research', *Progress in Tourism, Recreation and Hospitality Management*, Vol. 2 (1990).

4. J. Bale, *Sport, Space and the City* (London, 1992).
5. J. Bale, *Landscapes of Modern Sport* (Leicester, 1994).
6. R. C. Mitchell and R. T. Carson, *Using Surveys to Value Public Goods: The Contingent Valuation Method* (Washington DC, 1989).
7. See L. C. Kantorovitch, 'Mathematical Methods of Organising and Planning Production', *Management Science* (July 1960), pp.366–422; W. Leontief, *The Structure of American Economy* (New York, 1951); W. Miernyk, *The Elements of Input–Output Analysis* (New York, 1965); P. C. Newman, *The Development of Economic Thought* (New Jersey, 1952).
8. C. Gunn, *Tourism Planning*, 2nd edn. (New York, 1988), p.259.
9. D. Getz, *Festivals, Special Events and Tourism* (New York, 1991); M. Stone, 'Marketing Strategies for Leisure Services', *Long Range Planning*, Vol. 23, 5 (1990).

# 15

# The Stadium as Theatre: A Metaphor for our Times

*John Bale*

What metaphors can be used to describe the modern sports stadium? For Foucauldians and neo-Marxists the prison might seem appropriate.[1] After all, the stadium is a means of disciplining and controlling a large number of people. It serves to confine them under conditions of strict surveillance for prescribed and regular periods. An alternative but, nevertheless, still appropriate metaphor is that of the garden, the stadium being an undoubted blending of architecture and horticulture. Sports places are often referred to as 'parks' or 'gardens' and care is required in the maintainance of the 'sacred turf', which will otherwise, like the garden, return to nature. Other metaphors could be considered – the stadium as a machine for the production of sports events, for example, or the stadium as a cathedral in which modern religious liturgies and ceremonies are practised.

Metaphors are important because they permit us to see the world in different ways; but one must pick one's metaphor carefully, for appropriateness and potential fruitfulness.[2] The selection of the metaphor will influence not only the meaning we attribute to the stadium but also our attitudes towards it – whether we view it as a good or bad place, for example. In this chapter I want to suggest that an appropriate and fruitful metaphor for an exploration of the modern stadium is that of theatre. I choose theatre not simply because it draws our attention to some of the properties of stadiums but because it also highlights their ambiguities, and the ambiguity of the relationships between their two prime groups of occupants – the audience and the players. It will already be noted that the use of 'audience' and 'players' is appropriate to both theatre and sports stadium and I will proceed to argue that theatre – in all its forms – provides a helpful metaphor for exploring modern stadiums and their spatial dynamics.

Theatres and sports arenas share in the hosting of 'spectacles'.[3] Stadium events can be 'planned for and staged just as in the theatre';[4] 'the drama of a good game of football as it unfolds itself has something in common with a good theatrical play' each possessing mimetic tension, perhaps excitement, a climax and then a resolution of the tension.[5] Sport and theatre are both regarded as forms of *ludus*, that is, although they may be play-like they each have conventions imposed upon them with only limited amounts of 'carefree gaity' (*paidia*).[6] It has also been argued that among 'performance spaces', those of sports have more in common with theatre than with ritual or play.[7]

But is the stadium a theatre? A stadium sports performance and a dramatic presentation in the theatre are often said to differ fundamentally in that the former has an uncertain outcome whereas the latter is scripted and hence predictable. Cashmore, for example, is quite clear about this when he writes that 'as soon as the unpredictable element of competition is gone … [sport] … becomes pure theatre'.[8] Likewise, it has been argued that because sports are not rehearsed or simulated, they cannot be regarded as theatrical.[9] But most sports are carefully planned (as the American term 'game plan' explicates) and in some sports individuals' performances are choreographed – gymnastics, synchronized swimming and ice dance come to mind – and hence predictable, though the individual ranks in the competition are not, and the uncertainty of the final result is always there. The case of professional wrestling falls between sport and theatre: 'the matches are known to be fixed but a certain willing suspension of disbelief is practiced'.[10] At the same time, it could be added that the 'outcome' of a scripted play may *seem* to be different each time it is seen, according to an individual's 'reading' of it.

### 'Bad' Stadiums as Theatres

Theatre is often used more specifically as a metaphor for the *modern* stadium. It is also used to imply that the modernization (or the implied theatricalization) of sports has negative characteristics. For example, it has been suggested that by moving sports indoors, the new, often domed, environment reduces 'heroic myth to theatrical spectacle,'[11] and that in huge stadiums, sport becomes 'a spectacle presented on a remote stage'.[12] The rationalization of the body in civilized society has traditionally involved the careful deployment of passions and can be argued to include the 'ordered, mediated, cerebral and relatively passive pleasures of spectating'[13] and sports events 'as theatrical representations, with a clear differentiation in space between different types of players (the ground, the seating and stand) are undoubtedly a creation of modernity'[14] (see Figure 15.1). With modernity, the discriminating spectator represents a move from ritual to theatre, the participating audience fragmenting 'into a collection of people who attend because the show is advertised, who pay admission, who evaluate what they are going to see before, during and after seeing it'.[15] In other words, the negative

**Figure 15.1** A society of the spectacle? Confinement and geometry in a stadium setting

application of the theatre metaphor implies a more distanced, less involved, experience for the spectator, reflecting modern tendencies towards spatial segmentation and teritorialization.[16] Modernization implies a clear definition and spatial separation between players and spectators and this might logically lead to a situation where the fan becomes totally passive. In the orthodox ('modern') theatre, which I view as analogous to the modern sports environment, spectators have an 'almost private experience', sitting in the dark in their separate chairs, contemplating scenes 'out there' and putting an increasing stress on the eye, rather than on other senses;[17] the audience reflect upon a performance rather than experience corporeal participation; in the modern stadium the spectator's contribution becomes that of an outsider's gaze.

Stadium sports and theatrical performances have paralleled each other in their respective territorializations. Much early theatre was like early sport; in medieval streets actors sought active involvement from their audiences but after the mid-seventeenth century a growing distancing occurred between them,[18] exactly the same situation that developed in street football a century or more later. In eighteenth-century theatre, however, the distancing of a 'civilized' audience from the performers was far from complete and there was no shortage of crowd disorders inside theatres, involving fighting and the destruction of theatre property, often as a response to an unsatisfying performance[19] – not unlike football hooliganism. The 'intrusion of the audience into the actors' precinct

313

persisted until the middle of the eighteenth century'[20] and the convention of audience as voyeur, resulting from the dominance of the lighted stage over an audience in a darkened auditorium, has been dated from as late as 1880,[21] more or less the same time as football, cricket and rugby spaces were likewise being unambiguously separated from their audiences.[22] By the twentieth century, the theatre had assumed a rather different social setting with its more restrained audience, emotionally distanced and spatially separated from the performance with excitement being restricted to a 'feeling level'.[23] The more dialogical and spatially-interactive forms of theatre were now reserved for melodrama, and later for the more 'common' pantomime, music hall, circus, and cabaret.

Just as various dramatic genres vary considerably in their degree of 'theatricality', so too do various stadium-based sports. Theatres can host pantomimes as well as Shakespeare; stadiums can host football as well as tennis. Indeed, the genteel milieu of tennis may have been the Thatcherite dream for British football. This was an 'image of a stadium full of spectators silently watching the performance and not taking part in the drama, who consequently cannot change the result'.[24] This ideal type can be seen in many sports, but has existed for many years in the theatre, cinema, and in its extreme form, in television. The notion of a 'critical distance', imposed by a bourgeois economy of the body[25] and applied to players and spectators, is helpful here and can be interpreted as the emotional or physical distance which is reached between them when the spectators become so passive as no longer to influence the outcome of play, becoming merely 'imaginary participants'.[26] A 'spectacle' becomes a 'sight' as in middle class theatre and in total contrast to, say, working-class football or boxing.

### The Stadium as Liminal Space

It is clear, however, that the degree of theatricalization, defined here as the fundamental distancing (emotionally as well as physically) and separation (essentially, a form of territorialization) of the various participants (that is, the reaching of the 'critical distance' between players and spectators) varies considerably between sports, and between different periods of time in particular sports. For an example, let me return to professional wrestling which is virtually a pantomime performance masquerading as sport or, more accurately perhaps, a pre-modern theatrical performance where the audience is regularly engaged in the action while the wrestlers themselves often engage one another outside the ring. The spatial boundaries within an arena are constantly and deliberately violated, while the referee's 'authority' is always being upstaged by wrestlers and spectators.[27] Less dramatic examples of the liminal nature of sport's boundaries may

314

be found in, for example, football, though such liminality was not always favoured. For example, in a football programme for a Sheffield United game in 1907, polite, non-dialogical behaviour was encouraged among spectators, when it was noted that 'continued bellowing at the top of your voice … gets on people's nerves and takes away a lot of the enjoyment of the game'.[28] Such advocacy of polite behaviour in early modern football can be compared with the traditional attitude in tennis, for example, where the umpire often calls for silence. In such situations, the (middle-class) tennis audience concurs and applause is polite and at specific times, as in the theatre. The audience and the players engage in 'turn-taking'. Traditionally, tennis spectators have not shouted or urged on a player; they do not engage in singing or beating drums or in rhythmic chanting or clapping. Such behaviour could be regarded as assisting the competitors in some cases or putting them off or interrupting the performance in others. While acceptable in many sports – and indeed, contributing to the enjoyment of the game, rather than detracting from it as the 1907 football programme suggested – it is clearly unacceptable in others.

The involved attitude and behaviour of spectators at football or boxing matches contrasts with the more polite ('theatrical') applause traditionally (and I stress, traditionally) displayed at cricket and tennis matches. In football there are strong aural and visual links between spectators and players, including banners, flags, music, drums, chants and insults, as Kayser Nielsen's chapter in this volume makes clear. Should the same crowd involvement occur in tennis as occurs in football it would have exceeded the critical distance demarcating modern from pre-/post-modern spectating behaviour. The distinction between the different kinds of 'distance' between fans and performers in sports is graphically illustrated in a description of bullfights and baseball:

Unlike the *matador* who constantly communicates with the crowd, the baseball players are seen to remain distinctly aloof from them. The player's allegience is to the team, and he who performs ostentatiously for the crowd is ostracized as a 'grandstander'. Contrast, for example, the baseball player's downcast eye and turf-kicking toe after an outstanding move with the *matador's* haughty glance and proud posture following a good series of passes. … It might be said that in baseball the crowd is expected to observe, in a relatively detached way, the spectacle being performed for them on the field. At the bullfight, however, the crowd is expected to be one with the *matador*, to participate, fully, in the emotions of the fight.[29]

In recent years there does appear to have been a tendency towards the imposition of a critical distance as the modernist project would wish. In Britain all-seat stadiums and greater constraints on crowd behaviour reflect this trend and create milieux where loitering and aimless strolling are discouraged (see Williams's chapter earlier in this volume). The restrictions on where people can and cannot go in sports environments, when fans should and should not chant (as in the musically-orchestrated singing in North American ice hockey), what they can, and cannot, bring with them to a game (as in the example of police confiscation of flags and banners at some English football matches), or when they can or cannot shout at the players (as in tennis), are further exemplifications of control over socio-spatial interaction.

Paradoxically, however, in view of the modernization thesis, there are also signs that the critical distance between players and spectators is actually being reduced in sports which have traditionally been more 'theatrical' in this respect. The noise (involving singing, chanting and the use of various 'musical' instruments) and excitement now found in English cricket has created a more carnivalistic atmosphere at some of the 'stately homes' of the game. In tennis and badminton, crowd involvement is also more evident now than ever before while in track and field, the triple jumper, Willie Banks, started the idea of rhythmically orchestrating the chanting and clapping of the crowd in unison with the rhythm of his athletic performance. More recently high-jump events have been held where the athletes each select their own accompanying rock music, amplified to them and the crowd through the arena's sound system. Traditionally, the crowd had been hushed while athletes in jumping events took their approach run with applause being restricted to the completion of the jump (reminiscent again of tennis). But today 'de-differentiation' between player and spectator seems to be taking place.

In football and other sports, 'gesturing' or 'display' has become common among carnivalistic (or 'clown-like') characters such as the postmodern footballer Paul Gascoigne or the tennis player John McEnroe. Footballers display an increasing number of dialogical antics directed at spectators rather than other players, including various acrobatic feats, somersaults and brief spells of dancing, following the scoring of a goal. And in such relatively bourgeois sports as tennis, badminton or cricket, the growing liminality of boundaries suggests that they are merging with – or being appropriated by – the more working-class sporting behaviours associated with football and boxing. Attempts to bourgeoisify football stadiums (all seat stadiums, family enclosures, executive suites) have therefore been paralleled by the proletarianization of tennis arenas (crowds shouting, players gesturing) revealing, perhaps, a polarization of sporting milieux.

Such unrestricted kinds of body movements can be interpreted as forms of resistance to the 'modern' traditions of self-discipline, lack of ostentation, and the suppression of emotional display. In these ways, the 'clown' or 'fool', far from 'inhabiting the edges of staged and "real life"' as normally occurs, is able to assume a centre-stage position – an *inversion*, perhaps even a *perversion* – of modern hierachical society.[30] In postmodern sport fools can and do assume a centrality denied them in other areas of life.

Such boundary violations, therefore, appear more frequently than the apparently neat and tidy world of modern sport might lead us to believe. They exemplify the *liminal* nature of its boundaries, often appearing to be worlds of betwixt and between, or marginal play:

> In liminal or marginal play sport overflows the normal boundaries of the game. For instance play may spill over from the official players to encompass pseudo-players like spectators, managers, players on the bench or technical support teams. Play can become spatially marginal when the playing field's boundaries are temporarily breached to include the spectator stands or other peripheral areas as part of the play. In relation to time, play becomes marginal when it flows into periods before or after official play. Or when 'time out' periods become an important part of the play itself.[31]

The effects of the audience clearly spill over on to the field of play and appear to be crucial in influencing the outcome of sporting contests, clearly transcending the boundary between spectators and players in some of the most apparently theatrical of sports. Basketball and ice-hockey, for example, may appear theatrical in the sense that they take place indoors, 'in the round', on more or less identical plane surfaces in brightly lit environments with the seated and individualized audience in relative darkness. Yet it is in these sports, rather than in those played outdoors in more varied environments, that the 'home field advantage' is found to be greatest. In the absence of physical variables with which the home team might be more familiar, this has been attributed to the presence and close proximity of the audience whose participation is regarded as crucial in contributing to the home advantage.[32] In such cases as these, the audience is returning/going to pre-/post-modern traditions, becoming (or, perhaps, having always been) much 'closer' than the 'theatricalization thesis' might suggest.

Liminality is important in sports because, as elsewhere, it 'represents a liberation from the regimes of normative practices and performance codes'.[33] That is, the strictly-ordered world of rigidly-defined geometrical and ordered cells which sports and their stadiums ought to be according to their spatial rules and regulations, is often found to be one of shifting interstices, widening and narrowing over time and between sports.

My observations of stadium space as liminal space does not make the stadium less like a theatre, but more like alternative forms of theatrical performance and it is now appropriate to stress that, in addition to the orthodox (or 'modern') theatre, other forms exist, notably the confrontational and 'environmental' (or 'organic') theatre. In confrontational theatre the players make gestures to the spectators and *vice versa* (as in the case of the bullfight, and of the footballers, alluded to earlier). In the case of environmental theatre the spaces 'occupied by the audience are a kind of sea through which the performers swim … there is one whole space rather than two opposing spaces'.[34] The spectator and the performer share the same space and sometimes exchange spaces.

## A Note on Placelessness

The theatre-stadium metaphor is not so immediately apparent, however, if the significance of 'place' (even landscape) rather than 'space' is considered in each genre. The *modern* sports landscape can be described as tending towards 'placelessness' in its geographical sense of places looking and feeling alike with 'dictated and standardized values'.[35] When used in theatre, however, the word 'placelessness' describes the *post-modern* – or at least the avant-garde theatre (typified by Ionesco, Becket and Genet) – and refers to the result of the minimal attention paid to the spatial setting and the lack of spatial distinction between actors and audience.[36] Yet the amorphous nature of the post-modern stage/auditorium and the modernity of the isotropic sports field each in their own way serves to focus the attention of the various 'actors' on the basic message of respective 'performances'. In stadiums, place has often been rejected in order to focus fully on the quality of play and achievement, and in theatre in order to focus on the identities and relationships imposed by society. In each case, the objectives are facilitated by 'space'. Stadium and theatre become the same in the sense that 'place' and 'scenery' would simply distract 'players' from their 'performance'.

## Theatre as Stadium

Paralleling the tendency for sport to use theatre as a metaphor and, at the same time, to theatricalize and territorialize itself, the world of theatre has, implicitly and explicitly, used sporting practice as 'a metaphor, a structuring principle and an exemplary model for theatre practice and in doing so has continually provoked questions about spectatorship and identification'.[37] I now want briefly to note how theatre has seen the stadium as a model, rather than the more well-known and opposite relationship that I have been mainly discussing so far. Again, emphasis is placed on the spatiality of theatre and the centrality of segmenation and boundaries in critical observations of conventional theatre.

**Figure 15.2**   The Berlin Olympic Stadium during the 1936 Olympics. The photograph suggests a number of stadium metaphors

In the period of revolutionary activity in post-1917 Russia and 1920s Germany, when contemporary theatre was concerned with breaking down boundaries between players and spectators as part the transformation of established modes of representation and production, radical or 'organic' theatre used sport as its model.[38] 'The organic theatre tradition has always insisted that spectacle, sport and theatre are by their very nature public discourses but differ at the point of their social extension'[39] – the polite bourgois theatre with its traditionally passive audience contrasting with football or boxing with their working-class traditions and greater sense of crowd involvement. The radical and controversial Russian actor-director, V. E. Meyerhold argued that:

> we must remove the boxes and abolish seating in tiers. The only design suitable for a performance created by the combined efforts of actors and spectators is the amphitheatre, where there are no divisions of the audience into separate classes dependent on social standing and financial resources ... Also we must destroy the box-stage once and for all, for only then can we hope to achieve a truly dynamic spectacle ... the new stage will have no proscenium arch ...[40]

Conventional theatrical space was most emphatically 'destroyed' in the 1920s and '30s theatrical festivals for the masses, notably the Workers'

Olympics and the Nazi *Thingspiel*.[41] In such 'events', actual sports stadiums were used to host massive displays, often involving the audience. The introduction of stadium plays at sports events really did lead to the proscenium arch being replaced by an open-air theatre in the round. Hence, 'the spatial arrangement of the amphitheatre or arena became a structural principle of the *Thingspiel* theaters. The action – without background or curtains – was visible from all sides'.[42] The zenith of such mass events was reached in 1936 at the Nazi Olympics (see Figure 15.2). Indeed, the theatricality of the Olympic Games has continued with the elaborate, sometimes Disney-inspired, performances of the opening and closing stadium ceremonies (though since 1936 the theatricalization of western politics in this form seems to have declined).

Bertold Brecht took stadiums as his models, describing them as 'those huge concrete pans ... with ... the fairest and shrewdest audience in the world', adding that 'there seems to be nothing to stop the theatre having its own form of 'sport' and increasing its contact with the public, providing them with more involvement and fun'.[43] But this meant the opposite of being 'seduced' by a 'performance' and, in the interests of encouraging placelessness, he modelled some of his theatrical productions on the milieu of boxing and,

> ruling out all but a minimum of make-up, costume or setting, Brecht ... made the concert or lecture platform as unemotional and unhypnotic as the boxing ring; it became impossible for the actors to do more than demonstrate and illustrate; the audience could no longer be 'carried away'.[44]

Brecht's view was that the audience in the sports arena *knows*. The sporting environment would, he assumed, create 'a critical but dispassionate audience, which would regard the actor in the same wide-awake spirit as it judged a sporting event', alive to the performer's technique in the same way a sports crowd was appreciative of physical skills.[45] It should be clear, however, that Brecht failed to appreciate the extent of partisan attitudes and behaviour among crowds, especially at team sports. This is not to say that the average football crowd is anything but much more informed and much more analytically talented about the performances and the performers they are watching than is, respectively, the average theatre audience.[46]

## Conclusion

What can be seen in environmental theatre is a move in spectating behaviour towards ritual, 'when the audience is transformed from a collection of separate individuals into a group or congregation of participants',[47] more typical of the twentieth-century football stadium. Such tendencies in theatre sound strange when placed against the implementation of the British government's Taylor Report for all-seat football stadiums, taking as it does the modern, fully-segmented theatre with its passive and polite audience as its implicit model.[48] Yet, I have tried to show that sports which most approximate to modern theatre in their player-audience relations (e.g. tennis and badminton) do appear to have become more sport-like in this respect. And in sports like football which have been traditionally less like modern forms of theatre, attempts have been made by segmentation and control to turn them more into passive, theatrical events. Spectators have been far from neutralized, however. At the same time I have tried to show that the stadium as a theatre is a useful metaphor for illustrating, not the increasing passivity of audiences, but the ambiguity of stadium space. The fact that 'distance' between players and spectators may be breaking down at the same time as barriers are being set up reflects, in fact, the ambiguity of modernity itself.

## Notes

1. Michel Foucault, *Discipline and Punish* (Harmondsworth, 1979), provides a history of punishment, on which the prison metaphor is based. For an elaboration, and the incorporation of geographical ideas, see John Bale, 'The Spatial Development of the Modern Stadium', *International Review for the Sociology of Sport*, Vol. 28, 2/3 (1993), pp.122–33.
2. Victor Turner, *Dramas, Fields and Metaphors* (Ithaca, 1974), p.25.
3. Guy Debord, *The Society of the Spectacle* (Rebel Press, 1987).
4. Bero Rigauer, 'Sport and the Economy', in Eric Dunning, Joseph Maguire and Robert Pearton (eds.), *The Sport Process* (Champaign, Ill., 1993), pp.281–305.
5. Norbert Elias and Eric Dunning, *The Quest for Excitement* (Oxford, 1986).
6. Roger Callois, *Man, Play and Games* (London, 1962).
7. R. Schechner, *Performance Theory* (New York, 1988).
8. Ellis Cashmore, *Making Sense of Sport* (London, 1990).
9. Janet Oates, *On Boxing* (New York, 1987).
10. Schnecher, *Performance Theory*, p.10.
11. Michael Oriard, 'Sport and Space', *Landscape*, Vol. 21, 1 (1976), p.37.
12. J. Kilburn, 'County grounds of England', in E. W. Swanton (ed.), *Barclay's World of Cricket* (London, 1980).
13. Chris Shilling, *The Body and Social Theory* (London, 1993), p.165.
14. Eduardo Archetti, 'Argentinian Football: a Ritual in Violence?' *International Journal of the History of Sport*, Vol. 9, 2 (1992), p.214 (emphasis added).
15. Schnecher, *Performance Theory*, p.142.
16. The term 'territoriality' is used here in the sense adopted by Robert Sack, *Human Territoriality* (Cambridge, 1986).

17. Yi-Fu Tuan, *Segmented Worlds and Self* (Minneapolis, 1982), p.189.
18. Ibid, p.103.
19. W. Lawrence, 'The Drama and the Theatre', in A. Turberville (ed.), *Johnson's England* (Oxford, 1933), p.178.
20. Elizabeth Burns, *Theatricality* (London, 1972), p.74.
21. Ibid, p.77.
22. John Bale, *Landscapes of Modern Sport* (Leicester, 1994), p.72.
23. Elias and Dunning, *Quest for Excitement*, p.84.
24. Archetti, 'Argentinian Football', p.214.
25. Rob Shields, *Places on the Margin* (London, 1991), p.96.
26. Archetti, 'Argentinian Football', p.215.
27. Bradd Shore, 'Marginal Play: Sport at the Borderlands of Time and Space', in Otmar Weiss and Wolfgang Schultz (eds), *Sport in Space and Time* (Vienna, 1985), p.114.
28. Quoted in Tony Mason, *Association Football and English Society, 1863-1915* (Brighton, 1980), p.232.
29. Louis Zurcher and Arnold Meadow, 'On Bullfights and Baseball', in Eric Dunning (ed.), *The Sociology of Sport* (London, 1970), p.190.
30. I. Mangham and M. Overington, *Organizations as Theatres* (Chichester, 1987), p.121.
31. Shore, 'Marginal play', p.114.
32. For a review of the home field advantage, see John Bale, *Sports Geography* (London, 1989), pp.29–33.
33. Shields, *Places on the Margin*, p.84.
34. R. Schechner, *Environmental Theatre* (New York, 1973), p.39.
35. Edward Relph, *Place and Placelessness* (London, 1976), p.120. In a sports context see Bale, *Landscapes of Modern Sport*, Ch. 5.
36. Burns, *Theatricality*, pp.86–8.
37. Stuart Cosgrove, 'Football, Theatre and Social Pleasure', in Charles Jenkins and Michael Green (eds.), *Sporting Fictions* (Birmingham, 1982), p.125.
38. S. Kern, *The Culture of Time and Space, 1880-1918* (London, 1983), pp.201–2.
39. Cosgrove, 'Football, Theatre', p.126.
40. Quoted in E. Braun, *Meyerehold on Theatre* (London, 1969).
41. Henning Eichberg, 'The Nazi *Thingspiel*', *New German Critique*, Vol. 11 (1977), pp.135–50.
42. Ibid, p.139.
43. Quoted in Cosgrove, 'Football, Theatre', p.138.
44. J. Willet, *The Theatre of Bertold Brecht* (London, 1977), p.148.
45. Ibid, p.144.
46. Jan Needle and P. Thompson, *Brecht* (Oxford, 1991); B. Emslie, 'Bertold Brecht and Football', in G. Day (ed.), *Readings in Popular Culture* (London, 1990), p.165.
47. Schechner, *Performance Theory*, p.143.
48. Lord Justice Taylor, *Hillsborough Stadium Disaster, Final Report* (London, 1991).

# 16

# Stadium, Pyramid, Labyrinth: Eye and Body on the Move

*Henning Eichberg*

The sports stadium is not only external to us; it is also a part of us. Let me start with two stories and one question. In 1993 my son Malte took me to Old Trafford, the home ground of Manchester United. Malte was twelve years old at the time and identified strongly with Peter Schmeichel, the Danish goalkeeper of the Manchester club. We took the guided tour inside the stadium – Figure 16.1 shows Malte looking from the police control station down over the green grass.

When the tour was finished, I asked Malte about his impression of the stadium. 'Indeed, it is beautiful,' he answered, 'but it is smaller than I had expected. In some ways it is rather a normal stadium'. I could detect a slight undertone of disappointment in his voice. When leaving the building by one of the underground tunnels, Malte picked up a small piece of concrete from the ground. 'Shouldn't we – maybe – take a stone with us? As a memory?' After a moment's hesitation he put it into his pocket.

This story tells of a contradictory relationship: there is the 'normal' space, which can be 'seen'; and there is a 'holy' place, which is experienced – but the question is, how? The story is about the complex relationship between the visible and the evocative.

The second story does not seem to be about the stadium at all. Two strange men meet at a door where they get involved in a brawl:

As soon as Leuwenhoek had caught sight of his enemy Swammerdamm, he ... jumped and tried to bar the door ... with his back. When Swammerdamm perceived this, he pulled a small telescope from his pocket, pushed it to its full length and approached the enemy crying loudly: 'Pull, you dammed, if you have courage!'. Quickly, Leuwenhoek held a similar instrument in his hand, pushed it to its length too, and cried: 'Come on, I'll resist, and you shall soon feel my power!'

Both set now their telescopes to their eyes and lunged furiously against each other with sharp, murderous strokes by lengthening and

**Figure 16.1**  Malte Eichberg at Old Trafford, Manchester

shortening their weapons and by pulling and pushing them. This resulted in feints, parades and voltes; in short, all possible arts of fencing, and their minds seemed to grow hotter and hotter. When one of them was hit, he cried loudly, jumped high into the air, made strange caprioles, beautiful entrechats, pirouettes like the best solo dancer from the Paris ballet, until the other fixed him by staring firmly through the shortened telescope. When the other was hit in the same way, he behaved similarly. They were charging with the most frolicsome jumps, with the maddest gestures, with the fiercest cries. Sweat was dropping from their foreheads, blood-red eyes protruded from their faces, and as one could only see them staring through the telescopes and no reason for their St Vitus dance, one had to regard them as madmen escaped from a lunatic asylum. The event was, by the way, rather pretty to look at.

This story is from E. T. A. Hofmann's romantic novel *Meister Floh* (*Master Flea*), published in 1822.[1] The grotesque struggle between the two opticians tells us about the visual as a weapon – the gaze is used in the duel. Evidently, the visual is not only view, and to look is not only to see.

The story could be understood as a comment on another stadium picture, a view from the Olympic stadium during the Berlin Olympics in 1936.[2] The visual does not only involve seeing, but is connected with the 'shedding' of light. Light is 'cast' by projectors just like the anti-aircraft searchlights used for the enlightening of the Nazi *Parteitag* arrangements.

324

**Figure 16.2** Closing ceremony at the Berlin Olympics, 1936

The Olympia book, from which Figure 16.2 is taken, compared the television camera – which for the first time in history sent live pictures – with 'the gun of a giant ordnance'.[3] Gaze, camera, stadium, floodlight and enlightenment are all related to one another. Therefore, our reflections about the stadium contribute to the question: 'What is enlightenment?'

## Birth and Modernity of the Stadium

The history of the stadium is normally thought of as following a rather simple pattern: as a progression from societies without stadiums to stadium-building societies. Non-stadium cultures are more 'primitive', while stadium-building is a feature of 'high culture'. The stadium does not only represent development in terms of technology, etc., but it *is* development itself. The stadium makes development and progress visible in stone.

A rough periodization of stadium history might, at first sight, seem to underline this perspective. The classical modern continuity of stadium construction started at the end of the nineteenth century, especially with Olympic sport. Stadium, sport and technology moved forward hand in hand.[4] If we look further back in history, however, we can see the forerunners of the modern stadium in the early phases of industrial modernity in the (late) eighteenth century. The stadium has different roots, beginning in England one or two generations earlier than on the continent.

In 1720 James Figg built an amphitheatre in London. Figg, who had originally begun his career as a fencing master, presented in his building different forms of physical performance, mainly boxing matches, to a well-paying public. The social shift from the noble art of fencing to the vulgarities of boxing as entertainment was here driven by economic interests. This sounds like a modern phenomenon of sport, but it can also be seen in the framework of a much older, but newly-developing circus culture which presented, for instance, animal fights in the cockpit. But in spite of some configurational similarities, the view down in the cockpit was not the modern view of sports.

In 1724 John Wood presented his plans for the completion and new construction of the English town of Bath. In this town, there already existed some places 'for taking the Air and Exercise, in Coaches or on Horseback' and a course for horse-racing. But the new project included a 'Grand Circus' for the 'exhibition of Sports'.[5] When developing a new social leisure culture, England's imperial gentry and bourgeoisie tried to relate themselves to their Roman heritage.

In 1771, the Austrian Emperor, Joseph II, visited Verona. The Governor of the Italian town had prepared a special surprise for the Emperor: a bullfight in the ancient Roman amphitheatre. The Emperor was led from the entrance at the back to his seat and all at once the oval of the arena opened to his view as the thousands of spectators on the terraces rose to their feet and applauded him. It was, as a contemporary source tells, 'a sight which threw the Emperor completely off balance' (*ein Anblick, der den Kayser ganz außer sich setzte*).[6]

The reported words do not tell precisely whether the Emperor's feeling was negative or positive. It was, nevertheless, overwhelming, in spite of the fact that he was surely accustomed to seeing crowds of people assembled. Something novel had suddenly happened in the old ruins. A new configuration had arisen which only later observers could understand as innovation, while the Emperor could only vaguely feel it. His shock may therefore be understood as a state of mind produced by an ex-posure of the view, an (e)migration of the gaze from a pre-modern custom to the modern stadium view.

One of the later, modern observers was Johann Wolfgang Goethe. During his travels in Italy in 1786–8, he also visited the Verona amphi-theatre and was impressed by its majestic view. About a thousand paces outside the arena, however, he found a crowd of four to five thousand spectators watching a ball game between two teams of four men, the noble game of *pallone*. In his diary, Goethe asked himself why the players and the spectators did not use the existing arena. He also remembered the experience of Joseph II and the astonishment of the Emperor when standing face-to-face with the crowd. Goethe reflected back in history to the ancient origins of this – now little-used – edifice, 'when the people (*Volk*) was still more people than it is today. Because properly, such an amphitheatre is suitable for impressing the people (*Volk*) by itself.'[7] Goethe's observations illustrate again that it is not the physical stone structure itself that produces the view and the action, nor even its func-tion as a sports venue. The stadium at Verona had been a ruin for centuries, while sports and games had searched for other ways of displaying them-selves; the physical arena and the games inhabited different worlds. Goethe was one of the first individuals to 'see' the new connection, to express the modern view and to wonder about the relationship between the visual and the practice of past centuries. As an early modern man, Goethe took part in (re-)creating the stadium as a modern formation of the gaze.

The French architect, Etienne-Louis Boullée, did likewise, around 1790. In his *Essai sur l'art* he included a chapter about the *Colisée*.[8] Stim-ulated by the ancient Roman model, he devised a stadium for 300,000 spectators, but made it circular instead of oval as in the original. This colosseum was to be used for festivities and public ceremonies as well as for competitions (i.e. for sports, though this modern word was not yet available to him in the French language). Boullée represented the 'archi-tecture of the revolution' and, indeed, he could by his stadium project integrate some experiences from the French revolutionary process. On 14 July 1790, the people of Paris celebrated the first anniversary of the Revolution. For this 'Festivity of the Confederation' they constructed collectively a huge stadium on the *Champs de Mars* which is regarded as the first permanent stadium of modern times (see Figure 16.3). It was opened by a large procession, after which the four to six hundred thou-sand spectators watched political and religious ceremonies, which were

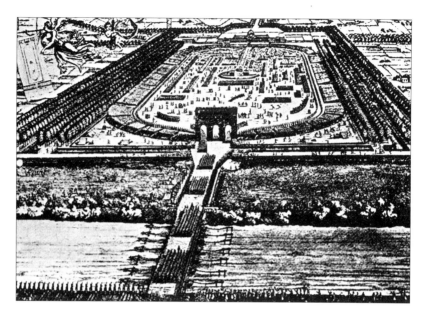

**Figure 16.3** Festivity of the Confederation, Paris, 1790. Procession and assembly

followed by some competitive games.[9] Thereafter, the commemorative festivities of the Revolution were repeated annually. They became, however, less and less political and more and more entertainment-oriented and sportive in character. In 1795–7, moreover, some technical deficiencies of the stadium became obvious and were discussed by a special commission. Because of the huge dimensions of the building, the spectators on the periphery could not – or not sufficiently – hear the speeches, the music, or the results of the competitions. This required technological remedies which were unavailable before early in the twentieth century. The social configuration, however, easily prefigured the technological development.

What had started as a revolutionary impulse, was soon turned into something new and different. In 1806–7, Napoleon ordered the erection of a provisional arena in Milan after he had conquered Italy. It had places for 30,000 spectators and its opening was celebrated with a dramatic representation of a sea battle.[10] The Imperial power, thus, tried to continue – and to transform – the revolutionary innovation based on new premises.

From about 1850, circus buildings were constructed in several European metropolises, and these new spatial and visual configurations were used for the commercial display of sports and for the entertainment of spectators. The stadium became, as it had been in England since the time of James Figg, a structure of economic interest. In the framework of world expositions, the model expanded and finally became related to Olympic sport.[11]

## The Stadium as an Innovation

The historical process of the stadium shows different and even contradictory driving forces: commercial interest, revolutionary energy and power strategy. They all went together in forming the new Western configuration of the visual.

But was the stadium really quite new? From the Olympic stadium of the late nineteenth century and the Roman references in the colosseum architecture of the late eighteenth century, we are tempted to jump back once more in history – back to the ancient stadiums of imperial Rome. The Roman emperors had developed the politics of *panem et circenses* and installed huge buildings – both the arena and the circus – as a central focus in the design of their cities. By means of the games, the imperial power tried to entertain the public in the interests of an inner discipline. The circus and arena architecture marked the cultural radiation of Rome, from the centre to the periphery, to Trier in the Germanic north as well as to the towns on the Libyan coast in the south.[12]

Indeed, here we find power and the stadium narrowly connected – but not at all in the modern way. While the eye in the modern stadium is directed towards a type of sport which is also practiced in the daily life of schools and clubs, the Roman circus presented bloody displays of an extraordinary type. The modern stadium exposes a part of our own identity – 'this is us' – while the Roman circus showed lions, gladiators, bears and prisoners of war dying – 'these are the others'. In spite of the hero-athlete as a connecting figure, the (Roman) circus was not sport.

So we need to be careful when following the modern neo-classic or new-humanist lines further back to ancient Greece and the architecture of Olympia. The Hippodrome of Herodes Atticus in Athens was excavated in 1869 and used as the stadium for the first modern Olympics in 1896, in order to make the alleged connection visible.[13] But what does this signify when the view in the stadium is not reconstructed from architectural ruins, but from the inside of a foreign and distant society?

Last but not least, we could consider the ballyards in some Native American societies.[14] Their constructions might show once more some inner connection between societal development in general – especially the development of state and rationality – on the one hand, and stadium development on the other. Yet again, these stadiums were places of killings and offerings, and this prevents us from reconstructing a single line of stadium development through history.

On a broader perspective, a more critical examination of the connection between stadium, power development and 'progress' in history should also be a warning to us. Some societies, like those of ancient China and Japan, have given birth to state formation and centralization without ever developing the spatial, visual and the architectural concepts of the stadium.[15] The arrangement of stage and public in theatre performances was highly developed, as was – since the seventeenth century – the *dohyo* arena of Japanese *sumo* wrestling, especially in local *shinto* shrines and temples. Maybe it is our own Western state-centric and evolutionist perspective that makes those strange lines of 'development', 'evolution' and 'steps' appear as if they were integral to history itself. As Pierre Clastres and other anthropologists have shown, there did not exist any quasi-natural evolution from stateless 'segmented' societies towards power centralization and state formation. Statelessness was, and remained, the norm in thousands of cultures, and only in a few of these did the 'accident' of state formation happen.[16] The same can be said about the stadium. Often, the two processes – state power and stadium building – seem to have been interconnected. Often, but – as Chinese and Japanese cultures show – not always.

So the birth of the (modern) stadium is much less 'logical' or 'evolutionary' than Western ethnocentrism would have us think. The stadium is not the result of a long-range 'progressive' rationality in society, but a very specific spatial organization of visuality, produced rather suddenly in the genesis of modern (pre-)industrializing society, between 1720 and 1850. The stadium does not tell the undifferentiated story of 'development', but the story of a specific view and rationality. What type of rationality?

### Towards Absolutist Enlightenment

Some comparisons may shed light on how different the human games and movements were even inside early modern Europe. In 1559 Pieter Bruegel prepared a picture of the kermis (carnival) in the Flemish town of Hoboken, diffused by the engraving of Frans Hogenberg, shown in Figure 16.4. Here, the crowd is seen occupying the space of the village in multiple ways. People are moving about in the built-up environment within the town as well as in the green fields outside; in sacred places around the church as well as in profane places; using them for games and plays, dances and sports, spectacles and processions. The activities and the watching public are not separated by any major barrier. Active and passive roles are shifting and diffuse (but can the spectator's role really be called passive?). In the background, people are gathering around an elevated stage: maybe an actor is showing off his art, or a balladeer, or a

**Figure 16.4**  Pieter Bruegel, 'The Festivity of Hoboken', 1559

travelling quack. The place of these activities is not a unitary scene, but the scene is – or the scenes are – integrated into the complex world of games and festivity.[17]

Bruegel presented the whole picture by use of central perspective. In a cunning way, he created the illusion of a three-dimensional view from above and downwards. This bird's-eye view might look like a logical step towards the view of the stadium; but it is not. What is crucial is not the optical 'logic' but the real, bodily activities of the involved people. Their activities are not arranged to be seen in any particular order. Their games and dances are labyrinthine and crowded. Compared with the modern geometry of the stadium, they act in 'disorder'.

Let us now try to imagine what sort of view we might encounter inside the church. Here we might observe – at the time of Bruegel – some tendencies towards another pattern which come nearer to the panoptical configuration of the modern stadium. During the 1560s, Calvinist Protestantism and the Catholic Counter-Reformation struggled in the Netherlands. Both transformed the medieval church into a new, hierarchical order where the line of sight was directed from the central altar and from the minister's pulpit towards the congregation sitting in rank-and-file order. And from the public viewpoint, the line of vision was directed – two-dimensionally and hierarchically – back to the altar and to the minister. What had earlier been a manifold pattern of holy places

331

(altars), of ritual as well as 'profane' activities (among these also games), now became a mono-functional, one-directional space. A new hierarchical order was shaped, with God's eye and the authority of 'the Word' – placed in the sermon of the priest – as the focusing point. The kermis games of Hoboken, in contrast, were still characterized by the labyrinth and crowding. The panoptical space had not yet won over their 'disorder'. The games did not structure a (functional) space, but they spread over (and created) a place.

When we approach the courtly societies of European absolutism, important changes become visible. The plays and exercises of the socially-disciplined nobility began to follow another, more geometrical pattern. The noble exercises organized the body in choreographies which gave priority to the view, to symmetry and observation, especially from the bird's-eye view. Courtly dance, graceful fencing, dressage equestrianism of 'the high school', and vaulting over the wooden horse, represented the standard set of this body geometry.[18] It is not by accident that the story quoted above of the view-duel between Leuwenhoek and Swammerdam – the two seventeenth century opticians – referred to some of these geometrical exercises of the nobility, to ballet and to foil fencing. In his grotesque narration, E. T. A. Hoffmann, as a romantic author of the early nineteenth century, pointed back to an epoch which was just closing. By presenting a 'decent' and courtly exercise with such satire, he made it appear absurd.

How were these noble exercises looked at concretely? In one of Jacques Callot's engravings of 1616 of courtly plays ('War of Love'), the observer is looking down (the bird's-eye view) on the tactical evolutions of infantry while a crowd of spectators forms a circle or oval around an open place in the city (see Figure 16.5).[19] In a similar arrangement, the 'War of Beauty' opens by a parade of festive carriages. Here, the festive games and plays employed geometrical configurations as they were developed contemporaneously in the framework of new military tactics. Since the early seventeenth century, Oranian military reform in the Netherlands put new stress on the exercises of soldiers in geometrical formations, under the key-word *disciplina*. The military 'evolutions' paved the way towards the lineal tactics of the seventeenth and eighteenth centuries.[20]

Another example can be provided from 1667 when a pompous horse ballet took place at the wedding of the Habsburg Emperor, Leopold I.[21] The imperial bridgegroom himself was a central actor in the display (see Figure 16.6). The equestrian game was constructed in strictly geometrical patterns, presenting the movement of riders and horses as a display of power and centrality. The game was, again, to be looked at both from a surrounding public and – imaginatively – from above, by graphic presentation. Pictures of the event were distributed by copper engravings which used the central perspective and the bird's-eye view to call forth

**Figure 16.5**  Jacques Callot, 'War of Love', 1616

the æsthetic geometry of sovereignty. In this display, view and power were interlaced directly – in a similar way to the contemporary art of the French-style garden, to the planning of 'ideal cities' and to the construction of bastions, fortresses and citadels.[22] The game gave a picture of 'natural' society – hierarchical, geometrical and exposed to the human view.

The stadium itself, however, was not yet installed in its modern form. The horse ballet of 1667 in Vienna could be watched from wooden balustrades, but these – together with temporary temples – were pulled down after the festivity. The location was still a place of everyday life, not a functional space for sport. It was place more than space. In this respect, the stadiums from around 1790, with their functional logic, were indeed innovative. And so was the panopticon, an idea which Jeremy Bentham presented in 1791, as the spatial model of a new, industrial society (see Figure 16.7).[23]

It is true that, in some respect, the social-geometrical exercises of the seventeenth and eighteenth centuries prefigured industrial panopticism as did the geometrical fortifications of that time with their panoptical and mathematical placing of the citadel, the bastions and the cannon batteries. The panoptical view of modernity was prefigured by the enlightenment of early modernity. But these prefigurations did not

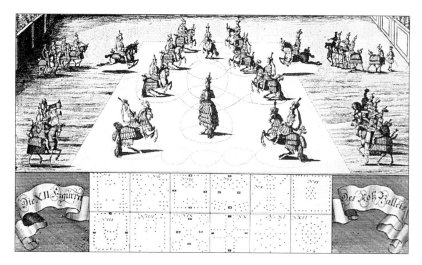

**Figure 16.6** Johann Josef Waldmann, the twelve figures of the horse ballet in Vienna, 1667

mean that there was 'development', 'evolution' or 'progress' in history. The revolutionary stadium of 1790 on the *Champs de Mars* was not a 'more developed' successor of the balustrades around the 1667 horse ballet of Vienna. And the displays shown by Callot in 1616 were not 'less progressive' than Napoleon's naumachia. They were different – and yet related. They were related to each other by European history – and yet separated by a deep crack in the process of configurational change, by the leap from early modern social geometry to industrial modernity. They were connected by discontinuity.

In other words, the stadium shows that modernity did not 'develop' along those long lines which we can use in our need for affirmation and self-elevation. But what we understand as 'the' modernity came into existence by a configurational leap. This means, that 'the' modern enlightenment does not exist either. Instead there existed several enlightenments. Enlightenment was not only the vision of rationalist and revolutionary intellectuals opposing the absolutist regime. Absolutism itself had, much earlier, developed its own enlightenment. Besides its highly scientific methods and its mathematical forms, this absolutist enlightenment acted very practically. By the enlightening (i.e. by lights and lamps) of the streets, disorder and criminality were cleared up.[24] By applying geometry and science to warfare, the killing of people was made more efficient.[26] And by the 'enlightening' of the festival – using firework displays – the eye was directed towards the beauty of order in representative play and games, in noble academic exercises – as well as in society. But not yet in the stadium.

334

**Figure 16.7**　N. Harou-Romain, plan for a prison, 1840

The ritual place and the mythological reference of early modern society was the theatre – *Theatrum Europaeum*, 'theatre of war'; *'Die Welt ist ein großes Theater'* (The world is one large theatre), as a writer of the absolutist enlightenment expressed it.[26] The ritual place of early modernity was not the stadium. (This marks the historical limits of the – otherwise very illustrative – comparison between stadium and theatre.)[27]

## Stadium, Panopticon and Pyramid

With the focus on the history of the stadium, the configuration of modern panopticism can be discussed in a more differentiated way. Let us try some comparative approaches. The stadium is connected with the panopticon by the hegemony of the view. All should be made visible. Nothing should be hidden from sight. The view is directed from above, from the ranks down to the field, from the tower of the prison down to the cells. This view from above has also found a further expression: the pyramid. The freemasonry of the eighteenth century placed God's eye at the top of the pyramid – and organized itself in hierarchical forms. In the pyramidal brotherhood of freemasonry, the individual could rise from the lower grades of relative ignorance towards the high grades of clearness and total view. Later on, pyramids became a model for industrial efficiency in many fields – from industrial corporations and revolutionary parties to academic school systems and Fascist states.

In some respect, however, the stadium is also the inverse of the pyramid. In the stadium, it is the people who can see all. In the football stadium, the 'base' sees 'the top'. It is as if the hierarchical visuality is turned upside down. The mass, the popular 'base', is sitting on high controlling the actions of the élite on the playing field below by their focused view. The stadium also inverts the panopticon. The panoptical view means the ability of the observer to see all without being seen. The tower of the prison may be empty but its control remains powerful. The stadium, in contrast, does not function when its terraces are empty. The visibility of the observers is an important part of the game; the play of a team before empty terraces is a metaphor of alienation.[28]

Visible while seeing. This takes us back to Goethe's observation on the amphitheatre of Verona: the crowd impresses itself. The masses stand face-to-face with each other. This is a metaphor of social identity. 'We are who we are' – God's eye for everybody. Furthermore, the views from the terraces of the stadium down to the playing area follow a certain direction of concentration, of 'con-centration'. The spectators concentrate on the action on the central field, focusing their view like a burning-glass. This is not the same as the centralization of control which is manifest in the panopticon, where the view from the cell to the central tower also runs on con-centrating lines. The centrality of the top of the pyramid in relation to its massive base has yet another character. But what they all – stadium, panopticon and pyramid – have in common in comparison with the labyrinthine configuration of play and games in Bruegel's world, is the directionality of the view. They all have a centre-orientation, which the folk games have not. By this con-centration, the stadium structure diverts the gaze from all other objects outside the focus, outside the stadium. While the view of Bruegel's games opens out into all directions and embraces the multiple world of life, the stadium gaze closes in. Sport in the stadium is, in this respect, literally a sort of 'di-version', of 'dis-traction', i.e. an entertainment turning the view off. A world disappears when the central game appears.

Stadium, pyramid and panopticon finally have in common the fact that they organize the space after uniform patterns. Where there has been place before – with its unique appearance – they create a universal order of directions and functions. Up and down, forward and backward, right and left – the abstract dimensions of space take over and are related to what is regarded as functional in movement. The three-dimensionality and functionality of space express in visible forms the rationality of a new, modern society.

Thus, what the philosophers of enlightenment had once praised and still praise as a way towards universal *Übersichtlichkeit*, towards the clearness of survey,[29] is not only a history of gains. It turns out to be a history of losses, too. What is being lost, is the place.[30] And where this loss is forgotten, modern totalitarianism begins. The totalitarian connection of stadium, pyramid and panopticon could be described in relation to details of the iconology of the German Nazi state. The Olympic stadium of 1936 arose in the context of the ornamental mass games of the Nazi *Thingspiel* and the Nuremberg *Reichsparteitag*. *Autobahn* highways were built and praised as 'the pyramids of the Third Reich'. Panoptical scientism was expressed in the form of universal race measurement and classification. And the panoptical striving for surveillance found its form in the hierarchies of secret services for the observation of the people …[31] While some of these institutions ended in 1945, the fundamental modernity of which they were born survived.


## In the Undergrounds of the Stadium

The panoptical dimension is, however, only one side of the living historical phenomenon of the stadium, albeit the hegemonic one. The experience of real people on the terraces is much more complex and more contradictory than the planned gaze. What else is happening there?

Sports stadiums are often places of disorder and tumult, in some cases even of revolt. This can appear – negatively – as hooliganism and violence, but also – interpreted romantically – as part of the popular or folk dimension of stadium culture. Whether regarded as one or the other, stadium culture also includes drunkenness and collective frenzy. At any moment, the hegemonic con-centration can collapse. The stadium can turn into a place of wilderness, of carnival, but also – as the 1985 occurrences in the Heysel stadium in Brussels have shown – into a place of death. Administrative pressure towards the all-seater stadium shows how seriously sports bureaucracy takes this dimension, seeing it as a menace and a challenge to 'good order'. This conflict involves a confrontation between hegemonic panoptical order and non-panoptical, subversive elements. What else does the eye see – and what do the rank-and-file bodies experience?

The eye does not only see what is happening on the playing field. If this was the case, it would not seriously bother to be a spectator in a – nearly – empty stadium. But evidently, this is a problem; the planning of the Copenhagen *Parken* in the 1980s illustrates the divergency.[32] By using high technology, the planners computed all details of what could be seen from every single place – this was the concentrating-panoptical aspect. But what would people see if the stadium was – relatively – empty? This other dimension of visibility – the view from section to section – was 'forgotten' by the planners. But the question arose almost as soon as *Parken* was opened for use – the result being a remarkable financial loss. The stadium corporation became financially bankrupt.

The alternative view in the stadium is, however, not only that from grandstand to grandstand. Underneath the stands, the stadium continues to exist. The building contains an entanglement of passages and tunnels leading to the seated areas, to club rooms, toilets, dressing-rooms and other installations. Recent measures of riot control even include the installation of prison cells inside the stadium underground. The way through this labyrinthine maze – starting from the riot-controlled entrance tunnels – is also a part of the experienced or imagined stadium structure.

This reminds us of the other side of the pyramid. What from outside looks like perfect visibility and panoptical geometry, contains, in its interior, hidden systems of passages leading towards secret graves and treasures. The industrial mass culture has – in novels, comic strips and movies – extensively played on the popular imagination of the interior of the pyramid. We see heroes like Indiana Jones fumbling through labyrinthine worlds of Egyptian tunnels and graves, searching up and down over flights of stairs, following exotic treasures, falling into hidden traps. It is the world of the living dead, of the awakened mummy and of strange rituals. This trivial mythology was preluded by the romantic

338

narrations of the genre of the 'freemason novel' or 'secret society stories' around 1800 – like Schiller's '*Geisterseher*' and the '*Zauberflöte*' of Schikaneder and Mozart: the hero goes astray through unknown labyrinthine buildings, meeting mysterious people from secret societies, finding himself confronted with entangling questions and unknown ceremonies. All sense of orientation and perspective is lost. But it is this very loss which is the focus of fascination.[33]

## The Maze, the Crypt and the Noise

The boom of this fantasy production – labyrinths and 'Egyptian' mazes – in the years around 1800 was paralleled by the new experience of urbanism as a 'labyrinth of the cities'. How ever this coincidence may be interpreted, it was not by accident that it arose contemporaneously with the genesis of the modern stadium. The 'new survey' of modernity had the fantasy of the secret labyrinth as its reverse. The panoptical view also produced a loss of orientation. Underneath hegemonic visibility, there opened a world of non-visibility. This is more than a creation of fantasy. The stadium has, during its recent history, again and again been used concretely as a concentration camp. In Chile, the military dictatorship of Pinochet used stadiums frequently in its strategy to make people 'disappear'. Eastern European and African states planned or practised on similar lines. What had arisen as a structure of modern visualization, turned out to be useful as an instrument of concealment and 'disappearance'.

Terror, fright and the strategy of power are, however, not the only aspects of this other side of visibility. When enthusiastic sports journalists describe the events in the stadium as a *Hexenkessel* or 'witch's cauldron', they refer to an element of fascination. The stands form a closed world full of mystery and secrets. The stadium is not only an open field, but also a crypt – an inside place of warmth and togetherness.[34] It is this aspect that we could discover in the story of my son Malte and his 'holy place', Old Trafford. The small piece of concrete is a memory of the 'sacred' event and the unique place – but there is also the disappointment at the 'normality' of the stadium as space. Or, in reverse – and this is the paradox of the stadium – there is organized space, but suddenly – here and now – we are in a place.

For these qualities of place, of crypt and 'holiness', the view or gaze does not work alone. The other senses contribute considerably to the experience. Of special importance is the noise of the stadium. We hear people on the terraces singing and shouting. By laughing and chanting, they produce a subversion of the pure view. Drums and instruments on the terraces accompany the game on the field. A common rhythm can arise.[35] Without the noise, there will rarely be any *Stimmung*, any mood, humour and 'spirit' – and no carnival.[36] In passing, it can be noted that when visiting the Manchester United Museum in Old Trafford, the difficulty of recalling the visual experience is obvious. The visual reproduction exhibited in the show-cases is poor in contrast to the noise from the television films which fills the museum and which gives a much stronger impression.

## Towards a Zapping Society?

To return to the world of views and gazes, some remarkable (also subversive?) contradictions can be seen in the most recent developments of the stadium. Increasingly, we see large screens inside the arenas used to present the events in visual detail. They are able to enlarge on selected scenes; they reproduce processes in slow motion and split the visual impression up into a multiplicity of pictures. This is no longer the visuality of the traditional modern stadium – it is hypervisuality. The hegemonic formation of the gaze changes. The eye is distracted from its concentration. The view is zapping from the grass to the screen, from picture to picture. And the zapping spectatorship opens up a new world of simulation in sports – virtual sports.[37]

This is not simply a development in the world of media technology; it carries a further significance, comparable to the genesis of the modern stadium in the context of industrial modernity around 1800. The zapping pattern may destroy some important traditional habits of sport spectatorship. Will, for instance, traditional stadium culture disappear, as it is imagined in the science fiction of Bilal and Cauvin?[38] But the technologies of hypervisualization may also reinforce some sports which have been marginal (or marginalized) in relation to stadium sports. This is what happened to boxing during the 1960s. After having degenerated for decades, boxing experienced a leap towards a new visuality and popularity as a result of American television. Suddenly, the boxer's face was brought into the sitting-room – and a new age and image of the sport opened.[39] However, the zapping pattern concerns much more than the world of sports. By actualizing a dimension of visuality which, to be sure, has always been present, it gives change, variation and multiplicity a new societal significance. This may be the view of a new type of society.

If the stadium is an indicator of behavioural transformation, as it was around 1800, then the question arises: what is the equivalent of the zapping view in the general pattern of society? Or, in other words, after the panoptical view of industrial culture, what does the zapping society look like and how does it relate to modernity?

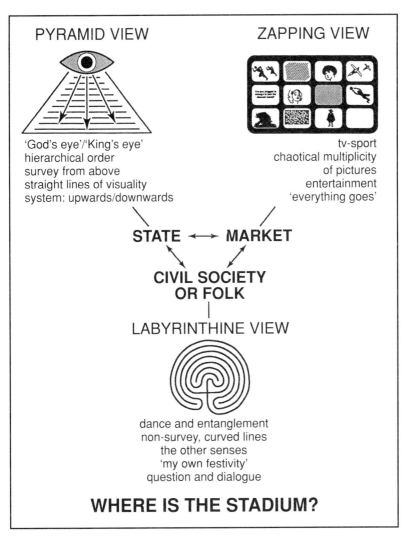

**Figure 16.8** Trialectics of the social view

## Trialectics of the Social View

The contradictions between the panoptical dimension of the stadium, its labyrinthine underground and the new zapping view are highly relevant for social analysis. They deliver categories for a more detailed description of what is going on in society in actual late (or trans-?) modernity (see Figure 16.8). The pyramid, labyrinth and zapping are not neutral or balanced in relation to social structure. The panoptical view has a tighter connection with the state, while the unfolding of zapping patterns is driven by the market. In contrast to both, the labyrinth had a special relationship to folk culture, or to what recent sociology calls civil society.[40] State, market and civil society are fundamental categories for the understanding of actual societal tension and change. All three dimensions are involved in the shaping of the stadium. The stadium manifests their contradictions and conflicts concretely and visibly.

The trialectical pattern should not be read as a harmonious equilibrium; it describes dynamic imbalances and contradictions. In any society, there is always hegemony and subversion. Modernity has established a hegemony where the space of sports, the stadium, is constructed panoptically – as is (or tries to be) the modern state. However, hegemony might glide towards the zapping view. This would have dramatic consequences for the configuration of late (or trans-) modernity. It is this shift on the level of hegemony which gives the labyrinthine underground a new significance. Why have people built new labyrinths since the 1970s, to be used for dance, for land art, or as tourist attractions?[41] When the philosophers of 'the modern enlightenment' deplore the *Neue Unübersichtlichkeit*, the new lack of surveillance in society[42] or the defeat of the reason,[43] their impression can be related to both the labyrinthine aspects of civil society and to the zapping processes on the market level. Modern man suddenly becomes afraid – and this also surely tells a new gender story. Whatever the case, the stadium helps to ask new questions of a society in transformation.

### No Place to Hide

To be sure, in the end there are more questions than answers. But we can, nevertheless, draw some conclusions. First, the visualization of game, play and movement by the stadium is not only 'practical'. Technological solutions are never innocent. But as the organization of (collective) senses they are part of a societal process. This social-bodily dimension is the world of myths and rituals. It is at this point that a place – or even a functional space – can turn into a 'holy' place. We pick up a stone – and it becomes a relic. Here and now, the event takes place. However, it is also on the level of myths and rituals that society shapes the panoptical view, by referring to 'God's eye' or to 'the good order', to the 'light' of enlightenment or to the pyramid. This means that modernity and enlightenment did not at all de-mythologize the world (as their own mythologies have always claimed). They created societal myths themselves – myths of 'light' and 'darkness' as well as (pan)optical rituals. Sport was one of their fundamental rituals, and the stadium its mythological place.

**Figure 16.9** Max Peintner, *'Die ungebrochene Anziehungskraft der Natur'* (The unbroken attraction of nature), *c.*1970

Myths and rituals, understood in this way, are not only 'symbolic' superstructures over the real material process in society. Nor are they ornaments of the real process, such as Pierre de Coubertin's 'Olympic religion' was a system of neo-humanist moral ideas and a set of ceremonies surrounding the 'real' sporting competitions. The competition itself is the ritual, and the achievement and its visibility is the myth. Myth and ritual are what materialist psychoanalysis has been observing.[44] To see is one of the fundamental conditions of human material life. How does the fascination originate when we are gazing into the whirl of the water or into the leaves of a tree? What do we see when looking into the face of an old woman or of a newborn child? Why can we look for hours – hypnotized – into the flames of a fire, and how can one become pyromanic?[45]

The stadium as a mythological and ritual place – seen from these psychoanalytical perspectives – is not only a luxury, established by a rich society as a means of leisure, i.e. as a superstructure to the world of 'real work'. Nor has it essentially to do with religion in the specific Western understanding as an emanation of a 'belief' in a 'Book', in 'God' or whatever. The mythological dimension of the stadium concerns – instead – the way by which a society manifests its basic principles of organizing senses and rationality. And manifesting means not only to affirm, but also to contest (see Figure 16.9).[46]

Second, to look and to see are not the same. The social geometry of the exercises of the nobility from the seventeenth and eighteenth centuries, the stadium sports of the nineteenth and twentieth centuries and the zapping sport of our late twentieth century are all based on a high

**Figure 16.10** Johannes Grützke, *'Er will nicht hingucken'* (He does not want to look), 1967

valuation of visualization. The visibility or hypervisibility of the body and its movements characterizes their respective configurations. But the configurations – manifest in the organization of display, among others in the stadiums – are different from age to age and from culture to culture. They relate to different configurations of society. The view is a 'weapon'. But weapons are of different types. The foil in the Leuwenhoek–Swammerdam duel of the (fictional) seventeenth century is different from the cannon of the television at the Olympics of 1936. History is not so much 'tradition' as a change of configurations. The *colisée* of Boullée cannot be understood as 'Roman'. The Olympism of Coubertin was not ancient Greek. And enlightenment is 'enlightenments' in – historical – plural. To see includes the historical crisis of seeing (see Figure 16.10).[47]

Third, the hegemonic view and the dominant configuration always have an underground. Underneath the light, the 'enlightenment' and the gaze, there are labyrinths and mazes. This does not mean that it is 'dark' beneath the enlightenments – as the modern mythology of 'the one enlightenment' suggests.[48] The noise is not in the shadow, but on a different level from light and dark. The other senses tell other stories of sociality. They tell distinctly, but are not exposed to the 'light' of the view. Their stories are about place, about 'disorder' and revolt, about the paradoxes and the changes of the hegemonic order. And why will it be interesting to follow these stories? To leave the power no place to hide: not even in the floodlights of the stadium.

## Notes

1. E. T. A. Hoffmann, *Meister Floh* (1822). In Hoffmann, *Werke*, Vol. 5 (Zürich, 1946), pp.418–19.
2. *Die Olympischen Spiele in Berlin und Garmisch-Partenkirchen. Offizielles Olympia Album von 1936*, Reprint, p.158.
3. Ibid., p.163.
4. For details see J. Bale, *Sport, Space and the City* (London, 1993).
5. F.-J. Verspohl, *Stadionbauten von der Antike bis zur Gegenwart. Regie und Selbsterfahrung der Massen* (Gießen,1965), p.53.
6. G. U. A. Vieth, *Versuch einer Encyklopädie der Leibesübungen, Berlin, 1794–1818*, Vol. 3, p.370, quoted in Verspohl, *Stadionbauten*, p.26.
7. J. W. Goethe, *Italienische Reise* (München, 1957), pp.27–30.
8. See Verspohl, *Stadionbauten*, pp.27–38.
9. Ibid., pp.39–48.
10. Ibid., pp.144–6.
11. R. D. Mandell, *Paris 1900. The Great World's Fair* (Toronto, 1967).
12. Verspohl, *Stadionbauten*, pp.33–34, 65–75; M. B. Poliakoff, *Kampfsport in der Antike. Das Spiel um Leben und Tod* (Zürich, 1989).
13. Verspohl, *Stadionbauten*, pp.163–64. Characteristic for neo-classic pathos is L. Drees, *Olympia. Götter, Künstler und Athleten*, (Stuttgart, 1967).
14. J. Bale, *Landscapes of Modern Sports* (Leicester, 1994), pp.21–24; L. Raesfeld, *Die Ballspielplätze in El Tajín, Mexiko* (Münster, 1992).
15. S. Brownell, 'The Stadium, the City, and the State: Beijing', Chap. 6 in this volume; J.Möller, *Sumo – Kampf und Kult. Historische und religiöse Aspekte des japanischen Ringens* (Sankt Augustin, 1990), pp.73–7.
16. P. Clastres, *La société contre l'état* (Paris, 1974); in German: *Staatsfeinde. Studien zur politischen Anthropologie* (Frankfurt/Main, 1976); P. Clastres, 'Über die Entstehung von Herrschaft. Ein Interview', in H. P. Duerr (ed.), *Unter dem Pflaster liegt der Strand*, Vol. 4 (Berlin, 1977), pp.104–40.
17. C. Brown, *Bruegel – Meisterwerke im Großformat* (Wiesbaden, 1975), p.59. See also p.69, 'Let the farmers have their kermis'.
18. H. Eichberg, *Leistung, Spannung, Geschwindigkeit* (Stuttgart, 1978).
19. Verspohl, *Stadionbauten*, p.114.
20. Eichberg, *Leistung*, pp.120–31; H. Kleinschmidt, *Tyrocinium militare. Militärische Körperhaltungen und -bewegungen im Wandel zwischen dem 14. und dem 18. Jahrhundert* (Stuttgart, 1989).

21. H. Handler and E. Lessing, *Die Spanische Hofreitschule zu Wien* (Wien/ München/Zürich, 1972), p.86.
22. H. Eichberg, *Festung, Zentralmacht und Sozialgeometrie* (Wien, 1989); H. Eichberg, 'Ordnen, Messen, Disziplinieren. Moderner Herrschaftsstaat und Fortifikation', in J. Kunisch (ed.), *Staatsverfassung und Heeresverfassung in der europäischen Geschichte der frühen Neuzeit* (Berlin, 1986), pp.347–75.
23. M. Foucault, *Discipline and Punish* (Harmondsworth, 1979).
24. W. Schivelbusch, *Lichtblicke. Zur Geschichte der künstlichen Helligkeit im 19. Jahrhundert* (München/Wien, 1983).
25. Eichberg, *Zentralmacht*; H. Eichberg, *Die historische Relativität der Sachen oder Gespenster im Zeughaus*, 2nd edn. (Münster, 1987).
26. J. B. von Rohr, *Einleitung zur Ceremoniel-Wissenschaft Der Privat-Personen …* (Berlin, 1728, reprint Weinheim, 1990), p.506; see H. Eichberg, 'Fremd in der Moderne? Über Zeremonialwissenschaft', *Zeitschrift für historische Forschung* (forthcoming).
27. Bale, *Landscapes*, pp.85–95.
28. For more on theatre before empty seats as a dream of alienation, see the novel of Gerz Feigenberg, *Grimmsburg* (Lindhardt & Ringhof, 1993).
29. J. Habermas, *Die Neue Unübersichtlichkeit* (Frankfurt/Main, 1985).
30. Y. F. Tuan, *Space and Place*, 2nd edn. (London, 1979).
31. H. Eichberg et al., *Massenspiele. NS-Thingspiel, Arbeiterweihespiel und olympisches Zeremoniell* (Stuttgart-Bad Cannstatt, 1977); R. Stommer (ed.), *Reichsautobahn. Pyramiden des Dritten Reiches* (Marburg, 1982); B. Müller-Hill, *Tödliche Wissenschaft. Die Aussonderung von Juden, Zigeunern und Geisteskranken 1933–1945* (Reinbek, 1984).
32. P. Jørgensen, 'Copenhagen's Parken: a Sacred Place?', Chap. 8 in this volume.
33. M. Thalmann, *Romantik und Manierismus* (Stuttgart, 1963), pp.55ff; H. Eichberg, 'The Labyrinth – The Earliest Nordic "Sports Ground"?', *Scandinavian Journal of Sports Sciences*, Vol. 11 (1989), pp.43–57; on the renaissance of the view on the 'secret' interior of the pyramid with New Age mythology, see M. Toth and G. Nielsen, *Pyramid Power. The Secret Energy of the Ancients Revealed* (New York, 1985).
34. G. Warming, *Fodbold – sprog og kult. Om det numinøse og frivole i fodbold (Football – Language and Cult. The numinous and the Frivolous in Football)* (Gerlev, 1987).
35. E. T. Hall, *The Dance of Life. The Other Dimension of Time* (New York, 1984), pp.153–76.
36. Bale, *Landscapes*, pp.139–42.
37. Ibid., pp.177–80.
38. E. Bilal and P. Cauvin, *Hors jeu* (Paris, 1988).
39. A. Rauch, *Boxe – violence du 20e siècle* (Aubier, 1992).
40. Eichberg, 'Labyrinth'; H. Eichberg, 'Das revolutionäre Du. Über den dritten Weg', *Die Neue Gesellschaft/Frankfurter Hefte*, Vol. 38 (1991), pp.1128–34.
41. Eichberg, 'Labyrinth'; A. Fisher and G. Gerster, *The Art of the Maze*

(London, 1990); see also current documentation in the review *Caerdroia*, eds. J. and D. Saward, Thundersley Benfleet, 1980ff.

42. Habermas, *Unübersichtlichkeit*.
43. A. Finkielkraut, *La défaite de la pensée* (Paris, 1987).
44. G. Bachelard, *L'eau et les rêves. Essai sur l'imaginaire de la matière*, 18th edn. (Paris, 1983), p.6.
45. G. Bachelard, *La psychanalyse du feu* (Paris, 1973).
46. Tyrol artist, from *Profil*, No. 50, 9 December 1985.
47. J. Grützke, *Werkverzeichnis der Gemälde 1964–1977*, No. 68 (Frankfurt/Main, 1977).
48. Finkielkraut, *Défaite*.